THE FAR SIDE OF REVENGE

Making Peace in Northern Ireland

About the Author

Deaglán de Bréadún, Political Correspondent with *The Irish Times*, is one of Ireland's most experienced journalists and a former Northern Editor of the newspaper. His reportage of the peace negotiations leading to the historic Good Friday Agreement won the IPR/BT Northern Ireland Press and Broadcast Award for daily news journalism. In a wide-ranging career he has covered news stories all over the world and interviewed major figures such as Yasser Arafat, Kofi Annan and Jimmy Carter. Born in Enniscorthy, County Wexford, he was educated at CBS Synge Street and University College Dublin.

THE FAR SIDE OF REVENGE

Making Peace in Northern Ireland

NEW UPDATED EDITION

Deaglán de Bréadún

The Collins Press

First published in 2001 by The Collins Press
West Link Park
Doughcloyne
Wilton
Cork

This revised edition published 2008

British Library Cataloguing in Publication Data

De Breadun, Deaglan
  The far side of revenge : making peace in Northern Ireland.
  - Updated ed.
  1. Peace-building - Northern Ireland 2. Northern Ireland -
  Politics and government - 1994-
  I. Title
  941.6'0824
  ISBN-13: 9781905172610

Printed in Malta

Sculpture in cover photo: Maurice Harron, *Hands Across the Divide*

CONTENTS

*To the unionist and nationalist families,
and to my wife, Maria, and our own beloved family.
This act of remembering is further dedicated
to my late brother Kieran, who lost his memory
through illness but will never fade from mine.*

A hunger-striker's father
Stands in the graveyard dumb.
The police widow in veils
Faints at the funeral home.

History says, Don't hope
On this side of the grave.
But then, once in a lifetime
The longed-for tidal wave
Of justice can rise up,
And hope and history rhyme.

So hope for a great sea-change
On the far side of revenge.
Believe that a further shore
Is reachable from here.

from Seamus Heaney's *The Cure at Troy*:
A version of Sophocles' Philoctetes.
London: Faber, 1990

PREFACE TO
SECOND EDITION

After the first edition of this book appeared in March 2001, publishers The Collins Press and I agreed that an updated version should be produced at such time as there was 'closure' in the conflict. Judgments must always be tentative but we seemed to have reached that stage on 8 May 2007 when DUP leader Ian Paisley and Sinn Féin's Martin McGuinness took office as First and Deputy First Minister, wearing the broadest of smiles upon their faces.

Whatever was to happen in the future, this certainly marked a very advanced stage in the peace process. As a result, I have added two new chapters to what appeared seven years ago. Chapter 14 describes how we got to our present stage and provides some new background information on various developments. With Chapter 15, I have stepped outside my role as chronicler of events and, instead of reporting the past, tried to discern what H.G. Wells called 'the shape of things to come'.

Some have been kind enough to say that this book could be helpful to negotiators seeking to end other long-running conflicts. I am pleasantly surprised that relatively few corrections and amendments needed to be made to the first edition. Both editions have been read in typescript by participants in the negotiations.

I wish to express my heartfelt thanks to those who helped with the second edition and encouraged me in the writing of it, especially my wife Maria and our family, Erica, Cillian, Ronan and Olwen. I rather doubt there will be a third edition, but you never know. I wish to stress that no slight or insinuation against the character, integrity or reputation of any person or organisation is intended in these pages.

Deaglán de Bréadún
January 2008

─────── ACKNOWLEDGEMENTS ───────

The title chosen by Hillary Rodham Clinton for her book about
rearing a child was *It Takes a Village**. The number of people who
helped in different ways to make this book a reality would easily populate a village or even a small-sized town. As with the
poet W.B. Yeats, 'My glory was I had such friends'. Some I cannot comfortably name because their positions as civil servants,
political leaders, party workers or just contacts of mine as a journalist might be put in jeopardy. If I have erred on the side of caution and someone feels undeservedly left out, I humbly apologise. Given the sensitivity of the topic, I have had few complaints
over the years for the care I always took to protect my sources.

It is easier to express gratitude and appreciation to colleagues and friends (usually the same thing) in the journalistic
profession. Pride of place must here go to the Editor of *The Irish
Times*, Conor Brady, who was supportive, tolerant and understanding of this unseen project which took up so much of my
time. The Sabbatical Committee of the paper also deserve grateful acknowledgment.

Colleagues North and South aided and assisted me in several respects. Some helped in practical ways, either with the book
or with the 'story', while others put the difficulties in perspective
when the mountain seemed just too high to climb. Journalists
and others in the North took this 'Free State' *émigré* under their
collective wing. The Belfast office of *The Irish Times* was always
on my side, and special thanks must go to my colleagues Jill
Russell, Gerry Moriarty and Gordon Houston. Whereas I am fully
and totally responsible for the contents of this work, it would have
been less complete without the kind assistance and encouragement of Ken Reid, Eamonn Mallie, Stephen Grimason, Martina
Purdy, Mark Simpson, Kate Fearon, Lena Ferguson, Toby
Harnden, Liam Clarke, Máirtín O Muilleoir, Darwin Templeton,
Nicholas Watt, Tim Attwood, Brian Rowan, Vincent Kearney,
Steven King, Chris Thornton, David Sharrock, John Mullin, Hervé

Amoric, Frank Costello, Chris Anderson, Deirdre Devlin, Kathleen Cavanaugh, Deric Henderson, Anne Cadwallader, and, last but not least, Trevor Birney.

Outside the North, special mention must be made of *Irish Times* colleagues who actively aided me or else ensured that the continuing demands of the 'day job' never halted the project in its tracks. I am thinking particularly of Willy Clingan, Séamus Martin, John Maher, Dermot O'Shea, Paul Gillespie, Pat O'Hara, Joan Scales, Mark Brennock, John Waters, Peter Murtagh, Dan Keenan, Derek Grant, Rosaleen Bamford, Donal Dorcey and Kathy Sheridan. Outside the paper, special thanks must go to Charlie Bird, Gabriel Burke, Niall O Muilleoir, Shane Kenny, Dick Spring, Emily O'Reilly, James B. Monaghan, Maolmuire Tynan and Mairéad Foley. Farther afield, in the great republic across the waves, I wish to thank Bruce Morrison, Congressmen Peter King and Richard Neal, Trina Vargo, Niall O'Dowd, Bill Finan of *Current History*, Bill Katz, Professor Laurie Lehmann and 'Skylark'.

Nobody gave more practical assistance in this project than Ingrid Gray whose patience and eagerness to help seemed endless. In addition, the itinerant author was given a roof over his head and ample quantities of peace and quiet in houses from Wexford to Connemara and from Kilkeel, County Down, to Castlegregory, County Kerry. My thanks to Michael Commane (who also helped with the footnotes), Seán Ó Tuairisg and Beatrice and Mark Keown. The Linenhall Library, Belfast, opened its doors to me as to so many others, past, present and future.

My wife Maria and children, Erica, Cillian, Ronan and Olwen have had to cope with me while I pursued this lonely obsession over the past two years. No words of mine can do justice to their love and support. Special thanks go to my agent, Jonathan Williams, whose enthusiasm never flagged from the day he took that first phone call.

The title grew out of a lunch in Belfast with my former *Irish Times* colleague, now with the *Independent*, David McKittrick, who was always generous with his advice and wisdom. When I informed Seamus Heaney that words of his were being borrowed once more, he replied with typical graciousness and generosity: 'It is a bonus to have a man of your gifts using a phrase of one's own as a title.'

ACKNOWLEDGEMENTS

The comprehensive history of the peace process will be written by someone with more time on his or her hands, but if this volume contributes to that enterprise I will be grateful. I was there and this is what I saw and heard. It is primarily an eye-witness account with a strong analytical dimension. The typescript was read at various stages by a considerable number of people in sensitive positions who also gave me the benefit of their experience and inside knowledge. I regret that it would not be appropriate to name them all, but they know who they are and they also know my gratitude is genuine. That exercise was in line with my effort to achieve the highest possible level of accuracy and impartiality. Readers who spot mistakes or wish to make observations or even complaints should contact me through the publishers, or at *ddebreadun@ireland.com* for email messages. No unwarranted slight or insinuation against the character, integrity or reputation of any person or organisation is intended in these pages.

DEAGLÁN DE BRÉADÚN
DUBLIN 2001

A Note on Style: Daily news journalism is a fast-moving, fast-talking business and the argot of this book may at times jar with the more artistic reader. My justification is that this is the way we talked about the 'story' among ourselves, as it developed before our eyes. With deadlines to meet, we did not always have time to hone the most elegant sentences. I was tempted to change some of the expressions and phrases here but decided against it: they may not always be poetic but they are authentic. I have also retained the journalistic habit of referring to 'Dublin' and 'London', as shorthand for the government/administration/ bureaucracy/political élite in both places. The precise meaning depends on the context in each case.

* Simon and Schuster, 1996.

GLOSSARY

Alliance Party. Middle-ground political party which draws support from both communities in Northern Ireland, mainly the middle classes.

Belfast Agreement. Document which emerged after protracted talks involving most Northern Ireland political parties and the British and Irish Governments; more usually known as the Good Friday Agreement because negotiations concluded on Good Friday, 10 April 1998.

Continuity Irish Republican Army (*CIRA*), also *Continuity Army Council* (*CAC*). Republican paramilitary splinter group opposed to the peace process; its political counterpart is Republican Sinn Féin.

Dáil Éireann, also the *Dáil*. Lower house of the Irish Parliament, sits at Leinster House, Dublin.

Democratic Unionist Party. Largest unionist party, currently in government with Sinn Féin. Rev Ian Paisley is party leader.

Fianna Fáil. Largest political party in the South; republican in ideology, in practical politics it is moderate nationalist.

Fine Gael. Second largest political party in the Republic; more moderate in its nationalism than Fianna Fáil.

Gaelic Athletic Association (*GAA*). Largest sporting organisation on the island of Ireland; almost entirely nationalist in its membership.

Garda Síochána. Police force in the Republic of Ireland.

Good Friday Agreement. See Belfast Agreement above.

Irish National Liberation Army (*INLA*). Republican paramilitary group that has been riven by violent internal divisions. On ceasefire since 1998, the INLA has been accused of heavy involvement in criminality. Its political counterpart is the Irish Republican Socialist Party.

Irish Republican Army. Republican paramilitary organisation. The title is usually applied to the Provisionals (see below) although this is disputed by others, e.g., the Real IRA (see below).

Loyalist. Theoretically, someone who is loyal to the British Crown. In practice, a militant working-class unionist who may also have associations with one of the loyalist political parties and/or paramilitary groups.

Loyalist paramilitaries. The main groups are: the Ulster Defence Association (UDA) which also uses the title Ulster Freedom Fighters (UFF); the Ulster Volunteer Force (UVF), associated with the Red Hand Commando (RHC). The latter groupings officially support the peace process. The main dissident organisation is the Loyalist Volunteer Force (LVF); others include the Red Hand Defenders and the Orange Volunteers.

Nationalist. Someone who supports the reunification of Ireland. Most nationalists are also Catholics. The category embraces supporters of the SDLP and Sinn Féin, but whereas all republicans are nationalists, not all nationalists are republican.

Northern Ireland Office (NIO). British government department set up with the imposition of Direct Rule from London in 1972 to administer Northern Ireland, it lost some of its functions with the establishment of the power-sharing executive after the Good Friday Agreement. The NIO has two divisions, one in Belfast at Stormont and the other in London. It retains responsibility for constitutional and security issues.

Officials. The IRA split in 1969 into Official and Provisional wings. The Official IRA, colloquially the 'Officials' or 'Stickies', called a ceasefire in 1972. Allegedly involved in criminality afterwards but now largely quiescent.

Orange Order. Grass-roots Protestant organisation, founded on 21 September 1795. In March 2005, the Order voted to sever its 100-year link with the Ulster Unionist Party. Its opponents accuse it of bigotry and some of its marches during the summer can be controversial.

Patten Commission. Body set up under the Good Friday Agreement to recommend reforms in the policing of Northern Ireland. Chaired by the former NIO Minister and last Governor of Hong Kong, Christopher, now Lord, Patten, its controversial report was issued in September 1999.

Progressive Unionist Party (P U P). Political counterpart of the Ulster Volunteer Force (UVF).

Provisional IRA. (Also known as Provisionals, Provos, PIRA and, most frequently nowadays, the IRA). The main Republican paramilitary group, it was formed out of a split with the 'Officials' (see above) in December 1969 and led the violent campaign to force the withdrawal of British troops and destroy Northern Ireland as a political entity.

Real IRA. Dissident republican paramilitary group formed in late 1997 because of dissatisfaction with the Provisional leadership and the peace process. Forced to go on ceasefire after the Omagh bombing of August 1998, but now active again. Its political counterpart is the 32-County Sovereignty Movement.

Republican. Strictly speaking, someone who supports a democratic republic rather than a monarchy. In Ireland it usually means a militant nationalist who seeks an end to the British presence in the North and the establishment of a 32-county government.

Republican Sinn Féin (RSF). A breakaway group formed when mainstream Sinn Féin under Gerry Adams and Martin McGuinness ended the party's policy of refusing to take its seats if elected to the Irish parliament in Dublin. Opposed to the peace process, RSF is the political counterpart of the

GLOSSARY

Continuity IRA, although there is no formal link.

RTE: Radio Telefís Éireann. Main broadcasting organisation in the Republic of Ireland, set up by the state but semi-independent.

Royal Ulster Constabulary (RUC). Northern Ireland's police force from 1922 to 2001, when it was reorganised and renamed as the Police Service of Northern Ireland (PSNI).

Sinn Féin (SF). Irish for 'We Ourselves' or colloquially, 'Ourselves Alone'. Republican party, the political counterpart of the IRA. Together they are known as 'the republican movement'. Formerly a propaganda vehicle for the IRA, Sinn Féin has become more important as the movement's involvement in politics has deepened.

Social Democratic and Labour Party (SDLP). Nationalist party which supports the achievement of Irish unity but strictly by non-violent means. Strongly supports and campaigns for reconciliation between the two communities.

Sunningdale Agreement. Pact agreed between mainstream nationalists and unionists in December 1973, to set up a power-sharing Executive in Northern Ireland and also to establish a Council of Ireland with ministers from North and South – seven of each. The administration subsequently established was brought down by a general strike of loyalists in May 1974.

'Ulster'. Strictly speaking and in nationalist eyes, the historic Irish province consisting of nine counties. Unionists use the term to refer to the six counties of Northern Ireland which they also call 'The Province'.

Ulster Defence Regiment (UDR). A regiment of the British Army recruited in 1972 from within Northern Ireland. Most of the initial membership was composed of prior members of the disbanded 'B-Specials'. Almost entirely Protestant in composition, the regiment was eventually merged with the Royal Irish Rangers to form the Royal Irish Regiment.

Ulster Democratic Party (UDP). Loyalist party, now defunct, political counterpart of the Ulster Defence Association (UDA) and the Ulster Freedom Fighters (UFF).

Ulster Unionist Council (UUC). Governing body of the Ulster Unionist Party until its powers were transferred to the UUP Executive in October 2007.

Ulster Unionist Party (UUP). Formerly the main unionist party, which governed Northern Ireland for over 50 years. Its principal aim is to keep the constitutional link with Great Britain.

Unionist. Someone who wishes to maintain Northern Ireland's position as part of the United Kingdom. The overwhelming majority of the Protestant community are unionists.

United Kingdom. The constitutional entity which comprises Great Britain and Northern Ireland. Beginning with the kingdom of England, it was created by three acts of union: with Wales in 1536, Scotland in 1707, and (the whole of) Ireland in 1801.

Drawn by M. Murphy

Chapter 1

'WHO'S AFRAID OF PEACE?'

Out of Ireland have we come
Great hatred, little room

Ireland is too small, as W.B. Yeats suggests, and the hatreds are too intense. His celebrated lines sum up the history of a conflict that has bedevilled relations between Ireland and Britain and among the people of the island themselves for centuries. It has brought tragedy and grief to untold numbers of families and communities. It has made Ireland, once known as 'the land of saints and scholars', a byword for violence and bigotry throughout the world. It has poisoned the country's political and intellectual life and undermined civil liberties and human rights in both Ireland and Britain. This book is the story of a determined effort to lay the foundations for a resolution of the Irish Question, once and for all, and to replace murder, terror, discrimination and inequality with the norms of a modern and civilised society.

How far back does one have to go to trace the roots of the conflict? The relationship between Ireland and England over the centuries, fortunately or otherwise, failed to culminate in the successful integration of the Irish into the British political and social system. There was a persistent demand for independence, expressed in its most militant form in modern times by the republican movement, founded as the Society of United Irishmen in 1791 by Theobald Wolfe Tone, a Protestant radical, and his friends, Samuel Neilson and Thomas Russell.

There is no need to rehearse the long history of strife and rebellion over the last 200 years. Suffice to say that there were regular outbreaks of armed revolt, finally leading in 1921 to the setting-up of an independent Irish state consisting of 26 of the island's 32 counties – today's Republic of Ireland.

In a sense, that was the easy part, because the 3.5 million

1

population of the 26 counties (now over four million) was over-whelmingly from the Catholic and nationalist tradition. Six northern counties remained part of the United Kingdom, with powers devolved from Westminster to a regional parliament at Stormont, on the outskirts of Belfast. The population of Northern Ireland was 1.68 million in the 2001 census. The religious break-down of that figure is almost 900,000 Protestants, the vast major-ity of whom wish to retain the British link, and 740,000 Catholics, who would mostly prefer a united Irish state. The rest belong to other religious groups or none. The dividing line between Northern Ireland and the rest of the island was drawn with the intention of ensuring there would be a permanent Protestant majority in favour of maintaining the Union.

For almost 50 years, apart from some republican violence in the 1950s, the pond was generally placid on the surface and few outside the region were aware of the bitter resentments and seething passions underneath. These boiled over eventually in the civil rights movement of the late 1960s, modelled on the black struggle in America whose methods of non-violence and passive resistance were adopted, along with the anthem, 'We Shall Overcome'. The civil rights marches and protests sought to end the second-class status of Catholics with regard to voting rights, job opportunities and housing. The movement was not overtly nationalist and did not put forward demands for unity and an end to the partition of Ireland. It merely sought the same equality that pertained in Great Britain itself, British rights for British citizens as it were. In the beginning there was a small but significant involvement on the part of liberal Protestant opinion.

The political system in Northern Ireland, dominated by an inflexible unionist elite, was unable to accommodate the demands of the Catholics and integrate them into a pluralist, inclusive society with equal opportunity for all. The fact that Northern Ireland was set up to maintain Protestant supremacy and the British link was not likely to facilitate pluralism in the first place.

As a mass movement of nationalists to end their second-class status, the civil rights campaign inevitably generated fear and loathing on the other side of the community divide. Attacks by loyalists on Catholic working-class enclaves in West Belfast in August 1969 quickly assumed the proportions of a pogrom[1].

Tragically, the civil rights leaders – for all their courage and dedication – had not thought things through. They underestimated the obduracy of unionism, the depth of loyalist fears and hatred, and the lassitude of Westminster when faced with a serious political challenge. They had not allowed for the eventuality, indeed inevitability, of ordinary Catholics being shot at and burnt out of their homes on a large scale. It was perhaps the first example of 'ethnic cleansing' in Western Europe since the Second World War. The Catholic working-class community turned for its defence to the Irish Republican Army. Here there was a further complication, because the IRA leadership had adopted a quasi-Marxist approach based on social agitation: in the process the organisation had become almost defunct as a paramilitary force. Legend has it that disillusioned nationalists chalked up 'IRA – I Ran Away' on the walls in West Belfast.

Veterans of former IRA campaigns, who were out of sympathy with the new political orientation, became active once again and formed the backbone of the defence of Catholic areas. At a convention in January 1970, the movement split into two wings, the left-wing Officials and the militaristic Provisionals. Over time, the Official IRA ceased to be a significant force, especially after it declared a ceasefire in 1972, and the Provisionals achieved virtual hegemony in the North's republican community. In time, too, the Provisional IRA adopted a socialist philosophy, although it was never formally Marxist. Its main focus remained a 32-county Ireland and, seeing the opportunity to achieve the long-cherished goal, it quickly moved from a defensive to an offensive role in the conflict. Recruitment soared in the wake of disastrous moves by the authorities such as the mistaken and mismanaged internment of suspected IRA members without trial in 1971 and the killing of thirteen civilians and fatal wounding of another by British soldiers during a march in Derry in January, 1972 which was quickly followed by the suspension of Stormont in favour of Direct Rule from London.

The conflict continued for a generation: the IRA could not be defeated but neither could it secure final victory. Whereas it enjoyed considerable popular backing in both parts of the island at the outset, a number of atrocities by the organisation led to a decline in public sympathy and support, especially in the Republic. The nadir of its activities was probably the Enniskillen

Remembrance Day bombing in 1987 when eleven Protestant civilians died in a blast purportedly intended for members of the security forces. The IRA still retained the support or at least tolerance of a significant element of the Catholic population in the North, especially in West Belfast, South Armagh and on Derry's 'West Bank', i.e., the mainly nationalist side of the River Foyle where Derry, or Londonderry as it is also known, is located. In the mid-1980s the IRA had received a number of substantial arms shipments from Libya. In October 1987, French customs officials intercepted a Panamanian-registered vessel, the *Eksund*, on its way to Ireland with a huge cargo that included ground-to-air missiles, heavy machine guns and plastic explosive. The IRA stepped up its campaign in the early 1990s with a series of devastating attacks in Britain. Republicans called these 'spectaculars', i.e. big operations with major physical and publicity impact. They were taking the war to the enemy: a huge explosion in the City of London in April 1992 killed three people and caused £800 million worth of damage and, a year later, the same district suffered £400 million damage when a bomb went off in Bishopsgate. According to an apocryphal story at the time, a top British civil servant asked one of his colleagues: 'Remind me again of the reasons we're holding on to Northern Ireland.'

If there were what republicans would consider 'successes', there were also disastrous blunders. The Shankill Bombing of October 1993, aimed at loyalist paramilitaries, resulted instead in the killing of nine Protestant civilians along with one of the two people who planted the bomb in a fish-shop on Belfast's Shankill Road. The IRA's activities were often counterproductive and hindered the growth of the republican movement's political influence. There had been a massive wave of public sympathy in 1981 when ten republican prisoners died on hunger strike rather than wear convict's clothing. The hunger strike leader, Bobby Sands, was elected MP for Fermanagh–South Tyrone and the base of support for the Provisionals in nationalist ghettoes was consolidated. Even greater political gains could have been made but the continuing IRA campaign acted as a drag on republican progress: Irish nationalists were prepared to turn out for a funeral or a by-election but were not ready for insurrection. To shore up moderate, as against revolutionary, nationalism the British and Irish governments concluded the Anglo-Irish Agreement in

1985 which, to the fury of unionists, gave Dublin a consultative role in the administration of Northern Ireland with Irish civil servants on the spot in Belfast as observers.

The conflict dragged on and, although the British Army could not defeat the Provisionals, the ultimate goal of unity still seemed no closer. However, the victory of Bobby Sands showed the political path could bring results. The old ways would not be abandoned just yet but, the argument went, what could be wrong with achieving Irish freedom with 'an Armalite (rifle) in one hand and a ballot-paper in the other'? It was a sign of growing pragmatism when in 1986 a majority in Sinn Féin (Irish for 'We Ourselves'), the political wing of the IRA, voted to end the policy of abstentionism towards the Dublin parliament, or Dáil. A small breakaway group, styling itself Republican Sinn Féin, held to the traditional stance of refusing to take seats in the Leinster House parliament which they believed had 'usurped' the true republican Dáil.

On 11 January 1988 the first of a series of meetings took place between Gerry Adams, president of mainstream Sinn Féin, and John Hume, leader of the moderate Social Democratic and Labour Party (SDLP), who enjoyed the support of the majority of nationalists in Northern Ireland. The Hume–Adams dialogue signalled a new development in modern Irish politics, the beginnings of a convergence between the constitutional and revolutionary traditions. There was a nineteenth-century precedent when physical-force republicans put violence to one side, for the time being at least, and sought to advance their aims by political means in a 'New Departure' with the leader of constitutional nationalism, Charles Stewart Parnell. At the same time that the Irish peace process was being born, other revolutionary movements in South Africa and Palestine were also exploring their political options. As an example of the new thinking, former Sinn Féin publicity director Danny Morrison wrote to Adams from prison in October 1991, quoting the South African revolutionary, Albie Sachs: 'We [the African National Congress] might find ourselves confronted with hard decisions, whether to hold out for generations if necessary ... or to accept major but incomplete breakthroughs now, transforming the terrain of struggle in a way which is advantageous to the achievement of our ultimate goals.'

British government policy was focused on containing the

IRA campaign and bringing together the mainstream parties on both sides with a view to establishing a power-sharing coalition that excluded Sinn Féin. The expansion of the middle ground might even lead to a situation where the security forces could crack down on and eventually crush the IRA. Yet one of the reasons the 1973 Sunningdale power-sharing agreement had ended in collapse and the resumption of Direct Rule was the failure to involve or at least neutralise the extremes.

A former British Secretary of State for Northern Ireland, James Prior, once mused that, 'The island of Ireland could become a Cuba off our western coast. What on earth would we do?' The dismantling of the Berlin Wall in November 1989 and the collapse of the Soviet system in eastern Europe may have contributed to a more relaxed British attitude: there was now little reason for even the most anxious Tory to fear a Soviet base on Albion's doorstep. One of Prior's successors in the job, Peter Brooke, delivered a potentially epoch-making pronouncement in November 1990 when he said that Britain had 'no selfish strategic or economic interest in Northern Ireland' (the subtleties of diplomacy meant that the absence of a comma between 'selfish' and 'strategic' was significant). He said later that the statement was premeditated and had followed consultation with John Hume, who had now been in dialogue with Adams for two years. Rarely can a nine-word phrase have been so carefully weighed and assessed before it was uttered: the Prime Minister of the day, John Major, describes it in his memoirs as 'a cornerstone of future policy'. An advance copy of the speech was sent to the Provisionals; in it, Brooke was echoing and expanding on the British commitment in the Anglo-Irish Agreement to legislate for a united Ireland if a majority in the North so desired. He had previously caused a mild sensation by hinting at the possibility of dialogue with republicans.

Republicans were interested but suspicious: pretending to be neutral was an old imperial trick and Brooke had not disavowed Britain's political as distinct from economic or strategic interest in Northern Ireland. Father Alec Reid, a Belfast-based priest who played a critical role as an intermediary, wrote in *The Irish Times* shortly afterwards that the Provisionals would only exchange their armed strategy for a political one if they were sure that 'the main nationalist political parties' would join them in pursuing the traditional aims of Irish nationalism. In other words, there would have to be some form of broad front or consensus with the SDLP and the government in Dublin, which at this time was led by Fianna Fáil.

Hume, who had been a bitter critic of the IRA's methods, saw a chance to wean the republicans away from violence and onto the constitutional path. Despite vitriolic and sustained criticism from elements of the southern media and strong reservations inside his own party, he persisted in his dialogue with Adams. It was arguably his finest hour.

Dublin was the missing leg of the stool. Sinn Féin had been in communication with Fianna Fáil: Charles Haughey, who headed the Irish Government at the time, was well-disposed and helpful to the process but kept the republicans at arm's length. A risk-taker was needed who would brave the misgivings of colleagues and media obloquy to provide the vital third element in the nationalist consensus and give Adams the basis for asking the IRA to call a halt to its campaign.

Cometh the hour, cometh the man. Another player arrived on stage who was to have a crucial role in consolidating the new nationalist consensus: Albert Reynolds became Taoiseach (Prime Minister) in Dublin in 1992. Fianna Fáil roughly translates into English as 'Soldiers of Destiny' but Reynolds had the swashbuckling approach of a Soldier of Fortune. 'Who's afraid of peace?' was his cry as he embarked on a politically risky programme of reaching out to the republican movement and its loyalist counterparts. At this time Sinn Féin representatives were still banned from radio and television, under the Irish Government's Section 31 censorship directive, and the IRA campaign had helped make the party a political pariah in the Republic. There was a climate of fear and suspicion surrounding the northern issue and establishment politicians approached it at their peril. I was on the political staff of *The Irish Times* and was sent to Reynolds' home county of Longford to cover his triumphant return after he had taken over as leader of the country's largest party and head of government. Like most reporters, I had a fairly hard-boiled view of politicians and, to most of the media, 'Albert' – he was always known by his first name – was a 'cute hoor' (clever manipulator) who had pulled a great 'stroke' by ousting the legendary Charles Haughey and grabbing the top job. Longford had never won a senior All-Ireland title in Gaelic games, a benchmark of first-class status among Irish counties, but now this neglected area of the Irish midlands had taken the prime political trophy.

Ruddy-faced folk from rural areas braved the February chill to greet their hero. In the ballroom of the Longford Arms hotel, they queued up to have their photograph taken with the new Taoiseach, no doubt to hang on the wall at home beside the customary pictures of John F. Kennedy and Pope John XXIII. In the schmoozy world of politics, Reynolds was that rare thing, a non-drinker. It was said to be the secret of his success in many late-night negotiations: like a certain brand of battery, he kept going long after his interlocutors had succumbed from too many fine wines and liqueurs. I can still recall, as he left the hotel that night, how he gave a little skip in the corridor. He had probably been on his feet since six o'clock that morning and it was now well after midnight, but he was still full of beans and clearly delighted with his newfound power and position.

A dynamo, yes, but to what purpose? I once described the wealthy pet-food manufacturer and former dance-hall propri-etor as 'the Frank Sinatra of Irish politics'. A close relative of his commented, 'You got that right'. The style of Irish politics had changed: instead of the carefully measured Haughey gravitas we now had the flashy Reynolds flamboyance. But surely the sub-stance would remain the same? The faces at the cabinet table would be different, but the North, the big issue of our generation not to say the entire century in Ireland, would continue to be kept at a distance, for fear the conflict would bubble over and engulf the South.

The media consensus can be a wall against reality. The ready cynicism, the shared jokes about the trickery and foibles of the political class, the endless supply of evidence that idealism and principle have virtually disappeared: these can almost blind you to sudden and startling turns of events. My sensibility was not quite so dulled, however, that I could not be stopped in my tracks by a speech Reynolds gave from an open-air platform in the cen-tre of Longford town that Saturday night. It was about the North and it was not so much the words as the tone, the determination, the obvious sincerity – in a politician, for heaven's sake – that gave me pause for thought. His ringing declaration, that all was not hopeless and something could be done to bring peace in our generation, pierced the cold night air. I gave a full report of this remarkable speech in Monday's paper but thought little more about it. There were other issues to distract one's attention: Reynolds sacked no fewer than eight members of the Haughey cabinet, revolving-door style, and there was a continuing fascination with appearances by himself and his colleagues at a tribunal over allegations of improper political interference in Ireland's multi-million pound beef industry. Unknown to most of us, Reynolds – whose critics said he was clueless when it came to Northern Ireland – was working away quietly on the peace process.

Reynolds had built up a good relationship with John Major, who had hardly ever visited Ireland but was also keen to grasp the opportunity to end the long conflict. The Taoiseach's special adviser, Dr Martin Mansergh, represented Reynolds in contacts with the republicans; London had already opened its own secret channel of communication, where the traffic soon intensified, although Reynolds knew nothing about it at this stage.[2]

Reynolds was the catalyst for the first significant public development in the peace process, the Downing Street Declaration signed by himself and Major on 15 December 1993. In this document Britain reaffirmed its long-standing pledge to place the constitutional future of Northern Ireland in the hands of the people of the region, who could decide by a majority vote to enter a united Ireland if they so wished. In a complex formula, Britain also accepted the right of 'the people of the island of Ireland' to self-determination and promised that Sinn Féin could take part in political negotiations once the party had established a commitment to exclusively peaceful methods.

Britain had held a referendum on the constitutional position in the North in March 1973: most nationalists boycotted the poll, which inevitably showed an overwhelming majority in favour of remaining in the United Kingdom. In the Anglo-Irish Agreement Dublin had accepted the principle that the consent of a northern majority was necessary to achieve unity: the Downing Street Declaration reaffirmed that position.

The Declaration reiterated Peter Brooke's carefully chosen formula that Britain had 'no selfish strategic or economic interest in Northern Ireland'. This was not the same as a declaration of intent to withdraw if a majority in the North opted for unity, but an Irish official commented privately that the document was 'suffused with the psychology of withdrawal'. It was also possible to read the statement as being completely in line with the affirmation in the Anglo-Irish Agreement that the constitutional position was a matter for the majority of the people of Northern Ireland. Hard-line republicans saw the Declaration as marking another stage in the 'sell-out' of nationalist fundamentals by Dublin, without serious objection from a Sinn Féin leadership that merely sought 'clarification'. There was a counter-argument that, despite the formal acknowledgment of the Union, the Declaration was the beginning of a process which would redefine and might eventually end the constitutional link between Northern Ireland and Britain. The statements of principle in the Declaration tended to support the status quo, but they were surrounded by ambiguous language which may have been intended to placate, but would certainly also encourage, nationalist and republican desires. Britain committed itself to encourage and facilitate dialogue and co-operation between nationalists and unionists and acknowledged that this might result in 'agreed structures for the island as a whole'.

Despite some tantalising language in the Downing Street Declaration, not to mention the prospect of Sinn Féin participation in talks about the future of the North, there were still many psychological barriers to cross before the IRA could be persuaded to halt its campaign. A previous cessation in 1975 had achieved little from a republican viewpoint and 'ceasefire' had become almost a dirty word in republican circles, where pacifist or moral arguments about the evils of violence carried little weight. Republicans were concerned that a prolonged cessation would be used by elements on the British side (the so-called 'securocrats') to undermine their movement. They were also worried that Sinn Féin would be sucked into conventional politics, becoming largely indistinguishable from Fianna Fáil and the SDLP.

Movement towards a cessation was achieved by a series of confidence-building measures, perhaps the most significant being the decision of President Bill Clinton in January 1994, in the teeth of strong British Government opposition, to grant a US visitor's visa to Gerry Adams. This ended a longstanding ban on entry to the US for Adams, who was seen as a spokesman for terrorism. Clinton's daring move demonstrated to Irish republicans and nationalists that the White House could be an impartial and even friendly entity in the developing peace process: the tradition whereby the US automatically took its lead on Northern Ireland policy from Britain no longer held. There was even a view that, as a post-war 'baby boomer', Clinton was less susceptible to the pull of the special relationship between Washington and London: his immediate predecessors had lived through the time when the US and Britain stood shoulder to shoulder against the Nazis while Dublin adopted a policy of neutrality.

In his autobiography Major tells of his 'astonishment and annoyance' when, in the face of a powerful lobbying campaign by himself and others, Clinton still gave Adams the go-ahead. Major's office had 'forcefully' told the White House that withholding the visa would be useful leverage in bringing an end to IRA violence. The Prime Minister's annoyance must have been all the greater when the Sinn Féin leader became the darling of the US media during his brief visit, but whether London liked it or not there had been a fundamental shift in US policy which would have huge effects further down the road.

Major implies that granting the visa delayed an IRA ceasefire but there is a counter-argument that it showed the republican leadership the advantages of a more political approach. Either way, speculation began to increase about a possible IRA ceasefire. When a Sinn Féin conference at Letterkenny, County Donegal, rejected the Downing Street Declaration in July 1994, most observers misread it as a signal that there would be no IRA cessation. It was a fraught and nervous time for everyone, journalists included. We knew our reputations were at stake as we tried to divine the intentions of a secret army. Opinion began to harden that they might do it, after all, but there was still a widespread belief that it would be time-limited. Some of us got word a week in advance that an indefinite ceasefire was on the way by the end of the month. Reynolds was under pressure to accept nothing less than a 'permanent' halt to violence but in the end the issue was fudged when the IRA announced a 'complete' cessation on 31 August.

I remember going home from the office one night after writing a page one report that the ceasefire was imminent. I was unable to unwind from a combination of nerves, the wear and tear of a difficult news story, and euphoria. Instead of the reporter's favourite, the BBC World Service, I listened for hours to a rock station on my transistor radio, which I normally would not dream of doing. The possibilities of the new situation seemed enormous: the Troubles, which had blighted our lives in many ways and in which many of my generation had lost friends or acquaintances, looked like coming to an end. Naively optimistic, few of us saw the many difficulties and obstacles that lay ahead. Some days later, I attended the all-Ireland hurling final at Croke Park in Dublin: people stood to applaud Reynolds when he arrived in the dazzling September sunshine. I mused privately that we might yet see the Ulster Unionist Party leader as an honoured guest at this quintessentially Gaelic, nationalist and, until recent years, Catholic event. Reconciliation was breaking out all over, it seemed: but like most others of my background, I still had a lot to learn about unionism.

The loyalist paramilitaries, who were taking new and more enlightened political advice from the likes of Billy Hutchinson, David Ervine and Gary McMichael, called their own ceasefire six weeks after the IRA. One of the surprise features of this intricate and absorbing process was that, despite the fearsome activities of loyalists on the ground, their political representatives were more pragmatic and flexible than many mainstream unionists.

There was now a widespread expectation that Sinn Féin would be admitted to all-party talks within months. However, Major's parliamentary majority was slim and the small contingent of Ulster Unionists in the House of Commons potentially crucial to his survival. Given the empathy between the two leaders, Reynolds might have had a chance, however remote, of persuading Major to adopt a different perspective. However, a political crisis blew up in Dublin over allegations of delay in processing an extradition warrant for a priest accused of child sexual abuse. Political life was convulsed with rumours of church–state conspiracy and allegations of scandal that would supposedly rock the foundations of government. In retrospect, it looks like a bottle of smoke but it was sufficiently serious at the time for Reynolds to lose his coalition partner, the Irish Labour Party, and then resign as Taoiseach. Having held his own with Charles Haughey, the British Government, the IRA and the loyalist paramilitaries, Reynolds finally lost his political nerve. Had he called a general election, he might well have swept the country. Loyalty within his own party was in short supply, but one of the few who stayed faithful remarked ruefully: 'He climbed Mount Everest and stumbled on a pebble.'

The new Taoiseach, John Bruton, leader of the Fine Gael party, did not have the special relationship with Major that Reynolds had. Nevertheless, Bruton's three-party 'rainbow' administration pressed ahead in negotiations with the British, leading to the publication of the Joint Framework Document in February 1995. Labour was a junior coalition partner in both the Reynolds and Bruton governments, but whereas the party's leader, Dick Spring, had been the cautious partner in the Reynolds administration, he now took a more adventurous stance. As Reynolds was to him, so he was to Bruton, but for his pains in helping to maintain the peace process at this time Spring was rapidly demonised by the unionists. For his part, Bruton went out of his way to show the unionists that he understood their fears and anxieties although he got little by way of public gratitude for this from any quarter. Bruton told me later: 'Without unionists feeling that they had a measure of understanding from responsible political leaders in the Republic, Trimble wouldn't have been able to go as far as he did subsequently.'[3]

In the Framework Document, Dublin agreed in principle to modify the territorial claim to the North in the Irish Constitution by making it subject to the wishes of a majority in the North, but the document also proposed a new North–South body or council to take decisions on an all-island basis on designated topics. A second paper in the name of the British Government envisaged an elected assembly to administer Northern Ireland. Advance leaks served to heighten the fears of unionists, who took fright at the proposals for North–South interaction which they saw as the high road to unity. 'Framework' became a dirty word in the unionist vocabulary and they would not accept the paper even as a basis for negotiation. However, the ideas in the document, representing as it were the collective wisdom of the two governments, were highly significant. Its publication meant that a lot of the groundwork had been done when the time came to tie up a deal between the parties and therefore little time was wasted on administrative detail.

Supposedly to placate the fears and anxieties of unionists over republican weapons, Brooke's successor at the Northern Ireland Office, Sir Patrick Mayhew, announced during a visit to Washington in March 1995 that partial decommissioning of weapons by the IRA was required before Sinn Féin could be admitted to all-party talks. This new, post-ceasefire, precondition became known as 'Washington Three' because it was third on a list of stipulations (the other two were non-controversial) set out by Mayhew.

Whatever London thought it was up to, this was not the way to do business with the leaders of the IRA who had been operating on the basis that, if they called a ceasefire, Sinn Féin would be admitted to talks. Prior decommissioning was not part of the deal as far as they were concerned. The view is still strongly held in some circles, mainly among the Provisionals, that Washington Three was part of a 'securocrat' agenda (the word was formed from 'security' and 'bureaucrat' and first came into use in the South African context), aimed at splitting and demoralising the republican movement. Although there had been declarations on the need for prior decommissioning from some Dublin politicians, before they realised its politically lethal implications, it only took off as a serious issue after Mayhew's speech. The unionists quickly took up the cry and it became their Number One issue in the peace process for several years.

The republican and broad nationalist mood soured still further when, after a controversial Orange Order parade along the nationalist Garvaghy Road in Portadown, County Armagh, the Rev Ian Paisley, leader of the hard-line Democratic Unionist Party (DUP), and the local Ulster Unionist MP, David Trimble, walked triumphantly hand in hand. Sourness gave way to near-despair among nationalists two months later when Trimble, widely perceived as a hard-liner, emerged as the surprise victor in a contest for leadership of the Ulster Unionist Party (UUP). A leading Sinn Féin member, when informed of the news, went white in the face.

As so often, events on the surface of politics distracted attention from the underlying reality. Reflecting their growing interest and involvement in the peace process, Bill and Hillary Clinton made an official visit to Belfast and Dublin at the end of November 1995. They were met by large and enthusiastic crowds: no US president had received such a warm reception since John F. Kennedy's visit to the Republic in 1963 and, by all accounts, it made a huge personal impression on the President. 'Why don't you love your neighbour? Go ahead and turn the other cheek,' sang rock stars Van Morrison and Brian Kennedy as Bill Clinton switched on the Christmas lights at Belfast City Hall. Before then, his interest in Ireland seems to have been utilitarian: it was a good issue to pursue, which won him friends in the powerful Irish-American community. After this visit, it was personal. Clinton told people these were some of the best days of his political life. It also said something about the Irish of both traditions and on both sides of the Border. A leading Irish-American writer summed it up for me: 'A needy man met a needy people.'

Bruton has told me how he and his colleagues used the imminence of Clinton's visit to secure agreement from London for the launch of a 'twin-track' approach whereby decommissioning would be dealt with in a separate channel from the broad negotiating process. He had 'a succession of phone calls' with Major that night and the 'twin-track' was launched 'while Clinton's plane was in the air'.[4]

There was much talk of the 'Clinton majority', the young Catholics and Protestants in the North who turned out to greet the most powerful man in the world and listen to his plea for peace. The presidential entourage included the former US Senate majority leader, George Mitchell, who was Clinton's economic envoy to Ireland. As with the Reynolds speech in Longford, I remember being struck by the obvious sincerity with which Mitchell spoke of his affection and regard for the people of Northern Ireland, from both traditions. The Clintons got an equally enthusiastic reception in Dublin, appearing on a platform outside the old parliament house in College Green.[5] In the background the US Ambassador, Mrs Jean Kennedy Smith, a sister of the late John F. Kennedy, could be seen rubbing her hands with delight at the size of the crowd and the success of the occasion.

Away from the spotlight, however, there was growing tension among Irish republicans over the lack of political progress. Warnings from Adams about the likely consequences went unheeded or were dismissed as sabre-rattling. In an attempt to overcome the impasse on weapons, the British and

15

Irish governments commissioned a report from a group of three respected international figures led by Senator Mitchell, whose involvement in the Irish situation was deepening. The International Body on Arms suggested the possibility of decommissioning in parallel with talks, instead of beforehand. Mitchell recalls in his book, *Making Peace*, how the trio were told by Major that, if they suggested parallel decommissioning, he would reject their report.[6] However, the group had come to the conclusion that seeking prior decommissioning was both impractical and unworkable.

London then tried another tack and asked that a reference to elections in the North be included in the final text. Responding to the Mitchell Report in the Commons on 24 January 1996, Major signalled that he was moving away from prior decommissioning, but most attention was drawn instead by his acceptance of the unionist demand for elections ahead of talks.[7] Nationalists and republicans had no time for Major's subtle manoeuvring, accusing him of 'binning' the Report and pandering to unionists. With hindsight, this looks like an overheated and politically unwise reaction: the view that elections were Major's device for getting off the hook of prior decommissioning seems plausible in retrospect. Indeed Bruton had told Major the previous September that the elections idea had potential, on the basis that 'this created a unionist cart onto which you could put nationalist baggage'.[8]

Major had left it too late and his response was the last straw for republicans: the IRA had been making preparations for renewed violence for several months and now the ceasefire came to a dramatic end with the bombing at London's Canary Wharf on 9 February.[9] Two people died, more than 100 were injured and there was over £85 million worth of damage. A friend who was in the bar at Leinster House, location of the Irish parliament or Dáil, said people knew something was up when cellphones started ringing all around the room. According to a Dublin source, the bombing operation was set up the previous September.

Euphoria gave way to despair. However, later in the month, the British and Irish governments announced that multi-party talks would be convened on 10 June, following elections in Northern Ireland. Despite their denials, it was hard to avoid the

unwelcome and disturbing suspicion that the bomb had gal-
vanised the two governments into action.[10] In the contradictory
way of the peace process, however, the governments excluded
Sinn Féin from the talks because of continuing IRA violence.

The governments published a set of proposed Ground Rules
for the forthcoming talks and named 30 May as the date for elections to a Northern Ireland Forum. Each party would nominate
delegates to the negotiations from those elected to the Forum, but
the talks would be completely separate in every other respect.
Since the Forum would determine who could sit at the talks, a
way had to be found to ensure that the smaller parties, particularly those linked with the loyalist paramilitaries, obtained seats
at the table. The civil servants devised an electoral system whereby each of the eighteen parliamentary constituencies elected five
members to the Forum, making a total of 90; there was a further
group of twenty seats, with the ten parties which secured the
highest votes on an aggregate basis throughout Northern Ireland
obtaining two seats each. Were it not for the 'top-up' system, the
loyalists would not have been eligible to take part in the negotiations. Despite being excluded from participation in talks because
the IRA campaign had resumed, Sinn Féin reluctantly decided to
take part in the poll. This was the election that precipitated the
collapse of the ceasefire and sceptics wondered how strong
republican objections had really been in the first place. The party
increased its vote dramatically and won seventeen seats although
it did not intend to take part in the Forum, which eventually
petered out for want of nationalist participation.

It was the beginning of a long road and the end still has to be
reached. Even at time of writing, the future of the peace process
remains in the balance. But if it succeeds in bringing about a just
and lasting peace, then the characters who took part will be long
remembered and a source of curiosity for generations to come. If
the process fails, few will care to know who the main players
were, never mind the bit parts. Who remembers more than the
main participants in the short-lived Sunningdale experiment?

Let us assume it will be a success and that future generations
will be curious to know what the key players and the major sec-
ond-ranking people were really like and what kind of atmosphere there was, as Northern Ireland groped its way towards
peace at the turn of the century.

Curious readers will want to know who started it all and made the first moves which brought such sweeping and significant results? The first name that comes to mind is inevitably Gerry Adams, though closely followed by John Hume. I first met Adams in 1986. A Dublin government minister had launched a fierce attack on him as a 'bird of carrion' feeding off the atrocities of the IRA from which he allegedly sought to make political gain. It was strong stuff, though not untypical of the time and I was asked to seek an interview with Adams, in the interests of balance: let's get the other fellow's point of view. In my first encounter with the man I found him surprisingly low-key in his approach, focusing on local issues on the Falls Road rather than the broad sweep of Anglo-Irish relations or the campaign the Provisional IRA was waging in the North. There was limited interaction in those days between the Dublin-based media and the republican movement, whose activities were generally covered by security specialists as part of the crime and terrorism brief, rather than political or general reporters. In the wake of the great H-Block hunger strike upheaval of the early 1980s, Sinn Féin had become a political force in the North, but had made little impact in the South where it was generally regarded in establishment circles as the propaganda arm of the IRA.

Slim, tall, bearded, Adams seemed grateful for the rare interest of a general news journalist. He wanted to speak Irish with me, while apologising for a lack of proficiency (he has improved a lot since.) Having had relatively little face-to-face contact with active republicans, I expected a latter-day Pádraig Pearse,[11] speaking in visionary terms about the 'sacrifice' and the 'struggle'. I might not approve of his views, but surely they would make interesting copy? Instead, as he chronicled the woes of his West Belfast constituents in wearying detail, I found myself thinking, 'He's a more militant version of Gerry Fitt'.[12] He failed to match the stereotype of the firebreathing subversive, choosing instead to act as a conduit for the grievances of the grass roots, more like his predecessor as MP for West Belfast than a tribune of the people.

It was some time before I encountered Adams again. IRA violence continued unabated and there was no let-up either in loyalist counter-attacks, which were usually directed at ordinary Catholics. Like most of my contemporaries, the situation in the

North plunged me into despair. There seemed little or no potential for political progress. The republican movement was caught up in a spiral of violence and the talks between mainstream parties appeared to be bogged down in boring minutiae, never going anywhere.

Unknown to me and most other observers of the political scene, Adams was working away on a possible solution, having joined with John Hume in the cause of achieving peace by non-violent means. Even his enemies would acknowledge that Adams looks at the Big Picture. Everything he says and does in politics is connected with a grand plan or strategy. His pronouncements are often enigmatic and hard to fathom at the time but this may be because he is so many jumps ahead of everyone else. His enemies and critics call him Jesuitical. His intellectual and tactical subtlety sometimes confuses and irritates people but he has brought the republican movement a long way down the peaceful road, in the process helping to create a large and powerful political consensus stretching from the White House to Leinster House. It has been a hard road for Gerry Adams. As a republican leader he has been sharply attacked over the great suffering inflicted by the movement, but he, too, has paid a price. Relatives and friends have died and he himself was the victim of an assassination attempt whose after-effects still remain. He pays close attention to detail and not all of his associates find him a delight to work with, but he would be the republican movement's nominee for the title of Ireland's Nelson Mandela. Like him or loathe him, Ireland's fate is inextricably bound up with the success or otherwise of his political project.

The other half of the peace process double act, John Hume, is a totally different proposition. All his life, the Derryman has combined an espousal of non-violence with the relentless pursuit of his community's legitimate aspirations for economic, social and political advancement. It has been a wearing and wearying struggle which has taken its toll, leaving him in a state of questionable health. While his achievements are monumental, his flaws are obvious. Without Hume, the nationalist community would have a lot less clout internationally and in the Republic of Ireland: there is no Basque counterpart of John Hume, for example. Without Hume, nationalist efforts to achieve equality and proper recognition would have been smothered years ago in headlines about terrorist atrocities. Interviewing the man is frustrating – he will often repeat simple slogans coined many years before, e.g., about the need to 'spill our sweat and not our blood' or the fact that 'you can't eat a flag'. The wits call it the 'single-transferable interview'. His critics complain that he is vain and egotistical, glorying in his many peace awards and prestigious foreign trips, not to mention his high-level political access in Washington, London, Dublin and Brussels, but his enemies and opponents know he is a formidable force. His energy and drive are not what they were, but he remains a political and moral colossus ranking in stature with the nineteenth-century nationalist leaders, O'Connell and Parnell.[13]

Hume was preaching the gospel of political activity by nationalists from the start; Adams came later and had to work his way through a lengthy phase of republican violence before finding the farther shore; there was a third player required, without whom the Hume–Adams project would end in failure. It was essential for their joint efforts to be reciprocated from the unionist side and the unlikely vehicle for this was one David Trimble.

Unionism has never wanted for hard-liners and Trimble had always seemed one of the hardest of them all. He was involved in the right-wing Vanguard movement, which had disturbing authoritarian trappings and was led by the former Stormont home affairs minister and scourge of leftists and republicans, William Craig. Trimble played a part behind the scenes in the loyalist workers' strike which brought down the power-sharing executive in 1974. His triumphalist behaviour after the Orange Order march along the nationalist Garvaghy Road in Portadown in 1995 horrified even moderates and when he became UUP leader the same year efforts to achieve a peaceful historic compromise in Northern Ireland looked doomed.

Closer scrutiny would have taken account of the fact that Portadown was in Trimble's own parliamentary constituency of Upper Bann. As the local unionist MP and a member of the Orange Order, he was unlikely to resist the temptation to share in the glory of a successful Garvaghy Road march. In the broader political sphere, even in his Vanguard days he had argued for a voluntary coalition between unionists and moderate nationalists. He had also developed an unusually close relationship, for a senior unionist, with the British Labour Party under its new modernising leader, Tony Blair.

Nevertheless, Trimble was a reluctant recruit to the peace process. He never seemed quite able to free himself of suspicions about the republican movement's real intentions, although he was by no means alone in this regard. He was also under constant pressure and attack from Paisley's DUP and disillusioned rightwingers in his own party, who took it badly when their hard-line hero turned around and made a deal with the ancient enemy.

While Adams, Hume and Trimble were the main leaders, all three had able, dedicated and talented people in their parties who provided essential back-up and in some cases substituted for the leader when he was not available. In republican circles, Martin McGuinness was looked on as a giant. Revered by the grass roots and hated by unionists in equal measure for his activities in the 'struggle' over three decades, McGuinness showed another side to his character and personality as the peace process developed. Where Adams contributed the broad, strategic sweep, McGuinness surprised some by proving a canny negotiator, pragmatic and with an eye to the main chance. The boy revolutionary developed into a mature and skilful politician – the latter description is not mine but comes from a senior Irish civil servant. More than the chief lieutenant to Adams, McGuinness got 'respect' in his own right, thanks to his formidable history as an activist and his direct and commanding personality. If Adams was the architect of the republican project, McGuinness was the engineer.

Hume, too, had a powerful and commanding deputy leader in the person of Seamus Mallon. Whereas Adams and McGuinness never seemed to exchange a cross word, the testy relationship between Hume and Mallon was a legend in northern politics. The early years of the peace process were necessarily discreet, even secretive. The term 'team player' does not readily come to mind in describing John Hume, and the SDLP often seems to have wondered what its leader was up to and if he knew what he was doing. In a celebrated meeting during the last, agonising month before the 1994 ceasefire, tensions almost reached breaking point, with Mallon, in particular, expressing serious qualms about the likely trajectory of events. Hume held up against the pressure and when peace talks eventually started

Mallon became a central figure, arguably more important on a day-to-day basis than his leader.

In the UUP there was little doubt that Trimble's most loyal, able and trusted lieutenant was Reg (later Sir Reg) Empey. Like Trimble he was a former member of Vanguard but began to show signs of moderation when, as Lord Mayor of Belfast, he braved the displeasure and protests of his fellow-unionists by addressing a conference in the city in April 1990 which was attended by the Taoiseach of the day, Charles J. Haughey. A tall, slim man with a pleasant, amiable manner, Empey could still talk tough when he felt the situation required it. He was seen as a critical index of middle-ground unionist opinion and Trimble had little chance of selling any deal, pact or package to his people unless Empey was also backing it. The UUP's official deputy leader, at least at Westminster,[14] was John D. Taylor, a former junior minister in the old Stormont government, who narrowly escaped death when the Official IRA tried to kill him in 1972. Taylor was a less-visible and politically more erratic figure than Empey: his waverings at critical moments set his colleagues' teeth on edge, although he had a good 'feel' for what the grassroots were thinking and always seemed to come down on the side of the angels in the end.

The local politicians in Northern Ireland were important. Without Gerry Adams and John Hume there would have been no peace process. Without David Trimble there might well have been no possibility of agreement. Those republican and loyalist paramilitary leaders who were looking for an alternative to 30 years of violence were also critical. There were other players, though, whose role, while not always visible, was probably crucial. The British and Irish prime ministers and the US President come into this category. Behind Tony Blair, Bertie Ahern and Bill Clinton there were teams of officials and advisers, many of whom worked long hours and displayed extraordinary patience and endurance as they strove to keep the ship afloat and bring it safely into port.

What of the media? Most of us would claim no credit for what was achieved: that was the business of politicians. From time to time our reports were criticised as 'unhelpful', but full disclosure and the public's right to know transcends the political process. We showed endurance, that's for sure, covering a story that was at times like watching paint dry and at other times full of drama and tension without respite. It was a privilege to watch history in the making and see the politicians, with all their faults and failings, and in some cases paramilitary records, struggling to reach agreement so that their children would not have to go through the whole thing all over again. It was an engrossing human story, but professionalism obliged the watching media to conceal their feelings: behind it all they probably cared more than they even realised ourselves. It is fair to say also that there were some in the media and in the political sphere who regarded the process with deep scepticism and were concerned that it had the potential to bring unreconstructed paramilitaries into the heart of the democratic process with catastrophic results.

This was the drama, these were the actors. Divisions which had grown wider and deeper over decades and even centuries had to be bridged because the killing and the mayhem could no longer continue and, if it did, the example of the Balkans showed that it might get even worse. Like one of those New York skyscrapers, a whole society was being shifted on its foundations to catch the light of a new dawn. Nobody said it was going to be easy ...

Chapter 2

RESTORING THE CEASEFIRE

The two Prime Ministers, Major and Bruton, came to Belfast for the opening of multi-party talks on 10 June 1996, almost two weeks after the Forum elections. At a joint press conference, Major left unionists and everyone else in no doubt that he hoped and expected George Mitchell would chair the negotiations. Major failed to mention the Framework Document although Bruton referred to it twice in his remarks. This deepened nationalist suspicions that London was taking its distance from the Framework in response to unionist pressure. There was a fairly cynical view of the talks at this stage in the media and indeed in the population at large. The notion that it was all a bit of a circus was strengthened by the public divisions and rancour among unionists. The cynicism missed the point: a deadly serious issue was being fought out. If Mitchell was rejected because of unionist objections to his alleged links with Irish-America, the consequences further down the line would be very damaging. Nationalist and republican confidence in the process would be dented and White House involvement halted at source.

The eventual appointment of Mitchell to chair the talks provoked a temporary walkout by the DUP and Robert McCartney's United Kingdom Unionist Party (UKUP). In the early hours of 12 June a unionist delegate tried to occupy the chair before Mitchell arrived. He was fended off by the Political Development Minister at the Northern Ireland Office,[1] Michael Ancram, who installed a civil servant to hold the seat for the Senator. Having walked out, the dissidents came back next day, arguing in the face of UUP sneers that their return did not imply an acceptance of Mitchell's chairmanship. McCartney addressed Mitchell as 'Sir' rather than Chairman.

The negotiations were conducted on the basis of three sets of relationships, or 'strands', to be debated concurrently. Strand One dealt with new arrangements for the internal governance of

24

Northern Ireland; Strand Two with the North-South relationship and Strand Three concerned relations between Ireland and Britain. Both Paisley and McCartney declared their intention of being involved in Strands One and Two but not in any sessions conducted under Mitchell.

There were bitter words for the UUP leader from the DUP's Rev William McCrea at Castle Buildings, the dreary office block at Stormont where the talks were taking place. Trimble was finishing a television interview and, with the cameras still running, McCrea accused the UUP of 'surrendering Ulster' and 'lying to the people' and he claimed Trimble had a 'guilty conscience'. An embarrassed Trimble gently demurred, addressing McCrea by his first name and seeking to mollify him. The gospel-singing MP for Mid-Ulster was having none of it. For a southerner like myself, it was an instructive illustration of the type of pressure Trimble was under from his right.

The following weekend the IRA bombed the centre of Manchester, injuring several hundred people and causing massive damage to property. There was outrage and incomprehension as the television news showed footage of Saturday shoppers with blood streaming from their injuries. Most of them were ordinary working-class people and many would have Irish connections. Trimble demanded a security crackdown to ensure the Provos could not bomb their way to the table. He drew in the IRA killing of Detective Garda Jerry McCabe at Adare, County Limerick in a botched robbery attempt on 7 June, shortly before, as evidence that 'Sinn Féin are not able to meet the requirements for participation in this process'.

With Sinn Féin remaining outside, the parties at the talks began to discuss rules and procedures. There was concern that the UUP's objections might lead it to walk away, but Trimble said a composite paper produced by Mitchell and his staff and incorporating proposals from his own party had gone a considerable way towards meeting their concerns. The UUP had been seeking to transfer many of Mitchell's powers to the Business Committee of the talks, which had a co-ordinating role and was chaired by General John de Chastelain, Canada's former chief of defence staff, who was also chairing the North–South Strand Two section.[2]

It amounted in effect to replacing Mitchell with de

Chastelain as the main chairman. Unionists were more comfortable with the Canadian military man, a Scots Presbyterian by birth, than with the Kennedy-linked US politician. It was not surprising to hear, given the seventeenth-century mindset of some in Northern Ireland, that the religious background of the two men was a factor, with de Chastelain regarded as 'one of ours' and Mitchell seen as some sort of Catholic, or at least an associate of Irish Catholics. De Chastelain's American mother was a Walsh whose grandfather probably came from Kilkenny, in southern Ireland, although that did not register with the unionists. Some nationalists were worried because both de Chastelain's parents had been wartime intelligence operatives but in fact Mitchell had worked with US Army counter-intelligence in West Berlin during the Cold War. The biographical permutations were endless, but the two governments had chosen Mitchell as their main chairman and so he remained.

The first of many serious complications developed over the relationship between the procedures being worked out with the parties and the Ground Rules for the talks agreed previously by the British and Irish governments. When a point of procedure was raised by the deputy leader of the DUP, Peter Robinson, Ancram told him this was covered by the Ground Rules. Ancram further suggested that the Ground Rules should operate in parallel with the new procedures and he proposed that the new procedures should include a clause recognising this.

Ancram's comments reportedly 'opened up a can of worms': the Ulster Unionists proposed that aspects of the Ground Rules be incorporated into the new procedures but that material reflecting the aspirations and desires of the two governments should have no special status in the talks. The precise legal standing of the Ground Rules document was also in dispute, with the UUP maintaining that it was no more than a position paper from the two governments and not binding on other participants. The Irish Government and the SDLP took the view, however, that the document was legally binding. Irish Government sources said that both Dublin and London were reluctant to 'let the Ground Rules go'.

The dispute appeared technical but was in fact political, reflecting the continuing desire of unionists to reduce Mitchell's influence and enhance the position of de Chastelain. There was no obvious difference of outlook between the two but Mitchell was the one with links to Clinton and Kennedy. The DUP and McCartney proposed that Mitchell's powers be limited to those granted him by the participants in the talks and that any powers previously given him by the two governments 'shall be of no force or effect'. The SDLP insisted on the primacy of the Ground Rules document and proposed that, in the event of any conflict of interpretation between the new set of procedures and the Ground Rules, 'the relevant chairman shall take the Ground Rules document to be the authoritative text'. Important issues were being discussed and decided and Sinn Féin leaders subsequently expressed frustration at being kept out of the talks when these debates were taking place. When they eventually got to the table the rules previously agreed meant that Sinn Féin carried little weight in arithmetical terms when it came to voting.

The extent of Dublin's interest and commitment was seen in the fact that four cabinet ministers – Dick Spring, Proinsias De Rossa, Nora Owen and Mervyn Taylor – as well as junior finance minister Hugh Coveney, arrived for a plenary session about the overall agenda on 19 June. However, because of the Ground Rules dispute the plenary lasted only three minutes.

As efforts to reach a compromise continued, the differences of emphasis between the main unionist factions hardened into a split. There was severe criticism of the UUP from its unionist rivals – known as 'The Cousins' in the Trimble camp. The DUP accused Trimble of forming an axis with Spring, whereas Trimble said the new rules of procedure incorporated 'significant changes' from what had been proposed originally by the two governments. McCartney responded that the Irish Attorney General, Dermot Gleeson, and the SDLP's Seamus Mallon had stated 'in no uncertain terms' that nothing would be changed in the Ground Rules. Although reporters were excluded from the talks, inside sources said the participants agreed to complete discussions on the procedures and the agenda before returning to the issue of the status of the Ground Rules. This meant that an obstacle to the progress of the talks had been put to one side, but not yet overcome. This became a pattern in the negotiations: issues were 'parked' but the engine was never allowed to get so cold it could not be restarted.

Relations between Dublin and Sinn Féin were seriously

disturbed by the discovery of a large quantity of arms and explosives in a bunker south of the Border at Clonaslee, County Laois. Senior Coalition Government sources said it was 'deeply disturbing'. Contact had not formally been broken off but it was 'becoming more and more difficult'. Spring was said to be particularly disappointed: he had put an enormous effort into securing the nomination of Mitchell to chair the multi-party talks. Spring's contribution to the peace process in general during the Rainbow administration was very considerable and even those who criticised him for pulling out of government with Reynolds were at least partially mollified.

At least there was some progress on technical matters in the negotiations, with participants agreeing on the basis for decision making on issues where unanimous agreement could not be reached. Decisions could be made if there was 'sufficient consensus', namely, the support of parties representing a majority of the total valid poll in the Forum elections, a majority of both communities in Northern Ireland as represented by the parties in the negotiations and, thirdly, a majority of the parties involved in the talks. This was known as a triple-lock mechanism. There were implications, not just for the talks, but for any future system of government or local assembly that might be agreed, where this approach was likely to continue.

There was little advance on issues of substance, however. A remark the previous April by Dick Spring's influential aide, Fergus Finlay, that talks without Sinn Féin were 'not worth a penny candle' had brought howls of criticism but events now confirmed the truth of his observation. The republicans were privately very eager to call a halt to their campaign so they could get to the talks table but first of all they needed certain guarantees from London. As the winter of 1996 approached, Hume and Adams launched a determined initiative – the first of two – aimed at persuading Major to create the conditions for a fresh ceasefire. The first approach to the British was on 10 October 1996. Major's response came on 28 November by way of a reply to a parliamentary question from Tory backbencher Andrew Hunter. Critically, the Prime Minister gave no date for Sinn Féin entry to talks, merely stating that any new ceasefire would have to be tested over 'sufficient' time. This lack of precision would not do, and the two main issues at this time were (a) how soon after a ceasefire would Sinn Féin be sitting at the table and (b) how would the decommissioning issue be addressed, once Sinn Féin was in the talks and had committed itself to the Mitchell Principles of democracy and non-violence.[3]

Hume and Adams met on 10 January 1997 and, at the end of that month, the SDLP leader faxed a list of questions to Sir John Chilcot, permanent undersecretary at the NIO. Believed to have been drafted with the aid of Irish officials, who played an active role behind the scenes throughout this period, the Hume–Adams questions were variations on now-familiar themes. Hume informed the NIO that 'suitable answers' would lead to an IRA ceasefire: in other words, the IRA was signed on, if London would send the right signals.[4]

The British stalled and decided to give Hume their own list of six questions for the Sinn Féin leader. If Adams answered them, London would in turn respond to the Hume–Adams list of queries. The British approach came across as minimalist and unenthusiastic. Keeping the heat on, Adams told a news conference in Belfast on 10 February that he had sent a fax to Major asking him to authorise contact between his officials and Sinn Féin. Downing Street sent an answer the same day, signed by a senior Prime Ministerial aide: 'If you are serious about peace-making you will call an immediate and lasting ceasefire.'

While Adams was sending his fax to Downing Street, the IRA was preparing to take a more traditional and lethal course of action. At 6.30 pm on 12 February, Lance Bombardier Stephen Restorick (23) was manning a checkpoint at Bessbrook, County Armagh. A friendly young man, he had just checked a woman through in her car and was apparently still smiling when he was hit by a single high-velocity round which struck him in the back below his flak jacket. The soldier was taken to Daisy Hill Hospital, Newry, within ten minutes, but was certified dead at 7 pm. The shooting came a week after an IRA spokesman had rejected suggestions that the organisation was engaged in a 'phoney war'. Observers believed the IRA was sending a message to the next British government, since it seemed virtually certain there would be no ceasefire before the Westminster election. The predictable republican response when challenged about the killing was given by Sinn Féin chairman Mitchel McLaughlin who said the ultimate responsibility lay with John

Major for failing to bring the republicans into the talks process.

The republican view at the time, according to sources close to their thinking, was along the following lines: the British government was prepared to engage in talks while the IRA campaign was at its height but, as soon as the first ceasefire was declared, all meaningful communication stopped, to be replaced by peremptory demands for a handover of arms – a gesture of surrender. However, the more politically-minded republicans knew a full-scale return to violence could wreck the pan-nationalist consensus, which was already under strain, and dissipate the political and propaganda gains made, especially in the US.

Therefore, it was not a case of 'Cry havoc and let slip the dogs of war' but pay out the leash slowly and allow some controlled and carefully calibrated forms of violence to keep London on its toes and at the same time placate the hard-liners in the movement. The strategy earned the disdain of diehard elements and there were sneers about a 'shoot to miss' policy, but informed sources said there had been a 'strong message' to activists to avoid civilian casualties. 'Quite significant efforts are being made to hold IRA activity at the level where the militants are happy and the politicals are still on board,' sources said.

The political side of the movement kept pointing up the alternative available to the British if they chose to adopt it. Sinn Féin's chief negotiator Martin McGuinness said at a news conference in Belfast that the Framework Document had not been advocated or pushed forward by either of the two governments since its publication two years before. He also took a swipe at Bruton: 'There are many people in the nationalist community – right across the broad spectrum of nationalists – in the North of Ireland who are less than happy with Mr Bruton's stewardship of his end of the peace process ...' Privately a senior Sinn Féin figure said the Framework Document was the 'bottom line' for the republicans but he suspected it was the 'top line' for Bruton. The criticism of Bruton reflected republican frustration with his approach and was probably quite helpful to Fianna Fáil as it geared up for the coming general election in the South. Later, republicans claimed in conversation with me that, after Canary Wharf, there were two occasions during the remaining life of the multi-party Rainbow administration in Dublin when the ceasefire could have been renewed, but the opportunity was lost. John

Bruton was intrigued when I put this to him later: 'I don't recall it being made clear to me.'[5]

The renewal of the IRA campaign was meant to give a short, sharp shock to the British, leading to a rapid restoration of the ceasefire and Sinn Féin's entry to talks, but that was not the way things worked out. It eventually got to the stage where the conditions for restoring the ceasefire included the return of Fianna Fáil to power in Dublin and a Labour victory in Britain. There was a cynical element in Fianna Fáil which wanted the IRA to hold back the ceasefire until after the general election in the Republic but, until they became disillusioned with Bruton and Major, this was not the attitude of republicans, who wanted to get into the talks as quickly as possible.

Adams replied to London's questions on 20 February, appending a highly significant article he had written for the following Saturday's *Irish Times*. He used the article to set out the republican terms for a ceasefire. He made clear that Sinn Féin would formally commit itself to the Mitchell Principles of democracy and non-violence upon entering the negotiations. The British based their reply to Adams on their previous policy statements. Again the answers were not sufficiently precise about the timing of Sinn Féin's entry to talks and thus failed to generate the necessary momentum.

As so often, Trimble was taking steps to ensure he would not be outflanked on the right. In a *Belfast Telegraph* article at the end of February, he urged the parties and governments to proceed without Sinn Féin and the IRA, which he described as an 'unreformable terrorist gang'. Yet even UUP sources acknowledged privately that, as things stood, there was only so far they could go with the SDLP before the majority nationalist party had to mark time while its republican cousins decided whether or not they wanted to go along.

The multi-party talks had been limping feebly on at Stormont. The day they adjourned on 5 March was particularly bleak: reporters and camera crews mooched about wondering how to breathe life into a story that was gradually slipping down the news agenda. One observer said it was not so much a case of *Four Weddings and a Funeral* (the title of a popular film) as 'Four Funerals and a Funeral'. A huge investment of time and energy, by a wide range of participants, had gone into the talks – but to little or no avail. It couldn't go on much longer like this.

Many believed only a British government with a clear majority of at least 30 seats (some said 50) would feel strong enough to resist unionist anger – and pro-unionist sentiment in the Commons – and give the republican movement the guarantees it was seeking. While there was a general expectation that Labour would win the election in May, at that stage few anticipated the eventual landslide victory by 179 seats. Lines of communication between Sinn Féin and elements in the Labour Party were said to be busy.[6] A strong Sinn Féin showing in the Westminster poll, combined with an offer of an IRA ceasefire, might well concentrate the minds of an incoming government. Yet very senior UUP sources claimed to regard the prospect of Labour in Downing Street with equanimity. 'We are very comfortable with Tony [Blair],' they told me, pointing out that there was a significant element of the Labour Party sympathetic to the unionist case. Trimble was relatively unusual as a unionist leader in having a cordial relationship with Labour. There was also more comfort for unionists than republicans in Blair's Northern Ireland pronouncements before becoming Prime Minister.

Sinn Féin had not openly given up on Major but the republicans seemed to be going through the motions in order to make a political point, rather than holding out any great hope that he would bring them into the talks. On 10 March, Mitchel McLaughlin urged the Prime Minister to take advantage of the period prior to the Westminster elections and authorise contact between the two sides. The Hume–Adams package presented to Major the previous 10 October was still on the table: 'We're talking about a commitment to inclusive negotiations without preconditions, a time-frame within which those negotiations will happen and a range of confidence-building measures – indeed Gerry Adams explained the IRA's role in confidence-building in those circumstances.' Around this time a republican leader told me his ideal British government would be a Labour majority led by John Major. This remark acquires added piquancy when you consider that the IRA tried to kill Major and his ministers in a mortar attack on 10 Downing Street on 7 February 1991!

Debate still continues as to whether it was the importance of the Ulster Unionists in the parliamentary arithmetic or the prevalence of unionist sentiment on the Tory benches – and in

Major's own outlook – that caused the Prime Minister to remain inactive when a ceasefire and a place in the history books were there for the asking. There is an argument that all Major's positive actions in the peace process were carried out at the urging of Albert Reynolds and that, when he was gone, there was no one with the same influence on the Irish government side. Doubt must remain, though, over Major's capacity to bring his party and the unionists with him even if Reynolds had remained at the helm in Dublin. Bruton points out that Major was weaker when he was Taoiseach than in Reynolds' time.[7]

All along, the republican side was eager and even anxious to restore the ceasefire: Canary Wharf was meant to be part of a short, sustained campaign which would come to an end quickly when Major invited Sinn Féin into talks. The invitation never came and the delay was causing concern on the republican side. Looking back on that period, republicans felt they missed a significant opportunity by being absent from the talks when ground rules were being agreed because these turned out to be very important when terms for agreement were being worked out.

It was now time for the annual migration of Northern leaders to the US for St Patrick's Day. It had got to the stage where most of the front-line political leaders departed for Washington, leaving the Belfast scene almost deserted. With all the political activity going on, it was inevitable there would be significant public statements and interventions.

The first of these – which was also the most moving and eloquent – came from George Mitchell. The setting was straight out of Cecil B. DeMille: the National Building Museum in Washington DC is an epic structure with Romanesque pillars rising hundreds of feet to the ceiling. Amid the pillars sat the great and the good of Irish America, their tuxedos and backless evening gowns a long way from the humble attire of their immigrant forebears. There, too, was David Trimble, chatting to his party colleague, Jeffrey Donaldson, both of them making a point about their Scots-Irish background by wearing tartan bow ties. Their party's security spokesman Ken Maginnis was seated nearby; John Hume was at a different table with his wife, Pat; Mitchel McLaughlin sat with friends in another part of the room. Senator Edward Kennedy, a long-time supporter of non-violent nationalism in the North, dropped in for the reception, and his sister, the US Ambassador to Ireland Mrs Jean Kennedy Smith stayed for the meal.

Perhaps it was during his years as a federal judge that Mitchell learned how to bring a hushed silence even to the largest of gatherings. He spoke in simple, clear sentences in a voice that was penetrating but not piercing: here was genuine gravitas and solemnity, a serious intervention on a life-and-death issue. When the Stormont talks were breaking up shortly before, journalists wondered yet again why a man who could be doing more pleasant and productive things in life could endure sitting at a table for nine months listening to dreary re-runs of the Ulster quarrel. Now he revealed he had often asked himself the same question. What had kept him going was his desire to 'help others to have a chance'. For that to happen there had to be peace and reconciliation: 'No one can really have a chance in a society dominated by fear, hatred and violence.' He made clear that he was motivated by feelings of common humanity towards the people on both sides, trapped as they were in the vice of history. The Senator was seeking to exorcise the twin demons of Northern Ireland – violence and intransigence – evil spirits which 'feed off each other in a deadly ritual in which most of the victims are innocent'. The twin demons did not want anything to change, ever, they wanted to re-create a past which could never happen again.

It was not so much the content as the impassioned tone and style of delivery which struck home to Mitchell's audience. His powerful oration was followed the next night by a forceful contribution from Senator Edward Kennedy, at a function in New York organised by *Irish America* magazine. The Massachusetts Senator, who was picking up the award for 'Irish-American of the Year', was introduced by John Hume. Kennedy was blunt and to the point: he urged Major and Blair to drop other preconditions and promise Sinn Féin entry to the talks in return for an unequivocal IRA ceasefire. It had become fashionable to dismiss the last ceasefire as a sham but, in a pointed dig at Downing Street, Kennedy said this 'comes with ill grace from those in high places who do not want to admit or accept their responsibility for failing to respond to the ceasefire'. He didn't mince his words either on decommissioning: it was 'a phoney issue because the IRA and the loyalist paramilitaries can each disarm today and rearm tomorrow'. Decommissioning in parallel with the talks was a 'good suggestion' but it should not be a precondition for getting to the table. As one observer said afterwards, 'That's an initiative from Kennedy – not just a speech'. It certainly was: Kennedy was not speaking just for himself but for the entire pan-nationalist consensus. The text was released in advance and carried on the wires: presumably London would have been well aware of its contents ahead of delivery.

Later in the week, Kennedy expressed disappointment with the reaction to his remarks. 'Many Americans have difficulty understanding how the Prime Minister can be talking to the representatives of the IRA when they are involved in violence, as Major was, and then to have a whole period of seventeen months when there is no violence – and refusing to engage in conversation.'

Back home, on 1 April, armed and masked IRA men appeared on the streets of Belfast – not in a funeral parade or reading a prepared statement in a graveyard but in a rare show of naked force. It took place during an Easter Rising commemoration in North Belfast. The two IRA men suddenly materialised while a message from republican prisoners was being read. The crowd responded eagerly to a call for a round of applause for 'the Irish Republican Army: these are the men that are protecting our community ... the only protection we have in our district'. One of the IRA men waved a Kalashnikov in the air, the other brandished an Uzi sub-machine gun. Both wore balaclavas. The crowd comprised about 1,000 republican supporters from Ardoyne, the Bone and Ligoniel districts. Prominent among the attendance was the republican Eddie Copeland, who survived a loyalist bomb which exploded under his car the previous December. After the display concluded and the IRA men had slipped away down a side street, the Sinn Féin councillor from Dungannon, Francie Molloy, gave the customary Easter oration. There were blunt words for the incoming Labour administration. He said memories of Roy Mason's hard-line approach as secretary of state 'makes us wary of any future Labour government'. He had a message for the current Labour spokeswoman: 'Mo Mowlam would need to come up with more than fancy words.' He went on: 'The British Labour agenda, let's be quite clear, is a return to Stormont under a power-sharing executive and, as we have said before, a return to Stormont is not acceptable to republicans.' Molloy asked what Labour in government was going to do for republican prisoners. 'Will they release Roisin McAliskey [daughter of the former MP, Bernadette Devlin McAliskey], not just because she is a young girl, pregnant and in jail, but because she is innocent, because she is an Irish republican hostage?'[8]

It looked as if a little political theatre was being enacted to send a message to New Labour. There had been a more conciliatory approach by Martin McGuinness at a republican rally in County Tyrone the previous day. McGuinness described Mowlam's statement that Sinn Féin could be in talks by 3 June if there was a genuine IRA ceasefire as 'encouraging' and he hoped it was a sign of 'new and progressive thinking within the British Labour Party'.

Four days after the Molloy speech, the IRA caused an international media sensation by disrupting the Grand National horse-race at Aintree, Liverpool. Nobody was hurt but the event had to be abandoned after an IRA bomb-warning which later turned out to be a hoax. Thousands of punters were obliged to evacuate the course. The political and media reaction was unfavourable but in the words of a former Taoiseach: 'The IRA doesn't care about bad publicity.' It was part of a sustained campaign of bloodless but effective disruption with warnings about bombs at railway lines and motorways. Republican prisoners had also been busy: a tunnel was discovered under the exercise yard at the Maze Prison on 24 March. Nevertheless, speculation about a renewed IRA ceasefire continued unabated. Even the attacks in Britain were an echo of similar activities which took place prior to the 1994 cessation. There had been forecasts of a lull in IRA violence in Northern Ireland for the duration of the election campaign, but it was said that this would not necessarily be accompanied by an immediate scaling-down of operations in Britain.

On 9 April, Trimble sent a message of his own when he spelt out 'the characteristics of a genuine ceasefire'. Introducing election candidates at party headquarters in Glengall Street, he declared it was up to 'Sinn Féin-IRA' to demonstrate there had been a genuine ending of violence. 'What one should focus on is the quality of the ending of violence, whether it is merely another cynical manoeuvre such as we've seen in the past and is being predicted at the moment, or whether it is a genuine change of heart and a genuine turning away from violence.' There was a hint, however ambiguous, that Trimble was less worried about the details of decommissioning than about the republican mind-set and whether a renewed ceasefire would be merely tactical.

The last high-profile act of violence by the IRA in this period was the shooting of a police officer on a busy street in Derry. Constable Alice Collins was shot and wounded as she stood guard outside Derry Crown Court. The attack took place only minutes before an IRA ceasefire was rumoured to be coming into effect. However, Sinn Féin sources failed to confirm reports that a de facto cessation had begun. Asked later if he had considered asking the IRA to suspend operations for the duration of the election campaign, Adams gave a cautious answer: 'I'm not going to get into any speculation at all about what the IRA is at.' Nationalist sources sympathetic to Sinn Féin claimed there was a well-orchestrated exercise in black propaganda underway and that the spurious ceasefire story was fed to journalists to put the republican movement on the defensive. Later, however, there were reports that Sinn Féin wanted the absence of IRA activity in this period to be taken into account by the British Government in deciding when to admit republicans to multi-party talks.

The most plausible interpretation of events was that IRA violence was being switched off until the ballots were counted, but republicans were not going to admit this was the case because it would lessen the value and impact of declaring a formal ceasefire sometime in the future.

Outsiders might find it strange that the IRA violence prior to the start of the election campaign was not expected to damage Sinn Féin's prospects in the Westminster poll. Local observers described the Sinn Féin support base as 'bullet proof' – they said a sex scandal involving one of Sinn Féin's leaders would lose the party far more votes than the activities of the IRA. Some said after the election, however, that the shooting of the police officer in Derry had prevented Sinn Féin from winning the West Tyrone seat (tragically, having survived an IRA bullet, Alice Collins later died of cancer).[9] IRA activity probably also slowed down the expansion of Sinn Féin's support base by alienating those who were wavering between the republicans and the SDLP.

Throughout the peace process there would be an unresolved argument: did the reality and the threat of IRA violence impel London to come to terms with the republicans or did it do more harm than good by reinforcing suspicions that the Sinn Féin leadership was not 'for real'? A long-time observer said at the time that the Provisionals were reminiscent of the Sandinistas, who had an unfortunate tendency to visit Moscow every time there was an important debate on Nicaragua in the US Congress.

Trimble called for the 'flawed' Anglo-Irish pact of 1985 to be replaced by a British–Irish Agreement. 'The broader agreement must look to the totality of relations within the British Isles which is the natural social and economic unit.' Such an agreement could include an appropriate cross-frontier relationship which would be based on pragmatic considerations of mutual benefit and not on a political agenda, he added. Nationalists and republicans were also seeking a new British–Irish Agreement: their list of demands was not the same as Trimble's but observers felt that with intelligence and imagination some common ground might be identified. The UUP leader's reference to 'an appropriate cross-frontier relationship' was also quite promising. It was hard to avoid the impression that a series of choreographed steps were being enacted.

I interviewed Gerry Adams at the start of the election campaign and the overwhelming sense from an hour's conversation was his deep and abiding distrust of the Tory government and his near-total disillusion with the Prime Minister. He said Major should have seized the opportunity to tie up a peace settlement but that military advisers and intelligence 'spooks' had persuaded him to use the peace process to wage war by other means on the IRA. 'They stretched it like elastic and then it snapped.' He believed Major was advised that if he waited long enough the IRA, being a voluntary organisation, would evaporate and its members go back to ordinary life in colleges, on the farm or on the factory floor. Thus, when Canary Wharf occurred it caught them all on the hop.

The other main thrust underlying Adams' remarks was his almost pathological determination not to split the republican movement. Others might argue that you could not allow the last ship in the convoy to set the pace and there was a strong feeling in the political establishment at the time that this was happening inside republicanism. However, Adams was determined that, next time the IRA laid aside its arms, the movement would remain as united as it was in 1994: 'We had no Hamas in that situation.'

Reflecting the private contacts with Dublin that were taking place, Adams saw the role of the Irish Government as crucial. If Dublin and London were speaking with one voice, then there was no space for the Americans and others to get involved. 'The international community will only act in the space between London and Dublin.' It was a revealing insight into the Adams approach: Dublin was not just important in itself, it was the key to getting the US involved.

When the Westminster election results came in, Labour's landslide victory combined with Sinn Féin's success in winning two seats clearly strengthened prospects for a renewed ceasefire. At sixteen per cent, Sinn Féin had the third-largest share of the vote in Northern Ireland, overtaking the DUP on fourteen per cent. Running under the slogan, 'A New Opportunity for Peace', the republicans went up six points on the ten per cent they received in the 1992 general election, although there was only a slight increase on the fifteen and a half per cent secured in the 1996 Forum poll. The SDLP also increased its share on 1992, from 23.5 per cent to 24 per cent but Adams won back the West Belfast seat from Dr Joe Hendron, reducing the SDLP team in the Commons from four to three. On the unionist side, the UUP had gone from nine to ten seats after winning the new constituency of West Tyrone; the loss of the Rev McCrea's seat in Mid-Ulster to Martin McGuinness meant that the DUP now had two representatives at Westminster instead of three.

Trimble had now lost any arithmetical advantage he enjoyed at Westminster and despite their leader's outwardly jaunty approach, Unionist sources privately expressed some trepidation at the prospect of dealing with a Labour government with an unassailable majority. They also foresaw a rescue operation being mounted by Dublin on behalf of the SDLP to keep a resurgent Sinn Féin at bay. The last such mercy mission resulted in the Anglo-Irish Agreement, which still seared the unionist soul. Where could the next one lead – joint authority?

The republicans had done well but it would be wrong to conclude that everyone who voted for them was an IRA supporter.

The peace process was good for Sinn Féin electorally. The party was also seen as a vehicle for nationalist anger on a number of issues. The first was the Drumcree/Garvaghy Road issue, which rankled bitterly. The crucial factor in the Mid-Ulster constituency was the decision by the sitting MP, the DUP's Willie McCrea, to share a platform with the prominent loyalist, Billy Wright, the leader of the Loyalist Volunteer Force which was blamed for many murders of Catholics. It was hard to imagine anything more calculated to arouse the ire and outrage of even the most non-political nationalists. Another factor was that even many moderate nationalists accepted Sinn Féin's analysis that the British Government and particularly Major were to blame for the collapse of the peace process. There was also a strong element in the nationalist vote of seeking to help those who were perceived as doves in the republican movement.

Dr Marjorie 'Mo' Mowlam took up duty immediately as secretary of state, saying there was a 'door open' if the IRA would allow Sinn Féin to pass through it. She introduced herself in her new role to the ordinary people of Northern Ireland in a 'walk-about' among the Saturday shoppers of downtown Belfast. At one stage the cabinet minister asked for a bite from a punter's apple: this extreme informality contrasted with Mayhew's more reserved demeanour. What became known as her 'touchy-feely' approach would later be cited as a drawback by some Ulster Unionists who would have preferred someone more 'ladylike' although their main objection was that she was not sufficiently on their side in political terms. An Irish minister later described her to me in enthusiastic terms as 'the first impartial secretary of state'. The previous April it was announced that Dr Mowlam had been undergoing treatment with radiotherapy and steroids for a brain tumour. 'I am a tough old boot'[10] was her characteristic response.

She rapidly signalled a new approach in a three-page statement issued on taking up her new post, which spoke of achieving 'a new settlement for Northern Ireland'. The key words were 'consent' and 'support': there would be no constitutional change without the consent of a majority, but any arrangements for government should have the support of all. She committed the incoming government to the reform of policing and ensuring equality in employment. She expressed a desire to see Sinn Féin in the Stormont talks provided there was an unequivocal IRA ceasefire. On balance, her words were more likely to appeal to nationalists than unionists, although her reassurance on the consent principle was clear and unequivocal. Republicans noted with approval the signals directed towards themselves. Cautious hopes were now being raised for the renewal of the ceasefire.

Next day, Adams told a Sinn Féin rally in Belfast that the new government had to recognise there would be no peace settlement 'unless every single political prisoner is freed from prisons on this island and in Britain'. With freshman MP Martin McGuinness standing beside him on the platform and the rain pouring down on their loyal followers, Adams said: 'Sinn Féin is ready to do business with the British government. We are ready to do business with the unionists.' Republican sources said Sinn Féin was examining the legal position on opening offices for the new MPs at Westminster, a move immediately interpreted by observers as the first step towards ending the longstanding policy of abstention from the House of Commons.

Some unionists were already speculating in private conversation whether Mowlam had the 'Right Stuff' for her highly demanding new job. The marching season would give her a chance to show if she had the political skill and courage required for her highly challenging assignment. Nationalists, too, would be watching to see if she would stand firm on the key issues or, like Labour in the mid-1970s, collapse ingloriously in the face of militant loyalism and unionism.

The new Prime Minister was not generally known for having a special interest in Northern Ireland and there was some surprise when he arrived in Belfast on 16 May, only two weeks after taking office, to deliver a major set-piece speech at the Balmoral conference centre. It was his first visit anywhere and his first major speech since the election. Republicans were taken aback by the apparent pro-Union emphasis in the speech and Blair's disparaging remarks about the likelihood of achieving a united Ireland.

'I am committed to Northern Ireland. I am committed to the principle of consent,' he said. 'My agenda is not a united Ireland – and I wonder just how many see it as a realistic possibility in the foreseeable future.' Pointing out that the North was, along with England, Scotland and Wales, one of the four constituent parts of the United Kingdom, the Prime Minister said: 'I believe in the United Kingdom. I value the Union.' Again and again, he stressed the centrality of consent. Of course, if supporters of a united Ireland won a majority without coercion, that would be respected. Then he made his most wounding comment of all, from a republican perspective: 'None of us in this hall today, even the youngest, is likely to see Northern Ireland as anything but a part of the United Kingdom.'

In his eagerness to set unionist minds at ease, the Prime Minister had gone too far for republicans. However, wrapped among all this pro-Union sentiment, there was the hugely important announcement that he was permitting his officials to meet Sinn Féin. It was about the only practical measure the speech contained. The Prime Minister's words were essentially a smokescreen.

Blair said his message to Sinn Féin was clear: 'The settlement train is leaving. I want you on that train.' The content of the speech was reportedly made known to the UUP at the highest level in advance. I found it a futile exercise making the argument to republicans that Blair clearly felt obliged to engage in union-ist rhetoric to allay the fears aroused as he opened the door to the political associates of an organisation dedicated to killing Crown forces. Blair's manoeuvrings had the republicans bemused: one of them described him as an 'enigma'.

Contact had been officially re-established between Sinn Féin and top civil servants in Dublin – although republicans said it was never broken off. Informed sources were now saying that if Ahern replaced Bruton as Taoiseach in the forthcoming general election in the Republic, then an IRA ceasefire was a strong pos-sibility. The Sinn Féin weekly, *An Phoblacht/Republican News*, made it clear that republicans wanted to see a change at the top. The main feature article on the forthcoming general election began by calling Bruton 'a national disaster' and the piece was illustrated with a smiling photograph of Ahern and Adams. A visit by Ahern to the Falls Road after he became party leader had been extremely important in developing trust with Sinn Féin because of the effect it had on the people of West Belfast who felt that Ahern understood what his role was in relation to northern nationalists. Bruton had worked hard on the North as Taoiseach and was centrally involved in such key developments as the publication of the Framework Document and the initiation of multi-party talks and he made a genuine effort to appeal to the unionists but there was better chemistry between Sinn Féin and Fianna Fáil, despite the latter's harshness towards republicans in the past. Chemistry, of course, sometimes leads to explosions but nobody was thinking about that just now.[11]

At noon on 21 May, Quentin Thomas of the Northern Ireland Office and Sinn Féin's Martin McGuinness headed separate delegations in a meeting at Stormont Castle. The British side was playing down the encounter in advance, ludicrously refusing even to confirm officially that it was taking place. Sinn Féin was full of suspicion and ready to make a rapid judgment on what it saw as the key issue: are the British serious or are they just stringing us along, like they did before for seventeen months? The meeting lasted three hours and was totally different in tone from the last such encounter. The fact that a new government with a different agenda was in office was reflected in the approach of the civil servants. While the two sides did little more than outline their respective positions, the 'mood music' had changed. McGuinness told reporters afterwards that a start had been made in overcoming difficulties in the peace process. Asked if he detected any change of attitude from the civil servants since they last met fifteen months before, McGuinness said: 'It was very clear to me from their demeanour at the meeting that they are now working under a new set of employers.' Although Mowlam was not present at the meeting, she was hovering nearby and said later at a news conference: 'The time is not yet set but if things remain the same on the ground they will meet again in the near future.'

The general climate between Sinn Féin and the British had improved. The new administration was expected at some stage to reopen the inquiry into the Bloody Sunday shootings of 1972.[12] London had also indicated that the decommissioning issue would not be allowed to block Sinn Féin's entry to substantive negotiations.

Writing in *The Irish Times*, Adams called on the British to state clearly that Sinn Féin would gain immediate entry to the talks following a ceasefire. London's reluctance was understood to be motivated in part by nervousness over the likely UUP reaction. The White House was observing progress and Mowlam travelled to Washington, where she met Ted Kennedy on 23 May. His speech the previous March left no doubt what his message would be.

There should have been time for a rest after the Westminster elections, but the northern parties had to embark straightaway on vote-getting in the council poll. The political map of Northern Ireland was being redrawn at local level as preliminary results indicated the main unionist parties were likely to lose control of councils in Belfast, Fermanagh and Tyrone. Belfast would shortly have its first nationalist Lord Mayor, the SDLP's Alban Maginness.

As the results came in, cars displaying the Tricolour and hooting their horns made their way through central Belfast. Sinn Féin supporters leaning through the windows cheered exultantly and exchanged taunts with passing loyalists. A loyalist woman on the footpath was incensed by the demonstration and shouted in anger at police for allowing it to take place. The completion of the count confirmed the rise in support for Sinn Féin, which gained 23 seats and increased its share of the vote by 4.7 per cent.

Later in the evening, loyalists organised their own victory cavalcade past Belfast City Hall, waving flags of the Ulster Volunteer Force, Ulster Defence Association, Red Hand Commando and Ulster Freedom Fighters from car windows. Election posters were used to black out car registration numbers. Sinn Féin had displayed no paramilitary posters and, as a person of a Catholic background standing virtually alone on the footpath, I found the demonstration somewhat chilling: loyalist paramilitaries had killed about a thousand ordinary Catholics in the Troubles. As I watched the exultant procession make its way past the seat of local government, I noticed a pair of newly-weds having a photograph taken in the grounds at the front of the City Hall. Only a set of railings separated the normal and everyday from the world of paramilitarism and terror: the happy couple on one side, paramilitary supporters on the other. The police watched the victory procession but took no action. It was a source of some comfort that, instead of celebrating a shooting or bombing, the paramilitaries were marking their successes at the ballot box. The Progressive Unionist Party, political wing of the UVF, now had six council seats, and the Ulster Democratic Party, linked with the UDA, had four. Previously they held one each. Inside the hall, Sinn Féin's Alex Maskey recalled how in 1983 he was his party's sole representative on Belfast City Council. At the time Sinn Féin activists were being assassinated in a campaign reminiscent of the Phoenix programme in Vietnam. Maskey himself had been shot and wounded in 1987, exactly ten years before. In those days, when Sinn Féin councillors got up to speak at meetings of different councils, unionist opponents would blow trumpets or spray deodorants into their faces.

Meanwhile, there were suggestions that London was being urged to take the current absence of IRA activity into account as part of a de facto decontamination period so that Sinn Féin could be admitted immediately to talks once there was an IRA ceasefire. Mowlam referred to the issue in an interview on Radio Ulster. Asked by the presenter, Jim Dougal, if she believed there was at the moment an unofficial IRA ceasefire, she replied that this seemed to be the case in Northern Ireland but it was difficult to know if it was also in operation in England. Dougal asked: 'If there was a ceasefire announced, would you look at a period before it, when there had been no activity, as part of a testing period?' Mowlam said: 'I think it would have to be taken into consideration, but I don't want to make a clear commitment that that time-period would be important.'

The second meeting between Sinn Féin and the British on 28 May lasted more than three hours. Insiders said that there was a lack of substance and no real dealing. Afterwards, normally talkative Sinn Féin spokesmen were tight-lipped. The IRA was quick to draw its own conclusions. Leaving a 1,000 lb van bomb in the Poleglass estate in Belfast two days later was.an obvious signal that, in a famous phrase used by Gerry Adams during the first IRA ceasefire, 'They haven't gone away, you know'.

Sinn Féin sources said privately the British side seemed to be marking time at the second meeting and speculated that London might be waiting until after the general election in the Republic. Republicans denied they had gone into the second meeting with a fresh shopping list and a new and more demanding attitude inspired by their success in the local elections. Party sources said the real problem was that the British side refused to 'put meat on the bones' and would not give specific responses to the standard Sinn Féin demands: immediate entry to talks, a time-frame for those talks, the removal of decommissioning as an obstacle to talks and a series of confidence-building measures.

Despite the difficulties, a third meeting was agreed in principle. While refusing to guarantee immediate Sinn Féin entry to talks, the British were stressing that there would be no unnecessary delay once a ceasefire had come into operation. Irish Government sources said that the adjournment of the talks for the summer holidays could be 'used creatively' in devising a formula to facilitate Sinn Féin entry in September. Two recent meetings between Sinn Féin and Irish Government officials had helped greatly in improving relations between the republicans and Downing Street. Considerable weight was given by both London and Washington to Dublin's assessment of the republican movement's intentions. In their meetings with Sinn Féin, the Irish officials stressed the importance of grasping the present opportunity and warned that any further IRA violence would have a major alienating effect on British opinion.

The North was said to be a key issue in Clinton's discussions with Blair during a presidential visit to London on 29 May and it was a focus of attention at their joint press conference afterwards. Downing Street sources insisted the two leaders were completely in tune on Northern Ireland. Clinton had reportedly offered any assistance Blair required and told Mowlam that peace in the North was 'an article of faith in my life and household'. At the press conference Clinton struck a balanced note between calling on the IRA 'to lay down their guns for good' and stressing the need for all parties to engage wholeheartedly in the peace process.

On the morning of 3 June, as the talks were resuming at Stormont's Castle Buildings, Adams arrived with a busload of Sinn Féin's elected representatives. The gates were closed to keep them out, but this meant also that members of the loyalist Ulster Democratic Party, who happened to come along at the same time, were obliged to wait outside until the Sinn Féin delegation had left. Yet everyone in Northern Ireland knew that the loyalist ceasefire was as much fiction as fact and there had been more loyalist than IRA paramilitary activity in recent months. Sinn Féin sources said this was an example of double standards, although they stressed they did not want the loyalist parties expelled from the talks. It was a neat propaganda coup for the republicans.

It was reported that Dublin and London were working on a joint paper aimed at breaking the decommissioning logjam. There had been an interesting signal of a new British attitude generally, in a message sent by Blair to a musical commemoration of the Great Famine at Millstreet, County Cork, the previous weekend. While in opposition, Ahern had urged in the Dáil that London should apologise for the Famine and it was hardly a coincidence that Blair was now saying that, 'Those who governed in London at the time failed their people through standing by while a crop failure turned into a massive human tragedy'.

Trimble departed from his usual hard-line language to hint at a possible climbdown on weapons when he said at the 10 June talks session that the parties should 'pigeonhole' the decommissioning issue. The political risk he had taken was underlined when Paisley immediately denounced him for 'the most serious surrender statement' any UUP leader had ever made. 'Pigeonholes are the cage for every unclean and deceitful bird when you're selling a country out to the enemy,' Paisley said.

Decommissioning was the last thing on the IRA's mind at this time. At 11.45 am on 16 June, two men, reportedly disguised as women out shopping, ran up behind two policemen on the beat in a Lurgan side street and shot them in the head at point-blank range. The assailants escaped in a car which was later found burnt out in the nationalist Kilwilkee estate. Constables Roland John Graham and David Andrew Johnston were the first RUC members to be killed by the IRA since the end of the first ceasefire. Their deaths left five children under ten without fathers and generated a wave of helplessness and apprehension in the community at large, heightened by the fact that the annual Drumcree church parade by the Orange Order in nearby Portadown was now only three weeks away.

What political aim, if any, lay behind the shootings? Sources in the peace process said at the time that the British government had been responding very positively to Sinn Féin overtures. Progress had been made and the scene was set for a successful third meeting between NIO civil servants and Sinn Féin. There had been encouraging noises from Clinton, and the expected replacement of Bruton by Ahern as Taoiseach in the next election south of the Border meant that, from a republican point of view, all the pieces would be in place.[13] Republican sources insisted, despite the sceptics, that the killings reflected the fact that the 'war' was still in progress. Yes, the Sinn Féin leadership was making progress with the British but no ceasefire had been called and the activists on the ground were doing what IRA members did – attack the security forces.

Publicly, at least, Sinn Féin was isolated as Blair called off the next meeting planned between the party and the Northern Ireland Office. Bruton, who was with Blair at an EU summit in Amsterdam, indicated there would be no further contact between his officials and Sinn Féin, and there was negative reaction too from the White House. A proposed meeting between Ahern and the republicans was in doubt, although the Fianna Fáil leader left the possibility open as long as the subject was a new IRA ceasefire. Bruton immediately said such a meeting would be 'terrible'. Even in the wake of this horror, the British government did not definitively close the door on Sinn Féin. The line coming from Blair and Mowlam was, no further talks 'in these circumstances'. Mowlam was not her usual jaunty self: she looked depressed, even crestfallen. However, she was working all-out for a ceasefire and privately republicans had kind words for her. 'She's good', a high-level Sinn Féin official said. 'She's in there trying to do it.'

In a statement on the killings which was considered stronger than usual on these occasions, Adams said: 'At a personal and at a human level I am shocked.' Bruton was dismissive: Sinn Féin had 'ransacked the dictionary'. While Ahern made no such public comment, he let it be known in unequivocal terms to Sinn Féin that there was deep and heartfelt dismay and despondency in his camp at the apparent perversity of the republicans, suing for peace with one hand and shooting policemen with the other.

It subsequently emerged that documentation had been given to the republican movement from the British side on 13 June – three days before the Lurgan killings. It reportedly conceded '95 per cent' of what they had sought – sources revealed that there weren't many i's to be dotted or t's to be crossed – and was apparently due for release in the form of an official statement on 19 June. Were it not for the shootings of the RUC officers, it was said this documentation would have set the stage for a renewed ceasefire by mid-August and Sinn Féin's entry to talks on 29 September. Blair said pointedly in the Commons that the Lurgan killings were 'a doubly wicked act because those who were responsible knew perfectly well of the chances that were being taken and the opportunities to try and put this process back on track and get a lasting political settlement'. Clinton was said to feel he had been 'taken for a sucker'.

If there was anger, there was also bemusement. Loyalist politicians I was speaking to at the time recalled that, just before Canary Wharf, there were persistent rumours the two governments were about to call all-party talks with Sinn Féin participation. On this occasion, Sinn Féin had reportedly been promised entry into talks six weeks after an IRA ceasefire and Irish Government officials were said to have recommended the deal. The attack raised a number of questions: did those who ordered it have prior knowledge of the British document and, if so, why did they proceed and in the process jeopardise the new relationship between London and Sinn Féin? Other IRA actions that year seemed to be part of a deadly and carefully worked-out political and military strategy but the effect of these shootings was anarchic. The location of the shootings also raised eyebrows, as North Armagh was not known for a high level of IRA activity. Was a dissident element trying to sabotage the peace process?

The stark and terrible circumstances in which Constables Graham and Johnston died, the heart-rending sight of their wives and children at the funerals, the wave of fear over a loyalist backlash: this was everyone's worst nightmares come back with a vengeance. The near-universal horror and revulsion generated by the killings showed the strength of the desire for peace North and South in the island. The fact that the IRA had carried out the killings, and at such a sensitive time, added extra voltage to the reaction.

Horrified reaction to the Lurgan shootings had a stalling effect on political activity but did not bring about a permanent halt. A twelve-page Anglo-Irish document on decommissioning was formally agreed by Bruton and Blair at a twenty-minute meeting in New York on 23 June. It was understood to have the same or similar content as the document given to Sinn Féin on 13 June. Additionally, there was a British aide-memoire setting out London's position on Sinn Féin's entry to talks. Although not published immediately, leaks indicated that the joint document would propose the setting-up of an independent body to deal with the weapons issue. This was in line with the Mitchell Report, which stated: 'The decommissioning process should take place to the satisfaction of an independent commission acceptable to all parties.' This body would be appointed by the two governments after consultations with the parties in the Stormont talks and report to a liaison sub-committee of the talks. The governments acknowledged that decommissioning required the full co-operation of paramilitaries. A key point in the document – and one that Sinn Féin would have been watching out for – was that both London and Dublin acknowledged their joint efforts to achieve progress on decommissioning should be pursued alongside political negotiations and without blocking the progress of those negotiations.

The aide-memoire, possibly the more important of the two documents, said the period for assessing a ceasefire prior to admitting Sinn Féin to talks would be six weeks and that talks should not continue beyond May 1998, by which time a settlement should have been achieved. In giving a time for Sinn Féin entry to talks, Blair was taking the political risk Major had avoided.

There was considerable criticism from some participants in the talks of the decision not to distribute the documents for discussion at the next day's plenary session. Robert McCartney, leader of the hard-line UK Unionist Party, described the scene for reporters: 'Despite the fact that they had handed copies of these documents to the three chairmen, they took those documents back without them being read. It is my belief that the reason they were recovered and were not handed out was because those documents may be altered pending negotiations with Trimble and the SDLP in an effort to get consensus.' Commenting on media reports of the joint paper's contents, Paisley said: 'This is a surrender document to the claims and the demands of armed gangsters that are destroying our province, incurring mayhem and murder around our streets, and it's an absolute disgrace.' He added that, when Sinn Féin came in through the door, the DUP would be out.

There was said to be a 'huge debate' going on inside the republican movement. The key question was whether decommissioning really had been removed as an obstacle to Sinn Féin's participation in negotiations on an overall settlement. There was still some distrust of the British Government's intentions although it was acknowledged the Labour administration had been more conciliatory than its predecessor. Sources close to republican thinking said the first ceasefire was a 'top down' affair; decided at the highest level and handed down to the rest of the movement as a fait accompli. The next 'cessation' had to be sold to the middle ranks of the movement at least. The difficulty for Adams was that, if there was a ceasefire and he led his party into talks, then the deal he came back with had to be seen by his followers as a significant step towards a united Ireland. He would not get a ceasefire unless the military wing of the movement was convinced that this was a better way of making progress towards the ultimate goal.

Blair spoke in the Commons of the need for 'a new Anglo-Irish agreement'. This echoed the 'new, more broadly-based agreement' considered during the Brooke–Mayhew multi-party talks in 1991–92 which did not include Sinn Féin. Obviously unionists would love to see the hated Anglo-Irish Agreement of 1985 gutted and the Irish civil servants packing their bags to leave the so-called 'bunker', the Anglo-Irish secretariat at Maryfield, on the outskirts of Belfast, which was set up under the terms of the Agreement. The republican movement, on the other hand, wanted an interim settlement which would be a down payment on unity. This implied a beefed-up role for Dublin in the affairs of the North: not necessarily joint sovereignty but stronger than the present position where the Irish had been able to put forward views and proposals on aspects of Northern Ireland affairs but were given no formal role in decision-making. This was where the part played by Bertie Ahern as Taoiseach could prove crucial. The republican perception of Bruton was that he would never push things so far, but at this time there was greater faith in Ahern and people around him – special adviser Martin Mansergh for example – to move things forward.

In terms of media coverage, the annual dispute over the Drumcree Orange parade overshadowed almost everything. After a Protestant religious service at Drumcree, on the outskirts of Portadown, the Orange Order wanted to march back to the town centre via the nationalist Garvaghy Road. The Garvaghy residents objected strongly to this and, the previous year, Drumcree had generated enormous tension and fears of a civil war. Now Mowlam was making very public efforts to resolve the dispute. On the nationalist side there was a fair degree of cynicism about proximity talks (same building but not the same room) scheduled to begin at the Secretary of State's residence, Hillsborough Castle on 27 June, and a suspicion that a decision to push the Orange march down the road had already been taken. Nobody expected a ceasefire before the parade, which was scheduled for 6 July: the republican debate was unlikely to conclude before then anyway. If the guns went silent it was more likely to happen in the second half of July, in time for the end-of-July deadline set by the two governments, but sources said the decision was in the balance. Against its scepticism of British intentions, the republican movement had to weigh the hard political reality that another chance like this might not come along for a decade or more. In the preamble to their new joint document, the two governments said that 'they share the view in the (Mitchell) Report that voluntary and mutual decommissioning can be achieved only in the context of progress in comprehensive and inclusive political negotiations'. That sentence was a step back from the Washington Three 'arms before talks' precondition and would unlock the gates of Castle Buildings to Sinn Féin, provided there was another ceasefire.

Fingers were tightly crossed on the unionist side as well, because Trimble had taken the gamble of his political life by refusing to denounce the decommissioning initiative, seeking instead to harden up the proposals and put Sinn Féin on the spot. In an eight-page and quite legalistic letter to Blair, Trimble had asked when 'Sinn Féin–IRA' would have to respond to the joint paper on decommissioning from the two governments. He pointed to the continuing IRA campaign, including the shooting of the RUC men in Lurgan. Would the British Government demand a 'genuinely complete, permanent' ending of IRA violence? He asked if any new IRA ceasefire would really be tested for six weeks, because the aide-memoire from the British government seemed to allow Sinn Féin immediate access to the talks process, with facilities and privileges enjoyed by other participants. Would assurances of Sinn Féin's expulsion in the event of IRA violence be adhered to? There was a timetable for the talks, would there be a timetable for decommissioning? Reflecting his background as an academic lawyer, he went into considerable detail and his questions were deeply probing, but he still stopped short of condemning the approach of the two governments. The measured nature of Trimble's response was considered helpful by those who were actively working to restore the ceasefire; republicans said it was important.

The results of the general election in the Republic allowed Fianna Fáil and the smaller Progressive Democrats to form a coalition government on 26 June, with Ahern replacing Bruton as Taoiseach. Caoimhghín O Caoláin, the first Sinn Féin candidate to be elected to the Dáil since the party dropped its abstentionist policy in 1986, voted for Ahern's appointment.

In an article which no doubt echoed what Sinn Féin had been saying privately to Fianna Fáil, Adams wrote in the Belfast-based nationalist daily, the *Irish News* that the new government in Dublin must advance the aim of Irish unity and independence along with the objective of achieving civil rights and equality for nationalists in the North. He claimed that Blair wanted a UK-based internal settlement in the North, with mere lip-service to cross-Border agreements (this was based on Blair's 16 May speech which was slanted a particular way to appeal to unionists) and said he was 'quite confident' Blair's stance was at odds with the views of other parties and the Irish Government.

Despite the declared intention of the two governments that decommissioning would not be an obstacle to Sinn Féin entry to talks, Adams expressed his continuing concern that the issue would re-surface 'further up the road' to prevent movement in the negotiations. He also stressed the importance of prisoner releases: 'There are five republican prisoners now entering their twenty-second year in prison in England and fourteen being held in special secure units.' It was the Provo shopping list and clearly the two governments would have to meet it if they wanted an agreement.

As Drumcree grew closer, the choice facing Mowlam, RUC Chief Constable Ronnie Flanagan and the British Army GOC in the North, General Sir Rupert Smith, was boiling down to halting the march outside the church or allowing it to proceed through nationalist protesters who would try to obstruct the Garvaghy Road. In the end the march was pushed through. The Chief Constable was concerned that loyalists would intensify their killings of members of the Catholic community if the parade were stopped.

Anxious not to miss the story, I had taken lodgings in a house on the Garvaghy Road. I was trying to get some sleep in the early hours of Sunday 6 July when a neighbour, who like many of the residents was 'on patrol' outside his house, rattled the letterbox shortly after 3.30 am. 'They're rioting up there, there's rioting going on,' he shouted. The British Army and RUC had overrun the estate and soldiers were engaged in running battles, firing plastic bullets at stone-throwing youths wearing masks. 'It's the subjugation of a people', said a colleague from a nationalist background. There were bizarre sights: a three-man Welsh choir sang left-wing and nationalist songs while the police manhandled several hundred protesters who were sitting down on the parade route. I saw an RUC man aiming a kick in the backside at the Garvaghy Road spokesman Breandán Mac Cionnaith as he challenged the police over their incursion. Another Garvaghy Road leader, overcome by the commotion, was being brought to an ambulance when the crowd shouted 'Halt!' so that the media would get a chance to take pictures. There was a continuous stream of hatred and invective against the police, the most popular taunt being 'Bullet in the head', a reminder of the dual murder of RUC men at nearby Lurgan. Rioting youths shook their fists in the air and chanted, 'No cease-fire!' Eventually the march went through, but after so much disorder it could only be considered a pyrrhic victory. There was a wave of disturbances in republican areas afterwards and, for the first and last time in the nationalist community, Mo Mowlam's political stock was near zero. Garvaghy residents further complained that Mowlam had failed to keep a promise to inform them of the march decision beforehand – an unsustainable pledge from a security point of view.

Shortly afterwards a confidential document dated 20 June was leaked from the NIO which indicated that the decision to force the march through had been taken a considerable time before. Mowlam played down the significance of the document as an 'initial consideration by officials'. However, one of her most senior civil servants had initialled the paper with the comment on the first page: 'I am sure this is the only way open to us that has any chance of success.' Backing Mowlam's claim that the leaked document was never endorsed by her, official sources told *The Irish Times* that a subsequent paper, drafted by the same civil servant, listed five options which specifically included the possibility of a total ban on the Orange parade. Reports of serious disagreement between Mowlam and Flanagan, with the former for blocking the march while the Chief Constable favoured allowing it to go ahead, were also denied but it was acknowledged that 'there may have been differences of emphasis'.

There were strong indications that the nationalists on Belfast's Lower Ormeau Road would attract massive outside support when the Ballynafeigh Orange Lodge, on the city's Upper Ormeau Road, sought to march through their district the following weekend. Derry activists were also making comprehensive preparations to oppose a similar march. The late-night decision on 10 July by the Orange Order to alter plans to march through key sectarian flashpoints was therefore greeted with widespread relief. Nationalist sources in the peace process believed it was 'people-power', the mass mobilisation of nationalists, which forced the cancellation or re-routing of the marches. However, a very senior Orange Order source told me: 'In fact the decisions were heavily influenced by reports from the RUC that the IRA were preparing to attack some of these parades with the resultant potential for carnage.'

The row over Drumcree and the adverse reaction from nationalists when the march was pushed through had served to reduce expectations of a renewed ceasefire. Behind the scenes, however, republicans were weighing their options. When the announcement came on 19 July it took most people by surprise: it was a better-kept secret than the first ceasefire and one of the reasons may have been that it was only decided to call the cessation a few days beforehand.

Most observers agreed the republican movement pulled a masterstroke by calling the ceasefire when it did. It badly wrong-footed the unionists, putting them in a position where, if they now rejected the Anglo-Irish joint document on decommissioning and walked out of the talks, they would be seen as unreasonable in the eyes of the world. As the ceasefire loomed, a very senior unionist admitted it would be 'a bit of a problem'. When New Labour had come to power, Sinn Féin strategists were among the first to sense that there had been, not just a change in government, but a fundamental alteration in the whole political landscape. They read the situation better than some unionists, who clearly did not expect the rebuff they got on decommissioning. It was not every day a London administration held firm and refused to budge in the face of unionist demands. Nationalist sources in the peace process were giving a great deal of credit to Ahern and Mansergh for creating the circumstances which led to the ceasefire. 'Bertie played an absolute blinder,' sources said. 'He got stuck in right away. He said to Blair, "Give me a month". He has been working on it night and day.'

As always at key moments in the peace process there was considerable activity behind the scenes, with positive noises coming from the US in particular. As with the previous ceasefire, there were concerns on the part of unionists in particular as to how genuine and long-lasting it might be. Every incident, however minor, over the next six weeks and more would be parsed and analysed for its meaning and implications. The mood in the unionist camp was extremely wary; among nationalists there was renewed hope and a determination to get results this time around. SDLP sources exulted: 'It's the opportunity we've been waiting for.'

Republican Sinn Féin forecast that the resumed ceasefire 'will expose as never before the Provisionals' reformist policy which seeks to make British rule in Ireland acceptable'. A paramilitary counterpart of RSF had now emerged, called the Continuity Army Council, or Continuity IRA. There were reports of scepticism within the Provisional movement itself about the likelihood that the traditional goal of a united Ireland could be achieved through the talks process. Adams provided ammunition for his critics when he wrote in the *Irish News*: 'During these talks Sinn Féin will press for maximum constitutional change, for a re-negotiation of the Union, for the political, economic and democratic transformation of this island.'

The phrase 're-negotiation of the Union' was seized on by the likes of Republican Sinn Féin who claimed its erstwhile comrades 'seek only a New Stormont rather than a New Ireland free of British rule'. Adams said later in an *Irish Times* interview that he was bemused by the reaction. 'The only interest we have in renegotiating the Union is to end it,' he insisted. 'We're not renegotiating the Union to strengthen it.'

It was an odd use of language for a republican, however.

Adams did not say things by accident and the suspicion remained that he was trying to draw unionists into talks by appearing to modify his ambition of Irish unity without actually doing so.

Mitchel McLaughlin was one of the least threatening Sinn Féin figures in unionist eyes, being identified very much with the political rather than paramilitary side of the movement. It often seemed that the main leadership used him to put forward positions that they could not yet publicly espouse. At this time he reiterated the party's belief in Irish unity during a Radio Ulster interview, but offered another option in the shorter term. 'I believe that we can actually conceive, as they did in South Africa, of the possibility of a negotiated agreement that provides for transition from the present failed political entity to a democratic structure that all shades of opinion on this island can give allegiance and authority to.'

Asked if Sinn Féin would 'sign up to a transitory agreement', McLaughlin replied: 'We've made it clear that that may in fact be the pragmatic outcome of negotiations – some form of interim or transition[al] political agreement.' The pragmatic note sounded by McLaughlin echoed the statement issued by Adams after the IRA ceasefire when he said Sinn Féin would be 'guided' by its aim of Irish unity and would be encouraging the Irish Government and others to join it in seeking an end to British rule and asserting the constitutional rights of nationalists.

During an interview he gave me, earlier in the year, Adams had referred to the need for a 'democratic peace settlement' but had not explained what he meant. Now Sinn Féin was beginning to supply greater detail. Immediate unity was not on the cards but the republicans wanted not so much power-sharing as shared sovereignty. This was the down payment on a united Ireland which could be sold to the IRA as the reward for a ceasefire. Talk of being 'guided' by the aim of Irish unity probably helped to calm unionist fears as there were always suspicions on that side of the community that a secret deal was being worked out between London and the IRA or Dublin to sell Ulster down the river. A pragmatic agreement with both sides coming halfway: this would not scare off sensible unionists who believed the Provos were war-weary and looking for an 'out' from armed struggle without losing too much face.

In the past Sinn Féin had been heavily criticised for refusing to accept the principle of consent, i.e. that there could be no united Ireland without the agreement of a majority in the North. A senior Sinn Féin figure told me privately in 1996 that the party did not want to give away its negotiating position before all-party talks had even begun. He admitted, though, that he could live with an 'interim settlement' leading to a United Ireland in ten or fifteen years' time.

At a talks session on 23 July, the Anglo-Irish document on decommissioning was rejected by the UUP and other unionist parties, but this had no practical effect since these parties had no veto over Sinn Féin participation.

The talks adjourned the following week, to reconvene on 9 September. The six-week period for assessing the IRA ceasefire would have passed by then and Sinn Féin was expected to take the opportunity to sign the Mitchell Principles as a condition of admission. The DUP, Paisley at their head, and McCartney's UK Unionist Party pulled out of the negotiations, never to return. The chances of eventual agreement were enhanced by their departure, as Trimble was no longer under direct and constant scrutiny from rival unionist parties.

The UUP delegates stayed in the talks but the prospect that they would talk directly to Sinn Féin under existing circumstances was an unlikely one. Yet, despite all the sound and fury over decommissioning, the fundamental reality was that Sinn Féin and the UUP were now in the same building. The only certain way for the UUP to remain totally free of contamination was to walk out and they had made clear this was not their intention. A very senior figure at the heart of the negotiations later told me that the departure of the DUP and UKUP made the securing of agreement considerably easier and that he felt those parties gained little from their action.

A speech by Bertie Ahern on 24 July strangely received little publicity although its content was very significant. It was the public affirmation of what was worked out in the private dialogue between Fianna Fáil and the republicans. The speech was addressed to an organisation in Dublin called the Solidarity To Organise Peace group (STOP) which had been active on issues relating to the troubles in Northern Ireland. Insiders blamed Fianna Fáil, not the media, for the modest publicity the speech received. It seemed that the party was shy about trumpeting to the world what it had formally agreed with republicans and this annoyed Sinn Féin, which felt stirrings of the old distrust for the bigger party. That agreement had gone through about fourteen drafts before it was completed. Ahern was making a fairly dramatic commitment, on the public record, to a re-opening of the negotiations which had closed with the signing of the Anglo-Irish Treaty in 1921, but there was some concern in republican circles that he was doing so in such a muted fashion.

In the speech, which some argue was the most important by an Irish government leader since the Treaty, Ahern said there must be a radical renegotiation, 'not just of the Anglo-Irish Agreement but of the 1920–21 settlement'. The key areas he identified were, equality, north-south institutions and 'a new approach to constitutional doctrines on both sides'. He said he would establish a committee, comprising his government and those northern parties who wished to participate, which would review progress in the process on a regular basis (the committee never materialised.) In a key passage, Ahern said: 'The Government of Ireland Act of 1920 and subsequent constitutional development failed to resolve the conflict of political allegiances within Ireland. A deep settlement, incorporating positive elements that have been identified, would address and overcome previous failures going back to 1920, to achieve the basis of a just and durable solution.' Privately, Fianna Fáil had pledged that Ahern would never repeat one of the more controversial decisions taken by the previous Taoiseach, when Bruton refused to meet Hume and Adams together, a move which had greatly annoyed the Sinn Féin president.

Between them, Adams and Hume had finally moved the mountain. Anglo-Irish, or as they were now being called, 'British–Irish' relations would never be the same again. The essential new reality was that Dublin was now centrestage with London in seeking an answer to the old quarrel with, not just northern nationalist and unionist leaders prompting from the wings but republicans as well.

Adams told me in an interview at this time that he saw a united Ireland as perfectly sensible and logical, considering the size, population and economic circumstances of the island. He also outlined a more immediate 'equality agenda' encompassing democratic and economic rights; an end to discrimination in employment; the right to education through Irish; tackling the issue of cultural symbols, flags and emblems; demilitarisation; the release of prisoners; and the disbandment of the RUC. Sinn Féin wanted 'the maximum constitutional, political and institutional change'. He added a pragmatic note: 'Negotiations are negotiations, you can't go in and dictate them and have a "take it or leave it" position. So we have to go in and listen. We will put our position and will obviously look at all sorts of suggestions, ideas and proposals put by others. We will consider all of that in the round as part of how you get a democratic peace settlement.'

I pointed out that Mitchel McLaughlin had mooted South Africa-style transitional structures but had not spelt out what he meant in detail. 'I don't think he should spell it out or that I should spell out what we mean, because we're going into negotiations,' Adams replied. He pointed out that the peace process was not like a football match which ends when the whistle blows. 'If this phase of negotiations does not bring about Irish unity, it does allow those of us who espouse that goal to continue to do so.' He recalled in this context Parnell's declaration: 'No man has the right to fix the boundary of the march of a nation.' Part of the difficulty in current circumstances was that 'the unionists never had to negotiate before'. As part of the 1920–21 settlement, 'the unionists got this place given to them on a plate'. At any time in the past 70 years, the unionists 'could have shaped things in a more inclusive way', but had failed to do so. 'The unionists never needed to have a leader. They always needed to have safe pairs of hands.'

I had been travelling up and down from Dublin on a regular and consistent basis to report on various events in the North – the Clinton visit, the Forum elections, the talks in their pre-Sinn Féin phase. From February 1997 I found myself permanently based in Belfast, as Northern Editor of *The Irish Times*. Having been brought up in a society that was generally stable and placid, it was hard to come to terms with the constant undercurrent of violence and sectarian tension in Northern Ireland. I could not accept or agree with the violence of the IRA. To take only three examples, I found the shootings of Lance Bombardier Restorick, Constable Alice Collins and the two Lurgan policemen deeply upsetting on a personal level. The activities of loyalists were at least as upsetting although, for some reason, they never seemed to attract the same level of condemnation and media coverage. I am thinking in particular of the death of RUC Constable Gregory Taylor, who was kicked to death by young loyalists at Ballymoney on 1 June 1997. He called for help on his mobile phone but no help came. There was the equally horrific stamping to death of the young Portadown Catholic, Robert Hamill, when the loyalist perpetrators reportedly danced on his head shouting, 'Die, you bastard, die', and it was alleged that a police jeep was nearby at the time. There were numerous other sectarian outrages and murders, bespeaking a society that for all its fine qualities and admirable features, nevertheless had a deep sickness at its heart, a cancer that needed to be excised before it spread and infected everyone and everything. A fundamental flaw in society had to be dealt with before communal conflict engulfed everybody. The task facing the talks participants was clear.

Chapter 3

THE ELEPHANT AND THE MOUSE

There was a long way to go. Martin McGuinness appeared on BBC television's 'Newsnight' programme with the feisty Ken Maginnis of the UUP in a head-to-head debate on 12 August. Such encounters eventually became commonplace, but it was a significant and remarkable development at the time. Sinn Féin had always been willing to talk, but the unionists held them at arm's length even after the ceasefire. Now the UUP was breaking the ice and, as so often, the Fermanagh–South Tyrone MP was the pioneer: he had already confronted Adams on CNN. Maginnis came out of his corner fighting and, as expected, dwelt in some detail on his opponent's associations with the paramilitary side of the republican movement. There were straws in the wind: McGuinness did not take fright at the notion of a Northern Ireland assembly, saying it should be considered along with everything else, including the Union with Britain, when the parties went to the table. BBC news programmes later showed footage from the aftermath of the debate, with McGuinness saying to his opponent: 'Would you like to shake hands, would you?' The UUP man declined the offer, pending the decommissioning of IRA weapons.

The long-awaited formal entry of the republicans to talks at Stormont on 10 September 1997, regarded by some as the most important event of its kind since the Anglo-Irish negotiations of 1921, turned out to be a quiet, almost staid, affair. The defining moment came ten minutes past midday when Sinn Féin affirmed its acceptance of the Mitchell Principles, which included a commitment to 'exclusively peaceful means' and 'the total disarmament of all paramilitary organisations'. No comets were seen in the sky, but maybe – just maybe – things would never be quite the same again.

Despite the best efforts of Lord Alderdice of the Alliance Party, the television cameras were still excluded from the deliberations but we heard that Sinn Féin sat beside the SDLP, across the room from Senator Mitchell and the representatives of the two governments. The Alliance Party and the Women's Coalition were also present: the five unionist and loyalist parties stayed away for the moment. A major storm erupted two days later, when an IRA representative told the Sinn Féin weekly *An Phoblacht/Republican News* on 12 September that the organisation would have 'problems' with the Mitchell Principles of democracy and non-violence.[1] There was unionist outrage and the future of the peace process was thrown into doubt for a time, with claims that a dual strategy of the Armalite and the ballot box was still in operation. A senior Sinn Féin figure said cryptically, 'We have backbenchers too.' This was taken to mean that elements in the movement were upset that the political leadership appeared to be forswearing violence as a means of achieving national liberation.

The Continuity IRA, paramilitary counterpart of Republican Sinn Féin, grabbed headlines for a day or two by exploding a 400 lb bomb at Markethill, County Armagh on 16 September. There was widespread damage but nobody was hurt. Privately, mainstream republicans dismissed Continuity as having only 'pinprick potential'. The UUP could have used the blast as an excuse to stay away from the talks for good but senior party sources said the bombing had 'upset our tactics but not our strategy'. Trimble immediately visited the scene of the bombing: nobody could accuse him of callousness or indifference towards the fate of the people of Markethill, seen as a good Ulster Unionist town in a sea of nationalism. This delayed his return to the talks but on 17 September he led his party back to Castle Buildings.[2] The unionists were accompanied by leaders of the fringe loyalist parties, the PUP and UDP, a move which brought them heavy criticism given the paramilitary connections. The phalanx of unionists and loyalists striding towards the gate inevitably reminded journalists of the famous scene from the film, 'Gunfight at the OK Corral'. Internally, for the first time, fractures were beginning to appear, with some of the party's members of the Northern Ireland Forum opposing a return to the talks.

Once inside the talks, the UUP sought the exclusion of Sinn Féin by the two governments, because of the IRA's belligerent interview in *An Phoblacht* as well as claims that the Provisionals were the real authors of the bomb attack in Markethill. Charging

Trimble with cynicism, Adams said: 'If that's his ticket into the room, then we'll suffer him on this.' Another talks participant said: 'Everyone knows they are not going to be expelled.'

The Ulster Unionist submission, headed 'Notice of Indictment', was read out by Ken Maginnis at the talks session of 23 September. When he was finished, Maginnis left the room with Trimble to give interviews to the media. However, it was seen as significant that, when they departed, other members of the UUP delegation remained.

In his remarks to the media, the UUP leader indicated that his party would pursue a strategy of negotiating with all the participants – except Sinn Féin. He pointed out that Sinn Féin's vote was not required under the sufficient consensus rule: 'There is no need for us to engage with Sinn Féin at all.' Observers were taken aback at the aggressive unionist posture towards Mo Mowlam. 'She had better be careful what she says in case her words turn round and bite her,' Maginnis said, adding that the Labour government was 'on trial' as well as Sinn Féin and the IRA. There were reports of a 'blazing row' between Mowlam and Maginnis when they met afterwards. While claims that Mowlam walked out of the meeting were officially denied, other sources reported that the Northern Ireland Secretary declared: 'I'm not going to have an argument, I'm leaving.' This occurred after Maginnis suggested she was being very unhelpful and was more concerned about having Sinn Féin in the process than the UUP. In the end, the row was said to have been patched up but relations were clearly deteriorating.

While the flim-flam was going on – about expelling a party that everyone knew would not be expelled – some real business was also taking place. It now appeared likely that a procedural motion from the two governments to move into substantive negotiations would be passed. The motion would provide for decommissioning to be considered in a separate 'track', probably under the chairmanship of de Chastelain. Although unionists were anxious to see the General in this post, they also wished him to remain as chairman of the Strand Two negotiations on North–South relations. There was a strong view on the nationalist side that one person could not do both jobs.

Finally, in what many saw as an historic breakthrough, unionists, nationalists, republicans and loyalists agreed with the

British and Irish governments on 24 September to discuss the 'three strands' of interlocking relationships – within Northern Ireland, between North and South, and between Ireland and Britain. Although it was the same basic design as the 1991–92 talks, the crucial difference was the presence of paramilitary-linked parties at the table. The participants applauded after the motion was passed around midnight and a delegate from one of the smaller parties has told me since that it was 'the moment when you knew it [a peace deal for Northern Ireland] was going to be possible'. The mood of optimism that developed after so many long days of doubt and despair was best caught by the words of the Irish Minister for Justice, John O'Donoghue: 'It is no exaggeration to say that a ray of light shines across the entire island of Ireland and will lift the hearts of all its inhabitants.'

At the same time de Chastelain was chosen as chairman of the independent body to oversee the disposal of weapons – still an aspiration rather than a probability. The unionists failed to achieve their objective of having the General appointed sole chairman of Strand Two, dealing with the ultra-sensitive issue of North–South relations: he became Number Three in this sphere of activity, after Senator Mitchell and a former Finnish Prime Minister, Harri Holkeri.

The agreement to move into substantive talks followed a day of hard negotiations in which the UUP had sought assurances, not only on decommissioning but on the principle that the consent of the majority in Northern Ireland was essential before any agreement could be implemented. By 6 pm UUP leaders were pronouncing themselves 'fairly comfortable' with the language in the procedural motion. However, objections were raised by the SDLP to aspects of the wording. Between 7.30 and 8 pm the UUP and the smaller loyalist parties went to the SDLP rooms in Castle Buildings and final agreement was reached there. 'There were climbdowns all over the shop,' said one participant. 'We're all nicely in the fold.' The episode showed that, for all the media attention to Sinn Féin, the SDLP could not be taken for granted.

There was comforting language for unionists in the declaration, as part of the motion, that 'resolution of the decommissioning issue is an indispensable part of the process of negotiation'. A unionist could insist this meant that a handover of arms at an early stage was de rigueur, whereas a republican could claim that 'resolution of the issue' did not necessarily imply immediate, or even early, disarmament. In allowing both unionists and nationalists to claim victory, this formula was typical of the constructive ambiguity underlying the whole process. It was a 'win-win situation'.

It seemed Trimble was right when he claimed the UUP could take part in the process with little or no contact with Sinn Féin. There would be an occasional plenary, but most of the business would be done on a bilateral or multilateral basis between the parties. The unionists had entered the conference room with the enemy, but insisted on acting as if he wasn't there.

Sinn Féin continued to find the new British administration more congenial than the old. One senior republican said it was 'like day and night', although there was a residual feeling that Labour's agenda might amount to nothing more than modernising the Union. Continuing in a benign vein, the senior Sinn Féin person said the vote on the procedural motion was 'a good night's work by everybody, including Trimble'.

Disturbingly, both a senior loyalist and a top Sinn Féin member had alluded around this time in private briefings to the danger of a high-profile assassination at the current sensitive stage in the process, although no further details were given.

The curtain had been lifted on substantive talks and an atmosphere of hope combined with apprehension developed at Stormont. There was a quickening sense of possibility but accompanied, as always in Northern Ireland, by the fear of disaster. If comings and goings could make a peace process, there was no lack of them. A Sinn Féin group visited the Labour conference in Brighton: they could be seen in the audience at a fringe meeting in the same Grand Hotel that the IRA had blown up so dramatically thirteen years before. Back home, further efforts by the Alliance Party to have TV cameras admitted to the Stormont talks were defeated. UUP sources were worried about 'pictures taken from a particular angle that puts you right up next to the Shinners'.

There were indications of discomfort, even mild alarm, on the republican side following reports of remarks made in the US by the Irish Minister for Foreign Affairs, Ray Burke, to the effect that Sinn Féin would settle for something less than a united Ireland in the Stormont talks. This might seem like basic common sense but not everyone in the republican community was ready to make that basic compromise and, besides, there was the additional question: would it stop there? A full page of *An Phoblacht* was devoted to the episode, warning that 'it suits the enemies of republicans to put out the message that republican leaders have changed their political objectives'. A declaration of intent by Martin McGuinness in a speech on 5 October to 'smash the Union' may have helped to calm those republicans who became unnerved from time to time about possible political compromises and who needed reassurance that there was no deviation from fundamental aims. If McGuinness and his colleagues on the Sinn Féin negotiating team accepted or even acquiesced to a deal in the talks they would have to explain to their grass roots how it brought a united Ireland closer and was not, as republican dissidents were already forecasting, just a modernised and reinforced form of partition.

The peace process used to resemble a three-ring circus, with the governments and the middle-ground parties in one arena, republicans and unionists occupying the other two. Now there was only one circus-ring, with the performance set to begin on the morning of 7 October at Castle Buildings. Strand One – new governmental structures within Northern Ireland – would be discussed at the first session, attended by the British Government and eight of the ten eligible parties (the Democratic Unionists and UK Unionists were of course staying away; the Irish Government was not officially eligible to participate in Strand One, because it concerned only the internal governance of Northern Ireland). They would be joined for the afternoon session by a delegation from Dublin, led by Justice Minister John O'Donoghue. He would be accompanied by Dublin's Junior Foreign Affairs Minister Liz O'Donnell: a member of the Progressive Democrats, the smaller party in the Republic's coalition government, she was to play a prominent role in the negotiations.

The afternoon session would be devoted to Strand Two, the relationship between North and South. This was the 'hot potato' of the talks, where the real dividing lines would be drawn. As far as the unionists were concerned, partition was not even on the table, whereas Sinn Féin sought, in the words of their founding father Wolfe Tone, to 'break the connection with England ... source of all our ills'. Each delegation was entitled to make an opening statement at the morning and afternoon sessions but it was understood the Ulster Unionists, in a hands-off spirit, would simply table their submission. Not only that, but Trimble himself was absent, as he often would be during the talks. The UUP leader was in Washington meeting President Clinton. Discussion of Strand Three, the 'East–West' or British–Irish relationship, was to commence at 7 pm. The only formal participants here were the British and Irish governments, but the other delegations would be kept informed of developments. The following week, a full day would be devoted exclusively to each strand.

There had already been a lot of discussion on Strand One in the Brooke–Mayhew talks, successively conducted under Secretaries of State Peter Brooke and Patrick Mayhew with no Sinn Féin involvement. Having finally made it to the table, Sinn Féin would doubtless have its own views on this subject. Its votes could not block agreement if the SDLP wanted to go ahead, although its political influence would have to be taken into consideration. Support from one of the loyalist parties was required on the unionist side, giving them at least technically a greater influence over the outcome. Strand Three was primarily for negotiation between the two governments, and rarely had Dublin and London administrations been in greater harmony; indeed Mowlam had described her Irish counterparts as 'wonderful' at a fringe meeting in Brighton the previous week.

Strand Two was clearly going to be the tricky one. One of the reasons the Sunningdale power-sharing experiment foundered was because unionists and loyalists balked at the concept of an Irish dimension 'with teeth'. The 1973 agreement provided for a Council of Ireland with seven ministers each from North and South taking decisions. This time the teeth had been replaced by 'executive powers' for North–South bodies. That was the issue which the talks would have to come to grips with sooner or later. Many unionists believed it was a Trojan Horse, cleverly designed to undermine the Union and act as the embryo for an all-Ireland parliament. There were hard negotiations ahead and the challenge would be to find some formula which the unionists could sell to their followers as innocuous and unthreatening but which at the same time gave nationalists a feeling of shared ownership in a new set of political and constitutional arrangements. It was known in American diplomatic jargon as the 'Elephant and Mouse' strategy: one side concedes what it regards as a mouse, but it looks like an elephant to the other side; and vice-versa.

The first day of talks was unhappily overshadowed by heavy speculation about the political future of Ray Burke, who was caught up in the imbroglio over political influence and property rezoning in the Republic. The rumour machine was quietly whirring all morning, putting out the message that Burke was on the last lap of his ministerial career. His resignation was announced during the day; it was a bitter irony for Burke to be stepping down as Foreign Minister at the very point when his work, and that of others over recent months, was coming to fruition. No friend to republicanism in the past and a strong supporter of keeping Sinn Féin off the airwaves when the IRA campaign was in progress, Burke had nevertheless been a heavyweight on the Fianna Fáil front bench in opposition when the party played a key role in negotiating the second IRA ceasefire. His departure probably delayed the process of reaching agreement.[3] More generally, the prospect of prolonged political uncertainty in the South where a rash of political scandals had broken out, was a cause for worry. Another Fianna Fáiler, and long-serving member of the Dáil, David Andrews, who took over the Foreign Affairs brief, was regarded as decent and honourable although he lacked Burke's recent background in the peace process.

In the negotiations proper, there was a noticeable difference of emphasis between O'Donoghue and Mowlam over Strand Two. The Irish Justice Minister made a sustained and carefully argued case for what he called 'a strong North–South Body invested with appropriate powers'. He did not hesitate to use the dreaded 'e' word (for executive) which frightened unionists so much. He argued that the concept of North–South institutions having 'executive powers' should not give rise to alarm: 'It simply recognises that such bodies should be able to carry out their own decisions.' But this was exactly what unionists were worried about.

Up to now, the received wisdom saw May as an unrealistically early deadline for agreement. Mowlam had caused some astonishment when she raised the possibility of agreement by Christmas. Sources said Mitchell had 'upped the tempo' of the talks by asking all the parties for papers on the topics under discussion.

The first meeting between Sinn Féin and the head of a British government since the Treaty negotiations over 70 years previously – when the party had 73 abstentionist MPs out of a potential 105 on the island – took place at Castle Buildings on 13 October. Held in private, the encounter was said to have lasted twenty minutes, which was longer than the meetings with other parties. Blair met and shook hands with Adams, McGuinness, Sinn Féin vice-president Pat Doherty, and a member of the party's administrative staff at Castle Buildings, Siobhán O'Hanlon.

Speaking to reporters afterwards, Blair did not explicitly acknowledge he had shaken Adams' hand, only that he greeted Sinn Féin in the same way as any other party. It had clearly been more relaxed than the encounter between Adams and Sir Patrick Mayhew when the latter was Secretary of State: Sinn Féin sources recalled how Mayhew's hands shook as he read from prepared notes and how he resisted Adams' efforts to engage him in genuine conversation. Smiling broadly, Adams described the meeting with Blair as a good one. Trimble was dismissive, telling BBC Radio: 'Sinn Féin are only bit players. They're a small group, a minority of a minority.'

London was anxious to be seen as a friend to both communities but it was not a particularly bright idea to arrange a visit for Blair to a shopping centre in the loyalist heartland of East Belfast immediately afterwards. The Prime Minister was also due to have a meeting there with the local MP, Peter Robinson of the DUP. Reporters covering the talks were tipped off during the afternoon that loyalist and extreme unionist elements were gathering at the Connswater shopping complex to give Blair a piece of their mind. On arrival, the Prime Minister's group quickly switched from a relaxed pace into fast-forward mode as they were pursued by about three dozen protesters who shouted 'traitor' and 'scum', cast doubt on the Prime Minister's genealogy, and without any sense of irony urged him to 'go on back to England'. Members of the RUC formed a circle around Blair to protect him. Some protesters had brought surgical gloves with them, intending to make the point while shaking hands with Blair that he was contaminated by Sinn Féin. They never got to the handshake stage and ended up throwing the gloves at him instead. Likewise, some wore large clothes pegs on their noses as they shouted at Blair: 'You stink.' Matronly loyalist women insisted they were just ordinary shoppers sparked to outrage at the sight of Blair, but did ordinary shoppers carry Union flags, surgical gloves and oversized clothes pegs with them at all times? There was a sinister side to the incident as a man who dissented from the protest was followed in the car park by loyalists seeking to note down the number of his car. The hatred was palpable and it was disturbing to see the Prime Minister having to get police protection from his own citizens. As I stood there watching impassively, Blair waved to me: since my face was not contorted in hatred and he did not know me professionally, he may have assumed I was a sympathetic or at least neutral resident of East Belfast! At one stage it seemed as if the Prime Minister would have to leave Connswater by the back door, which would have compounded the disaster, but in the event he faced his tormentors and made his way back through the boos and chanting to his car. Although a statement issued very rapidly from No. 10 Downing Street said he was unfazed by the 'orchestrated' protest, nevertheless the depth of fanaticism lurking in the corners of Northern Ireland must have been brought home to him.

The annual UUP conference took place at Newcastle, County Down, on 25 October against a rapidly changing political landscape. The era of a Protestant state for a Protestant people[4] was gone and an increasingly self-confident and articulate nationalist minority was carving out a place for itself under the North's clear blue skies. This minority had the backing of a powerful pan-nationalist consensus, embracing Dublin and Irish America, with the keenest interest from the White House. In Britain, a government which was paralysed when it came to the North had been replaced by a confident administration full of pent-up energy and ideas. Tony Blair, with the wind of a huge majority behind him, was clearly determined to sort out the Northern Ireland problem and wipe this blot off Britain's political escutcheon.

At this stage, there was still deep scepticism at the highest level of the UUP about the talks process. Sinn Féin wanted a united Ireland and that, as Margaret Thatcher would say,[5] was 'out' as far as the UUP was concerned. The only hope they saw was for a deal with the SDLP, but it was very early days yet and parties were still only producing position papers. Soon it was expected that Mitchell would tabulate the points of difference and agreement. Then the real talking could begin. Interestingly, the UUP's more politically sophisticated members said it was important to have a Fianna Fáil-led government in Dublin if a settlement was to be reached. Fianna Fáil in government could deliver, Fianna Fáil in opposition might cause trouble by playing the 'green card' and taking a hard-line nationalist stance. This was the equivalent of the republican/nationalist view that it was better to deal with a Tory government in Britain, on the same principle that only De Gaulle could have withdrawn from Algeria.[6] The UUP had not the slightest intention of yielding to what it saw as Fianna Fáil's sentimental hankerings for Irish unity, but it was prepared to go quite a long way concerning internal arrangements – further than Sunningdale.

Trimble got a standing ovation even before he delivered his conference speech, which must have been very welcome to a man who had been under unremitting pressure and condemnation from other unionist parties for the previous eighteen months. He pressed all the required buttons: echoing the phrase used by Gerry Adams a few months before, he said there would be no renegotiation of the Union; nationalists would get a hearing on the question of identity, but there would be no Trojan Horse to trundle unionists into a united Ireland;[7] and if Dublin wanted to press their territorial claim on Northern Ireland then they could 'jolly well take it to an international court of law'. He called on nationalists in the North to outline 'in realistic terms' what they needed in order to validate their sense of identity, but he cautioned that unionists would not agree to anything which undermined their British constitutional rights. He argued that there was no alternative to participation in the talks process: 'Does anyone really think that a new process, made necessary by unionist boycotts, will be more favourable to unionists?'

During a debate on constitutional affairs some speakers disagreed with the decision to take part in the talks at Castle Buildings. One young delegate quoted the party's general election guide which stated that Sinn Féin would not be let into the talks without a partial handover of IRA weapons. 'The subsequent action of the leadership has made a liar out of me,' he complained. There was an attempt to reach across the community divide by the party chairman, Dennis Rogan, who recalled King George V's historic 1921 appeal to all Irish people to stretch out the hand of forbearance and conciliation.

The most interesting moment occurred almost casually and without apparent stage management. During a panel discussion, the issue of whether Gerry Adams should be 'challenged' by UUP representatives on television came up. The existing policy was one of refusing to participate in such debates, apart from the occasional outing by Ken Maginnis. There was strong applause when one of the panellists, the Rev John Bach, said: 'It's absolutely wrong. Of course he should be challenged.' Reg Empey admitted the party leadership 'may well be trailing behind opinion in our own community' on this issue. In time and almost imperceptibly, the unionists softened their stance, with party representatives appearing on television panels where they would speak directly to the interviewer and avoid looking at or addressing the Sinn Féin participant.

Unionism might be quiescent but all was not well on the republican side. Reports in early November of resignations by senior members of the IRA caused widespread concern and alarm. The extent of the split was not immediately apparent and it seemed at first as if a sizeable chunk of the organisation might have broken with the leadership. The IRA's Quartermaster General – a key position – had left and so, too, had a number of other senior and experienced operatives, although mainstream republicans and others denied suggestions that the breakaway elements were strong in number. Estimates varied from 30 to 120, depending on the source. Even 30 activists could do a lot of damage. How many members did the IRA have? Answers varied from 300 to 700 and 1,000. The most plausible figure was 350 core members, with a lot of ancillary assistance. Dissident claims of a massive breakaway in South Armagh were considered overblown. And whatever might happen down the road, there was no immediate threat to the IRA ceasefire. Significantly, it was understood that the dissidents and retirees were not crossing over to the Continuity IRA.

In time, more detailed reports of events inside the IRA began to emerge – although it was always wise to treat such reports with caution as most of them emanated either from hostile security sources or from non-leadership elements who held a grudge against the high command. However, it was understood that around 100 delegates had attended a General Army Convention in County Donegal in early October. The mood was described as sceptical: there was a fair amount of disillusion with the political path. Sources close to republican thinking believed the dissidents could even have won the day had one of their number, a woman activist who originally hailed from Belfast, not launched a bitter personal attack on the role of Martin McGuinness. If she had expressed her case in cold, logical terms it would have proven more effective than the more emotional approach she adopted. Such was the regard in which the prominent Derry republican was held, going back several decades, that the convention was swayed into majority support for the leadership. The dissidents, led by the Quartermaster General and his partner, the Belfast woman activist, quit the Provisional movement to found what in time would become known as the 'Real IRA' although they preferred the title *Óglaigh na hÉireann* (Irish Volunteers), which was also, confusingly, claimed by the Provisionals and indeed the Republic of Ireland's regular army. Close observers believed the dissidents made a tactical error by leaving when they did and that they could have taken over the IRA eventually had they stayed. This assessment gave a revealing insight into the mind of IRA activists at a time when Sinn Féin was foraging deeper than ever into the political jungle. Decommissioning was at the heart of it: Sinn Féin's adherence to the Mitchell Principles, including 'exclusively peaceful means' and 'the total disarmament of all paramilitary organisations', was a matter of such sensitivity on the paramilitary side that it had been deemed necessary for an IRA representative to distance the organisation from Sinn Féin's stance in an interview with *An Phoblacht*. The dissidents also believed the talks would lead to a refurbishment of partition rather than Irish unity, with the neutering of the claim to the North in Articles 2 and 3 of Dublin's constitution and acceptance of a unionist veto over further progress.

Events in the IRA found an echo inside Sinn Féin and nine members of the party resigned at a meeting in Dundalk, the town where the former Quartermaster General and his partner lived. Names of those who left Sinn Féin soon resurfaced in connection with the newly established 32-County Sovereignty Committee, which had Bernadette Sands McKevitt, a sister of the IRA hungerstriker, the late Bobby Sands, as its main public voice. A local councillor in Omagh, Francie Mackey, was the first elected representative to join the Committee although he did not resign from Sinn Féin at the time. The Committee shared the same analysis of the situation as the Real IRA, although as usual in republican politics there was no formal link or connection.

In the talks nearly a month had gone by and the ice was melting, but not quickly enough for nationalists and probably too rapidly for unionists. Adams complained that, 'Paisley thinks he can wreck the talks from outside; David Trimble appears to think he can wreck them from inside'. Rather than seeking to wreck the process, however, the unionists seemed genuinely ambivalent about it. Senior UUP sources were anxious to see Dublin's proposed wording for changes in Articles 2 and 3: 'If there is going to be North–South co-operation it has to be predicated upon the basis that the people you are working with don't have a constitutional imperative to take you over.' Intelligent UUP insiders knew they could win significant gains from the negotiations, e.g. a Northern Ireland assembly with devolved powers; the continuation of the Union with Britain; and an end, or at least significant redrafting, of the 'hated Diktat' – as unionists termed the Anglo-Irish Agreement. There was a price to pay: 'The downside is the cross-Border stuff and power-sharing.'

The first month of substantive talks had been taken up with the submission of papers by the parties on different aspects of the agenda; there had also been an unwritten understanding among at least some of the participants that Trimble would have to be allowed to get through his party conference and a subsequent meeting of his executive before any kind of serious pressure was brought to bear on the Ulster Unionists to reach a compromise. As far as Sinn Féin was concerned, the unionists just weren't trying and were only in the talks to make sure the process didn't go anywhere. Loyalists, however, countercharged that Sinn Féin had its head in the clouds, was putting forward 'outlandish documents' and failing to get down to the brass tacks of real negotiations.

Socially, the talks had loosened up somewhat. At the start there was fairly strict segregation in the canteen with 'Prods' on one side, 'Taigs' on the other and the two governments in between.[8] That unofficial segregation had come to an end. True, delegations still stuck together over their chicken and chips but it was a question of taking the next available table rather than lining up in the green or orange corner. There was now what one source called a 'variable geometry' without any clear demarcation, although the Ulster Unionists still tended to sit in a small alcove partitioned off from the other groups. A microcosm of the the island perhaps? As for the food: 'The quality of the coffee and tea is still bad; the grub is mediocre.' Recalling the notorious detention centre where republicans were so often involuntary guests, Gerry Adams quipped that Castle Buildings was 'Castlereagh with coffee'.

The UUP was still maintaining its refusal to fraternise with Sinn Féin. *An Phoblacht* reported that McGuinness, having exchanged 'Hellos' several times with a unionist delegate, finally asked him: 'Can you not say anything but hello?' Quick as a flash, the unionist switched to the Donegal Gaelic salutation: *'Cad é mar atá tú* (How are you)?'

Reporters and camera crews were not allowed into the complex. There were security considerations here, according to Northern Ireland Office sources. There was even an official reluctance to discuss the layout in case some terrorist group took advantage of the information to launch an attack. Insiders said the layout and office arrangements were not particularly conducive to interaction. The ministers and civil servants from Dublin, as well as the SDLP, Sinn Féin, Northern Ireland Women's Coalition and a locally based Labour grouping, took up one floor, whereas the unionists, loyalists and Alliance occupied another. The British Government and the independent chairmen had their offices on still another floor, which also housed the conference room for plenary sessions. There was a committee or 'mini-conference' room on each floor but most of the hard talking was believed to take place in party offices. Thus, final agreement on the motion to move into substantive talks was hammered out in the office of the SDLP leader, where unionists found themselves gazing on a portrait of the Apprentice Boys' hall in Derry! Another reason given for not admitting the media was that it would be more difficult for the politicians to cut a deal. If the talks were to prove successful, both unionists and republicans would have to move away from long-standing positions on basic issues and many felt that this would be infinitely more difficult if every word was being relayed via the media to their support base outside. There would also be the natural temptation for politicians to grandstand in front of the cameras, instead of coming to terms with opposing viewpoints. No credence was given at official level to the view that open and transparent debate might be the best approach in the long run, ensuring that the public was being educated along with the politicians. The journalists were kept outside in the car park, where a number of prefabs had been provided, for holding press conferences and filing reports. Some participants expressed the hope that, when the talking got really intense, delegates would not be 'running in and out to the media' but concentrating on the real business in hand. However, there were frequently a lot of media people outside Castle Buildings, hungry for soundbites, and it was a rare politician who declined to supply them.

There was a fair degree of comment on the way Sinn Féin delegations tended to vary in composition, as if a conscious effort were being made to give everyone a 'taste' of the talks and a sense of responsibility for what was taking place. The skill of Martin McGuinness as a negotiator was remarked upon by observers who would not normally be admirers of republicans or their ideology. However, UUP sources said the Sinn Féin delegation seemed 'very down-in-the-mouth' at the 10 November session, possibly as a result of the republican movement's internal difficulties. Ironically, while republicans were blaming their internal problems on the slow pace of the talks and the reluctance of the Ulster Unionists to 'engage', UUP sources said they were becoming more wary about participation precisely because of those internal republican difficulties. UUP insiders worried that the divisions could be serious enough to lead to a breakdown in the ceasefire. It was a classic chicken-and-egg situation.

There were continuing noises offstage. Paisley was in top rhetorical form at a 'United Unionist' rally of more than 250 people in the Orange Hall at Omagh, County Tyrone. He declared in ringing tones: 'The time has come when we must indict David Trimble, call him to the bar of public trial and remove him forever.' As the cry of 'Lundy' – the notorious traitor whose effigy is traditionally burnt each December[9] – rang out, Paisley intoned: 'Everything that makes me an Ulsterman cries out against this treachery.'

In his address to the SDLP annual conference in Belfast on 14 November, John Hume emphasised the need for 'equality of allegiance'. His speech was seen as an implicit response to Trimble's Newcastle plea to nationalists to spell out their demands more precisely. Hume said if the parties agreed on arrangements which enjoyed equally the allegiance of national-ists and unionists, 'would that not allow unionists a greater sense of confidence in the stability and viability of those arrange-ments?' Equality of allegiance would change political relation-ships in the North and provide a basis for real and developing partnership. None of this would threaten unionist traditions, ethos or identity.

The precise meaning of Hume's 'equality of allegiance' was not clear. It seemed to be a compromise between an internal set-tlement and joint sovereignty. The unionists would get their assembly but nationalists would have an institution such as the proposed North–South Ministerial Council as well as built-in safeguards internally which acknowledged their identity and aspirations.

The conference mood was one of cautious optimism. In help-ing to set the Strands One, Two and Three agenda for the Stormont negotiations and talking the republican movement off the window-ledge of paramilitary violence, the SDLP had already achieved two of the principal objectives for which it was set up. Quoting Nelson Mandela, a speaker unwittingly gave an exposition of the party's basic philosophy: 'The real question is not whether the system works but for whom it works.' Some purveyors of gloom and doom had suggested the SDLP could be eclipsed by Sinn Féin in future years. Confronted by that sug-gestion, a former Northern Ireland Secretary reportedly asked: 'What on earth would we do?' If facilitating a republican con-version to exclusively political means and helping bring about an end to violence meant taking second place to Sinn Féin even-tually, not everyone in the SDLP would feel they had got a bad bargain. After all, by setting up the peace process with Adams in the first place, Hume ran the risk his own party could be eclipsed at some stage.

It emerged over the weekend of 15/16 November that round-table sessions in Strands One and Two featuring all the participants were being suspended for two weeks to allow the parties to hold bilateral meetings and discussions with Mitchell. Nationalist sources said they expected to know by Christmas if the Ulster Unionists were 'serious' about reaching an agreement. Participants would discuss Strand Two, covering relationships between North and South, in bilateral meetings for the first three days of the first week. The second week there would be three days of discussions on Strand One, covering internal arrangements in Northern Ireland. Finally, the new programme of work envisaged that a three-day plenary in Week Three would review progress.

The first week of bilaterals got off to a promising start on Monday 17 November. There was a busy round of meetings and word was that an encounter between the Ulster Unionists and the SDLP had gone quite well. Then on Tuesday, the best-known figures on the UUP side decamped to London to meet the Prime Minister. Nationalists felt deflated by these guerrilla tactics and there were dark mutterings about the unionists not wanting to engage or take the talks seriously. Why Blair facilitated the unionists in effectively playing truant was a mystery to nationalists. But in the contradictory way of things, a meeting in London between the Taoiseach and David Trimble on 20 November gave the process a fresh injection of hope.[10] It was clearly one of the more positive encounters between the Dublin administration and Ulster Unionism although, as one seasoned talks participant put it, 'Every hope has to be tinged with caution'. Nobody knew what might be around the next corner and there were still many in public life and in the shadowy recesses of the paramilitary and perhaps even security worlds who wanted the process to collapse.

There was nervousness on the republican side. The perceived slow pace of British demilitarisation was causing problems with their followers. There was a feeling also that the Dublin administration had lost some of its edge, combined with a worry that the Ahern government might go too far on Articles 2 and 3 out of anxiety to draw the unionists into a settlement. Sinn Féin's Francie Molloy raised unionist hackles when he told an audience in republican South Armagh that the current phase of negotiations might not succeed. 'And whenever that does happen then we simply go back to what we know best.'[11]

Senior British government sources remained optimistic about the progress of the talks. They believed Trimble was keen on a settlement: the internal arrangements would not be a problem, the difficulty was still North–South relations. The final package might be such that even Sinn Féin could live with it – like the Scottish and Welsh nationalists, they might see it as a means to an end.

The talks would focus on Strand One in the week starting 24 November, covering internal arrangements in Northern Ireland. The Framework proposals had envisaged that any new assembly would have some of its key decisions subject to veto by a three-member panel elected by the whole population. This idea now started receding as the notion of sufficient consensus took hold in the talks: this meant that decisions must have the support of a majority in both communities.

The UUP and SDLP met at Stormont on 24 November and there was some preliminary discussion of a Hume proposal suggesting a European Union model for new North–South structures. Based on the structures and procedures of the European Council of Ministers, it envisaged a North–South executive body comprised of members from the Irish Government and a Northern Ireland assembly which would have joint decision-taking powers. After decisions were made it would be up to the Dáil and the Northern Assembly to dictate separately the pace of implementation in each jurisdiction. Trimble had hitherto opposed a North–South executive, primarily on the grounds that it would be a 'united Ireland in embryo'. The SDLP was arguing that its model could not be so construed, as it would be for the Assembly itself to govern when and how decisions were taken. Mallon said: 'The cross-Border institutions would have executive power as exercised by the respective ministers in charge of their respective departments.'

In the talks, the mood on the nationalist side was broadly-speaking upbeat. Unionists were more reserved, still worried about decommissioning. Both sides agreed that the parties were at last getting down to the real issues. A nationalist source rejected the word 'breakthrough' but allowed that there was emerging common ground. Credibility problems would begin to arise for the talks if there was not some evidence of progress in the near future.

Unionists I spoke to acknowledged that the talks participants had begun to get down to serious work. They said one of the first issues that had to be decided was, 'based on the principle of consent, the reality that Northern Ireland will remain part of the United Kingdom'. Unionists were 'very, very disappointed' at the lack of progress on decommissioning and this would be reflected at the forthcoming review plenary in the talks. They would also be seeking a general recognition that, whatever the details of any outcome, Northern Ireland would remain in the United Kingdom firmly and without equivocation. The UUP had not seen the detail of the SDLP's proposals on North–South relations, but there was 'a long way to go' on this issue. 'We will not be agreeing to all-Ireland bodies with executive powers.'

It was originally intended that the review plenary planned for the third week in the programme, with all the parties sitting around the table, would run through Monday, Tuesday and Wednesday, 1–3 December. Now, in line with the stop-start pattern that was beginning to emerge, Monday would be devoted to preparing for the plenary proper, which would not commence until the next day, probably at 1 pm. Mitchell had asked the parties for submissions indicating the key points that needed clarification. The hope was that the plenary would agree a timetable for discussion of these topics. It might be decided to set up subcommittees on different topics, with two members from each delegation instead of the usual five; not so much 'small is beautiful' as 'small might be more productive'. Obviously a sub-group dealing with North–South relations would attract most attention.

There seemed to be a fairly benign attitude on the part of moderate nationalists to the unionist notion of a 'Council of the British Isles', although the preferred title might be a 'Council of the Isles' or a 'British–Irish Council'. This would include representatives of the Republic and Northern Ireland as well as London and the new devolved administrations in Edinburgh and Cardiff. There might also be a parliamentary tier. It was not clear what powers such a council might have, but it could well be part of what David Andrews called the 'institutional architecture' emerging from the talks. It might also help the unionists to swallow some of the less palatable aspects of a North–South council.

There was an urgency now, given that the talks would probably break for Christmas. If the parties were to keep to the original timetable, there would be only three months from early January to tie up an agreement which would be put to referendums North and South in May. Although significant progress was being claimed on Strand One, highly contentious issues remained, such as the composition and acceptability of the police force.[12] Discussion on these issues would have to continue even after a settlement, it was said. On Strand Two, the SDLP proposal that the implementation of joint decisions by a North–South body would be a matter for individual jurisdictions was a possible basis for solving the Rubik's Cube of the talks: how to give solid recognition to the identity of nationalists without alarming their unionist neighbours. Without a solid North–South body, voters in the Republic might not be willing to modify Articles 2 and 3 of the Constitution,[13] redefining the aim of Irish unity as an aspiration rather than an imperative. Nationalists would wish to see corresponding changes in Britain's Government of Ireland Act which partitioned the island in 1920.

The South's new Foreign Minister put his foot in it with some ill-chosen words in a BBC interview broadcast on 29 November. There was a storm of unionist anger when Andrews suggested that decisions of a cross-Border council of ministers would be implemented by a secretariat with strong executive functions 'not unlike government'. This was seized upon by the unionists who demanded his resignation less than two months after taking office. Andrews withdrew the remark and he revealed later that he even considered resignation but was urged to stay by the Taoiseach and others.[14]

Mitchell managed to sideline the affair to some extent by proposing – and securing – a new working-group format for the talks. It was seen as a way of increasing the pressure on participants to identify the key issues for resolution in a peace settlement. What to put in and what to leave out was highly contentious: Sinn Féin did not want an Assembly but for the unionists it was a *sine qua non*. The republicans had their own shopping list with items that set unionist teeth on edge. The final balance would be critical.

Until now, each of the ten delegations had been represented by an average of five persons. On some occasions as many as 70 were taking part in round-table discussions. The new, more workable format would reduce this number to ten delegations of two members each. These were expected to be made up of the party leader and one other representative. The first meeting of the new working group was scheduled for the morning of 3 December and would discuss a timetable of meetings leading up to the next plenary session of the talks set for 15–17 December. When he was questioned about the fact that Trimble would be absent from the first meeting of the working group, Mitchell told reporters that this was 'readily explainable' as there had been less than 24 hours' notice and Trimble had other commitments: the party leaders had indicated that, whereas they might not be present for every meeting, they would attend when decisions were being made. It sounded pretty lame and Adams may have been closer to the mark when he accused Trimble of having a 'semi-detached attitude' to the negotiations.

First reports from the talks in their new format – and new, smaller room – on 3 December were positive and cautiously upbeat. One observer claimed that, 'Mitchell has taken the process by the scruff of the neck'. This note of restrained optimism had been heard before: the intensive bilaterals the previous month were meant to come up with a similar list of key issues, but got overshadowed by Trimble's meetings with Blair and Ahern. Ironically, the success of the Ahern–Trimble encounter on 20 November had injected fresh optimism into the talks but that gave way to renewed gloom after the Andrews gaffe. Now the process was back on the rails, at least until someone stepped on another banana skin. Through his meetings with Blair, Ahern and Clinton, Trimble had almost created a parallel negotiation process. Mallon publicly criticised attempts to reach a settlement outside the formal negotiations: 'The real centre of gravity should be the talks process itself.' The SDLP deputy leader was more and more taking on the burdensome role of mediator between the demands of unionism and republicanism although he was likely to get little thanks from either side for his efforts during those tense days.

If the Castle Buildings talks ever agreed a final package, it would have to be put to referendums on both sides of the Border. This would be a unique democratic exercise, the likes of which had not been seen since the so-called 'Sinn Féin election' of 1918 when the republicans won a majority of seats in an island-wide poll. A mass plebiscite, admittedly in different juris-dictions and with primacy given to the result north of the Border, would adjudicate on the efforts of the parties at Stormont. The unionist community would have to decide between dire warnings that their birthright was for sale and equally doom-laden predictions that, if they rejected what was on offer, the two governments would impose something far worse. Nationalists and republicans would be asked to accept a precondition on their cherished objective of a united Ireland by formally making it subject to the consent of a majority in the par-titioned six counties. To some extent, the debate had already begun in the North, but south of the Border it had not really started. The notion that supporters of the Rev Ian Paisley might end up having a say on the deployment of tourism resources in, say, Tipperary had not really sunk home. Ambivalent attitudes in the South towards Northern nationalists had emerged over the candidacy of Mary McAleese[15] in the recent presidential elec-tion. A parochial antipathy towards 'pushy northerners' con-tended with the more inclusive approach of traditional national-ism. Republicans, too, would have to make unpalatable choices in the coming months.

The new wording of Articles 2 and 3 was still undecided and Adams put down a marker when he warned against any redefi-nition of the national territory: 'No Irish government can change the Irish Constitution in a way which seeks to change the defin-ition of the Irish nation as being the island of Ireland – all 32 counties. The constitutional change that is required is the end of British sovereignty in Ireland.' The occasion he chose for his remarks was a commemoration of the famous War of Independence ambush at Kilmichael, County Cork. In an inter-view with the *Independent on Sunday*, published the same day, 7 December 1997, Adams said the present talks were a phase and, if there was no agreement on a united Ireland, Sinn Féin would continue to pursue that objective.

The pressure he was under emerged more clearly next day when Bernadette Sands McKevitt of the 32-County Sovereignty Committee denounced the Stormont talks for offering only a 'modernised version of partition'. This new grouping described the principle of consent, i.e., that a majority in Northern Ireland must consent to Irish unity, as 'a unionist veto, dressed up in another way', and it rejected the Mitchell Principles. Ms Sands McKevitt told RTE Radio she was 'just more or less invited along because of me being a member of the Sands family'. When asked if the group was connected to the resignations from Sinn Féin or the IRA, she replied: 'I wouldn't know.' She emphatically denied she was a member of Sinn Féin or the IRA.

If internal republican relations were under continuing strain, so too was the relationship between Mowlam and the UUP. Trimble said his party was 'astonished' at the way she had conducted matters in Northern Ireland since the summer. 'I got the feeling she was trying to drive us out of the talks in September. I've got the feeling again in terms of the way in which she has constantly over the last few days been handing out concession after concession to Sinn Féin.'[16]

There had also been some infighting among nationalist parties over the itinerary for a visit by the Taoiseach to Belfast. Fearing a Sinn Féin jamboree, the SDLP made representations and persuaded Ahern to include a visit to City Hall and a meeting with the SDLP Lord Mayor and the first nationalist to hold the post, Alban Maginness. Ahern would see both the present and former MPs for West Belfast, Adams and the SDLP's Dr Joe Hendron respectively. When the visit took place on 8 December, UUP sources took particular interest in comments Ahern made about Strand Two at a press conference. He defined this strand as 'mutual co-operation in the interests of developing the issues that would be common to the island of Ireland'. This was as far as possible from the Andrews formulation about an embryo government.

Trimble was encouraged by what he saw as movement on the issue of setting up an 'umbrella' institution representing parliaments and assemblies throughout the two islands. What were currently called North–South and East–West issues would be addressed within that structure: 'The realities of the situation are that while there are linkages and matters of interest on a Belfast–Dublin axis, those are dwarfed by the interests that Dublin has on an east–west axis, and ditto Belfast'. It seemed that the UUP leader hoped to submerge the proposed North–South Council within a British–Irish body, but nationalists would do little to facilitate him on that score.

One of the tunes that could be heard quietly but insistently in the background at this time was the lament of the moderate nationalist. As the SDLP and its friends saw it, the party had carried the torch of reason and tolerance in the bad times. It would be one of the two main signatories to any future settlement, the other being the Ulster Unionists. The party had worked closely with different Irish governments for many years and benefited from the political support and back-up of Dublin and its bureaucracy. There was a close relationship between the Anglo-Irish division of the Department of Foreign Affairs, based at Iveagh House on St Stephen's Green, and the SDLP, indeed the mandarins were believed to have an input into SDLP speeches at times. Lately, however, the party seemed to be feeling squeezed, neglected and, to some extent, taken for granted. The 'feelgood factor' generated by November's Trimble–Ahern meeting in London left the SDLP cold – one senior member felt the 'spin' about the success of that meeting was exaggerated to make Dublin look good. Dublin and London both seemed to be walking on eggs as far as relations with the UUP and Sinn Féin were concerned. In the process it was perhaps inevitable that the loyal and reliable SDLP should feel aggrieved.

'Passivity' was the charge laid at the door of the two governments by senior SDLP sources. During the week beginning 8 December, the SDLP secured a deal with the Ulster Unionists on the list of key issues: they had agreed what was described as a 'very anodyne' selection of core topics to be dealt with. It was a synthesis of a list presented by Mitchell, which in turn was based on papers submitted by all the parties. The UUP had not submitted a paper but this did not prevent it from having a significant input. Inevitably Sinn Féin objected to the vagueness of the formulation on North–South bodies and wanted special emphasis on the equality agenda, demilitarisation and political prisoners (the release of prisoners was an issue Sinn Féin pursued at every stage of the process with the two governments, both of whom were holding republicans in jail). The SDLP looked for support to the administration in the South, but this was not forthcoming, because Dublin feared that Sinn Féin would walk out of the talks.

In the circumstances, SDLP sources felt Dublin should have 'put the heat' on the republicans. Instead, Dublin sat on its hands. The rationale for Dublin's behaviour was that the situation inside the republican camp was still too delicate for such robust handling. The emergence of Bernadette Sands McKevitt as a focus of the political opposition and doubt over Sinn Féin's role in the peace process could yet be the tip of a larger iceberg. 'Sinn Féin could only sign up to certain things as part of – and in the context of – an overall package,' according to Dublin sources. 'There's a dilemma in every direction,' was how a well-placed insider put it. 'It is essential to the talks process to embrace everybody's concerns.' The ceasefires must be kept intact; David Trimble's position had to be shored up; the loyalists were essential to sufficient consensus on the unionist side – the list went on. Meanwhile, there was deep and growing worry in the Catholic establishment north of the Border about the position of the SDLP. Sinn Féin had been making huge strides in recent years and its new-found electoral strength was mirrored by an impressive network of community activists. At the same time, the SDLP was not getting any younger.

I wrote in *The Irish Times* that, despite its perhaps understandable impatience, the SDLP would, in retrospect, have been wiser to ensure the open support of Dublin for the joint list.[17] The time might come when Dublin turned its back on Sinn Féin, but to do so at this time would have placed the whole process in jeopardy, or so Dublin sources believed. As a result the SDLP had found itself on its own on the nationalist side. Indeed, UUP sources claimed that when push came to shove, only Seamus Mallon was prepared to stand by their earlier deal. There was angry SDLP reaction to this and outright rejection of persistent suggestions in some quarters that Hume had been less enthusiastic about the initiative.

The Sinn Féin view was that the party would not block the inclusion of any item on the agenda by another party (by implication, the UUP proposal for a Northern Ireland assembly) provided the list addressed republicans' own concerns. The obvious ones were prisoners, demilitarisation, the equality agenda, executive powers for cross-Border bodies, and issues of sovereignty and Britain's constitutional claim to the North. Insiders claimed Sinn Féin had highlighted the issue of an assembly as a form of retaliation for being left out of the SDLP–UUP arrangement. It would also have caused serious problems among republicans on the ground if the final list included an assembly but left out, say, equality and demilitarisation. That was why Dublin was refusing openly to take sides. On the other hand, it can be imagined what hay Paisley would make if the UUP agreed that demilitarisation was a key issue to be addressed. Insiders believed Sinn Féin could be persuaded to accept an assembly as part of an overall comprehensive settlement and that the party would go on to win a sizeable number of seats in it.

My report led Mallon to condemn breaches of confidentiality in the talks. 'We have respected the confidentiality of the talks process at all times – even when misleading facts and interpretations were being leaked by others who chose to break confidentiality. Over the past two weeks the SDLP sought to build an understanding with the UUP and the other parties about the key issues to be agreed. Last Monday week we reached an understanding with the UUP on a formula which we both hoped might achieve consensus within the talks.'[18]

Responding to a suggestion in my article that the SDLP had failed to ensure the backing of the administration in Dublin for the joint formula, Mallon said the Irish and British Government delegations had in fact been consulted and had given no reason to believe that they would not accept it. 'The meeting then reconvened and it quickly became clear that consensus would not be reached on the basis of this paper.' This was another way of saying there was not sufficient support. During discussions at a later meeting the SDLP and UUP agreed a further amendment to be proposed by the UUP. In a subsequent discussion, this also failed to achieve consensus. In an apparent rebuke to Dublin, Mallon added: 'Those who have chosen to distort or misrepresent this serious attempt to reach agreement have damaged the trust which is needed if these talks are to succeed. We hope that damage can be repaired when we return on January 12th.'

At this time, and notwithstanding the SDLP's complaints, an almost relentlessly positive message was coming from the Dublin direction about the turn of events. However, the public would have to see some concrete results from the Stormont deliberations soon. Although no agreement was reached, there was 'teasing out of issues', Dublin sources said. Pushing for agreement at this stage was going beyond what the market would bear. 'There may have been an assumption on the part of some that things could go further than in fact they did.' The problem as Dublin saw it, and as outlined by Minister of State Liz O'Donnell at a press conference, was that even trying to list heads of agreement inevitably drew you into issues of substance. Be patient, said talks insiders. Most of the advances in these negotiations were likely to be achieved in the final stretch. 'Once you get people in the mood to do a deal, anything becomes possible.' Dublin was essentially telling the Mallon wing of the SDLP to slow down for fear of losing passengers off the wagon. It was a d i f ficult time: if a deal were not done soon the talks would probably collapse but if Sinn Féin went too far ahead of its base it could only benefit militarists in the republican movement.

The apparent reluctance of the UUP to commit itself to anything on paper was being attributed to fear of Paisley and McCartney[19] on the outside, but perhaps more importantly to potential dissidents inside the party. Memories of the political fate of former leaders Terence O'Neill[20] and Brian Faulkner[21] were still fresh. The UUP leaders wanted to ensure that the Christmas skewer was in the turkey, not in themselves. Such was the tentative choreography of peacemaking, or perhaps mere political survival in Northern Ireland. Now it was believed that the UUP had problems with the dates set for the proposed temporary transfer of the talks to Dublin and London in the New Year – an idea the party was not particularly keen on anyway. The nervousness of the Ulster Unionists in particular suggested that the parties at Stormont, left to their own devices, would probably never arrive at a settlement. The two governments yet again would have to put their shoulders to the wheel to get the process out of the mud. Indeed Dublin and London would have to remain in the driving seat all the way to a referendum in May.

The 10 December meeting of the leaders' group in the talks achieved little in concrete terms but, like an amateur stage production, it seemed things would be all right on the night. There was talk now of a further meeting of leaders the following Monday, 15 December, before that week's full plenary session. The likelihood was that a paper of sorts would be presented to the delegates with a general list of key issues. Specifics would be few and far between but it should be possible to move the process another slow, painful step forward. It was not helpful that legislation on the future of policing in Northern Ireland would be debated in the House of Commons on 15 December, leading to the unavoidable absence of some senior politicians from Stormont.

The latest attempt to advance the process ended in failure on the night of 16 December amid recriminations between the Ulster Unionists and the SDLP. The so-called sub-group, consisting of the party leaders and one other representative, met at Stormont throughout the day, but failed to reach agreement on the key issues for discussion in the process. SDLP sources said that the Ulster Unionists had 'got it in the neck' from all the other parties because of 'gratuitous leaking' about an 'alleged agreement' on the key issues between themselves and the SDLP. For their part, sources in the UUP insisted that an agreement had been made with the main nationalist party but that Mallon was the only SDLP representative prepared to stand by the deal. Questioned about this, Mallon said that he was not going to break confidences. 'Our party stands by its word,' he added.[22]

It was a bleak moment, although Mitchell and other senior politicians remained resolutely optimistic that progress would be made when the talks resumed on 12 January. Mitchell told reporters that, while the participants had not reached agreement, there was a significant measure of common ground. He added: 'The real question is whether the participants are prepared to deal with the issues in a serious way. I believe they are.' This point was repeated by Andrews who said that the exercise had been valuable in establishing 'a lot of common ground'.

Ahern, who was visiting Boston, was in expansive mood. He had 'no great worry' about the failure to reach agreement. He believed the parties had effectively agreed the heads of agreement already and there was some 'play-acting' going on. 'The line of disagreement is that the unionists are saying that Sinn Féin won't talk about Strand One issues unless policing and demilitarisation are on the agenda, but all these things are going to be part of the discussions anyhow.' Ahern was briefing members of the Irish media accompanying him on his US trip, on the basis of the most recent reports he had received on the talks in Belfast which had not concluded at that stage. He said the most 'significant' aspect of the day's talks was the fact that McGuinness had stated his party would discuss a Northern Ireland assembly in Strand One. 'That will allow us to move on to Strands Two and Three,' Ahern said. While McGuinness had linked Sinn Féin's agreement to discuss an assembly in Strand One to negotiations on the reform of the RUC and demilitarisation, it had already been decided that these matters would be discussed. 'The unionists would have thought that Martin McGuinness would say "I'm not talking about Strand One issues". I think McGuinness has been cute ... he did not say that. He said "I'll talk about Strand One issues with policing and demilitarisation". I think that's a clever card, frankly, to play on the day that was in it.' The Irish Government had done a lot of work on Strand Two issues dealing with North–South bodies and it was important for nationalists in Northern Ireland that these bodies would be 'real, meaningful and not just useful, ad-hoc advisory chat shows'.[23]

For all the Taoiseach's optimism, the Stormont talks were running into problems of credibility. The failure of the leaders' group to reach agreement on the core issues was well-forecast, giving the great and the good ample time to prepare their messages of resolute optimism afterwards. Yet the fact remained that the new format failed to achieve its objective within the stated time. Likewise, the previous format of breaking the talks down into intensive bilaterals also proved a failure. But if the talks were bogged down, good news was coming in from other fronts. A much-heralded meeting between the Prime Minister and a Sinn Féin delegation at Downing Street on 11 December was generally regarded as a success. It was reported that Blair found his visitors quite fascinating: it would certainly have been different from meeting Labour councillors from Hackney.

Chapter 4

A ROAD MAP TO AGREEMENT

Shortly before 10 am on Saturday, 27 December 1997, at H-Block 6 in the Maze Prison, near Belfast, the name of Billy Wright was called out as a signal that a visitor was waiting to see him. Leader of the notorious Loyalist Volunteer Force, 'King Rat', as he was also known, boarded a transit van on the H-Block fore-court to go to the visiting area of the prison. He was accompa-nied by another LVF inmate, with a prison officer as escort. As the van was about to leave the forecourt, three men jumped down from the roof of A wing of H-Block 6, the section which housed prisoners from the Irish National Liberation Army (INLA). One of the men pulled back the sliding door at the side of the van and fired several shots point-blank at Wright, hitting him in the chest. As the firing started, the victim sprang forward and tried to defend himself by lashing out with fists and feet, to no avail. A witness claimed that the killer laughed as he left the scene. When the shooting was over, the second loyalist prisoner tried to revive Wright, but realising this was futile, he jumped out of the van and, covered in the victim's blood, shouted to the other LVF inmates watching impotently through the bars of their cell windows.

The likely consequences of the INLA's action struck fear into many hearts in the North. Conspiracy theories abounded: the killing was part of a plan to destabilise the peace process; it was intended to consolidate the peace process; it was a plot between mainstream loyalists and republicans to remove a thorn from both their sides. None of these theories was substantiated, although the ease with which the assassination was carried out did raise questions, as did the decision to house LVF and INLA inmates in the same prison block, a move that was bound to lead to trouble.

There was speedy retaliation against the Catholic community in general that night when an LVF group killed a security guard outside a hotel in Dungannon, County Tyrone. New Year's Eve saw a gun attack on the Clifton Tavern, a public house in a republican area of North Belfast, in which one man died and five other people were injured. The LVF claimed responsibility, but this was greeted with scepticism in some quarters. The Irish Republican Socialist Party, political counterpart of the INLA, issued a statement blaming the Ulster Freedom Fighters, a cover-name for the largest of the loyalist paramilitary organisations, the Ulster Defence Association. I could not help recalling Winston Churchill's phrase about Belfast's 'murky underworld'.

In a separate development, loyalist prisoners in the Maze were growing increasingly agitated about the conditions of their incarceration and their prospects for release. The leader of the UDA prisoners, Sam McCrory, warned that the loyalist ceasefire 'probably is more shaky than ever'. The UDA/UFF prisoners voted to withhold support from the peace process and it looked as if their political counterparts in the Ulster Democratic Party (UDP) might have to withdraw from the Stormont talks. The Progressive Unionist Party (PUP), which was aligned with the Ulster Volunteer Force (UVF), was also making noises about withdrawal. Under the sufficient consensus rule, at least one of the loyalist parties was needed at the table to approve an Agreement.

Mowlam took an unprecedented initiative in agreeing to meet loyalist inmates at the Maze on 9 January. Her purpose was to prevent the formal collapse of the loyalist ceasefire and the possible disintegration of the Stormont talks. This was a highly controversial move – meeting UDA prisoners at a time when the UDA was being blamed for murder. It was easy to believe that her civil servants were not overjoyed at the notion, but it was typical Mowlam, gutsy almost to the point of recklessness, and it seemed to work: the loyalist prisoners were mollified. Speaking from Japan, Blair claimed she had 'saved the day'.

But while the prisoners might have calmed down, loyalists on the street continued their deadly activity, striking again on the night of 10–11 January when they shot Terry Enright, a young Catholic cross-community activist who was working part-time as a security guard at a nightclub in Belfast. A Ford Sierra car pulled up outside the club: one gunman pointed a gun at the doormen through the window while another got out and fired over the top of the vehicle. As the shooting started, the victim made a run for it but was hit four times. The staff and clientele at the club came from both sides of the community. Married with two children, the dead man had taken up the job to raise money to improve the kitchen at his home.

The murder created a coalition of grief in the peace process, since the victim's wife was a niece of Gerry Adams and the club was owned by a sister-in-law of the loyalist politician, David Ervine of the PUP. Adams was visibly upset when he met reporters the following afternoon. There was universal agreement with David Ervine's description of the victim as 'a fine and reputable young man, a community worker with a vision for the future'. The funeral was the biggest in West Belfast since the hunger strikes in the 1980s and over 250 death notices were placed in the main nationalist paper, the *Irish News*. In the talks there was a significant crack in the ice when Reg Empey of the UUP offered his sympathy to Adams: this was not the result that Terry Enright's killers intended.

Earlier in the week, there was a meeting in London of the liaison group of top civil servants which maintained continuity between meetings of British and Irish government leaders and laid the groundwork for future initiatives. Although virtually everyone in the peace process knew it was happening, Dublin would not admit officially that the meeting was taking place. Reflecting Blair's personal concern at the stalemate in Castle Buildings before Christmas, the British side produced a document listing heads of agreement for possible presentation to the talks on 12 January. Dublin responded with a longer document of its own.

The following weekend in Belfast, officials from both governments were busy meeting representatives of the political parties and trying to hammer out a consensus for the resumption of the Stormont talks the following Monday. The *Daily Telegraph* caused a stir when it reported that Blair was in broad agreement with Trimble on the need for an Assembly and a British–Irish 'Council of the Isles'.[1] Nationalists and republicans wondered what had happened to the North–South bodies and there was concern that the British government had lost its nerve in the face of recent loyalist violence. Unionists had been arguing that North–South interaction and exchanges should be subject to the overall British–Irish relationship but even moderate nationalists could not accept emasculated North–South bodies that would be the footstool of a council representing assemblies which, in the case of Scotland and Wales, still had to be established under New Labour's devolution programme.

Senior Dublin sources were reassuring. The British were willing to live with North–South bodies with executive powers. Unionists would have to swallow that, just as republicans would have to accept an Assembly. The great phrase of the weekend was 'possible propositions', which were being put to the parties by civil servants (there always seemed to be a phrase or motto in the air, which set the tone for the proceedings). Ideally there would be equal amounts of comfort and discomfort for all in the forthcoming heads of agreement: not so much parity of esteem as 'parity of pain'. Dublin played down the draft leaked to the *Daily Telegraph*: 'Ourselves and the British have been running off different texts.'

While their civil servants were meeting the parties in Belfast, the Prime Minister, who was still in Japan, and the Taoiseach in Dublin were busy working the phones to try to bring the various leaders on side. It was said that 'Blair took a very prominent role in bringing Trimble on that last few inches'. The final text was hammered out by the two government heads between 7 am and midnight on Sunday, 11 January, and a senior civil servant from the Department of the Taoiseach drove to Belfast at 6.30 next morning with his copy.

The fruit of all the negotiations, soundings and meetings was a document entitled 'Propositions on Heads of Agreement', unveiled when the talks resumed on 12 January. The 'Propositions Document', as it became known, included proposals for changes in Articles 2 and 3 of the Irish Constitution and Britain's Government of Ireland Act 1920. These changes would be 'based on commitment to the principle of consent in all its aspects'. A joint British–Irish statement stressed that the two-page document was 'only the outline of an acceptable agreement'.[2] The proposals included a Northern Ireland Assembly, elected by proportional representation, and 'a new British–Irish Agreement to replace the existing Anglo-Irish Agreement'. On the key issue of cross-Border relations the governments proposed establishing a North–South Ministerial Council. There would also be a body reminiscent of the council of the isles, which would hold summit meetings twice a year and include representatives of the parliaments in Dublin and London and the new assemblies in Belfast, Edinburgh and Cardiff.

The propositions were described by officials as 'the two governments' best guess as to where the outlines of an agreement might lie'. Most participants, including the UUP and the SDLP, responded favourably. Dublin, in particular, was anxious to tie Trimble further into the process. Sinn Féin reserved its position and cautioned against any 'dilution' of the 1995 Framework Document. In private, republicans were concerned over what they saw as 'a sop to David Trimble to keep him in the talks'. Not for the last time, republicans charged that the two governments had 'leaned over too far in the unionist direction'. It was said that one leading republican 'had to be tied down' when he saw the final text. Nevertheless, republicans emphasised that the proposals were not set in stone. They would not walk out, because that would only play into unionist hands.

Already unionists were arguing that, under the terms of the document, the North–South Ministerial Council would be firmly under the control of the Assembly and within the umbrella of the British–Irish regional council or council of the isles. Dublin sources took a different view: 'We see it as being a stand-alone body; we don't see it as in any way subservient to the British–Irish Council and it would be in charge of agencies with executive functions.' The relationship between the two was not spelt out in the document, but an accompanying statement from the two governments said they would operate independently 'in their designated areas of responsibility'.

When the document was circulated, all eyes had focused at once on the provision dealing with cross-Border relations. The stark terms 'North–South body with executive powers' did not appear, nor were they likely to, since unionists and loyalists would immediately have felt obliged to walk out. The question was whether the provisions that were published amounted to the same thing. Advance leaks had suggested that the key-word 'executive' wasn't in the document; then journalists were told that it was, but in a particular context. The compromise formula devised by politicians, diplomats and civil servants in the end was: 'A North–South Ministerial Council to bring together those with executive responsibilities in Northern Ireland and the Irish

Government in particular areas.' This could be interpreted in different ways, which presumably was the intention. Both sides could put their own 'spin' on it, each with a fair amount of plausibility. Nationalists could point out with satisfaction that, yes, the 'e' word was there. Unionists could counter with the fact that the new council would be accountable to the proposed Assembly in Northern Ireland as well as the Oireachtas (the houses of parliament in Dublin), and that all decisions would be by agreement between both sides. We were walking the fine line between interpretations and negotiating positions. The point stressed by representatives of both governments was that this document was intended to be a basis for negotiation and not a definitive, take-it-or-leave it proposal. Few disagreed with the unionists when they said that 'the many ambiguities and gaps in the paper need to be explored'.

For some time now, SDLP sources had been expressing the hope that the two governments would 'take the talks process by the scruff of the neck', and this was what they had now done. Republicans had balked at the idea of a six-county assembly but there it was, in black and white. The pain barrier had to be crossed some time because *realpolitik* dictated that there was always going to be an assembly as part of the deal. John Hume, who did not criticise the republicans lightly, said Sinn Féin was 'being either deliberately destructive or failing to face reality'. Mitchell comments in his book, *Making Peace*,[3] that it was too early for the Sinn Féin leadership to accept an Assembly but, like everyone else, they knew it was essential to an Agreement. Broadly speaking, it looked as if the unionists had won the day but a Dublin civil servant hinted at a deeper game plan: 'We have lost three-two but our two scores are away goals.' There was a view that the immediate problem was to lock the unionists irreversibly into the talks; there would be other opportunities for nationalists to claw back ground they had lost in the preparation of what was, after all, only meant to be a discussion paper. Dublin, which before Christmas had refrained from openly supporting a package that included an assembly, had now judged that the time was right. David Andrews described the document as a 'road map' for the parties: he might have been more accurate in calling it a 'middle-of-the-road map'.

Seamus Mallon exuded satisfaction and seemed a different

man from the tense negotiator of previous press conferences. In many ways 12 January was the 'Day of the Moderate' at Castle Buildings. Talks insiders who observed the activity behind the scenes over the weekend admitted the document 'had to be at times a bit vague, to keep people on board'. The Framework Document was thought to be too green for Glengall Street but now the unionists had a paper they could use as a basis for negotiation. There had been discreet contact between Irish Government officials and the unionists over the Christmas period, so Dublin was well aware of Glengall Street's views.

The great talks cliché was that 'the devil is in the detail' and some of the formulations in the British–Irish paper were fiendishly clever. One kept coming back to the all-important section on the North–South Ministerial Council. Anti-talks unionists had claimed that this body would have executive powers because the two governments' paper stated that it would 'take decisions'. Republican sceptics countered by pointing out that such decisions would be 'within the mandate of, and accountable to, the Northern Ireland Assembly and the Oireachtas respectively'. They foresaw a situation where the unionist parties in the assembly would hold the North–South council on a choking leash. Writing about it afterwards, Andrews said the biggest difficulty in the negotiations was that the unionists wanted to keep the North–South bodies at civil servant rather than ministerial level. He said it was 'imperative to the future of the negotiations that the paper was co-authored by both governments'.[4]

There were differing views of the importance of the so-called 'council of the isles' and the influence it might have over the cross-Border structure. Trimble appeared to draw comfort from the fact that this body was mentioned ahead of any cross-Border arrangements, making it 'clearly the first and most important element' in a new British–Irish Agreement. Peter Robinson of the DUP dismissed the inter-island council as 'a luncheon-club for politicians'. Well-informed talks insiders insisted that the activities of the North–South council could not be frustrated by the Assembly because ministers and civil servants taking part in it would have a 'duty of service' obliging them to make it work. They also pointed to a provision in the Framework Document which hinted at a type of 'failsafe mechanism' that could be brought into operation if cross-Border co-operation was being mischievously frustrated.

A considerable amount of work had been done by officials on the detail of issues like cross-Border co-operation. 'There are papers out there', one talks insider said, and some of these might be introduced to the negotiations at a later stage. For now, however, the priority was to 'bed down' the participants in discussion of the three strands of internal, cross-Border and British–Irish relations.

Sinn Féin's complaints about the document grew louder as days went by, reflecting the mood among the grassroots who were already very angry about the loyalist attacks. 'We were not consulted about the document,' party sources told me. 'Nor were we given sight of it. But from the conversations with the two governments we had a good sense of what was coming and that it was intended to appease David Trimble.' In language apparently intended to reassure republicans, Andrews said 'any new agreement must have as its fundamental basis the need for profound change'.

The Business Committee of the talks, chaired by General de Chastelain, agreed on 14 January that Strand Two talks on North–South bodies would move to London for three days at the end of the month, with a further three-day session in Dublin in mid-February.

In a statement on 22 January, the IRA rejected the Propositions on Heads of Agreement as pro-unionist. The liaison group of British and Irish officials met at Iveagh House in Dublin the same day to discuss another joint document on the powers and authority of the North–South Ministerial Council. John Taylor had warned that, in the event of a retreat from the Propositions paper by the two governments, his party should review its continued participation in the talks. Nevertheless, most observers expected to see an attempt in the new document to bring the republicans back on board. One wag joked that this could be the 'Sinn Féin Fightback Document'. Dublin had produced the first draft on 22 January and London responded with a counter-text late that evening. The liaison committee failed to arrive at an agreed text that day and the to-ing and fro-ing continued over the telephone on 23 January. By that evening agreement was said to be close and the final five per cent was due to be agreed over the weekend. Dublin wanted a paper that would be fairly prescriptive in tone and as close as possible to the pro-visions of the Framework Document. London was happy to see the Framework provisions included but as one of a number of options. This was because the Ulster Unionists were such strong opponents of the Framework.

The final format adopted was a series of questions aimed part-ly at outlining the views of the two governments but also at elicit-ing the real positions of the various parties, as distinct from the rhetoric reserved for press conferences. The questions format was not likely to appeal to the SDLP because it smacked too much of an 'options' approach. Other documents on the Strand Three rela-tionship between the two islands and the state of existing North–South co-operation were also in the pipeline. Taylor complained about the delay: no party could allow itself to be 'bounced into a position' by the delayed release of background papers.

While these high-level political negotiations were going on, the RUC Chief Constable, Ronnie Flanagan, publicly confirmed what was already widely believed, namely, that the UDA/UFF was involved in recent attacks. This was followed next day by a statement from the UFF admitting it carried out a number of murders in response to INLA activities – what it called 'a mea-sured military response' – but was now back on ceasefire. It was now virtually inevitable that the organisation's political wing, the Ulster Democratic Party, would be expelled from the multi-party talks. Within hours of the UFF announcement a Catholic workman was shot dead in a loyalist area near Belfast's Crumlin Road. Taxi drivers were being heavily targetted at this time and, in a tragic aside, a cabbie told me his colleagues were being shot down 'like clay pigeons'.

Trimble played down the importance of the forthcoming joint document – 'There is no document being prepared that has the status of the Propositions on Heads of Agreement'[5] – but for nationalists it was the key paper, the one that went to the heart of the matter. Crudely put, if nationalists were going to agree to an Assembly and tolerate a dilution of Articles 2 and 3 they would require a strong and vibrant North–South council with executive powers. Through this body, the Republic would be inextricably involved in the North's life.

There had been second thoughts about specifying the areas the proposed North–South council would deal with. These had been tentatively identified as culture, heritage, marine research, education, agriculture and tourism. These were known in peace process-speak as 'Division Two' issues because they were relatively uncontroversial. Issues like justice and security would come into Division One. However, in the interests of delicacy it had apparently been decided not to have a list at all.

Unionists essentially wanted little more than a North–South version of the Rotary Club where ministers from Dublin and Belfast would meet perhaps once a month with their opposite numbers in a Northern Ireland administration to discuss entirely voluntary co-operation on matters of mutual interest. Republicans wanted at the very least an embryo governmental structure to facilitate the transition to a united Ireland in ten or fifteen years. Ahern commented: 'If they were not executive agencies, then they would be seen to have no teeth, and quite frankly, we know it's no good debating this issue. We know that that would not be acceptable.'[6] The Taoiseach had come to Belfast for a Chamber of Commerce lunch at the Wellington Park Hotel. About a mile away four men from Portadown, who were believed to have links with the LVF, were detained by police: it was not clear whether the two events were connected.

If the ministers and mandarins got it right, the discussion could be brought onto a new level over the next few weeks. Many conflicting interests were involved and it would take something close to political genius to satisfy or at least placate them all.

Finally on the afternoon of 27 January at Lancaster House, the new but temporary home of the talks in London, the governments produced a paper entitled 'Strand Two: North–South Structures'. The start of substantive talks had been delayed by the issue of the UDP's eligibility to participate: the loyalist party withdrew in advance of its formal expulsion but was re-admitted four weeks later.

The new paper contained fourteen questions for the parties and Mitchell sought to initiate a discussion around them. Unionists professed themselves relaxed about the document. They said that, although the Framework Document was mentioned, this was only to keep Sinn Féin quiet: the substance was in the 12 January Propositions paper which, they insisted, placed the North–South relationship firmly under the control of the majority community.

For their part, the SDLP and Dublin were delighted at the affirmation of support for the Framework. Dublin had argued vigorously for the formula in the Strand Two paper which stated that the two governments were 'firmly' committed to the Framework. 'London only agreed to this at the very last moment and following extremely tough inter-governmental negotiations,' according to an insider. 'Dublin refused to budge on the need for the British to commit themselves to the Framework Document.'

There was a moment of theatre, courtesy of Trimble's colleague and putative rival, Jeffrey Donaldson. In what looked like a move that was planned in advance, the Lagan Valley MP tore up a copy of the Framework Document in front of the television cameras at a packed news conference. 'We as a party will not put our hand to any agreement based on the Framework Document,' he declared. A *Guardian* report observed: 'It was not an impulsive gesture as he had half-ripped it before taking his seat on the platform.' A Dublin insider commented that Donaldson's gesture 'showed the significance of what we had achieved'.

There was a division between the two largest parties on the powers a Northern Assembly should have. The Ulster Unionists wanted minimal powers for a non-legislative assembly: in that sense, at least, they did not want a return to Stormont. The SDLP wanted substantial authority and functions to be devolved. This was where Strand One became intertwined with Strand Two. The two governments had proposed that the North–South Ministerial Council be accountable to the new parliament or assembly in Belfast and the existing one in Dublin. If the council was to have real power, the Northern Assembly would therefore have to be a strong body with legislative functions.

Sinn Féin renewed its efforts to secure direct talks with the UUP and Adams complained that a leading unionist had rebuffed his approaches with, 'I don't talk to f***ing murderers!' Martin McGuinness approached the UUP leader to say that a meeting between their two parties was inevitable, but Trimble replied abruptly to the effect that communication could take place through the chair.

In the House of Commons on 29 January, Blair announced a fresh inquiry into Bloody Sunday. At long last the end of a painful and grief-laden episode seemed to be in sight. For 26 years the relatives of the dead and a few friends and supporters had kept the issue alive. The questions never went away: why were thirteen civilians, six of whom were only seventeen years old, shot dead by the Paras in Derry that day? The administration in Dublin, headed first by John Bruton and later Bertie Ahern, could claim its share of the credit for the announcement. There had been a time, in the 1980s especially, when the Dublin establishment did not particularly want to know; when issues such as Bloody Sunday or the Birmingham Six were kept at arm's length; when a McCarthyite atmosphere reigned and campaigners who spoke of truth and justice were in danger of being maligned as outriders for the IRA, whose violent activities were then in full spate. Although many people rightly resented the inquiry being linked to progress in the peace process, it was nevertheless seen as a confidence-building measure calculated to enhance the 'feel-good factor' among SDLP and Sinn Féin supporters. Certainly Blair's standing on the nationalist side improved and many were impressed by the firm manner with which he dealt with Trimble's objections in the Commons.

The UUP's relationship with Mowlam was at this stage only marginally better than its relationship with Sinn Féin. The return of the talks to Castle Buildings provided further evidence of this when, during a meeting of the confidence-building committee, Ken Maginnis objected vehemently to the fact that Mowlam did not know the first name of his UUP colleague, Dermot Nesbitt, whereas she knew the first names of Sinn Féin and SDLP delegates. Mowlam explained that she had met Nesbitt only once. Maginnis also complained that Mowlam looked at the nationalist side of the table only during the discussions. She replied that the UUP delegates were talking among one another in what she claimed was an unmannerly fashion. Maginnis, who had called for Mowlam's resignation a few weeks before, walked out of the meeting.[7]

On a visit to Dublin, Mowlam spoke in general terms about the shape of a possible settlement, which she suggested would have 'some kind of devolved body', a North–South council, an intergovernmental structure and 'something between east and west'. She believed that 'in that ballpark somewhere, things are going to fall'. In a meeting with the Taoiseach, she was encouraged by his optimism on the talks. 'It is possible I think to make progress quite quickly now,' she said later. Dublin, too, exuded optimism that a settlement package would go ahead by May. 'What are those guys smoking?' mused one of my fellow-journalists. Their upbeat mood was more likely based on the conviction that the republicans were, broadly speaking, 'on side' and the IRA would probably not oppose the emerging Agreement. The optimism of the governments was not reflected at inter-party level. UUP contacts said they had not held a bilateral in which serious negotiations took place with the SDLP for about six months. 'The two governments are making it up.'

There was a sudden and dramatic hitch when an alleged drugdealer and a leading loyalist were gunned down in Belfast over a 48-hour period.[8] Mowlam was officially informed by the Chief Constable that the IRA had been involved in both killings; a major question mark was now raised about Sinn Féin's place in the talks. Trimble said if IRA involvement in either attack was established, Sinn Féin's position in the process would have to be reassessed. The widely held view was that the republicans felt under pressure to respond to the wave of sectarian killings since Christmas, in a climate where the INLA was gaining ground and the Thirty-Two County Sovereignty Committee was alleging a sell-out in the talks. Beginning with Billy Wright, twelve people had died at the hands of loyalist and republican paramilitaries over a six-week period.

Unlike the UDP, Sinn Féin did not go quietly, even though they knew that, as in the case of the loyalist UDP, their expulsion would only be for a few weeks. The talks moved south, to the former seat of crown rule in Dublin Castle for a week on 16 February but, instead of Strand Two discussions, the proceedings were dominated by republican protests against their expulsion. As an increasingly frantic media tried to keep up with events, Sinn Féin took the matter to the Four Courts on the other side of the River Liffey, but the case was later dropped. If the republicans had not been expelled, then the sizeable unionist contingent would in all probability have returned to Belfast as a protest, which would have been profoundly embarrassing for the Ahern administration.

Adams caused a stir when he told a television interviewer he was 'absolutely pissed off' at the turn of events. Republicans in Belfast later made this into a T-shirt with the motto, 'I'm pissed off too'. Adams brought the house down at a crowded meeting of supporters in Liberty Hall with a quip about the pictures of former colonial rulers he had seen on the walls of Dublin Castle: 'I like to see the Ascendancy class [pause for effect] hanging.'

It was a difficult week for the SDLP, which remained largely silent while its colleagues and rivals in Sinn Féin were consigned to purgatory. London, in particular, was said to be 'rock solid' that the republicans had to be penalised over recent events. In a sense, the Sinn Féin imbroglio came as a godsend to the unionists, who had no intention of being seen by their followers making an enthusiastic contribution to the Strand Two debate in the Irish capital. I was dining with about ten unionists at a Chinese restaurant in Dame Street, near Dublin Castle, and was surprised how they were keeping their voices so low, since northern accents were quite common in Dublin. Had the other customers known who they were, they would either have let them be or come over to shake them by the hand. But it was a nervous time and all Northern politicians were conscious of their security.

Tension was high and became higher the following week with explosions at Portadown and the County Down village of Moira. The reflex reaction of many was to blame the Provisionals although their supporters denied responsibility. It was reported that an old IRA code word, not used for the past decade, was given in telephone warnings of the Portadown bomb.

If the bombers wished to derail the talks, they were too late. Already there was speculation that the final agreement would be a 'three–all draw', with the unionists getting an assembly, a Council of the Isles and changes in Articles 2 and 3 of the Irish Constitution, while nationalists gained a North–South council, a Bill of Rights or its equivalent and reform in the area of policing, justice and equality. In the prevailing climate, there were few to make the point that these changes might benefit both communities.

The atmosphere in the talks was described as one where the parties exchanged opinions in the knowledge that their real audience was not one another but the civil servants and government ministers who were listening, taking note, and trying to work out a set of proposals everyone could live with. A participant told me there was no real negotiation taking place: 'The sense is almost palpable that we're not negotiating. We're trying to sell our case to others who are going to do it for us.' The unionists were described as being 'in denial' on the North–South issue and someone would have to take them aside and talk them down from the clouds. 'They need a reality check.'

The ugliest and most vicious attempt to undermine the political process at this time took place on 3 March. Just after 9 pm that evening, two masked men, members of the LVF, entered the Railway Bar at Poyntzpass, County Armagh, shouted 'Get down, you bastards!' and then fired repeatedly at the customers as they lay on the floor. A Protestant lorry driver, Philip Allen (34), and a Catholic motor mechanic, Damien Trainor (25), were fatally wounded. Like their fathers before them, the two were lifelong friends and Philip had recently asked Damien to be best man at his wedding. The parents of the dying men arrived on the scene and were able to talk to their sons before they lost consciousness. This was tragedy on the Shakespearean scale: Mowlam said the killings were 'soul-destroying'. There was a general welcome when Trimble and Mallon were shown together on the evening news, jointly commiserating with the bereaved relatives. Mallon knew the younger of the two victims and his family. Instead of wrecking the peace process as intended, the Poyntzpass killings brought parties closer together. A wreath in memory of the victims summed it up: 'Great friends in life, now greater in death.'

In the talks, insiders said the level of agreement between the parties was 'allowing the shape of an agreement to emerge' and the outstanding differences were being identified and isolated. The last week in March and the first week in April were seen as crucial in forging a deal. 'It's going to be an incredibly tight squeeze.' If all went well, there was talk of a referendum on both sides of the Border to be held on or near 22 May.

Sinn Féin's expulsion period expired on 9 March and the following day Adams issued a document entitled *A Bridge to the Future*, which aroused considerable interest as an indication of what Sinn Féin's 'bottom line' might be. The republicans wanted minimal alteration in the Irish Constitution and maximum change in the British constitutional link with the North. After the current phase of negotiations, there might not be a united Ireland but neither should there be a United Kingdom. Sinn Féin would view any agreement in the current phase as part of a 'transitional process' to unity. The party's demands included powerful cross-Border bodies independent of a Northern

Assembly, RUC disbandment, courts and policing to be under the remit of new all-Ireland institutions, withdrawal of the British Army and the release of all political prisoners. 'It wasn't unhelpful,' talks insiders confided. The statement, in cold print in the document, that a 32-county republic was 'unlikely to be achieved by May' was seen as significant. There was, of course, no chance whatsoever of a united Ireland in such a short time – but it was not every day a republican leader spelt it out. The Sinn Féin emphasis on the equality agenda, a new note in republican rhetoric over recent years, was also considered encouraging. Other participants in the talks considered the 'wish-list' in the document as unrealistic and primarily aimed for internal party consumption, but one source close to the negotiations conceded: 'At last there's an agenda there to be discussed.'

Dublin sources described the Adams document as 'very significant'. The Sinn Féin leader had been 'quite subtle and clever' in outlining a nationalist agenda rather than traditional republican aspirations. Adams had shown both courage and leadership: 'A lot of it isn't that far removed from the Framework Document.'

Adams himself said the document contained Sinn Féin's assessment of the position of 'popular nationalism', which wanted to see 'an accord between unionism and nationalism'. Adams was at last spelling out his basic negotiating position, but he was also by implication making a bid for the allegiance of the broad mass of the nationalist population which had hitherto given majority support to the SDLP.

Sinn Féin's hope was that the more realistic elements of unionism would come to realise that the 'old days of domination are finished' and nationalists were not going to put up with the 'nonsense' their parents and grandparents had endured. Nationalists in the North also wanted to see their representatives taking up common positions, with Dublin being 'very much in the leadership'. There was a fear that 'Dublin doesn't understand what it's like to live under unionism', Sinn Féin sources said.

Sinn Féin was having a series of meetings at Downing Street which the party felt was 'quite unprecedented' because they provided an opportunity to outline their views at first hand to a prime minister for the first time since the 1920s. Adams flew to the US in the aftermath of one such encounter on 13 March. At a news conference he gave an insight into the quality of communication between Blair and the republicans. He said the Prime Minister's style was 'much different' from that of his predecessor. 'In our engagements with him, we have found a frankness and an ability to discuss matters which, as an Irish republican, I find very intriguing ... and we are able to hear his views of the situation.' All their engagements had been 'good and positive and frank and cordial'. Blair had read *A Bridge into the Future.*

In a public lecture at Seton Hall University in New Jersey, the Sinn Féin president said Blair had told them the status quo had to be changed and the question was how much change. 'What we have said to him is that we want absolute change. We have said, "We wish you well, we want you to be the last British Prime Minister with jurisdiction in Ireland (*cheers and applause*)". I made the point, half-jokingly, the first time we went to Downing Street, since the waiting room has portraits of different English statesmen, Lloyd George, Balfour and Gladstone, that it seems to me a very strange English custom that they put portraits of all of their failures up in their front room. I wasn't just jesting, I was trying to show the different cultural values, because, of course, these were great statesmen in terms of English interests, in terms of what England or Britain or the Empire represented. But as far as Ireland is concerned they are the people that partitioned the island, that have given us suppression, that have brought about the type of policies which continue even to today.'[9]

But behind the official optimism about the talks, there were nagging doubts. 'I don't know if the scope available to David Trimble is in any way sufficient to deliver nationalism,' one source confessed. Trimble, who had also travelled to the US for the St Patrick's Day events, said he was 'somewhat uneasy' about the way the British Government was 'talking up' the prospects for the Northern talks and giving the impression a settlement could be easily achieved. Perhaps the most problematic area was the possible relationship between a future Northern Ireland administration and the Republic. 'We will not have a third centre of government on the island of Ireland.'

An American reporter asked him if he had changed since taking over the UUP leadership. He quipped that change was like old age, you don't notice it creeping up on you. Yet, although he did not say it himself, he had indeed changed, not perhaps in terms of fundamental principles but in terms of engagement. While he might not appear enthusiastic about it, Trimble was up to his neck in the peace process at this stage and the dynamics of the situation were drawing both unionists and republicans more and more towards the middle ground. His theatricals with Paisley after the Garvaghy Road march in 1996 made Trimble look extreme in nationalist eyes but behind the rhetoric there was a layer of pragmatic realism that was becoming more evident with the passage of time.

At his news conference in the National Press Club, Trimble displayed a red and white St Patrick's Flag which he intended presenting to President Clinton at the White House. Two of his young advisers had been sent to the republican heartland on the Falls Road to buy it, the only place it was on sale.

Immediately on his return from Washington, Trimble had to undergo the annual re-election process required of unionist leaders. Addressing the party's annual general meeting, there was a typical Trimble touch when he made a potentially significant departure from the script distributed to the media beforehand. The original text stated that until 'Sinn Féin–IRA' accepted the principle of consent and abandoned violence, 'we have nothing to talk to them about'. In delivering the speech, he changed this to 'we cannot regard them as a normal democratic party'.[10]

From my conversations with senior unionists after the meeting, it was clear that their earnest desire was still to cut a deal with the SDLP and leave Sinn Féin out in the cold. Apart from the obvious political differences, they simply did not trust the republicans and were worried that recent acts of violence might have been sanctioned by the IRA leadership. If only, they mused, John Hume was prepared to turn his back on Sinn Féin.

With implicit approval, Trimble had quoted a statement by Professor Paul Bew of Queen's University that 'a North–South body of some sort – leaving aside the whole argument of executive powers' would be 'epoch-making – potentially an end to our own internal cold war'.

A North–South body of 'some sort' – but what sort? This was always going to be the key issue and was likely to dominate discussions in the lead-up to Mitchell's deadline. Republicans were said to have considerable confidence that Ahern knew what was required and what the bottom line was for them but, based on the experience of the Propositions on Heads of Agreement the previous January, Sinn Féin had less confidence in some members of Dublin's civil service apparatus. Meanwhile, the mandarins in Dublin were frustrated by Trimble's refusal to show his hand more clearly: 'It's like the Dance of the Seven Veils but he never sheds anything.'

As the debate ground on, Mitchell recalls that he became more and more convinced there had to be an early, hard deadline, partly because of the continuing threat of violence. The Easter weekend of 10–12 April was the obvious time. He estimated it would take two intense weeks to reach agreement, which meant starting on 30 March. The first week would allow the participants to make their final comments which could be incorporated into the first draft of a comprehensive accord for presentation to the parties on Friday, 3 April. After weekend discussions, a second, final draft would be made available on Monday, 6 April. He set the ultimate deadline at midnight on Thursday, 9 April. He made it deliberately early in case the talks had to continue until Friday or Saturday of the Easter weekend. However, when he announced his schedule on 25 March, he laid repeated emphasis on the absolute and inflexible nature of the deadline and the urgency of meeting it. The mood of the time was caught in an *Irish News* headline next day: 'Bloodshed Looms if Parties Fail to Settle.'[11]

Everyone was clearing their diaries for the ordeal ahead. In general, nationalists were more excited at the prospect than unionists and one of the latter was heard to moan about 'this godawful peace process which the (British) government has engineered'. Unionists had also begun to beat the decommissioning drum with greater intensity of late. However, the two governments were turning up the heat on participants and had even offered to pay lodging for delegates who came from outside the Belfast area. David Andrews told me in an interview: 'I'll be there 24 hours a day from Monday [30 March] until the following Friday and from the following Monday until April 9th.' He knew how high the stakes were: 'It's the biggest issue, in political terms, that has confronted the island of Ireland since 1918. From any point of view it's a historic time and we're all up there trying to make history together.'[12]

Chapter 5

THE LONG GOOD FRIDAY

The period in April leading up to Good Friday could truly be described as Ten Days that Shook Northern Ireland. Not since the Treaty negotiations of 1921 had such a determined effort been made to resolve the Anglo-Irish conundrum. These were days when participants scaled the heights of optimism only to be plunged into the depths of despair – and then lifted up again just as quickly. Each day leading up to Good Friday had its own character.

WEDNESDAY 1 April: As Mitchell's 9 April deadline for agreement grew closer, the talks shifted up several gears. Negotiations between the two governments had begun in earnest the previous Friday and now inter-party dialogue was reaching new intensity. The level of activity can be gauged from the fact that on this day the SDLP, for example, took part in meetings with: the UUP (twice); the three chairmen (twice); Sinn Féin; the loyalist parties; the Alliance Party; and the decommissioning subcommittee.

John Taylor weighed in with a broadside at the Irish Government for not revealing the full and final text of its proposed amendments to Articles 2 and 3. Dublin didn't rise to the bait: hadn't Martin Mansergh, 'the primary draftsperson' of the amendments, attended in person at a meeting with the UUP where the issue was discussed? Liz O'Donnell told reporters Taylor was being 'politically immature'. He and his colleagues had been given a full briefing on the changes envisaged: 'They are aware of the outline of the text.' But the unionists weren't satisfied with outlines, they demanded full disclosure. They wanted their lawyers to vet the new text to ensure it was 'judge-proof' – a reference to a past court case in the South which ruled that Dublin was under a constitutional imperative to seek Irish unity. From Dublin there were reports of deep concern among elements of Fianna Fáil over mooted changes in the Articles, and up to 30 drafts were said to have been written at this stage. Fianna Fáil TDs were anxious that any change should be supported by Sinn Féin as they were not keen on entering a referendum campaign in which Adams and his followers would be accusing them of a sell-out. Ironically, some of those who worried most were not necessarily the most republican members of the party.

Gerry Adams, fresh from a lengthy meeting at Government Buildings with the Taoiseach, was taking the nationalist high ground by echoing Daniel O'Connell's[1] demand for a repeal of the Union. There was no chance of that but changes in the Government of Ireland Act 1920 which partitioned the island had been mooted for some time. Sources in the SDLP remarked drily that Sinn Féin had adopted 'observer status' in the talks but when this comment was reported by me in *The Irish Times*, the republicans were furious. The incident reflected the delicate relationship between the two nationalist parties. Martin McGuinness later complained that even getting meetings with the SDLP at this time was very difficult: the republicans always had to make the initial approach. Mallon acknowledged that he refused a meeting with Sinn Féin on Strand One arrangements for the internal governance of Northern Ireland. As far as he was concerned, the republicans had refused to discuss this issue for two years, leaving the SDLP to carry the can, so it was a bit rich for Sinn Féin to be jumping on the bandwagon now. Republicans complained further that some SDLP people – they did not mention names – were personally standoffish during the talks but might talk to republicans who were not from the same constituency!

From the other side of the house, the UUP was also continuing its policy of refusing to meet or acknowledge Adams or his people: UUP delegates would not even return greetings in the corridor or dining room. At one stage the UUP's Peter Weir retreated into a cubicle of the men's toilet to avoid having to talk to Adams. As Weir closed the door behind him, the Sinn Féin leader joked: 'Now that's what I call a siege mentality!'

The Taoiseach was talking tough in advance of a meeting in London with Blair, sowing doubts over the possibility that an agreed joint position would emerge from the encounter. The focus was on Strand Two and Ahern told reporters as he left Dublin that there were 'large disagreements that could not be cloaked'. The Framework Document had to stand and he did not know if the differences could be overcome. His comments provoked anger in Whitehall. Although Ahern did not spell out the implications, clearly this would have knock-on effects for the outline agreement Mitchell was expected to produce by the weekend. While on the surface there appeared to be a serious stand-off between Dublin and London, it was far more likely that Ahern was seeking to demonstrate to the unionists – as well as to Sinn Féin and his own followers – that he meant business. Earlier in the week, Ahern had even floated the possibility of a referendum about the Border every five years.

Although Ahern never said it explicitly, he had to have been conscious of the imperative that the final deal should not provoke the IRA and the mainstream loyalists to end their ceasefires. For good or ill, the entire process was built on the absence of shooting and bombing from these groups. For an agreement to be successful, the men and women in balaclavas must be prepared at least to acquiesce in its operation if not actively support it (the word 'acquiesce' was heard a lot at this time, especially in relation to the likely republican attitude). For that reason, observers said, it was highly unlikely the nationalist side could agree a cut-and-paste document, put together at the last minute with the unionists. There had to be a significant improvement in the position of the Northern minority, expressed primarily through a North–South Ministerial Council (NSMC) (more generally known at this time as the 'North–South Council') and ancillary bodies, with de facto executive powers. So far, the hardline position of the unionists had proved disappointing ('There is no sense of convergence,' one nationalist source said), and there were growing if unspoken doubts over Blair's willingness and capacity to bring about a unionist change of heart. Getting the unionists to move without losing Sinn Féin was the great challenge in the coming days.

THURSDAY 2 April: Battling a dose of flu, Gerry Adams was sitting in the front seat of a BBC van at Castle Buildings with a reporter and a technician, giving an interview. Looking on, a journalistic colleague quipped: 'They are all getting Gerry's germs.' Talking to other reporters afterwards, Adams denied having influenced the Taoiseach, at their lengthy Dublin meeting the previous day, to take a more hard line position in advance of the London summit. He said Ahern's latest remarks were in line with other recent statements from the Taoiseach. Using the American management school jargon that he sometimes favoured, Adams said the Taoiseach was 'very focused' and knew what had to be done; however 'the big challenge' in all this was for Tony Blair.

Back in Dublin prior to a further trip to London that evening, Ahern laid the responsibility for agreement firmly on the shoulders of the UUP leader: 'David Trimble would need to understand that my compromises are completed.' Dublin was standing by the need for North–South bodies to be established on the basis agreed in the Framework Document, i.e., on a legislative footing, and Ahern wanted to see the SDLP satisfied over the internal government structures in Strand One.

The independence of the proposed North–South bodies from a new northern Assembly was indeed reported to be a key issue in negotiations between British and Irish civil servants working on a joint position paper for presentation to Mitchell. The Irish wanted the NSMC and its associated implementation agencies to be established by legislation at Westminster and in the Oireachtas, and to come into existence at the same time as the Northern Assembly. Unionists did not accept that the establishment of the North–South Council required special legislation. Their view was that the Council and any implementation agencies should be completely subordinate to the Assembly. The Irish Government, well aware that the unionists wanted to keep cross-Border co-operation to a minimum, pressed for the fullest possible autonomy and independence for the North–South bodies.

The British position was inevitably more ambiguous: London was said to be anxious that any proposals agreed between itself and Dublin be 'palatable' to unionists. 'Where does the North–South council get its authority from?' was how Dublin sources characterised the issue. 'Is it from legislation or will it be entirely hemmed-in by a perpetual need to move at the pace dictated by the Assembly?' The unionist fear was that the nationalists, particularly Sinn Féin, would eventually wreck the Assembly, but that the North–South bodies, since they had been established on a legislative basis, would continue in existence and ultimately open the door to all-Ireland government. Timing was also critical: if the Assembly were to meet in advance of the North–South bodies, once formal powers had been devolved, then unionist members might be in a position to exercise a veto on the powers of such bodies. Dublin favoured establishing the bodies simultaneously because otherwise, in the words of one talks participant, 'the Assembly could emasculate the North–South Council from Day One'. Asked what the British position was, talks insiders said, 'That's what's being negotiated'. UUP sources claimed Dublin was endeavouring to limit the accountability of the North–South Council, confining the Assembly to a 'scrutiny' role.

Mitchell was meant to take account of the position of the two governments in his forthcoming 'synthesis' paper; if a joint London–Dublin position were not agreed, it would create difficulties for the chairman. Following presentation of his synthesis document on 3 April, he was expected to hold bilateral meetings with the parties over the weekend, with a view to narrowing the differences as much as possible before formally tabling a refined version of the paper on Monday 6 April. That document should be the Agreement – or pretty close to it.

Policing was also set to re-emerge as a major issue and there were predictions that it would cause 'an almighty row' before too long. The SDLP favoured a commission for police reform but the UUP was concerned about demoralisation in the RUC. Nevertheless, observers regarded it as a healthy sign that the UUP's Dermot Nesbitt and Mark Durkan of the SDLP had given a joint BBC television interview on the state of play in the negotiations the previous night.

It emerged that Wednesday night's meeting between Blair and Ahern in London had been 'a lot quieter in tone' than might have been anticipated from the Taoiseach's tough talk beforehand. Dublin sources denied unionist claims that there was a plan to postpone the proposed 22 May date for a referendum in the Republic so that it could take place after the result in the North was known, but the fact that such a rumour was going around showed the depth of suspicion between the two sides. The dangers that lurked elsewhere were illustrated by the arrest of a man boarding the Dun Laoghaire car ferry to Britain. Gardaí said there was a 980 lb bomb in his car.

FRIDAY 3 April: The atmosphere at Castle Buildings six days ahead of the deadline was low-key. The real action was taking place in London. Ahern had met Blair for three hours on Wednesday night and for almost an hour on Thursday, and would meet him twice on this day. The meetings were facilitated by the Taoiseach's presence at the Asia–Europe summit in London. The rumour-mill was busy: Bertie had hardened his line, it said, raising his voice much louder than David Andrews had been wont to do. Loyalist sources expressed confusion and charged that Dublin was speaking with forked tongue. The media were in the position of people expected to cover a wrestling match without being admitted to the hall, but from snatched conversations and strategic phone calls it was clear everyone on the inside was feeling under pressure. The plaintive cry from more than one party was: 'We've got to sell this thing to our people too.' There were further rumblings from hardline unionism in the form of a meeting at Belfast's Ulster Hall where one of Trimble's dissidents, West Tyrone MP William Thompson, shared a platform with Robert McCartney and Ian Paisley jnr. These rallies were not attracting large crowds, generally speaking, but it was early days yet.

Taylor was again harping on the need to see Dublin's latest redraft of Articles 2 and 3 – the last version he had seen was now a week old. He was not prepared to compromise on North–South bodies, for example, only to find at the last moment that 'Eire' – his use of the Irish name for the state was at variance with current fashion which preferred the Republic of Ireland – was not going to deliver on the Articles.[2] He warned unionists about being lured into a trap by the 'wily' government in Dublin. Taylor still believed there was only a five per cent chance of agreement because, 'Eire remains too greedy'. A UUP source recalls: 'Taylor was telling people to get off side because the show was "going down".'

The relatively relaxed mood at Castle Buildings continued while the parties waited for Dublin and London to get it together on Strand Two. Trimble and Mallon had enjoyed a couple of drinks together – relations were good at this early stage – and a cross-party group including the UUP, SDLP, Women's Coalition and even, on the fringe, a prominent Sinn Féin spokesman, watched the latest episode of the television comedy series *Father Ted*. Next thing they would be watching *Friends*, a wit remarked.

Mitchell notified all the parties in the late afternoon that they could expect to receive the first draft that evening, 'hopefully by nine o'clock'. In his book[3] he recalls that at 6.30 pm he was the recipient of a conference call on the telephone from Blair and Ahern. The Prime Minister told him work was not yet concluded on Strand Two and suggested there should be no Strand Two section in the draft given to the parties later in the evening. Mitchell, who must have missed the hints in *The Irish Times* that agreement between Dublin and London was unlikely, says he was stunned. Then the Taoiseach chimed in that an agreement was close but more time was required: the weekend should be enough. Mitchell made clear that this created a serious difficulty because getting a first draft to the parties that night had been an important part of his deadline strategy. He would try to oblige, but first he wanted to talk to his co-chairmen and the party leaders.

He called the parties together at 9.40 pm on the top floor of Castle Buildings to tell them there were problems. Happily for Mitchell, the parties did not want to receive a partial document. The whole point of the initial draft was to have a comprehensive paper for the first time and, given the importance of Strand Two, a draft that didn't include those issues would be incomplete. Some parties would have had their own lines of communication with Dublin and London anyway. Mitchell called Blair and Ahern and told them he was delaying the draft. The British and Irish civil servants at Castle Buildings were worried that their heads of government might be blamed for the delay. Quite bluntly, they asked that the independent chairmen assume responsibility, or at least make the explanation so vague that no blame could be assigned. Later, flanked by his fellow-chairmen, Mitchell told a well-attended press conference that 'we' were not able to get the full document ready on time. He denied that the two governments had asked him to hold the document back. This was technically correct, although Blair and Ahern had created the set of circumstances which led to the document being delayed. Mitchell told reporters it was hoped to produce the 'full package' within days. He and his fellow-chairmen were disappointed, but still intended to meet the 9 April deadline. They would work with the parties over the weekend. He said it would be 'unwise' to establish a new deadline for producing the draft text.

The fact that the two prime ministers were not in a position to give Mitchell a joint paper on Strand Two was being reported in the media. There were conflicting versions of what was going on behind the scenes, with some sources suggesting there was a gap between the British and the Irish on Strand Two whereas others claimed a position had been agreed but Blair had pulled back because of a growing unionist backlash. Reports that Ahern had won the argument about having the North–South bodies established by legislation in Westminster and Leinster House were described by Dublin as malicious. A rumour went about that Trimble had flown to London for an emergency meeting with Blair: this turned out to be false but there was said to be extreme unease in the unionist camp at the trend of events.

SUNDAY 5 April: Stormont was relatively quiet over the week-end and an Irish civil servant quipped that the plane back to Dublin on Friday night had been like the last helicopter out of Saigon when the Communists took over. The parties were meant to be in the limelight, but the governments had become so involved it was now impossible for them to step aside.

The theme song in a weekend profile of Trimble on Radio Ulster was M People's *Search for the Hero Inside Yourself*. It was a theme that applied to all the participants in the talks as they entered the final stretch. The delay in the Mitchell paper had led to claim and counterclaim from unionists and republicans. UUP sources vehemently denied that the party leader had sight of, much less vetoed, a joint paper on Strand Two from the two governments the previous Friday. Indeed my UUP contacts counter-charged that the republicans had persuaded Dublin to urge the chairman to withhold his paper – although Mitchell had gone out of his way to exonerate Sinn Féin of blame.

Remarkably, sources close to republican thinking were now suggesting that, instead of merely acquiescing in whatever was agreed, Sinn Féin might very well be able to *support* the agreement proposed by the two governments. The package seemed, from what was known of it, to be about right on the key issues for re-publicans: policing, prisoners, North–South arrangements and changes in British constitutional legislation. They were not getting everything they wanted, of course, but there was suffi-cient movement in the right direction. Republican fears that Ahern would not be able to withstand the pressure from London and the unionists had also been allayed, at least for the time being.

It later emerged that Trimble discussed Strand Two issues with Blair over the weekend. UUP sources, meanwhile, said that if a North–South body was set up by legislation at Westminster and in the Oireachtas and was given responsibility for, say, tourism, that body would then be the government of the 32 counties on tourism. They believed this was 'a bridge too far' for the UUP and probably for London, not to mention some elements in the South. Trimble's people were developing quite a sophisticated awareness of the differences in Southern public opinion and the benefits of appealing to what one of them typified, in rather sexist terms, as 'doctor's wives in County Tipperary'.

At Stormont, the feeling continued that the real action was taking place in London and Dublin. As one insider put it, the parties were 'beating down the doors' of the two governments. A talks source summed up the interaction between Dublin and London: 'It's not a question of the governments agreeing, it's a question of the governments finding a formula that is miraculously complex enough to bring the parties on board.' An official from the Dublin side confessed that his colleagues had prepared so many versions of documents that they were 'drafted out' at this stage, although he expected the civil servants to get a second wind in the coming week.

Blair and Ahern finally worked out a common position and their officials brought a document to Mitchell's office on Sunday evening. Mitchell describes it as the most difficult meeting of its kind since he took over as chairman. As he read the document he says he knew that Trimble could not accept it. It was a tribute to Mitchell's impartiality that the hostility he encountered from some elements of unionism, when he became chairman, never tempted him to take an unsympathetic or biased view of the unionist case.

The document was precise on the independent authority of the cross-Border bodies to be set up to implement the decisions of the North–South Ministerial Council. It also referred to Annexes – still in the course of preparation – that would detail the potential areas of North–South co-operation. To add to Mitchell's anxieties, the high-level civil servants asked on behalf of Blair and Ahern that the chairmen should (a) make no changes of any kind in the text and (b) present it as their own draft, not the work of the two prime ministers. The chief Irish concern was that the document not be changed; the British were adamant that the true authorship be concealed, even though it was universally known that Blair and Ahern had been negotiating over Strand Two in London.

The implication to be drawn from Mitchell's account is that Dublin had pushed London into the present position and that London, given its special relationship with the unionists, was nervous about the risk it was taking. Blair still wanted to keep some distance between himself and what he had agreed with Ahern. At the same time, Dublin did not want the progress it had made in negotiations to be diluted.

In the end the three chairmen consented to have the ghost-written Strand Two draft appear as their own. Mitchell's view was that if the governments split on the issue, there wasn't enough time to heal the rift and still meet the deadline. Presumably the split would have come when London, having inevitably come under heavy fire from unionists, had to back away from or disown the Strand Two draft. It looked like London was going along with a green-tinted draft, using Mitchell as cover, in order to persuade the unionists to take the negotiations seriously and get down to business at long last. If the Mitchell figleaf were blown away, London might have to go into denial mode. Commenting later on this episode in the talks, Dublin sources pointed out: 'It was always understood that the proposals would *formally* come from the Chair – and not just on Strand Two.'

MONDAY 6 April: The Strand Two annexes listing areas for North–South co-operation were not ready until nearly midnight. Mitchell was surprised by their length and completeness: this pudding would not want for eggs. There was a last-minute technical hiccup when Mitchell's photocopier broke down and his chief aide, Martha Pope, had to carry out a frantic search for another machine.[4] At long last, the party leaders received the draft text, complete with annexes. At a meeting after midnight, Mitchell pleaded with them not to leak the document. A nervous talks delegate told me at the time that the version given to each party was 'coded', i.e. there were subtle stylistic or typing differences between them which would make it obvious to the chairmen where any leak had come from. This was confirmed later by another talks delegate: the device certainly worked because the detail in the document remained largely confidential until after Good Friday.

At a news conference after his meeting with the party leaders, Mitchell said the 65-page document was 'predominantly a synthesis of the views of the participants themselves'. This was correct if you included the two governments as participants, although the fiction that it was a multi-party discussion with the two governments merely advising from the sidelines still had a lot of currency. Intensive discussion and negotiation based on the document would begin at 1 pm the following afternoon. 'I have encouraged the parties not to leak the document to the press,' Mitchell said. It was a difficult enough process without being made more difficult by leaks for 'narrow and partisan advantage'. 'Lives and deaths are at stake here', he added and it would be 'incredible and dismaying and deeply disturbing' if the document were leaked. He also appealed to the media to call off the hunt for the document. This plea probably had little effect on individual journalists, but may have eased the pressure from their offices to get the 'scoop' before anyone else did.

The SDLP and UUP had held lengthy bilateral meetings earlier on Monday, without resolving their differences over the structure of a Northern Assembly and the status of North–South bodies. The SDLP, with tacit support from Dublin, argued for a power-sharing cabinet-style executive. For the moment, the UUP stood by its plan for a loose structure of committees to operate government departments, without an executive holding overall power.

The other major disagreement remained the question of establishing the North–South Ministerial Council by legislation in Westminster and the Oireachtas, and whether the council would begin to function at the same time as the Assembly – or even in advance. It appeared that London had come down on the nationalist side of the argument. Meanwhile, nationalist sources warned against any temptation to 'split the difference' on certain issues. On Strand One, for example, they argued that there was no halfway-house between having a cabinet and not having one. One of the fears of unionists, which grew as the days passed, was that setting up a power-sharing cabinet-style executive would lead to one or more portfolios being assigned to Sinn Féin. Unionists stressed this would cause major difficulties among their grassroots: they were prepared to contemplate Sinn Féin chairing departmental committees provided there was no overall collective authority.

The Mitchell document had been described in advance as a 'synthesis' paper attempting to narrow the differences between the parties. By the weekend it was being spoken of as a draft text for a settlement but on Monday night its status had begun to revert to that of a discussion document. Indeed Mitchell had 'Draft Paper for Discussion' printed at the top of each page.

TUESDAY 7 April: Early in the day John Taylor made the immortal remark to the media that he wouldn't touch the Mitchell document with 'a forty-foot pole'. Nobody was very surprised that the Ulster Unionists were having problems as the shape of the final agreement started to become clear. What caused some eyebrows to lift was the negative response of the loyalist groupings, particularly the UDP, and the centre-ground Alliance. Sinn Féin's comparative equanimity may have heightened unionist fears, according to one talks insider on the nationalist side, who suggested that it would have been better from a strategic viewpoint if the republicans had been their usual cantankerous selves. Strand Two was the main problem but, curiously, the provenance of that section – the real authorship must have been suspected if not known – did not seem to be an issue with anyone.

Trimble called Blair three times on Tuesday morning, and even the normally sanguine Alliance Party leader, Lord Alderdice urged the Prime Minister, through the media, to 'get here fast'. A meeting between the UUP and Mitchell was not one of their more amicable encounters. Dublin sources commented: 'This is a negotiating process. It's going to be a long three days.'

The UUP leader released the text of a message he was sending to Blair, stating that his party could not recommend the Mitchell document. Before contemplating alternative proposals, he wished to know if the two governments were prepared to consider 'radically different measures'. It appears that none of the points he had discussed with Blair at the weekend was included in the Strand Two section; instead, there were what

Trimble later described as 'huge, long lists' of areas for cross-Border co-operation, over 60 in all.

At the same time Mitchell was telling Mowlam that the chairmen did not believe Trimble was bluffing. Interestingly, the British civil servants welcomed Mitchell's empathy with Trimble on the draft paper: they had been uneasy over the Strand Two result all along. Dublin was less sanguine, as agreeing to renegotiate on Strand Two increased the possibility that Sinn Féin would walk away from the table. Obviously the final decision on Dublin's approach would have to be taken by the Taoiseach.

Blair arrived in the evening, but stayed at Hillsborough Castle for the moment. He insisted that it was not a day for soundbites, then without batting an eyelid went on to deliver the soundbite of the year: 'I feel the hand of history on our shoulder in respect of this, I really do, and I just think we need to acknowledge that and respond to it.'

As for Ahern, in addition to political pressure he now had to cope with personal tragedy as his 87-year-old mother Julia had died early on Monday morning. According to Mitchell, Ahern had initially decided to hang tough on Strand Two. Attending a church service for his mother on the evening of 7 April in Dublin, he was approached by aides who briefed him on the crisis at Stormont. The officials urged Ahern to reject unionist demands that the Strand Two section be renegotiated. The two governments had reached an agreement in good faith and should now devote themselves to persuading the parties to accept it. Ahern concurred but, later in the evening and after further consideration, as Mitchell tells it, the Taoiseach changed his mind. Originally intent on remaining in Dublin until after the funeral the next morning, he decided instead to fly to Belfast for a breakfast meeting with Blair, returning in time for the Mass. He was agreeing to renegotiate on Strand Two.

Unionists dispute this version of events and claim that it was pressure from Blair which forced Ahern to soften his stance. It was certainly the case that the Strand Two section negotiated by the two governments was particularly 'green' by unionist standards, but it acted as an incentive to Trimble's party to engage in a process about which it had often appeared very half-hearted. I remember thinking at the time, 'They've gone too far, the unionists will walk away', but it is a plausible analysis in retrospect that, in the shotgun wedding between unionism and nationalism, the Strand Two draft was the shotgun. Besides, the possibility of making concessions on prisoners to Sinn Féin still gave Blair and Ahern room to manoeuvre.

Adams wondered aloud and very pointedly how the Ulster Unionists could have assessed the lengthy Mitchell report in such a short time. UUP insiders insisted that 'the guys worked on it overnight' and that there had been a thorough discussion on Tuesday morning. The UUP attack on Dublin was unremitting: 'The Irish Government are fully batting for Sinn Féin and giving Sinn Féin a veto.' It was noticeable that the SDLP came in for little or no unionist flak. The motivation was clear from a remark by a UUP insider, who said Dublin 'should be bolstering the SDLP and helping them to get an agreement with us'. Some unionists were inclined to blame their problems on British civil servants, perhaps the same people who were regularly branded as 'securocrats' by Sinn Féin. Mandarins just couldn't win. 'Once you bring Sinn Féin into the loop, we go out,' UUP sources thundered. 'It's us or them.' Unionists were not going to be 'blackmailed' by threats of an IRA return to violence.

For reporters, the endless round of angry press briefings was reminiscent of the talks in the early days. Commenting on the UUP position over North–South bodies, Dublin contacts said: 'They have this notion that a lot of things should be left for the Assembly to decide. Nationalists just won't buy that.' On Tuesday night a number of key negotiators still insisted that an agreement could be reached, despite the combined unionist and loyalist rejection of Mitchell's first draft.

The UUP leader met Blair that evening at Hillsborough: party dissidents complained later that there were not supposed to be any 'one-on-one' meetings and Trimble had breached this rule. Taylor had gone to London for the fiftieth birthday party of the composer Andrew Lloyd Webber. Trimble may have been expecting a brief exchange about the situation over tea but the conversation turned out to be much more detailed than that. The Prime Minister had clearly come to do business and had already worked out, on the basis of his discussions with Trimble over the weekend, the changes he believed were necessary to secure agreement. Trimble left by a back gate, avoiding the media and loyalist demonstrators. Alderdice also met Blair and complained to him that the Mitchell paper 'took us backwards rather than forwards'.

WEDNESDAY 8 April: The last phase of the talks began in earnest with a Blair–Ahern breakfast meeting at seven and continued with few pauses until almost five o'clock on Friday evening, a total of 58 hours. As Mitchell told the two prime ministers, it had to be clear that they intended to stay to the end.

Some apprehension was expressed by Sinn Féin sources who could not see how the gap between Trimble's position and the Mitchell text could be bridged without making concessions unacceptable to nationalists. Adams said he told the Prime Minister that Sinn Féin could only support an agreement 'aimed at removing the causes of conflict as opposed to appeasing the extremes of unionism'. He accused Blair's press officials of exaggerating progress in the talks: 'I said to him that his people were spinning this up out of all proportion.' Sinn Féin sources said if the Mitchell text was recast to accommodate the fundamental objections expressed by Trimble, then there would be nothing but worthless 'scraps' left for nationalists. Republicans recalled afterwards that Dublin had held firm on Strand Two in a meeting with the UUP, but came back later with compromises. Sinn Féin had to 'try to halt the slippage' and there was a 'frank exchange' between the Irish Government and the republicans as a result. Sinn Féin was also understood to be pressing for bigger concessions on the issue of prisoners.

Dublin sources said they still didn't know what Trimble's bottom line was: 'We are not going to start rewriting the document.' If Blair agreed to rewrite the Mitchell draft, 'we'll be here for another 21 months'.

The drive to find an acceptable version of the Mitchell text followed a tripartite meeting of Ahern, Blair and Trimble, which took place shortly after the Taoiseach arrived back in the evening from Dublin. On his way into the meeting, Ahern told reporters that the Mitchell text was 'certainly the basis for an agreement' and invited parties to outline the changes or alterations that they 'can live with or that they require'. Significantly, he said everybody would have to 'move a little bit'. Blair's spokesman gave an upbeat report afterwards on the tripartite discussion: 'There was real progress tonight. It was a good meeting. From it, considerable work is ensuing.' Highlighting the pressure the parties and governments were under, he added: 'The will is very strong. The imperative is that nobody wants to fail. That is a very strong force driving this on.' It was said later that this was the key meeting of the week with Ahern conceding enough to reassure Trimble it was worth his while staying at the table.

A member of Trimble's talks team, Steven King, disputes the contention that Ahern decided independently and without significant prompting to renegotiate on Strand Two. He recalls warning Trimble against meeting Blair and Ahern together as he would most likely find himself in a minority: 'I was wrong. As David gleefully reported to me immediately after the meeting, "I have just witnessed the ritual humiliation of an Irish Prime Minister".'[5] A similar version of events[6] has been given by Professor Paul Bew of Queen's University, one of the key intellectuals in Trimble's circle: 'At a critical moment in Easter Week ... Mr Blair had to persuade Mr Ahern to alter significantly the Irish Government's negotiating wish list. Not only did Mr Blair exert pressure, he made it clear that London would publicly criticise any continued Dublin intransigence. The result was the Good Friday Agreement.' Dublin sources reject this interpretation: they are adamant that the Taoiseach realised he had to 'reach out' to the UUP leader if there was going to be a deal that both sides could sell.

In short order, the three annexes with Strand Two were reduced to one and a list of over 60 'subject areas' was cut down to twelve. Dublin had originally drawn up a list of about 100: the SDLP was privately very critical of this approach and would have preferred a shorter but broader list, with fewer minor matters and greater depth. 'There was a sense that Dublin had blown it in that list,' SDLP sources said afterwards. 'David Trimble took advantage of it by picking out the things he wanted.' Iveagh House sources said the list had been drawn up in the Department of the Taoiseach and they agreed with the SDLP critique. This begs the question of whether Trimble would have yielded to pressure if presented with a stronger list.[7]

The Taoiseach left the talks shortly after 1 am and flew back to Dublin. He was to travel north again for a 9 am meeting with Blair at Hillsborough Castle where they would assess the situation in the light of their officials' work. A Dublin spokesman said: 'A huge effort has gone into the attempt to work out a package of proposals designed to secure agreement. The Taoiseach and his delegation have been involved in meetings all evening: there has been positive engagement but it is too soon to say whether a final breakthrough will be possible.' Andrews recalled later that there had been so many difficulties with the unionists, especially over the North–South bodies, that the Irish Government was preparing for the possibility of withdrawal: 'Our view was that if there was no movement by Thursday lunchtime, it would be best to plan an exit strategy. The contingency plan accordingly was for the two governments to take stock around lunchtime on Thursday and, if necessary, to advise the Chairman at that point to set a deadline in the late afternoon for the conclusion of the talks.'[8]

Meanwhile the amiable Gary McMichael, also leaving early in the morning, said that 'the nut is far from cracked' but he refused to rule out the prospect of agreement: 'Never say never.' Officials from the two governments, acting on the instructions of their prime ministers, worked late that night in consultation with the parties to revise the Mitchell draft with a view to producing a settlement ahead of the following night's deadline. The key compromise was that 'at least' six North–South implementation bodies would be negotiated within a matter of months and assume their functions at the same time that powers were devolved to other new institutions such as the Assembly.

THURSDAY 9 April: Congressman Peter King, a member of the Republican Party in the US and a long-time friend of the very different Irish brand of republicanism, was keeping an eye on developments from afar. He recalls[9] that he spoke with a very senior figure from the NIO on Thursday morning who was highly critical of Trimble's 'childish' behaviour. The NIO person was also concerned about a half-page newspaper advertisement that day, sponsored by a number of Irish-American organisations and calling on the Taoiseach not to 'buckle to British pressure' by diluting Articles 2 and 3. King was asked to call Ahern[10] about the advert, which was having a 'depressing effect' on him. King reached a leading Irish civil servant, Dermot Gallagher, by phone at about 5 pm Belfast time and asked him to tell the Taoiseach not to worry about the advert which King said was not representative of opinion in the Irish-American community generally: 'This is not Irish-America.'

There was a pressure-cooker atmosphere in Castle Buildings. UUP dissident Jeffrey Donaldson later complained that negotiating into the night added greatly to the pressure on delegates. He also complained that the media were being briefed prematurely by the NIO that a deal was imminent. The Lagan Valley MP had been growing visibly uneasy with the trend of events. A fellow-dissident reports that, 'As the talks entered end-game in spring of 1998 ... Donaldson was asking increasingly awkward questions and taking verbatim notes of Trimble's answers.'

Shadowy figures now began to arrive at Castle Buildings in substantial numbers. This new type of talks delegate was more used to doing business in rather more robust ways than polite conversation across a table. David Ervine later admitted that the PUP was trying to spread the load across all elements of loyalism and not just the politicians, and he firmly believed there were IRA men present also.[11] The SDLP's Bríd Rodgers[12] was said to be alarmed when she saw a man wearing a balaclava but he pulled the garment off and told her he just wanted to keep warm riding his bicycle! The drinks bar may also have helped to attract some of these unusual visitors.

Later in the evening, many of the loyalists left the building to attend and heckle at a news conference called by Paisley who, after a long boycott, had come to Castle Buildings to condemn the impending 'sell-out' of his province. It was not Paisley's most successful outing: the sight of loyalists heckling the man who had been regarded by many of them in the past as their spiritual leader and political guru was an unusual one. I was in the room when it happened and it seemed to me that Paisley and his colleagues were holding their own reasonably well under difficult circumstances but it became clear later that it looked a lot worse for the DUP leader to the huge audience that was now watching events on television. Thanks to the small screen, the abrasive encounter came to be seen as a defining moment in the process: members of the loyalist and unionist community facing up to extremism in their own ranks was not an everyday occurrence in Northern Ireland. There was loud cheering and laughter as delegates and their friends watched the news conference on television in the small Castle Buildings bar. It could not have come at a better time: if Paisley was breaching his own boycott, there must be a deal cooking. When it became clear from the television coverage of Paisley's press conference that loyalists were actually prepared to confront the DUP leader, then talks participants knew there was a big difference from 1974, the year that loyalist workers went on strike to bring down the power-sharing executive.

It is likely that some important meetings were held away from Castle Buildings because of fear that the premises were bugged. There were even suggestions – so far unsubstantiated – that, not just the British, but the IRA also was 'listening in'. Eavesdropping can be a mixed blessing as republicans were quite capable of holding an entirely artificial discussion meant to sow a false trail for their unseen listeners and this almost certainly happened on occasion.

The focus over the previous two days had been on winning the unionists around to an agreement without abandoning elements of the deal that were regarded as essential by nationalists. Hard information was scarce but, to judge from the cordial reception and backing that he received at a meeting of his party executive at UUP headquarters in Glengall Street, Trimble had convinced his followers he was winning the argument.

GOOD FRIDAY 10 April: The deadline of midnight on Thursday slipped past almost unnoticed. About this time, Congressman King, having received a number of messages to the effect that the republicans felt the talks were going against them, called Sinn Féin at Castle Buildings and spoke to a party official who told him things did not look good, the Irish Government was giving in too much on the North–South aspect and there was a feeling that last-minute concessions were being made to Trimble at the expense of nationalists and republicans. The official called King again in Washington 'about an hour or two later' to tell him: 'It's really at the breaking-point, because I wouldn't be surprised if Sinn Féin walks out, it's that bad it's gotten.' King wondered if he should pass this on to the White House and the normally-understated Sinn Féin man said: 'I wish you would, this is very serious.'

The Congressman called the White House and spoke to a senior official from the National Security Council, who felt the talks were 'going better, or not as bad as I [King] said they were'. King then received a call some time between 1 and 2 am Belfast time from a senior Irish official who was 'calling me in Washington to find out what Sinn Féin was telling me, when Sinn Féin was, I guess, down the hall from him'. He passed on the version of events given by the Sinn Féin official, and the civil servant replied: 'Well, we still have the prisoner issue in reserve.'

Reporters on the ground also got a distinct sense at one stage that there was a question mark over Sinn Féin's continued presence at the talks. Mitchel McLaughlin indicated that the republicans would have difficulty backing an agreement but were not planning to leave the table. 'We will be here until the process either succeeds or collapses, but I think we are coming very close ... to the point of collapse,' he said. Sinn Féin sources have flatly denied since that there was any explicit threat to walk out and SDLP contacts are dubious that this was ever the republicans' intention.

A Strand One agreement reached at 3 am between the SDLP and the UUP on a cabinet-style executive, with as many as twelve ministers to run Northern Ireland (the number was not specified, apparently in deference to unionist sensitivities), gave the process a critical boost. Mallon played a central role on the SDLP side and, when the deal was finally done, one of his party colleagues who was present said it was like hearing that 'click' which tells you the combination lock is open. There was a light and unseasonal fall of snow outside as solemn-faced SDLP representatives emerged to brief selected journalists on what they considered a major development. The committee structure suggested in the UUP's Strand One document would also come into being, but only to monitor the activities of the ministers. An earlier UUP–SDLP meeting which involved Jeffrey Donaldson failed to produce agreement but then the Lagan Valley MP was detailed to attend a discussion on Articles 2 and 3 with the Irish Attorney General, David Byrne. The previous Monday, the UUP sent barristers Peter King (no relation to the Congressman) and Austen Morgan to meet Byrne in Dublin and this meeting was a follow-up. However, UUP dissidents say, 'Donaldson up to that point had no input into this contact and did not know any of the issues discussed'. A further UUP–SDLP encounter, minus Donaldson, reached agreement very quickly. UUP talks delegate

Thomas Hennessy has since confirmed my view that Donaldson was sidetracked 'to a meaningless meeting between the UUP and the Irish Attorney General on Articles 2 and 3 – the negotiations on which had already been concluded.'[13]

Outside, the media were able to watch the scene as Mallon arrived in the SDLP rooms with the glad tidings. Television cameras captured Bríd Rodgers, in silhouette, hugging Mallon and other colleagues in delight.[14] This was the critical element of the Agreement from the SDLP's point of view and Sinn Féin sources later complained that, having secured a power-sharing executive, the SDLP showed a tendency to sit on its laurels and let the republicans fight the good fight on North–South issues and on prisoners. However, sources both in Dublin and the unionist camp insist this is both untrue and unfair to the SDLP.[15]

While the governments had been stressing the importance and near-immoveability of the midnight deadline, one talks participant said it 'kinda came and went'. There were several meetings between Sinn Féin and the two prime ministers, one as late as 3 am in which Adams and McGuinness finally hammered out agreement with Blair and Ahern on the prisoners issue. Republicans say that, once the two governments conceded that all politically motivated prisoners would get out, negotiating the time-frame for release was relatively straightforward. Decommissioning had already been dealt with by changes in the text of the Mitchell draft, notably removing the specification that decommissioning was an 'indispensable part of this agreement'. The watered-down final version recalled that the procedural motion at the start of the talks described it as indispensable to 'the process of negotiation'. There was an attempt to balance this major negotiating gain for republicans to an extent by the insertion of a two-year time-frame within which parties would use 'any influence they may have' to achieve total decommissioning of paramilitary arms. However, this would take place 'in the context of the implementation of the overall settlement', which republicans could argue meant two years after the institutions had been established and were operating successfully. In the drive to secure agreement, someone got their numbers wrong and, although the decommissioning section has only five clauses, the fifth one appears incorrectly in the final text as No. 6. McGuinness said afterwards that Blair and Ahern were told very clearly that the

Sinn Féin leadership could not deliver on the decommissioning demand; it was a 'walking issue' for Sinn Féin.[16]

According to Donaldson, the Sinn Féin leaders made it clear at the 3 am meeting that they were leaving the talks process at that point unless London dropped the requirement that decommissioning was an indispensable part of the Agreement and permitted the release of prisoners within two years.[17] The republican version, however, is very firmly that the change on decommissioning had already been made before Good Friday, with that section of the Agreement being rendered sufficiently vague for Sinn Féin to find it tolerable.

On prisoners, Sinn Féin said total release within three years was not acceptable and eventually the two-year figure was agreed. From their dealings with Blair, republicans decided that an even shorter period for release might be possible ('He was in a giving mood,' says one insider.) Gerry Kelly, Sinn Féin delegate and long-time republican activist, went to the PUP rooms and asked to speak to Ervine. The PUP spokesman later spoke of the bemusement on the part of his fellow-loyalists – there were about 50 of them in the building at that stage – when Kelly came to the door.[18] Kelly proposed a common front between republicans and loyalists on the one-year term but the PUP declined.

Given the history and temperament of some of the loyalist prisoners in particular, some observers believe in retrospect that it was wise to keep the release programme at two years. McGuinness said the Sinn Féin negotiators were in direct communication with republican prisoners in the Maze[19] but he would not say how this was done (presumably by mobile phone.)

Around this time, Monica McWilliams of the Northern Ireland Women's Coalition was assured by a Sinn Féin negotiator that 'things were going to be OK' and the republicans were going to remain in the talks. An hour later she met an exhausted and exasperated-looking Mowlam, who was uncertain of Sinn Féin's intentions; the Northern Secretary was reassured when McWilliams told her the republicans intended to stay. In *Women's Work*, a valuable memoir of the participation in the talks by the Women's Coalition's Kate Fearon[20] writes that, even as late as 5 am, Sinn Féin presented Mowlam with another fifteen demands, including the withdrawal of named regiments of the

British Army. Earlier, the republicans had submitted 65 amendments or counterproposals to the Mitchell draft and they also proposed amendments to the final document when it was circulated; this was consistent with their view that negotiations were a 'phase of struggle'. Irish Government sources have also told me that, during the night, they still did not know if Sinn Féin was coming on board or not.

Trimble afterwards explained that his comparatively relaxed demeanour on issues like the prisoners arose from the fact that the primary focus for the unionist leadership was on the constitutional issues and structures which were the 'meat' of the Agreement. 'The other issues, although they captured a lot of attention afterwards, actually are the matters which are consequential on there being peace, on there being a genuine end to violence.'[21] It was reported afterwards that a top Irish civil servant successfully explained the relationship between the Assembly, the North–South Ministerial Council and the British–Irish Council by comparing them to a necklace. He pointed out to the unionists that all the beads on the string are separate, but when you want to wear the necklace you put them on at the same time.

The main focus had been on securing agreement with and between the parties but now it began to emerge that, provided these talks reached a successful conclusion, Blair and Ahern would almost immediately move to the signing of a new British–Irish treaty, superseding the 1985 Anglo-Irish pact, early on Friday morning. This had indeed been flagged up in advance but there had been no indication that it would follow so hard upon a multi-party deal.

Some of the likely provisions of the multi-party agreement began to emerge in the early hours of what David Andrews calls 'that long, nerve-wracking and sleepless night': the Assembly and North–South Ministerial Council would be established by legislation; there would be a prior commitment by the parties to establish implementation bodies; a short Bill at Westminster would establish the Assembly in 'shadow' form, pending the eventual transfer of powers to Belfast; the shadow Assembly would have a role in defining the remit of the implementation bodies and framing the legislation to bring them into being; it was envisaged that the North–South Ministerial Council and the

British–Irish Council (colloquially still known as the Council of the Isles) would come into being in shadow form at the same time as the Assembly; ten executive ministers or secretaries would run the Northern Ireland departments (this was not formally agreed at the time but the unionists were expected to give their consent to it eventually); departmental portfolios would be allocated in proportion to party strengths in the Assembly; Executive Ministers or Secretaries would be responsible for the allocation of the budget and policy co-ordination, and would effect decisions by weighted majorities or some alternative form of 'sufficient consensus'.

There would be a symbolic first meeting of the Assembly in early July. Legislation to establish the Assembly and the North–South bodies could not be completed in Westminster and the Oireachtas until the following February; hence the use of the 'shadow' format. If the Assembly – expected at that stage to have 110 members, although the figure later dropped to 108 – blocked the North–South bodies in February, then it would be abolished. Republicans were understood to be disappointed at the modest range of cross-Border responsibilities nominated for the North–South implementation agencies – animal health, drainage, transport, environmental protection and tourism were being mentioned. It was said the Dublin argument was that these bodies had the potential to grow. Their scope was more modest than I, personally, had expected. The legislative basis for the North–South bodies was seen as a victory for nationalists, but an enhanced role for the Assembly in overseeing their operations was seen as the balancing concession for unionists. The new wordings for Articles 2 and 3, leaked to *The Irish Times*, recognised that unity could only come about by the consent of a majority in both jurisdictions,[22] but even after this change was approved by referendum it would be held in abeyance pending the establishment of North–South bodies with executive powers.

Sources said a complicated formula on paramilitary prisoners would allow for their release over a two-year period. Policing reform would be the remit of a commission, which would report within a specific timeframe. There would be 'a very beefed-up equality agenda'.

As the night wore on, something of a party atmosphere developed in the press huts with old hands swapping yarns and trading jokes to while away the hours. An old country-and-western song was rephrased: 'If I said you were a cross-Border body would you hold it against me?' Eventually energies petered out: reporters and camera crews literally slept where they sat, on bare boards or in easy chairs. A kind colleague told me there was an empty bunk in a caravan belonging to one of the television stations. The hum of an air heater kept me awake, but not for long and I slept till dawn.

At about 6 am Alderdice gave a brief press conference – reporters and camera crews, their sleeping bodies strewn everywhere, stirred themselves to listen to the Alliance leader, who clearly found difficulty believing that so many yawning gaps had been bridged and that there was, in fact, a deal. He described it as 'quite remarkable'. Another participant said it was 'quite an extraordinary night'. Even those who had predicted the deal would be made, found it difficult in the end to believe that no wheels had fallen off the wagon.

The deadline had passed and food had run out in Castle Buildings. Coffee and rolls from a nearby supermarket were now the staple diet. Given the day that was in it, devout Catholics like Martin McGuinness and the NIO Minister for Political Development, Paul Murphy, would not eat sandwiches with meat in them.[23] Meanwhile, delegates got the final draft of the Agreement around 11 am and a plenary was expected around lunchtime.

When it was midday in Belfast, it was only 7 am in Washington. Congressman King was woken by a call from his senior contact on the National Security Council who said, 'I told you last night everything was going to be OK'. It looked like an agreement would be concluded in the next few hours. King, who had gone to bed thinking it was 'all over, you know' simply replied, 'Jesus!' He was told the President had been on the phone to people in Castle Buildings 'all during the night'. When King called the Sinn Féin rooms in Castle Buildings, Adams picked up the phone. 'You know we've been asked to swallow an awful lot,' Adams said, adding that one of the main reasons they agreed was because Clinton had assured them of continued US involvement. 'Gerry made that clear,' King recalls. 'And he said it was a very tough [judgment] call on their part.'[24]

Trimble had left Castle Buildings in the small hours of

Friday morning, after the deal with the SDLP on a power-sharing executive, to grab some sleep at the nearby Stormont Hotel. He had to come back before eight o'clock because there was a problem in his own ranks over decommissioning. Not everyone in Trimble's party had figured on an executive with cabinet ministers – and republican cabinet ministers at that. The spectre of 'the IRA in government' presented itself. The unionists discussed the agreement in an atmosphere of high tension for four hours. This became famous as 'the meeting from hell' and it was reported that one delegate actually fainted from the strain. It had become clear that the deal envisaged Sinn Féin ministers being appointed without a prior handover of weapons. Donaldson complained later that the pressure was intensified by the fact that Blair's chief of staff, Jonathan Powell, knocked on the UUP's door every half-hour to see if the party had made up its mind.[25] There was also the 'adamant' stance of Tony Blair that he could not change the final text of the Agreement.

McGuinness recalled afterwards: 'I met a senior civil servant of the Irish government and I said "Well what's the problem, I've met people who are saying it's this, this and this".'[26] The official was the Taoiseach's adviser, Dr Martin Mansergh, who replied in semi-humorous tones: 'It's you, Martin'.[27] Mansergh went on to give his assessment that one of the biggest problems the unionists were now faced with was the dawning realisation that they might have to go into government with Sinn Féin.

Donaldson later recalled that when he read the final agreement and saw what he regarded as 'significant slippage'[28] on issues like prisoners, decommissioning and the RUC, he then realised this was an agreement he could not support, on moral grounds.

Trimble said further details were sought on the conditions for prisoner release. He was also concerned that there should be an effective mechanism for ensuring members of the new administration were committed to peaceful means. The main UUP negotiators, including Donaldson, went to see Blair. Donaldson made it very clear to the Prime Minister that unless the document specified decommissioning as a prerequisite to holding ministerial office, or the release of prisoners for that matter, he could not give his backing to the Agreement.

There was stalemate among the UUP negotiating team. The

party's general secretary, Jim Wilson, suggested to Trimble that he put the matter to a meeting of his officer board, a more flexible group than the negotiators (there was a bonus in that many of the more moderate negotiators were also members of the officer board). Many of the party's officers were already in the building and, as the discussion with this group was taking place, Trimble received a phone call from no less a person than the President of the United States; Clinton had already contacted Mitchell who agreed with his proposal to call some of the party leaders. The President had been in touch with the talks earlier and it has been established, for example, that he spoke to Blair at least twice, at 4 am and 4.10 am not to mention numerous conversations with other key participants during the night.

Trimble later recalled telling Clinton there was a problem over decommissioning but the Prime Minister was working on a solution and would the President phone 'other parties' to persuade them to give it 'space'. Trimble told Clinton that his plan was to secure a letter of comfort on the issue from Tony Blair. As the 'other parties' waited, Trimble was up and down the stairs to Blair's top-floor office to consult about the letter.[29]

Donaldson complained afterwards that the pressure at this stage was enormous with Blair ringing every fifteen minutes and politicians from other parties calling to the UUP rooms. He took particular exception to the attitude of the Alliance leader whom he described as 'very aggressive'. Alderdice remained unapologetic: straight talking was needed at this stage because a delay of a few days or a week would cause the process to unravel.[30]

In his letter to Trimble, the Prime Minister said that if the Agreement's provisions on decommissioning were shown to be ineffective, the British Government would support changes to ensure that people connected with paramilitary organisations which still held their weapons would not hold political office. 'Furthermore, I confirm that in our view the effect of the decommissioning section of the agreement, with decommissioning schemes coming into effect in June, is that the process of decommissioning should begin straight away.'

Trimble took the view in discussions with his colleagues that, while the situation was not ideal, there would be time to get it right. He said: 'Well look, we've got to make a decision; I mean, it has to be Yes, and we'll have to go up now.' Donaldson saw the deals on decommissioning and prisoners as a blurring of the lines between terrorism and democracy and made it known to Trimble that he could not support the Agreement. Trimble was undeterred: 'There's a time when you have to take a deep breath and decide.'[31] According to sources, he said, 'I am doing it,' and walked out of the room.[32]

Seeing that their line on decommissioning was being over-ruled, Donaldson as well as Weir and the other 'baby barristers' (the name for the young, right-wing lawyers in the party) walked out. It was a difficult judgment-call and even John Taylor admitted to Eamonn Mallie in a documentary programme for Channel Four News a year later that he would 'possibly not' have signed the deal, if he had been party leader.[33] The letter of comfort would surface later in political controversy but nation-alists and republicans never conceded that it had any status since it was not in the text of the Agreement and they had not been consulted as to its contents.

There was intense media interest in Donaldson's departure. Trimble said the Lagan Valley MP had 'got his own commit-ments'. Another UUP source said Donaldson had left to go on holiday, which may have been true but was not the full story. Journalists were frantic and it took a while to confirm that the reason Donaldson was leaving was that the final document was unclear on decommissioning and the letter of comfort from Blair had been insufficient to quell his doubts.[34]

A leading UUP dissident comments: 'The overall impression the talks left with me was [of] a pre-cooked deal, with the Castle Buildings circus used to give the back-room deals the respectability of an open and public process. The problems of Easter Week within the UUP were caused when the truth of the process dawned on the team. I am not aware of any team dis-cussion of the prisoner release until the day before Good Friday.' Afterwards, Trimble's predecessor as unionist leader, Lord Molyneaux, who was not present at the negotiations, said: 'Changes were made to the document in the final hour. That was followed by what amounted to an ultimatum: decide the future of Ulster within fifteen minutes or else. So in my humble opinion that was pressure and blackmail amounting to brutality and in my time as a Justice of the Peace I held to the view that confes-sions made under duress were inadmissible.'[35] When I asked

Trimble about this, his response was blunt: 'The only question is who's been telling him this tosh. It didn't happen. Unless he thinks I browbeat the others into it, which I didn't.'[36]

Trimble confirmed to the Chairman at 4.45 pm that his party was on board for a deal. Mitchell had learnt over the years, especially as Majority Leader in the Senate, not to let the grass grow under a political pact, so with Trimble's consent he convened a plenary for five o'clock – only fifteen minutes later. When Trimble's group arrived, Donaldson was, of course, not among them. Mallon recalled that Trimble was 'in a white heat of pressure'. Others felt he could still go either way. My own recollection of seeing Trimble shortly afterwards was of a man with an electric current running through him, his normally ruddy complexion scarlet from excitement and pressure, dashing from Castle Buildings to a makeshift television studio set up in the car park.

The formalities of the plenary were gone through and each party leader was asked, 'Do you support or not support?' For the first time, television cameras were allowed into the room, which was crowded with delegates, their relatives, friends and former foes, all united now on a platform for peace. Responding to Mitchell, delegates said, 'For the Agreement', or 'Agree'. Adams said, 'Agree subject to consultation'. Trimble paused for a moment and said simply, 'Yes'. After all those years when unionists campaigned against the Anglo-Irish Agreement with the slogan, 'Ulster says No', Ulster had finally said Yes. The Senator declared at 5.36 pm: 'I am pleased to announce that the two governments and the political parties in Northern Ireland have reached agreement.' Politicians, some of them sworn enemies for decades, applauded Mitchell and his team. One participant recalls[37] how, in a separate ceremony conducted 'in a small room with dirty coffee cups', the two prime ministers signed the new British–Irish Agreement.[38]

After his lengthy ordeal, Blair inevitably looked pale and worn as he announced the successful conclusion of the talks from the steps of Castle Buildings. He was standing alongside the Taoiseach, who had also had a long night without rest; Ahern's black tie was a reminder of his recent bereavement. At their joint news conference, Blair said: 'I believe today courage has triumphed. I said when I arrived here that I felt the hand of history upon us. Today I hope that the burden of history can at long last start to be lifted from our shoulders.' It no longer seemed like a soundbite. Ahern said: 'This is a day we should treasure – a day when agreement and accommodation have replaced days of difference and division.' Hume, original architect of the Agreement, appeared in a remarkable photograph on the next day's *Irish Times*,[39] palms raised to heaven as if persuading the unbeliever that miracles really did happen. 'Only once in a generation does an opportunity like this come along, an opportunity to resolve our deep and tragic conflict,' Hume said. A colleague turned and pumped my hand in delight. Mallon said later he saw hard-boiled journalists in tears. I remember feeling pressure rather than emotion: there were copy deadlines to meet and everyone was 'knackered'.

The efforts to reach an agreement had kept Blair in Belfast from Tuesday afternoon until teatime Friday. Indeed, his spokesman revealed that the Prime Minister had not slept at all from the beginning of the last intensive round of talks until he left for Madrid on Friday night, a period of some 36 hours. Although anxious to join his wife, Cherie, their three children and his mother-in-law on holiday in Spain, Blair stuck with the hard grind. Eyewitnesses said a forest of paper had been consumed making drafts and counter-drafts, amendments and counter-amendments. As for Ahern, Mitchell described meeting him at two o'clock on Friday morning. He had never seen anyone so exhausted and at the same time so determined: 'His eyes burned like hot coals as he said to me: "George, we've got to get this done. We've got to get this done".'[40] According to another observer, Ahern showed 'phenomenal energy' and Andrews, admittedly a partisan source, recalls that the Taoiseach 'could and did out-sit anyone and was prepared to listen forever so that we could at last find peace'.[41] Ahern's determination to secure a deal, using the skills developed in his time as Minister for Labour, was a fairly consistent feature of the peace process.

Trimble said on television shortly after the deal was announced: 'I have risen from this table with the Union stronger than when I sat down.' The UUP had 'saved the future of the RUC' in the negotiations. These were bold claims from the UUP leader and they would soon be challenged by the sceptics in his community. Echoing sentiments expressed from the other side of the political divide by republican participants, Trimble said:

'It's not perfect; it's the best we can get at the moment.' He pointed out in a UTV interview that the UUP was getting the Republic's territorial claim removed, and insisted that there were no significant changes in the UK's constitutional legislation on Northern Ireland.

He said later in the evening: 'We know that the consent principle has been accepted by all nationalists, but with one conspicuous exception, and will be accepted and enshrined in the fundamental law of the Irish Republic.' Asked when he would be speaking face-to-face with Adams, he told a press conference he would be prepared to deal with Sinn Féin as democratic politicians. Snow was falling as Trimble spoke from the steps of Castle Buildings. He called on the republicans to declare that their 'squalid' terrorist war was now over. A leading Sinn Féin activist standing beside me with a South African observer was incensed. Red in the face, he exploded: 'He's like a f***ing child!' Clearly all was not as rosy as it might appear.

Sinn Féin was reserving its public position on the document. Adams said that while the text contained elements which were positive, 'there are others yet to be resolved'. The party was expected to hold a meeting of its *ardchomhairle* (executive council) in the coming week to hear a report on the talks from its negotiators. The council would assess the document, reporters were told, and decide whether or not to recommend it for discussion at the party's *ardfheis* (annual conference) in Dublin that weekend. Alternatively it might hold a special *ardfheis* on the matter. Despite Adams' caution, there were few who doubted that the republicans would come on board.

Reactions were coming thick and fast: Albert Reynolds, who had wound the clock but was not there to hear it strike, declared, 'It is a new beginning. There is a lot of hard work ahead. The feeling of history in the making is there. It's nice to be a political leader who sets out on a mission and gets there before he is buried.' Andrews said it was truly a day when history had been made: 'The success of these negotiations will, I believe, come to be seen as a turning point in the affairs of this island.'

Whatever about being a turning point, it was certainly a point of no return.

Chapter 6

LIFTING THE SIEGE

Right to the end, Trimble had kept everyone guessing, including some of his own people. He was clearly determined not to suffer the fate of some of his predecessors and gave his opponents inside and outside the party little time or forewarning to prepare his overthrow. Talks insiders commented that the UUP leadership 'kept everything very tight', e.g. the official party document on Strand One envisaged a committee structure to run government departments and this remained the UUP stance until the very last minute. It was written by Peter King, an articulate young lawyer with a tough attitude to Sinn Féin who later became a leading dissident. There was no interim position paper: such a document would undoubtedly have set the alarm bells ringing on the party's right wing.

More generally, while decommissioning was already beginning to blot out everything else, there was considerable initial interest in the North–South bodies. How much autonomy had they got? Could they be aborted or impeded by a unionist bloc in the Assembly? Could they expand over time to become a government for the whole island, as republicans hoped and some unionists feared? In a UUP policy document of 11 February, North–South bodies were not even mentioned, and the unionist view was that they should be no more than talking shops, meeting at infrequent intervals to discuss minor matters where minimal co-operation was, if not unavoidable, certainly voluntary. The Good Friday pact contained a good deal more than that – though not quite as much as nationalists, and particularly republicans, would have wished. Nationalists won their demand to have the North–South Ministerial Council established by legislation at Westminster and in the Oireachtas, thereby at least ensuring that it would not be a forgotten sub-committee of the Assembly. Nationalists also won the requirement that participation in the Council be an essential responsibility of relevant ministers in the new northern administration.

All council decisions were to be 'by agreement between the two sides'. It would probably have been better from a unionist viewpoint if unanimous agreement were specified as there would clearly be a tendency for Northern nationalist ministers to want to line-up with their counterparts from Dublin on particular issues. All ministers would be subject to 'the rules for democratic authority and accountability' in the Assembly and the Oireachtas. Further on, in some fairly tortured language, the document permitted ministers to take decisions within their 'defined authority'. Where ministers sought to go beyond that, Assembly approval would be required but 'through the arrangements in place for co-ordination of executive functions', which implied that the executive committee or cabinet would play at least a mediating role between, say, an adventurous nationalist minister and angry unionist Assembly members.

The council would meet in plenary format twice a year, with heads of government participating. In specific sectors – the example often given was tourism – it would come together 'on a regular and frequent basis'. Unionists would doubtless make much of the fact that the first duty of the Council would be 'to exchange information, discuss and consult'. This sounded like one of the 'ad hoc chat shows' so distasteful to Bertie Ahern, but nationalists could point to the provision allowing the Council 'to *take decisions* by agreement' [emphasis added]. The thought occurred that there could be some fat legal fees derived from arguing over this part of the Agreement.

Nationalists wanted the Council to come into operation at the same time as the Assembly – or even before – lest the time-lag allow unionists to sabotage the new body. This demand – yet another indication of the great lack of trust between the two traditions – was incorporated into the document. The Agreement also laid down that a work programme be undertaken by the Council, 'covering at least twelve subject areas'. There was a deadline of 31 October for the Council to identify and agree these areas, propose implementation bodies where they did not already exist, and draw up a substantial list of projects.

David Andrews had been in trouble for stating that the Council would be 'not unlike government' and a major question for both nationalists and unionists was whether an all-Ireland administration could develop out of them. The answer was Yes, but only by consent: 'Any further development of these arrangements to be by agreement in the Council and with the specific endorsement of the Northern Ireland Assembly and Oireachtas.' The unionists would have a veto on progress towards all-island consultation, co-operation and action.

The Council was to receive funding from the two administrations and the extent of the monies available looked like another potential battleground. There would also be a standing joint secretariat of civil servants from North and South and there was a hint that the Council might have its own representation at 'relevant European Union meetings'. The Assembly and the Oireachtas would consider setting-up a joint parliamentary forum, along the lines of the British–Irish Interparliamentary Body[1] and there might also be a North–South consultative forum representing the social partners and experts in various fields.

Militant nationalists were inevitably somewhat disappointed at the modest list of topics suggested for North–South interaction and co-operation. Animal health, teacher qualifications, inland waterways and accident and emergency services were not the commanding heights of social and economic activity. Tourism was the weightiest topic on the list, except perhaps for the one called 'relevant EU programmes'. Nationalists argued that the potential for further growth was there, to which unionists could respond, 'Not without our consent'. At the end of the day, it all came back to trust. The Agreement was an acknowledgment by both communities in the North that there was no way around one another: unionists could not be driven into the sea, nor nationalists cowed into silence. Great political tests of strength lay ahead: the shooting might be over, the shouting had only begun.

The language of the Agreement in general was complex, at times almost Byzantine. Many students of the text would find it hard to figure out who won and who lost. They might decide the game ended in a draw or that we had moved to a new plane where there were no winners or losers, just a blueprint for a joint effort to achieve permanent peace and stability.

Unionists were already claiming victory on Articles 2 and 3. The proposed Article 2 made Irish nationality a matter of entitlement – the concept was not new but the *mot juste* was claimed by a young Irish civil servant (the claim is disputed) – rather than implicit compulsion. The original bald definition of the national territory had overtones of the Italian nationalist Giuseppe Mazzini's assertion that first you must create Italy and then you can create Italians. Some Northern commentators said that if you wanted to remove the unionist siege mentality then you must 'lift the siege'. This was effectively what happened under the new Article 2. Irish nationality became a matter of choice rather than duty or obligation. This might alleviate the siege mentality of unionists but it would not enhance feelings of security among Northern nationalists. The *quid pro quo* for them was the North– South Ministerial Council.

The old Article 3 was an assertion of Dublin's right to rule the North, implying that the reintegration of the national territory was a matter of unfinished business. The amended version made unity a matter of 'firm will' rather than a constitutional imperative.[2] It amounted to saying: We want a united Ireland, but only by peaceful means and by agreement. There was an ambiguity where the amended version stated that this voluntary unity should be brought about by a majority of the people 'in both jurisdictions'. It would probably have been more comforting for unionists if the wording read 'in each jurisdiction'. The amended Article 3 could also be said to claw back some ground with its provision that North–South bodies might exercise powers in respect of 'all or any part of the island'.

Less attention was given to London's part of the deal, namely, the repeal of the Government of Ireland Act 1920. The significance of such a move had previously been assessed by John McGarry and Brendan O'Leary in their 1995 book, *Explaining Northern Ireland* where they pointed out that the 1920 Act expressed 'unqualified Westminster sovereignty over Northern Ireland'.[3] Dropping it would make Westminster's sovereignty 'clearly conditional upon the consent of a majority of the people of Northern Ireland to remain within the United Kingdom'. In that sense, Sinn Féin had a point when it said the new dispensation represented a 'loosening of the knot' with Westminster. Unionists disputed this interpretation, maintaining that the 1920 Act had effectively been amended by Acts in 1949 and 1973, with the Good Friday Agreement merely restating the status quo and that the original Act of Union was still in force.

The setting up of the Assembly was a clear gain for unionists, although the rules and procedures contained major safeguards for the nationalist population. It would be a far cry from the old Stormont, according to one leading nationalist intellectual, who said it would be as though Grattan's Parliament[4] were reconvened in the 1840s, after Catholics got the vote. Without doubt, nationalists would have a bigger voice in the Assembly's affairs than they ever had at Stormont. However, Trimble, writing in the *Daily Telegraph* around this time, described the procedures for cross-community decision-making as 'cumbersome', adding that they could lead to deadlock.[5]

The SDLP wanted a power-sharing cabinet; the UUP said all decisions should be made by the Assembly as a whole. We had ended up with a hybrid, closer to a cabinet than not. The question was: who would be on this 'executive committee'? Since seats would be allocated in proportion to party strength, Sinn Féin would inevitably be entitled to at least one seat. This was not a prospect to delight unionist hearts and here decommissioning reared its head once more, as a supposed precondition for taking a cabinet post. Some unionists were deeply unhappy with what they saw as loose provisions in the Agreement on this score and voiced their concerns about sitting down with Sinn Féin while the IRA was still in business. Hence Tony Blair's letter of comfort to Trimble on the issue.

The establishment of a British–Irish Council comforted unionists without discommoding nationalists. It would encourage and foster co-operation on an 'east–west' basis but had no power to inhibit or interfere with the activities of the North–South bodies and individual members could opt-out of implementing its decisions.

Provisions for the release of prisoners within two years and the promotion of greater equality in Northern society were claimed as a 'win' by members of Sinn Féin, although the SDLP had also fought on the equality issue. Meanwhile, unionists boasted that they had saved the RUC. Policing was perhaps the most sensitive, complex and difficult of all issues. It had been long-fingered in the sense that a commission had been set up, but this body had to make its final report by the following summer. Unionists understood there would be no member of the commission from the Republic.[6] The governments and parties would 'discuss' implementation of the report. The existing police service was said to be three times the size required if Northern Ireland were a stable and peaceful society while containing eleven times more Protestants than Catholics.[7] How to reduce the overall size while recruiting substantial numbers from the nationalist community was a daunting arithmetical challenge. Whatever happened would be expensive and it would be a difficult balancing act to convince nationalists that rapid change was in train without accentuating the fears and insecurities of the unionist community. Engels defined the state as 'bodies of armed men' and tackling this issue in a meaningful way would constitute a reshaping of the Northern state. The political fallout would be huge, and if any issue had the potential to bring about a renewal of widespread violence this was it.

The more one read and studied the Good Friday document, the more it seemed like an interim settlement, the 'best guess' of the parties and governments – for now. There were many unresolved issues – decommissioning, policing, the precise role and function of the executive committee and the North–South bodies. The hope was that all these matters could be worked out in a non-violent manner and that, for once, power wouldn't grow out of the barrel of a gun. One moderate unionist summed-up the essence of the Agreement from his viewpoint as, 'Ulster is dead. Long live Northern Ireland'.

The scale of the philosophical recasting of Irish nationalism was breathtaking in its ambition. The territorial basis was, on the face of it anyway, being thrown out and the claim to unity would now be a matter of argument and persuasion rather than doctrine. The sleeping dogma that underlay the old Articles 2 and 3 was a 'given' of Irish life, south of the Border at least. This was being junked in favour of real, practical, hands-on, day-to-day engagement between the two parts of the island. There would no longer be the consolation of knowing that, whatever happened on the ground, a basic ideological cornerstone remained in place.

Articles 2 and 3 were originally in part a formula to permit militant republicans to square their consciences with participation in the institutions of the southern State, which they had initially tried to abort. They were also an implicit guarantee to Northern nationalists, although many of these – including some Sinn Féin members – had placed little store by them over the years. It was only when unionists began to make an issue of the Articles that nationalists, and the Dublin administration in particular, woke up to the fact that this rusting vehicle in the constitutional garage might be a tradeable commodity rather than a candidate for the scrapyard. While there might be cynicism about their true value, amending the Articles represented a major change in the nationalist and republican mindset. It was not something republicans could come to terms with overnight or even at the forthcoming *ardfheis* in Dublin, set for the weekend after Easter. Nevertheless, the pressure was there for Sinn Féin to clarify its position on the Agreement. There was little or no room for cherry-picking or sitting on the fence. If Sinn Féin opposed the Agreement, as it had the Downing Street Declaration, or took a limp-wristed position on the sideline, there was a possibility the deal could be defeated or else fail to secure a convincing majority. Dublin, London and Washington were watching and waiting: it was a particular source of anxiety to Fianna Fáil. There seemed to be no way out and no space for Sinn Féin to fudge or seek 'clarification' as it did on the Downing Street text. Adams and his friends could play for time, but not much.

There was talk of a special meeting to consider the document a fortnight after the *ardfheis*. By that stage, the pressure would be almost unbearable, and there were hints that the special session could take place within a week. The prospect of some members falling away and joining the hard-line 32-County Sovereignty Committee or Republican Sinn Féin was considered very real. There were no indications so far that members of the leadership were about to splinter off. The cadre which had steered the Provisional movement over the years was holding firm.

Adams had described the recent talks as a phase in the struggle and asked his followers to look at the 'big picture'. The comparison with Michael Collins and his stepping stones[8] to freedom was a tempting one.

If the North–South bodies had a wider remit and the policing reform were 'nailed down' better, the document would have been easier for the Sinn Féin leadership to sell to its members. At the same time there was a sense in Sinn Féin circles that if the party rejected the document it would be playing into the hands of the unionists. The issue of whether the new Assembly was a truly partitionist institution or not was bound to surface. Given

the safeguards for the minority and the link with the North–
South Ministerial Council, there was an argument that this was
a fundamentally different institution from the old Stormont.
Some Sinn Féin members felt the North–South bodies would
never be more than token institutions unless the party was represented on them. For that to happen, Sinn Féin would have to
stand for the Assembly, take its seats and overcome any decommissioning obstacle that might exist to becoming ministers.
Although Sinn Féin would not put it this way, in order to push
for a united Ireland there would have to be *pro tem* acceptance of
partition.

Even if the referendums passed on both sides of the Border
– or perhaps especially if they passed – we would see further
violence. However, the Adams group seemed to be keeping a
firm grip on its support base in the republican ghettos and heart-
lands of the North. That was the importance of the 'equality
agenda', the release of prisoners and the reforms in policing. Life
'on the ground' had to improve for ordinary nationalists, who
had no great interest in theory and dogma, the finer points of
voting procedures in the Assembly or the rules pertaining to
North–South bodies. When traditional militarist republicanism
fused with the social grievances of Northern nationalists, with
the civil rights movement as the catalyst, the consequences were
explosive in every sense of the word. Now there was a New
Departure,[9] with the bread-and-butter concerns of nationalists
and the political structures necessary to accommodate them taking precedence over the bomb and the bullet. The old methods
still had their adherents, and there would probably be some
form of guerrilla activity in Northern Ireland for the foreseeable
future. The question was the scale: we might be seeing the development of a Catalan-style nationalism in the North where the
vast majority supported political activity and participation in a
new set of structures while the paramilitary path was chosen
only by a few.

In many ways the equality agenda espoused by Sinn Féin –
the SDLP was active in this regard as well – was the key which
unlocked the door to republican participation in the Assembly
and the northern executive. The ultimate objective of a united
Ireland would be maintained but, in the meantime, what could be
wrong with achieving the maximum level of rights and equality

for nationalists within the existing set-up, especially if you were also undermining partition in the process? Mainstream republicans argued that unionism was based on sectarian supremacy and that, by campaigning for equality, you were helping to remove the basis for unionism. There was a historical precedent: the civil rights movement – which, unlike Sinn Féin, hardly even mentioned partition – had destabilised Northern Ireland and reopened the issues that were meant to have been settled by the Anglo-Irish Treaty of 1921. However, the dissidents rejected the Provisional analysis out of hand: collaboration with six-county institutions would end up with republicans being absorbed into the existing scheme of things or else pushed to the margins of political life: look what happened to the 'Officials'[10] when they tried a similar approach, the argument went.

In the end, Sinn Féin decided two weekend gatherings were needed to reach a decision. The sense at the first session was that most of the Northern delegates would follow the current leadership. This was the cadre which took guerrilla tactics as far as they could possibly go, over the longest possible period. Was there anyone waiting in the wings who would dare more and push the limits of conflict against a massive military and police machine farther than they had? There was a different tone emanating from the Southern delegates. Perhaps to ward off the sneer that they were 'armchair generals', one speaker pointed to the part that activists from south of the Border had played in the IRA campaign of the previous 30 years. It was obvious from the speeches that there was a real difficulty for Sinn Féin in the South when it came to voting Yes in the forthcoming referendum. There was an expression of northern sentiment on Articles 2 and 3 from one delegate who said: 'I wouldn't give you tuppence for the entire '37 Constitution.'[11]

Senior figures hinted at a Jesuitical approach, involving a Yes vote in the North and a No in the South. This could cause problems for Sinn Féin internationally. The mixed signal would be confusing for observers abroad, unversed in the subtleties of partition. The word 'cop-out' might be heard from across the Atlantic. The one point all speakers were agreed on, at least publicly, was that the current leadership was the best ever, had put a huge effort into the negotiations and could not be criticised for anything. The document was another matter. Nobody was ecstatic about it, but some saw it as a basis for advance, whereas, in John Taylor's phrase, others would not touch it with a barge-pole. The question which those who damned the document failed to answer was how such an excellent leadership could have a hand in producing such an allegedly inferior agreement.

There would no doubt be some erosion of republican ranks, but at this time anyway the circumstances did not exist for a massive split. There was a war-weariness in the air, and several speakers from the North, older and more experienced than most of the Southern contributors, voiced the desire that their children and their children's children would not have to go through what they had suffered. Watching the debate, one was tempted to conclude that when this document was accepted and when, as expected, Sinn Féin entered the new Assembly not as a servant but as one of the masters of the banquet, then it could indeed be said that the war, if not over, had at least lost most of its soldiers.

Whereas Sinn Féin decided two weekends were necessary to decide on the Agreement, the Ulster Unionist Council completed its deliberations in a single five-hour session, which took place in the Europa Hotel in Belfast on 18 April. On their way into the meeting, UUC delegates had to pass two opposing groups of loyalists, one pro, the other anti, who shouted insults at each other across police barriers. A motion to endorse the document was carried by 540 votes to 210. A delighted Trimble said he hoped it was the end of 'the era of misrule, called direct rule'. Adams speaking the same day at the Sinn Féin *ardfheis* in Dublin said, 'Well done, David'; the phrase was used to taunt Trimble afterwards by his opponents.

A body not noted for radicalism, the UUC voted overwhelmingly for a programme of fairly sweeping change in the society around it, up to and including participation in government by the political wing of its sworn enemy, the IRA. A leading unionist dissident snorted afterwards that many of the 'brain-dead old duffers' on the UUC had not even read the Agreement and that their average age was higher than their average IQ. A more generous assessment might be that the spirit of reconciliation had permeated the ranks of the solid citizens of 'Middle Ulster' and that the ceasefires and subsequent political rapprochement were allowing them to display, however shyly, their more tolerant and forgiving side. If you want to lift the siege mentality, lift the siege.

The siege might be ending, but murder still stalked the land. The euphoria generated by Good Friday was punctured when a young Catholic local authority worker in Portadown, Adrian Lamph, was shot dead by the LVF on 21 April; at 29 years, the dead man was the same age as the Troubles. The recycling depot where he worked was only half a mile from the Lamph family home on the nationalist Garvaghy estate, but crossing that short distance brought him to the other side of a 300-year sectarian conflict. He was said to be on his knees cleaning up at the end of the day when the killer rode in on a mountain bike.

I covered Adrian Lamph's funeral, which was a striking demonstration of silent grief by the crowds of people who attended. There was no wailing, no histrionics, but the shock and outrage on the faces of the mourners – any of whom could also be a future target – were plain for all to see. There were no big-name politicians to the fore, just the ordinary people of the area. The victim's fiancee Nicola, small son Jude and father, Tommy, led the mourners and it was hard to find anyone over 30 at the front of the cortège. In the church, friends played music and sang beautiful tunes, and there was a haunting traditional air on the fiddle. There were recollections of a 'decent guy' who liked dogs, birds, music, get-togethers and parties and had a sense of humour. And who was killed by someone who did not want peace.

Continuing violence underlined the need to copper-fasten political progress. Those who negotiated the Agreement had reason to feel cautiously optimistic in the early stages about securing a substantial majority in the referendum. A joint *Irish Times/Guardian*[12] poll conducted the weekend after Good Friday found almost three in four, or 73 per cent of respondents in Northern Ireland, in favour of the Agreement.

A multi-party Yes campaign was a logical requirement and an attempt was made to have one established. A pro-Agreement activist, Quintin Oliver, describes in his valuable memoir *Working for Yes*, how an ad hoc group from the voluntary and business sectors arranged a meeting for the morning of 22 April but, as they assembled, a call came through from the UUP to say they could not come on board. The rationale was that the battle for the hearts and minds of Unionists could be jeopardised by a premature alliance with other parties, including Nationalists –

not to mention Republicans, if Sinn Féin came on board. The SDLP representative took the view that, if the UUP weren't on board then neither could the other parties, because there would be a permanent focus on Trimble's absence, with questions raised about his commitment to the Good Friday deal. This was probably true but had the other parties proceeded anyway they could have (a) generated a strong and united drive for a Yes vote and (b) conceivably drawn in the UUP eventually, since the latter was always a reluctant participant in anything to do with the peace process. Breakfast meetings organised by the campaign attracted a good attendance by politicians.

Oliver, whose background was in the voluntary sector, went ahead with colleagues to set up a non-party Yes campaign.[13] The group got the best professional advice, on an informal basis, from Alan Bishop, chairman of the multinational advertising firm, Saatchi and Saatchi. One of the campaign's more successful events was a victims' press conference where people who had lost relatives in the Troubles voiced their support for a Yes vote. The campaign was small but very busy: it was fighting a fairly lonely battle since the business community and the trade unions were adopting a lukewarm stance and support on the ground was tacit rather than active.

It was a fairly daunting scenario. The group also had to contend with the suspicion, which was never substantiated, that it was a 'front' for the Northern Ireland Office. Conspiracy theories find fertile ground in the North and they gained sustenance when Paisley gave journalists a leaked copy of an eight-page NIO memo on the referendum, prepared over a month in advance of Good Friday by the newly appointed director of communications, Tom Kelly. While much of the paper was unexceptional, anti-Agreement unionists highlighted a remark in the text that 'it will be important to ensure that not all of the results of opinion-polling, etc., will be in the public domain'. The document revealed that the NIO had commissioned a firm of consultants to carry out research 'without it being seen to be government-inspired'. It also proposed enlisting the help of key people 'to champion our cause', e.g., the Church of Ireland Primate, Lord Eames.[14] 'While any overt manipulation could only be counter-productive, a carefully co-ordinated timetable of statements from these people will be helpful in giving our message credibility with those they represent,' the document added. A data-base of 'key movers and shakers' was being drawn up and there were plans to target 'influential media people'. There would be co-ordination with Dublin. The No people made considerable use of the leaked document and the taunt 'Kelly's Heroes' was cast at those who were considered to be in the NIO's sphere of influence.

With the polls showing solid support for the Agreement among nationalists, the real referendum battle was within the unionist community. Though outwardly confident, pro-Agreement unionists harboured fears of some as-yet-unknown calamity which would cause their community to take fright.

On the republican side, a senior figure with a formidable history told me of being verbally assailed and accused of betrayal at a middle-class soirée in Dublin by one of the well-heeled guests whose father or grandfather had taken part in the independence struggle of 1920-21. But there was encouragement in an IRA statement issued on 30 April which said that, while the Good Friday document fell short of what was required, it nevertheless marked 'a significant development'. The organisation maintained its hard line on the weapons issue: 'Let us make it clear that there will be no decommissioning by the IRA.' In the usual stilted republican language, the IRA wished Sinn Féin further success in the development of its peace strategy. There were unconfirmed reports that the IRA had approved participation by its members in a Northern assembly, implicitly clearing the way for a similar vote by Sinn Féin.

The Sinn Féin *ardchomhairle* was due to meet shortly to discuss its recommendation to the party's special meeting to decide on the Agreement which was scheduled for 10 May at the premises of the Royal Dublin Society. It was likely the executive body would recommend taking seats in the new assembly but that would have to be approved by a two-thirds vote from *ardfheis* delegates. The interventions by representatives from the African National Congress, both at the ardfheis and various other meetings, were helpful to politically-minded republicans. It was very hard to argue with revolutionaries who had won in their own country when they said tactical flexibility did not imply selling-out on principles. At a rally in the Ulster Hall, the PM of Mpumalanga (former East Transvaal), Mathews Phosa said he regarded Adams as 'Mr President' adding, 'I'm in his country. He's my leader.' Cyril Ramaphosa, ANC chief negotiator during the transition to democracy, told the crowd: 'Negotiations are about give and take. Had we wanted everything or nothing, we would have ended up with nothing.'

Meanwhile, those dissident republicans who never signed on for the peace process were trying to raise cash to continue the war. A security van was held up outside Ashford, a peaceful village 30 miles south of Dublin. Despite the fact that uniformed police had taken sick leave en masse that day over a pay dispute, the Emergency Response and National Surveillance units, clearly aware of what was planned, were on the scene almost immediately. One of the raiders, Rónán Mac Lochlainn, was shot dead in the fracas under circumstances that remained unclear. His funeral took place a few days later at the republican plot in Glasnevin Cemetery where he was buried in the grave of 1916 veteran Joe Clarke, described as 'the ultimate republican'.[15] Round about were the headstones and monuments of republican legends like Cathal Brugha, Harry Boland, Frank Ryan and James Stephens, bringing home the extent to which the dead generations still weighed upon the lives and mindsets of present-day activists. Adams might be able to marshal logical arguments in support of his position but the question posed by W.B. Yeats after 1916 still stood: 'Is there logic to outweigh MacDonagh's bony thumb?' Downtown in Parnell Square, a short distance from Sinn Féin's Dublin office, posters of Adams and McGuinness could be seen with the motto: 'Wanted for Treachery'. The Sinn Féin leaders were accused of betraying 'the memory of the Irishmen and women who made the supreme sacrafice *(sic)*'. Though the posters lost a lot of their force through being anonymous, they were a disturbing indication of the climate developing in some quarters of the republican movement.

There were sceptics around who said the Sinn Féin debate on the Agreement was a total sham, a charade for the benefit of the voters and the media. The delegates would vote whatever way the IRA said they should vote and the IRA leadership was dominated by prominent members of Sinn Féin. However, the first debate in the aftermath of the Agreement was clearly genuine, with Southern delegates obviously plagued by doubts. Then the IRA gave a qualified blessing to the Agreement and who in Sinn

Féin was going to speak against the IRA? By the time the 10 May meeting came about, the problem for the leadership was to keep it from looking too easy. There were so few opposed to taking seats in the Assembly that it was like looking for a needle in a haystack. One Sinn Féin delegate said plaintively that the document agreed on Good Friday 'takes away the main basis of my republican beliefs' but he still pledged to continue working within the party. Whatever other political leaders thought of Adams and McGuinness, they must have envied them the loyalty of their followers.

If there was any prospect of substantial public opposition at the meeting, it melted with the surprise arrival of the Balcombe Street Gang – four republicans who had wrought havoc in the early 1970s in London and were now in the twenty-fourth year of their prison sentences. They had recently been transferred from Britain to Portlaoise Prison in the Republic and the Irish government had approved a temporary release. It was an event of high emotion: embraces, a standing ovation, fists in the air and, quietly in the background, a few very hard men wiping away a tear. One had seen photographs of this group – police pictures in the newspapers, other 'snaps' in Sinn Féin publications – but they had been in prison for so long that one wondered if they really existed. Few in the modern era who claimed the label 'political prisoner' had served so much time: Adams compared them to Nelson Mandela. Other prisoners also appeared, spoke from the platform and mixed in the crowd, laughing and joking and shaking hands. It was uncannily like dead people come to life: these were the subversives from beyond the Pale who had been locked up and the key thrown away. Now, much to the annoyance of the unionist community, they were almost on the point of release, some of them still young, others with half a lifetime spent behind bars.

The demeanour of Gerry Adams in the aftermath of victory at the RDS was worth observing. If he felt any temptation to break into a broad smile, he successfully resisted it. His expression was sombre and in his concluding speech to delegates he went out of his way to console the opponents of change. Perhaps he was thinking of the much larger number of 'antis' who were not in the hall but would still consider themselves part of the republican movement. There may also have been significant numbers in attendance who voted the right way out of loyalty rather than conviction.

The *ardfheis* was jam-packed with delegates, visitors and observers: Martin Mansergh could be seen listening to the speeches with his usual thoughtful demeanour. A few years before, it was difficult to persuade some journalists to treat this gathering as a serious political event: covering it was not a good career move. Now you could hardly get a seat in the area reserved for reporters. Meanwhile, the media were full of reports all week that Provisional dissidents had regrouped in a new organisation, variously dubbed 'IRA Nua' (Irish for 'New IRA') or 'Real IRA'. Nobody doubted that even a handful of paramilitaries could cause mayhem if they 'got lucky' but mainstream republicans and independent observers were still rejecting suggestions that the new group had attracted substantial numbers. The point was being made by others that the Provisionals themselves were a mere handful at the start of the Troubles.

Mainstream Provisionals had become more and more politicised to the point where eventually Adams might be able to oblige David Trimble by confirming that, yes, the war was finally over. Would Sinn Féin end up like Fianna Fáil, strong in one jurisdiction – the North in their case, the South with Fianna Fáil – but unable to make progress on the issue of national unity? That was not how senior party members saw it. They claimed their role in the new assembly would be 'subversive'; they were a dynamic force in politics, North and South; they had already brought about massive political change through the peace process, constructing a nationalist consensus that even spanned the Atlantic, and bringing about the Good Friday Agreement which, though flawed, nevertheless opened the door to an eventual United Ireland. The critics and the cynics sneered that an ageing, war-weary movement had come to terms with reality and settled for political advances within Northern Ireland while accepting that the Border was there to stay.

The truth of the matter was that it was still all to play for. Each concession boasted by the unionists in the Agreement could be matched with a gain claimed by nationalists. The unionist veto had been secured but the link with the Crown weakened. The challenge for Sinn Féin was now to persuade a deeply suspicious unionist community of its peaceful intent. Adams attempted, in his concluding remarks to the *ardfheis,* to reassure unionists that when Sinn Féin spoke of ending the British presence it did not mean driving the Protestants into the sea.

The Taoiseach and the Northern Secretary took a chance by releasing republican prisoners to attend the Sinn Féin gathering. They presumably thought it would help copperfasten support for Sinn Féin leaders as they sought to turn the republican movement on its axis. It went down like the proverbial lead balloon among unionists. 'It has certainly not helped things one little bit,' unionist Yes campaigners said gloomily. 'It was like Christmas for the No lobby.' A significant proportion of unionists remained undecided, and the prisoner issue was the one that probably concerned them most. The subtleties of constitutional legislation were for another day, but the prospect of persons convicted of paramilitary offences being freed to walk the streets – possibly people you knew who had killed other people that you knew – was alarming and upsetting. The significance of a high No vote went beyond the referendum. It had implications for the Assembly elections at the end of June. If the anti-Agreement forces won enough Assembly seats, they could prevent it from functioning properly with consequences also for the operation of the North–South Ministerial Council.

To make matters worse, the Northern Ireland Office let the loyalist prisoner Michael Stone – jailed for his attack on a republican funeral ten years earlier in which three people died – out on parole. The fact that Stone had become a supporter of the peace process did not appear to register with public opinion. He took the opportunity to attend a pro-Agreement rally organised by the Ulster Democratic Party in the Ulster Hall and received an ecstatic reception. It was a turn-off for middle-ground Protestant opinion, which felt almost as much distaste for loyalist paramilitaries as for republicans.

There was near-despair in the Yes camp when a poll in *The Irish Times* on 15 May showed a sharp drop in unionist support. Support for the Agreement stood at 56 per cent, compared with 73 per cent in the previous *Irish Times* / MRBI survey conducted with the *Guardian* after Good Friday. The figures showed 55 per cent of unionists against the Agreement. This echoed private NIO polls, which estimated the Balcombe Street episode had increased the No vote in unionist ranks by ten per cent. The figures also reflected an energetic and well-focused campaign by the No lobby, which contrasted with the lacklustre pro-Agreement effort on the unionist side. Blair decided to visit Northern Ireland again – he made three visits before voting day. The Taoiseach tried to help with a tough-sounding statement on decommissioning. The battle was now focusing on a small percentage of voters. If the overall Yes vote was less than 65 per cent, Trimble's position would be extremely difficult.

The poll showed that the highest percentage of undecided voters was in the 18–24 age group. In an attempt to attract young voters, Trimble and Hume made a unique joint appearance on the stage at a rock concert in Belfast starring U2 and the Northern band, Ash. The idea for the concert was attributed to Tim Attwood, a party worker with the SDLP and brother of Alex Attwood, one of the party's more prominent spokesmen. He had been lobbying U2 and the breakthrough came when the film director Jim Sheridan, of *My Left Foot* fame, arrived in Belfast to aid the Yes campaign. Chatting in the lobby of the Wellington Park Hotel, Attwood mentioned the U2 plan to Sheridan who used his cellphone to put in an immediate call to Bono, lead singer of U2. Sheridan's phone call was the clincher: the gig was on. There was some nervousness on the unionist side and one of them asked me discreetly whether U2 had any republican skeletons in their cupboard which could be exploited by Paisley. Tickled at the idea of a journalist being the arbiter of political respectability, I confirmed that the band was well known for its rejection of violent nationalism.

With the Yes campaign in deep trouble, Trimble went on the road with the opposition leader in the House of Lords, Viscount Cranborne, and Labour MP, Kate Hoey, a native of Northern Ireland. Putting false modesty aside, the Viscount recalled that he was one of 'those 27 heroes' who voted against the 1985 Anglo-Irish Agreement at Westminster – and would do so again today. The subtext for doubting unionists was: if this pillar of the British establishment was urging a Yes vote, then it must be OK. Standing on Derry's Walls at the site of the old custom whereby Apprentice Boys used to throw pennies down at their nationalist neighbours in the Bogside, Trimble made the startling claim that, under the Agreement, the Bogside was as British as Bangor or Bournemouth. I said afterwards to a prominent unionist that this was unlikely to win nationalist hearts, but he laughed: this was about winning unionist votes, not nationalist affections. Trimble still had a good deal to learn about PR. After he had recalled that his ancestors were in the Siege of Derry in 1689, someone pointed out a gravestone in an adjacent cemetery with the name Trimble on it. The UUP leader was heading straight for the spot when friends frantically intervened: 'Don't do it, David.' He wheeled around, much to the disappointment of a waiting photographer: 'You've just ruined my caption.'

A third *Irish Times*/MRBI opinion poll published the day before the vote showed that support for the Agreement had recovered, with 71 per cent in favour, 29 against. Among unionist voters, the figures were: Yes, 48 per cent and No, 52, compared with the previous week's percentages of Yes, 45 and No, 55. The more aggressive and energetic approach by Ulster Unionist leaders and successive interventions by Blair appeared to have paid dividends. The Yes campaign's emphasis on young voters seemed to have worked, with support in the 18-24 age group increasing from 39 to 50 per cent.

When 22 May arrived, a total of 3,922,829 people, North and South, were entitled to vote in the concurrent referendums, the first all-island poll since the 'Sinn Féin election' of 1918. This included 1,175,741 eligible voters in the North, where queues formed at some polling stations before they opened at 7 am. 'I've never seen anything like it before. It's quite extraordinary,' an electoral official said. The question was whether they were voting Yes or No.

The count took place next day at the King's Hall on the outskirts of south Belfast. Votes were sorted and counted at one end of the vast auditorium and the politicians and media were kept well back, which caused some resentment. The atmosphere was low-key, with the usual advance figures, predictions and wild guesses bandied about. When the final result was announced around six in the evening it came uncannily close to the latest *Irish Times*/MRBI poll, with 71.12 per cent in favour and 28.88 per cent against. There were 676,966 Yes votes as against 274,879 who voted No. When I phoned a nationalist contact with the figures, he declared: 'The war is over!' The Yes vote for the Agreement in the Republic was a massive 94.5 per cent but there

160

was a relatively poor turnout, reflecting the low level of campaigning by some of the political parties.

His eyes glistening, Seamus Mallon said it was the most important moment of his political life. It was no longer a case of Ulster Says No, he declared, but 'The North of Ireland Says Yes'. John Hume was elated. 'We are overcoming,' he said, an advance on the old civil rights song, 'We Shall Overcome'. Sinn Féin figures were relatively muted and, if the unionists were pleased, they dared not show it. Loyalists were more open about their feelings as they taunted Paisley, whom they had revered so much in the past. The DUP leader left the hall to the chorus: 'Cheerio, cheerio, cheerio!' and shouts of 'Easy! Easy!' A senior Sinn Féin member was standing beside me, watching the scene from the balcony. 'A very interesting sight,' he said, with quiet satisfaction, before walking away. I stayed to watch, reflecting that the IRA campaign had never split loyalists from Paisleyites like this.

There was a great deal of hair-splitting about the meaning of the No figure of almost 29 per cent. The dispute began even before the vote was announced. It was not so much a case of 'getting your retaliation in first' as 'getting your interpretation in first'. Whether or not an actual majority of unionist voters opposed the Agreement, it was undeniable that the unionist community was split down the middle. The imponderable was whether the No voters would be demoralised by the scale of the Yes victory. Certainly Trimble was the one who looked like the winner on the day.

Chapter 7

Two Minds, One Country

The Ulster Unionist Party's campaign for the Assembly elections on 25 June was a triumph of 'hype' over experience. Trimble gave a keynote speech to the business community three days before polling. The choice of audience was significant: in the old days a unionist leader would probably have opted for a group of Orangemen. Instead of the traditional horse-and-buggy style of unionist campaigning, the leader's image was multiplied on the screens of a 'video wall' at his back. With hindsight, it was the wrong approach: he stressed the value of modernisation and pluralism when he should have argued that his approach was the best one to protect the interests of the unionist community at this uncertain time. An emphasis on unionist self-interest rather than broad liberal values would have won him more votes even though it would have played badly with the two governments and the media and run counter to the mood of post-Good Friday euphoria. The political imperative was to chip away at the Paisley bloc by offering a different pro-unionist alternative, but Trimble opted instead for a more idealistic, cross-community approach. The line was Blairite when it needed to be Carsonian,[1] and Robert McCartney had a point when he said the speech 'could have been written by the Labour Party spin doctors'. A senior unionist agreed with me afterwards that Trimble should have appealed to his 'core vote'.

Meanwhile, word was coming from all shades of the political spectrum that the punters were more interested in watching World Cup soccer matches on the telly than talking to canvassers on the doorstep. The turnout on the day was 68 per cent, well below the 81 per cent figure from the Referendum. Periodic heavy rainfall probably kept voters away from the polling booths and a bomb in County Armagh the day before, attributed to dissident republicans, didn't help either. It seemed those elements of unionism which bestirred themselves to vote on 22

May lacked the conviction to turn out a second time.

There were 108 seats in eighteen constituencies. Although the SDLP took the highest share of the vote at 21.96 per cent, compared with 21.26 for the UUP, the vagaries of proportional representation and six-seat constituencies saw the UUP emerge with 28 seats to the SDLP's 24. The DUP won twenty and there were eighteen seats for Sinn Féin, which also secured its highest share of the vote so far at 17.6 per cent. As for the rest, Alliance secured six seats; the UK Unionists, five; Independent Unionists, three; Progressive Unionist Party and Women's Coalition, two each.

The PUP seats meant there was a majority of two for the Agreement among unionist Assembly Members: 30 votes to 28. It was a poor result for Trimble, guaranteeing that he would always have to worry about defections to the No camp. The prospect of having to enter government with Sinn Féin also loomed large: assuming there were twelve ministries in all, the republicans would get two as of right, with the UUP and SDLP entitled to four each and the DUP also getting two ministries.

The Assembly held its inaugural meeting at Castle Buildings on 1 July. It was an extraordinary and, at the same time, ordinary day. Ordinary because the main business was carried out without stunts or protests. Extraordinary, because many participants and observers thought such a day would never come. This was the birth of a new form of democracy in Northern Ireland but, far from the drama, tension and excitement of a human birth, the atmosphere was low-key and almost routine. Everyone, whether for or against the new development, kept their feelings in check, although there was plenty of emotion underneath the surface.

There was emotion in Hume's decision to step aside and allow his deputy, Seamus Mallon, to take the senior political post available to nationalists, that of Deputy First Minister-designate. Since the Derryman had written much of the script, and given the length of time that script had languished on the shelf before going into production, few would have disputed his right to a director's chair. As usual, Hume kept his counsel and even Mallon himself knew absolutely nothing about the plan. He did not even know about the meeting in Belfast's Wellington Park Hotel where Hume was planning to announce his decision. The MP for Newry–Armagh turned up at Castle Buildings in the morning to prepare for the afternoon opening of the Assembly and only then became aware that the real action was taking place several miles away. Apparently some attempt had been made to contact him in advance, but without success.

Mowlam's nominee for Presiding Officer or Speaker was Lord Alderdice, another move that came as a surprise to many. His Alliance colleague Seamus Close had been strongly tipped to get the nod from the Secretary of State. Clearly disappointed, Close accused Alderdice of acting from self-interest rather than party interest when he suddenly quit as party leader a few hours before being named to the Speaker's post with, it was said, the support of Tony Blair. Alliance had not won enough seats in the Assembly elections to secure a portfolio under the special d'Hondt[2] system of proportionality for allocating ministries. Alderdice took up his place and chaired the initial meeting, but members on all sides failed to respond when he put the question of his permanent appointment to them. There were believed to be other eyes on this plum job, particularly in the SDLP, but Alderdice continued to hold the post on an interim basis under the title of Initial Presiding Officer. Predictions that the anti-Agreement members would turn the proceedings into a farce proved incorrrect. Television viewers may have been appalled by some of the bad manners displayed, especially when Sinn Féin members were speaking in Irish, but to anyone familiar with local councils in Northern Ireland over the years it was pretty tame stuff.

The issues, on the surface, were decommissioning and the perennial trauma of Drumcree, which was looming in a few days' time. But there was a sense also that these were transient factors and that the real significance of the day was the fact that virtually all shades of the political spectrum – the failure of the loyalist UDP to win any seats was a cause for concern – were sitting together under one roof and behaving in a reasonably civilised manner towards one another. The only weapons in use were words. As one looked around, spotting a high-profile republican here or a staunch unionist there, it was hard to avoid the feeling that at long last we had the bones of a settlement.

As members delved with uncommon zest into the detail of party representation on the Standing Orders committee, it was impossible to suppress the first shoots of optimism that maybe it was all going to work. Of course there were bound to be long and bitter debates ahead. The gaps and divisions were enormous: there had been much hurt on both sides and the healing process was only beginning.

The standard of oratory was high, compared to what I was used to from years of reporting Southern politics and it was interesting how few speakers relied on notes, much less prepared scripts. Trimble and Mallon were among those who spoke impromptu and from the heart. Mallon paid tribute to Trimble's courage, dignity and integrity and, with some emotion, spoke of the 'awesome sense of responsibility' he himself felt. As Adams listened with close attention, Mallon pledged there would be 'no exclusions in this new arrangement'. Trimble nodded when Mallon said any disagreements between the pair of them would be sorted out 'face-to-face'.

Trimble referred to his friend, the late Edgar Graham, a unionist contemporary who was exploring new approaches but had been gunned down in his prime by the IRA. 'There are a number of people present in this room who have in the past done terrible things,' he said. Trimble was not known for profligacy in the matter of dispensing olive branches, but on the question of going into government with the associates of paramilitaries he said the important thing was to establish that they had irrevocable democratic credentials, and the fact that someone had a past did not mean they couldn't have a future. It must have been an extraordinary experience for the UUP leader to sit across the floor from Sinn Féin representatives, with every apparent prospect of having to form an administration with them eventually.

Trimble and Mallon were jointly elected First and Deputy First Minister by 61 votes to 27. There was a majority of both nationalists and unionists, as required under the terms of the Agreement when these positions were to be filled. There was a roll-call vote: Sinn Féin abstained but all Trimble's Assembly party, including some who were thought to be dissidents, supported the motion.

Nationalists and republicans privately felt this would be a good time to move ahead with appointing the full executive, even though the number of departments and their responsibilities had not been formally agreed, but in the event it was decided to wait.

The final swearing-in of the two new senior ministers-designate after a four-hour debate was a moment of quiet but no doubt deeply-felt emotion. They made their declaration under the tutelage of Lord Alderdice, shook hands and patted each other on the shoulder. The Assembly would move from Castle Buildings to the old Stormont parliament when it resumed deliberations on 14 September. The wheel had come full circle.

The start of that July was a strange week. People were walking on eggs and opening champagne bottles at the same time. Even Blair said he had to pinch himself to believe it was real. The PM was in town for talks about Drumcee, now only days away, and he grinned broadly as he shook Trimble's hand. The British Army and RUC presence in Portadown for the Drumcree weekend was staggering. The town was, in effect, under martial law. Even old hands had never seen anything quite like it in the North. This year, the Orange parade was banned from the Garvaghy Road and the barricade put up to halt its progress recalled newsreels from the First World War, with barbed-wire fences and stretches of No Man's Land. Orangemen walked down to examine the medieval-style moat which had been made out of the modest stream beside Drumcree parish church. On a pile of mud from the excavations a lone Union flag fluttered. A visiting American politician, the well-known anti-Vietnam War radical, Tom Hayden, compared Blair's position to that of President Kennedy when he sent US Marshals into the Deep South to enforce civil rights laws, despite heavy pressure to the contrary from the Southern Democrats.

There were fears the Orange Order would direct its traditional Twelfth of July parades from all over Northern Ireland to Drumcree. That would mean a build-up of 80,000 to 100,000 Orangemen, heading for trouble. Such an action, along with a programme of protest throughout Northern Ireland, could make the place ungovernable and force the authorities into a change of tack. Much would depend on the true state of mind of the Protestant community and whether the referendum result had any real meaning in the 'parliament of the streets'. In Belfast, loyalists launched gun attacks on the RUC, and police families were intimidated out of their homes. Violent clashes occurred between supporters of the Orangemen and the security forces at Drumcree. Unionists felt a visit by Martin McGuinness to the

Garvaghy Road on 9 July was not helpful in efforts to reach a settlement but some nationalists thought it sent an essential signal to loyalists and Downing Street, that the Garvaghy residents' leader Breandán Mac Cionnaith and his people were not alone.

In public relations terms, the Orange Order[3] was suffering tremendous damage. The soft-spoken pillars of Ulster society who led that body bore not the slightest outward resemblance to subversives seeking to undermine the law and bring about anarchy and chaos. Yet they had been unable to halt the attacks on mostly Protestant police officers at Drumcree and elsewhere, not to mention the violence, burning and intimidation all over Northern Ireland. From an Orange point of view, the story which should have been dominating the headlines was the suppression of their 'inalienable' right to walk 'the Queen's highway' on the Garvaghy Road. Instead, the organisation found itself riding a tiger that snarled and bit at the security forces night after night. Instead of civil and religious liberty, the issue had become the rule of law versus the law of the jungle.

While there had been church-burnings and arson attacks, in a strange way it was the small, almost workaday incidents that affected one most. As the Orangemen marched to Drumcree, a young loyalist camp-follower taunted Garvaghy Road Catholics by jumping up and down, shouting 'Robbie Hamill! Robbie Hamill!'. He was re-enacting the horrific murder of a young Portadown Catholic whose head was stamped on by loyalists in the town centre while armed police who were nearby in their Land Rover failed to intervene. Then there were the leaflets depicting Blair visiting the burned-out ruins of St James' church at Aldergrove outside Belfast on 2 July, one of ten Catholic churches attacked in the North. Biblical quotations proclaimed this was the right and proper way to deal with the infidel ('ye shall destroy their altars ... and burn their graven images with fire'). There was the militant loyalist who spoke with equanimity about marching down the Garvaghy Road even if it meant walking across dead bodies. In my presence, a protester who was not wearing an Orange sash informed a member of the RUC across the 'Drumcree Canal', as the moat dug beside the barricade became known, that he would 'cut the throats of his wife and children'. At the barricade itself, thugs taunted soldiers with indecent homophobic jeers and suggestions. I saw mothers of young families on the Garvaghy Road keeping vigil outside their homes, fearful, not so much of marching men in sashes as of other men in balaclavas coming to burn them out.

Then tragedy struck. In the early hours of 13 July, three young Catholic boys, Richard, Mark and Jason Quinn, aged seven to ten years, were burned to death in a petrol bomb attack on their home in the mainly Protestant Carnany housing estate at Ballymoney, County Antrim. Pressure on the Portadown Orangemen built up after the RUC said the attack was sectarian. The report of the three children's deaths – they were found in the foetal position – created a wave of grief that transcended the community divide and led to the first major public rift in Orange ranks since the standoff began. The Rev William Bingham, grand chaplain of the County Armagh Orangemen, made a courageous appeal in a sermon at Pomeroy, County Tyrone: 'After last night's atrocious act, a fifteen-minute walk down the Garvaghy Road by the Orange Order would be a very hollow victory, because it would be in the shadow of three coffins of little boys who wouldn't even know what the Orange Order is.' The Portadown Orangemen wouldn't back down, but they were on their own: the Grand Lodge announced that protests elsewhere in the North would be scaled down 'with immediate effect'.

There was nothing to link the Orange Order with the murder of the Quinn boys and the killings were said to have been carried out by loyalist paramilitaries. However, the stand-off at Drumcree was considered by many to have contributed to the climate in which atrocities like this took place. The Orangemen maintained a token presence at Drumcree but after the Quinn murders the violent forms of protest petered out and the storm subsided. It had been an exhausting year, physically and emotionally: the politicians heaved a sigh of relief and headed off on holidays.

Nobody realised that this was to be the North's shortest summer ever and that tragedy even greater than the callous murder of the Quinn children lay just around the corner. The Real IRA exploded a bomb at Banbridge in early August, which caused extensive damage and injured 35 people. But it was only a curtain-raiser.

As so often in the Troubles, there were conflicting claims about the nature and extent of the warnings given prior to the

Omagh bomb on 15 August. The police said they were told it was at the courthouse. The Real IRA claimed to have given a location 300 to 400 yards down the main street. Sadly, it doesn't matter now to the victims who, instead of being moved away from the car that had the 500 lb bomb in its boot, were actually herded towards it. Twenty-eight people died at the time, along with two unborn babies, and a twenty-ninth victim succumbed three weeks later; 310 people were injured, some for life.

The whole of Northern Ireland was traumatised, and normal political activity and debate virtually suspended. Leading politicians who were quietly preparing for the resumed sitting of the Assembly the following month spent their time instead attending funerals and trying to impart some form of consolation, however feeble, to the devastated relatives.

The obscenity of the Omagh events put the two governments under pressure to come up with instant solutions to the tangled problem of coping with tiny but elusive paramilitary groups. The isolation of the Real IRA could hardly have been more complete. The Omagh bomb was interpreted by republican insiders as an attempt by the dissidents to show they could operate freely in yet another part of the North: staking a claim over territory and cocking a snook at the leadership of the 'parent' organisation, the Provisionals. It emerged that the vote at the IRA convention in County Donegal the previous November on the issue of continuing with the peace process was quite a narrow one. The success of the mainstream leaders in outmanoeuvring their opponents had left a legacy of personal animosity between some of the leading figures on both sides. Yet a traditional republican like Ruairí O Bradaigh, president of Republican Sinn Féin, was clear and unequivocal in his attitude to Omagh. In a statement which surprised some observers by its bluntness, he deplored the 'absolute inhumanity' of the 'slaughter of innocents' and concluded: 'It is a severe setback to the project of achieving British government disengagement from Ireland and blurs British responsibility for the situation here.'[4]

Within a week of the blast, the Real IRA announced an indefinite ceasefire. Dublin said it was 'the pressure that we put on in the South that made the difference'. The announcement came in the wake of an ultimatum delivered by the Taoiseach, who called on all republican organisations not yet on ceasefire to make their positions clear, adding this dire warning: 'If they don't, we will intensify every single effort that I can physically and possibly do, legislatively and with the security forces, to break these organisations.' The announcement from the RIRA stated that as a result of the Omagh tragedy, and in response to appeals from Ahern and others, it was 'currently embarking on a process of consultation on our future direction.' The statement added that 'in the meantime, all military operations have been suspended'. It was reported Father Alec Reid was a central figure in the negotiations to achieve the ceasefire. There had also been 'visits' by mainstream Provisionals to the dissidents in previous weeks. Whether these visits had any effect is a moot point. A leading dissident republican told me return calls were made at the homes of some of those who made the original visits. Since they were not masked, it was known who they were.

Fifteen of the Omagh victims were buried in a single day, after twelve separate funerals. The funeral of three young boys from Buncrana, County Donegal, who were on a visit to Omagh when they were caught by the blast, was attended by President McAleese and David Trimble. Not just Northern Ireland but the whole island was a sea of grief that week. Public life became one long, heartbreaking funeral dirge. The sheer cumulative force of so much tragedy and the constant stream of funerals, especially those of young people, had a strong impact on public conscious-ness. Things would never be the same again, people were say-ing, although a still, small voice reminded us that this had also been said after Enniskillen, the Shankill bomb and other atroci-ties going as far back as Bloody Sunday.[5]

The Taoiseach moved fast, taking the initiative and using the moral authority of the united vote, North and South, in favour of the Agreement, to bring in his package of measures against the last of the republican diehards. The spirit of the Agreement was one of relaxing emergency legislation: it pledged the British Government to 'the removal of emergency powers in Northern Ireland' and the document also committed Dublin to 'a wide-ranging review of the Offences Against the State Acts 1939–85 with a view to both reform and dispensing with those elements no longer required as circumstances permit'. That was then, this was now. Trimble travelled to Dublin to seek tougher laws but he was pushing an open door. UUP sources recalled that Ahern had given commitments on security during the multi-party talks: 'He knew, once David said he was going to fly to Dublin, that he had to live up to them.'

Trimble wrote to Blair expressing his concern that London's response to the Omagh attack should be no less forceful than Dublin's. It was not every day, especially over the previous 30 years, that we had seen an Ulster Unionist leader praising Dublin for cracking down on republicans and warning of 'the potential situation of known terrorists from the Republic of Ireland fleeing to Northern Ireland for sanctuary from the Republic's new measures'. The notion of republicans finding refuge in, say, Newry instead of Dundalk, was startling indeed.

Civil liberties groups and others with long memories were sceptical about the impact of moves like the increase in the period of detention for paramilitary suspects in the South from two to four days. This was a step in the direction of the infamous seven-day detention which had to be curtailed following a spate of allegations in 1976–77 that a Garda 'Heavy Gang' was using it to ill-treat paramilitary suspects.

There was a terrible silence in Omagh itself: it seemed that not even birdsong could be heard in a town that was full of life and joy and laughter the day the world turned upside down on 15 August. The ambiguous nature of the Real IRA ceasefire announcement had left some observers guessing. A colleague who spent many years in Lebanon recalled a phrase from his Beirut days: 'Ceasefire means reload.' Others believed the Real IRA stoppage would last and was not just a tactical move. The imminent INLA cessation meant the Continuity IRA would soon be the only republican paramilitary organisation on active service.

To those who know nothing of Northern Ireland it may seem distasteful to engage in the arithmetic of tragedy, but what was different about Omagh was that the casualties came from both sides. Atrocities in the North have tended to affect mainly one side of the community or the other: the Shankill bomb, Greysteel, Darkley, Loughinisland,[6] are examples. Cross-community loss brought a cross-community response and Trimble's people, for example, were amazed at the number of ordinary members of the public from both sides who told them, everywhere they went, 'Keep it going, don't stop'. Trimble attended two Catholic and two Protestant funerals. In a normal society, to note such an occurrence would seem bizarre and uncalled for but in a deeply divided community that kind of balance was important.

There was continuing pressure on Sinn Féin from Trimble, although his words were becoming more measured, calculated and subtle. On UTV he said he wanted to hear 'something' to convey that Sinn Féin was 'condemning the violence on the basis that it was something they will put behind them permanently'. For its part, Sinn Féin had averted a considerable amount of odium by its relatively early condemnation of the Omagh blast and even some unionists had privately acknowledged this. However, there was a note of gloom in the main commentary piece in the Sinn Féin weekly, *An Phoblacht*. Referring to the bombers only as 'the splinter group', the anonymous author summed up the effect of the Omagh blast: 'Repression has moved to the top of the political agenda; the sterile decommissioning argument has been revived; the name of Irish republicanism has been sullied.'

While both the Dublin and London parliaments returned early from summer recess to pass the new repressive measures, an article by Blair in the London-based *Observer* indicated that he still believed this was not the sole or primary answer to the Northern conflict.[7] It was a firm declaration of commitment to and support for the peace process, even in the wake of one of the worst atrocities of the Troubles. 'There is no issue about which I feel personally more deeply committed, or more respons-ible,' Blair wrote. Looking back to the period before the Provisionals put their guns aside, Blair recalled that 'a host of different security measures, emergency legislation and sanctions' including internment, were tried in the fight against terrorism – 'but the truth is they didn't defeat it'. On disarmament, he said: 'It is – again, a blunt truth – a deception to claim there is a finite amount of weapons that, once decommissioned, can never be replaced'. In what had been a fairly difficult week for them, Sinn Féin leaders would take comfort from Blair's assertion that 'Gerry Adams and Martin McGuinness are serious about peace'. While pledging that 'whatever is required will be done' on security, if this revealing insight into the Prime Minister's thinking could have been boiled down to one simple message it was this: politics comes first in Northern Ireland and the peace process will continue. This article, reportedly penned entirely by himself, was a declaration of political intent at a time when it would have been much easier and more popular to beat the law and order drum in public, which was what politicians in the South were mainly doing.

Exactly a week after the bomb, a huge crowd including many prominent politicians gathered outside the Omagh court-house for a ceremony of remembrance. At the other end of the long street, the bomb site was a mass of flowers. Omagh was the flower capital of the world that day. People picked their way through the bundles to read the heartfelt messages. Some of the bunches were arrayed behind proper flower-shop cellophane; others were clumsily gathered into humble plastic bags; but each spoke the same message of heartbreak. 'Wishing their absence was only a dream,' said one. Another: 'We weep for the inno-cents and the loss of our children's innocence. Signed: An Omagh Family.' There were scores and scores of teddy bears: soft and cuddly, they were the kind teenage girls might give one another on their birthdays along with a present and a funny card. Sadly, the teenagers and other innocents who lost their lives in Omagh would have no more birthdays. No more for them that magic day every year when friends rejoiced and par-ents took pleasure and pride to see their youngster blossom and grow. Instead, there would be only one black date, 15 August, and it would forever be mired in sorrow and sadness.

If there was despair, there was also hope and uplift, notably in the song, *Broken Things*, so hauntingly rendered by a local singer, Juliet Turner, who accompanied herself on the guitar. Written by the American folksinger Julie Miller, it was said to be inspired by the Biblical message that the Lord is close to the bro-ken-hearted and crushed in spirit:

> *You can have my heart, if you don't mind broken things;*
> *You can have my life if you don't mind these tears;*
> *Well, I heard that you make old things new*
> *So I give these pieces all to you*
> *If you want it you can have my heart.*[8]

The singer's voice almost broke at one point, but her wonderful performance was the emotional high point of the day. People shed tears who had been crying all week and thought no more tears could come.

One was used to seeing politicians putting on an act, but even they could not be accused of fakery on a day of such deep and intense feeling. Bertie Ahern's face was contorted with grief; Liz O'Donnell wept freely; others such as President McAleese, John Hume and former Taoiseach Garret FitzGerald were obviously very moved. Everyone, from church leaders and dignitaries to political figures as diverse as John Prescott,[9] Peter Lilley,[10] David Trimble, Seamus Mallon and Gerry Adams, had come to show their solidarity with grief-stricken Omagh.

Father Kevin Mullan, eloquent as a prophet, summed up people's feelings best. 'At this hour last Saturday,' he said, 'twenty-eight good and deeply loved people, one carrying twins awaiting birth, were alive in these streets. Each of them, each of us, at this hour last Saturday had a future for some time on this Earth. But the future had already been brought among us. Evil had already possessed some human hearts and minds to do evil unto other human beings. At ten minutes past three the future came. Death and life were blasted together. Death carried life and peace away. It searched for many more of us with its savage scorching breath. Its bloody greed was fought in the street and the hospital by those who love and treasure life and dearly loved the lives for whom they fought.'

The mass outpouring of grief was reminiscent of the aftermath of Bloody Sunday, but now the two sides of the historic conflict were united in grief. There was no wailing or beating of breasts, but the depth of feeling could be gauged from the fact that several people collapsed under the weight of grief and had to receive emergency attention. Afterwards, as the estimated 40,000 crowd dispersed, people lingered to read messages and look at the wreaths outside business premises down the street: killing shop assistants seemed a long way from the vision of Wolfe Tone. The public grieving was coming to an end; for many the private sorrow would last forever. Yet as families made their way home, some stopped to let their kids take a turn on the slides and swings in a local park, and the silence of the afternoon was broken by peals of childish laughter. Even in griefstricken Omagh, life went on.

The Omagh tragedy notwithstanding, plans for the release of republican and loyalist prisoners proceeded apace. At a news conference in Belfast at the end of August, officials responsible for overseeing the releases said the first seventeen or so could be out within two weeks, with as many as 200 back on the streets by the end of October. It was also time for normal politics – if that adjective could ever be applied in Northern Ireland – to resume. In an interview with the *New Statesman*, Trimble gave a revealing insight into his view of the Sinn Féin president, not to mention the Taoiseach. He suggested Adams should have taken advantage of the revulsion after Omagh to declare an end to the war. 'We need to have that from them before we can move on.' He described Adams as a cautious leader who was careful not to advance too far ahead of his support base: a fair description of Trimble himself. He suggested Adams could play a similar compromise role in republican terms as Michael Collins, adding that he believed Adams to be concerned about avoiding the same fate as Collins, who was killed during an ambush by an opposing republican faction in 1922. On the Dublin administration, he said: 'Bertie Ahern is a practical man, interested in practical measures. I would say that this government is no longer concerned with ideology and harking back to the dictates of the past, perhaps the first Irish government really to be so.'

Trimble's interview acquired extra piquancy from the fact that Adams was about to make what some would herald as his declaration that the war was at an end. In a statement on 1 September, he said: 'Sinn Féin believe the violence we have seen must be for all of us now a thing of the past, over, done with and gone.'

The Sinn Féin leader's words would be parsed and analysed for days afterwards. There was an unspoken understanding that, like Trimble, he was in a difficult position and could not be as forthright as many would like. It was generally agreed that the key phrase was 'over, done with and gone', which echoed the words 'finished, done with, gone' used by Blair in a similar context when he spoke in Belfast during the referendum campaign. The unspoken subtext was that this was as far as Adams could bring his movement: under republican theology there could be no unilateral forswearing of violence because that would be tantamount to an admission that there was only one side to the conflict.

The statement opened the door to face-to-face talks for the first time between himself and Trimble. Almost immediately, Sinn Féin was invited to attend a round-table meeting at Stormont the following week, along with representatives of other Assembly parties. Clinton joined Blair and the Taoiseach in welcoming Adams' statement. The White House was understood to have been centrally involved with Dublin and London in brokering what many regarded as a breakthrough. Indeed it was said Blair's legendary spin-doctor, Alastair Campbell had an 'input' to the Adams statement.

High expectations were now being placed on the forthcoming Trimble–Adams meeting, although UUP sources insisted in the usual po-faced manner that it would have taken place anyway because the two ministers were required to give a progress report on issues such as the formation of the shadow executive in the new Assembly.

There was also a widespread expectation that Sinn Féin would soon formally nominate Martin McGuinness to liaise with the decommissioning body headed by General de Chastelain. This was the next act in the well-choreographed peace dance. However, there was extreme touchiness over a newspaper report that McGuinness would act as a facilitator between the Army Council and the commission, a claim republicans angrily denied and attributed to over-eager Dublin government sources. The IRA was not directly involved in this at all, whatever it may have consented to behind the scenes. There had been similar touchiness the previous June when, in an interview with the *Financial Times*, the leader of the republican prisoners in the Maze, Pádraig Wilson, used new and conciliatory language on decommissioning. Wilson was quoted as saying: 'I think a "voluntary" decommissioning would be a natural development of the peace process once we get a sense that the arrangements envisaged in the Agreement are beginning to function.' Wilson's remarks were seized on by unionists and others to show that republicans were weakening under pressure. But republicans moved quickly to disown or downplay the interview; one source claimed it was the product of an initiative by a Sinn Féin backroom worker which had not been authorised at leadership level in either Sinn Féin or the IRA and had caused ructions in both organisations when it appeared. Wilson had moved too far ahead of the 'base'.

Trimble gave a 'cautious welcome' to the Adams statement but added that 'carefully crafted words alone' were not enough. In the aftermath of the Adams gesture and the expected meeting between McGuinness and de Chastelain, republicans were expecting reciprocal gestures from the UUP leader. Clinton was making another trip to Belfast on 3 September, which would increase the pressure. However, political insiders played down the likelihood of significant moves by Trimble during the presidential visit. Even speculation about an Adams–Trimble handshake during the visit was finding few takers, while there was some expectation they would appear in the same photograph along with Clinton and others. However, the possibility loomed of a direct Trimble–Adams meeting, possibly including Seamus Mallon, after the round-table encounter.

Clinton arrived in the North just as the sex scandal involving the young White House intern, Monica Lewinsky, was reaching a new level of intensity. He had just flown in from Russia and looked like a man getting by on very little sleep. Mallon was the unexpected star of the show at the Waterfront Hall, where the President was greeted by political leaders. The SDLP man's speech, written by his new special adviser seconded from Brussels, Hugh Logue, quoted lines which the African American poet, Maya Angelou, had read out at Clinton's inauguration in 1993.

> *History, despite its wrenching pain,*
> *Cannot be unlived, but if faced with courage,*
> *need not be lived again.*

Clinton was not the same man we met in 1995: the hero's feet of clay had become all too evident. Be that as it may, Ireland would probably always be the one ineradicable bright spot on his record: in the words of the song, 'They can't take that away from me'. The New York *Daily News* columnist, Jim Dwyer, encapsulated the difference between Clinton and other presidents with an anecdote about an encounter twenty years before between an Irish-American activist and a senior official in the Carter administration. Asked when the Carter administration was going to take an interest in Northern Ireland, the White House official replied that it did not involve any US security or economic interests, only a few hundred people a year were being killed and there were much bigger fish to fry.

In important ways and at key moments, the peace process had been Clinton-driven and the President – close up, a surprisingly emotional man – was clearly moved when Blair paid heartfelt tribute to his role in helping to bring about the

Agreement. There was the physical commitment: Blair recalled that no call had been left unmade, no step untaken. There was also his detailed knowledge and understanding of the North. In a memorable phrase which also summed up the essence of the conflict, Blair paid tribute to his grasp of 'the subtlety of the competing claims for justice'. Clinton mouthed 'thank-yous' as the Prime Minister spoke the obvious truth: 'There's no President of the USA that has done more for peace in Northern Ireland than you.'

The one sour note, which provided the main talking-point in the Waterfront lobby afterwards, came with Trimble's pointed comments on the alleged past, evolving present and possible future of the republicans in the audience. He spoke of the 'reconstruction' of those who were previously associated with Omagh-type violence and were now 'crossing the bridge from terror to democracy'. Looking in the direction of Sinn Féin representatives, such as Gerry Adams and Martin McGuinness, he presented an olive branch wrapped in barbed wire. In essence he appeared to be saying: I thoroughly disapprove of what you were but I acknowledge that people can change and, if I am convinced the transformation is genuine, then I will meet you and we shall work together.

Although his blunt words for republicans attracted most attention, there was a phrase in Trimble's speech that one was not used to hearing from unionist leaders and spokesmen. He believed the Assembly could be 'a pluralist parliament for a pluralist people'. It was an implicit repudiation of Sir James Craig's statement that Stormont and Northern Ireland were 'a Protestant parliament and a Protestant state' and the dark, dank decades of exclusion it signified for nationalists.

For Adams it must have been reminiscent of the night he sat at a dinner in Washington and listened to the then-Taoiseach, John Bruton, pleading with and imploring the republican movement to turn away from violence. They still talked about that speech in Iveagh House, which in terms of tone and timing was not seen as a high point in Irish diplomacy. Republicans felt Trimble was talking down to them and privately there were mutterings that only so much of this 'aggressiveness and taunting stuff' could be accepted. Republicans had a constituency too, they said, and if Trimble was out to wreck the possibility of a rapprochement then he might very well succeed. The republican view of Trimble was at least as jaundiced as his view of republicans. They complained that he had to be 'dragged, pulled, pushed and persuaded' every step of the way in the peace process and, as far as they were concerned, had never taken a positive initiative of his own.

Party colleagues of Trimble's defended his remarks and described them as 'balanced', but there were concerns among leading SDLP members, one of whom wondered in the lobby afterwards: 'How is Seamus going to do business with this man?' The normally supportive *News Letter* rapped Trimble on the knuckles for giving a party-political speech on an occasion where the mien of a statesman was required: 'This confrontational demeanour was more suited to a UUP rally in the Ulster Hall.'[11]

The President's speech outlined a programme of action for the North's politicians, including decommissioning of weapons, formation of a multi-party executive, changes in policing, an end to paramilitary beatings, the early release of prisoners, the strengthening of human rights and the pursuit of equality measures. He appealed to the people: 'Do not let it slip away. It will not come again in our lifetimes.' Referring to Adams' 'over, done with and gone' statement, he said the words 'were music to the ears all across the world and they pave the way for the progress still to come'. Strangely to some ears, Clinton expressed the belief that the Omagh bomb would be followed by others. 'The terror in Omagh was not the last bomb of the Troubles; it was the opening shot of a vicious attack on the peace.' Around this time and despite their recent ceasefire announcement there was persistent speculation about a swoop on RIRA members, with reports that prison space was being cleared for a fresh intake. The organisation's political counterpart complained of intimidation and harassment by mainstream republicans. The 32-County Sovereignty Movement said: 'This sullies the name of republicanism and we want these people to stop making threats against us.'

Republican Sinn Féin, which was politically aligned with the Continuity IRA, also protested against the 'highly co-ordinated intimidation of members of the 32-County Sovereignty Movement by groups of Provisionals'.

A war of words on decommissioning erupted between

Trimble and Adams, in advance of the round-table meeting of party leaders. Trimble reiterated his stance that decommissioning was essential before he could enter government with Sinn Féin. Adams hit back in a prepared statement and through media interviews, asserting very strongly that there was nothing in the terms of the Belfast Agreement to exclude the immediate establishment of a Northern Executive which would include Sinn Féin ministers as of right. It was at this stage that republicans must have had their worst fears confirmed – that Trimble was not going to reciprocate Adams' 'done with and gone' statement by opening the cabinet door to Sinn Féin. Republicans were insisting that Adams had gone to the limit of acceptability with his words about the end of violence, but Trimble clearly did not feel that there was enough in them to justify taking the risk of forming an inclusive executive. Most observers agreed that, technically and under the letter of the Agreement, there was no obligation to decommission prior to the formation of an executive. Otherwise why did Jeffrey Donaldson walk out on Good Friday? Indeed there was a private acceptance in some unionist quarters that Adams was right in strict legal terms, but that the politics of the situation made prior decommissioning a *sine qua non*.

There was a new unity in Ulster Unionist ranks on the decommissioning issue. Most members of the party's executive, meeting in Glengall Street on 3 September, were prepared to live with the forthcoming round-table meeting and the likely Trimble–Adams bilateral, but the line in the sand was said to be 'no guns, no government'. Some might say it was very clever of Trimble to secure at least tacit assent for a face-to-face with Adams while reassuring supporters that, of course, this did not mean they would end up in government without decommissioning. He secured permission to give way on one front by pledging to hold the line on another and, in a way, it was the obverse of what the IRA had done in giving implicit approval to the Agreement and the Assembly while stressing simultaneously that, of course, decommissioning was not on the cards.

At the long-awaited round-table meeting Trimble and Adams reportedly addressed each other in a businesslike manner although there was some tension when the weapons issue was raised. Discussion mainly centred on a document prepared by civil servants outlining a variety of proposals for restructuring government departments in Northern Ireland. There were six departments under the existing dispensation, but everyone expected the number to increase to ten which, with Trimble and Mallon, would mean twelve ministers in all. Proposals were being considered for a new Department of Equality to promote and monitor the rights and opportunities of citizens. A Department of Regeneration and Development was under consideration, to undo some of the damage caused by 30 years of conflict; it would probably also have a significant brief in the area of community relations. A Department of Arts, Culture and Heritage was also envisaged. After the meeting, John Hume stressed the importance of moving ahead with the formation of an executive as soon as possible.

The Trimble–Adams bilateral took place three days later. Seeking to play it down, Trimble described it as being 'in the margins' of a larger meeting between himself and Mallon, on one side, and a Sinn Féin delegation consisting of Adams, Bairbre de Brún and Alex Maskey[12] on the other. That meeting lasted from 9.30 to 10.15 am. Then Trimble and Adams went into the annex off the main room. A Trimble wellwisher outside was almost in tears when he heard the meeting was one-to-one and entirely private. Did the man know what he was doing? Speaking briefly in Irish afterwards, Adams described the discussion as *cairdiúil*, which is usually translated into English as 'friendly', although the Sinn Féin leader preferred 'cordial'. It would probably sink Trimble if he was seen as friendly to his long-time opponent. Adams described the UUP leader as a man with whom he could do business. During a UTV interview, Trimble astonishingly referred to Adams by his first name, as 'Gerry'. The meeting at least had been polite, by all accounts. Cleverly, it appeared Adams raised the decommissioning issue first, without waiting for Trimble. It was understood he reminded the First Minister of Sinn Féin's recent gestures in this regard but added that he could not 'deliver' the IRA on the issue; Trimble was said to have reiterated in frank and direct terms the difficulties which the lack of progress posed. Speaking to the media in the main entrance hall of Stormont after the meeting, Trimble drew attention to the statue of Sir James Craig, one of his predecessors as leader of Ulster unionism, who had met Eamon de Valera[13] while the latter was on the run and later concluded a series of agreements with Michael Collins.[14] Trimble was finding cover even in the history books.

The political process seemed to be moving into a higher gear when, on the same day as the Trimble–Adams meeting, it was announced that military patrols in Belfast would cease from the weekend. Though dismissed by Sinn Féin, it was generally seen as a significant gesture. The closure of British Army bases in South Armagh was now considered a live possibility in some quarters, but not until an assessment of the true intentions and capacity of the Real IRA had been made. In another significant step, the first group of paramilitary prisoners to be released under the Belfast Agreement were to be freed next day.

The meetings and the optics notwithstanding, Trimble kept beating the decommissioning drum. Addressing the Assembly, which sat in the old Stormont parliament chamber for the first time on 14 September, he said: 'I simply cannot reconcile people in positions of government with a failure to discharge their responsibility under the Agreement to dismantle terrorist organisations.'

This was the Assembly's second sitting and it opened with a period of silence in memory of those who died in the Omagh bombing, which had increased to 29 with the death of another victim on 5 September. One prominent unionist summed up the general tenor of the day as 'nice and dull'. He added hastily: 'Dull isn't a bad thing.' No doubt he, like many others, could remember days that demeaned the name of parliamentary democracy, when instead of consensus we had a bear-garden. Even bitter opponents of the Good Friday pact were restrained in the Stormont chamber. David Trimble said it was a day for 'nuts and bolts' which provoked one wag to murmur that it was a change from 'just nuts'. A foreign visitor unversed in Northern politics would have assumed from the tone of debate that this Assembly had been sitting for years. There were times when old hands in the media had to pinch themselves to be sure Martin McGuinness really was sitting eight or ten feet away from Ian Paisley and that the Rev William McCrea was queuing just ahead of Gerry Adams in the basement canteen at lunchtime. Having campaigned and fought for years to bring down the hated Stormont regime, nationalists and republicans had now taken partial ownership. The old building still retained some of its unionist trappings: Carson was as defiant as ever outside and Sir James Craig lorded it at the top of the stairs. In time, the nationalists would doubtless have their symbols too, in the spirit of equality of treatment and parity of esteem, but perhaps it could be done without ruffling too many unionist feathers.

The hurried nature of the transition to the new system was evident from the wooden pallets and remnants of carpet propped against the walls of the basement although, as Trimble himself remarked, the chamber itself had been 'splendidly refurbished'. Taylor, who had been a minister in the old Stormont government,[15] boasted that neither the Scottish nor Welsh assemblies would be housed in so fine a building. Some observers even claimed that the fact the parties were now operating in a proper parliamentary environment rather than the aesthetic nightmare of Castle Buildings was having a subliminally positive effect on their deliberations.

Republicans remained unmoved by the plight of David Trimble and his supporters in the UUP leadership. As far as republicans were concerned, the Agreement was the Agreement was the Agreement. They also alleged that the UUP was 'milking' the arms issue for political gain: the unionists painted themselves into a corner on decommissioning and then Sinn Féin came under pressure to get them out of it. In the process, the 'green' elements of the Agreement became fainter and fainter. Republicans had set their face against 'trading off' Semtex and weapons for a place at the cabinet table. The firm message was: 'We are not going to collude in the negation of our mandate. It's not on.' The next move, as far as they were concerned, was up to Trimble: he had to establish the Executive as soon as possible. Instead of appeasing the reactionary elements in unionism, he should be drawing on the support of those members of the unionist community who demonstrated their willingness to embrace change by voting Yes.

The unionists and republicans were looking at decommissioning through opposite ends of the telescope. The UUP leadership was said to be 'very worried' about the 'D-word' and still looking over its shoulder at Jeffrey Donaldson. Decommissioning as an issue was growing all the time and unionist attitudes were hardening. Let Dublin and London come up with what schemes they might, was the cry, Trimble needed 'hardware'.

Sources in the peace process, with long experience of these recurring crises, were obdurately refusing to panic. Both sides needed 'a bit of time and space' to get around the problem. On the broader stage, significant progress had been made. The Assembly discussions were dignified and constructive and, instead of megaphone diplomacy, there was now a face-to-face relationship between Trimble and Adams. The two men knew they had to help each other. 'Throughout the whole history of the process there has been a series of obstacles which, if you look at them straight, seem impossible to overcome,' one insider observed. 'Somehow the process survived, because the political will was there and because people didn't realistically have an alternative. That's true of this situation as well.'

Trimble told the Assembly that because of the timetable on cross-Border co-operation laid down in the Agreement, and the fact that he and Mallon were making an industrial promotion tour of North America, the inaugural meeting of the North–South Ministerial Council would have to take place 'towards the end of September or in the first few days of October'. This was a startling suggestion, since the Executive had not been established, nor any sign of it. He appeared to be trying to exploit the eternal rivalry between the SDLP and Sinn Féin by holding out the prospect of a go-it-alone strategy for the larger nationalist party.

Ulster Unionist sources said a meeting was arranged with the SDLP, to take place at Parliament Buildings on the afternoon of 17 September. The UUP requested the meeting to discuss the formation of the NSMC, although the SDLP could raise other issues. However, UUP sources claimed the SDLP had cancelled the meeting that morning. The UUP said the 'logic' of the progress report recently presented to the Assembly by Trimble and Mallon was that the North–South and British–Irish Councils should be set up, irrespective of whether the shadow Executive had been formed or not. They attributed the cancellation of the meeting to 'tensions' between leading members of the main nationalist party. An SDLP spokesman had a different version of events: the meeting had been requested by the UUP at short notice and several prominent SDLP members were out of the country. An alternative date could be found, but the SDLP view was that, not just the NSMC, but the shadow Executive should be established at the earliest possible date. The following week Mallon intervened, with a series of interviews, to state that he would not assent to an inaugural NSMC meeting unless the shadow Executive was set up first.

Sinn Féin was expressing concern at comments by Trimble indicating that, in the absence of IRA decommissioning, the other parties in the Assembly could form an executive without it. Donaldson got in on the act, as Trimble's unofficial spokesman, after reports that his leader had threatened to resign as First Minister: 'He is not bluffing. He is aware of the deep unease within the party and this warning accurately reflects what he has been saying privately over the last couple of weeks.'[16]

The notion of a timetable surfaced as a possible way through the weapons impasse. Mowlam, who was in Dublin for a meeting with the Taoiseach, said: 'It's no longer a question of if decommissioning is going to take place, it's a question of when.' Ahern agreed: 'The argument about decommissioning was signed-off in the Agreement and now it is a question of when, and we have to get agreement on that.'[17] However, Adams told Ahern it was not within Sinn Féin's 'gift' to name a date.

Dublin had been at the end of its tether trying to come up with a formula. Clearly there were attractions in the idea of focusing on timing: would the guns be handed over before or after the formation of the Executive? Maybe that issue could be fudged while the ball was edged over the line.

It was understood Sinn Féin could live with a statement from General de Chastelain asserting his confidence that all parties to the process were sincere in their efforts to achieve decommissioning within the agreed two-year period. For its part, the UUP wanted 'product', whether it was left outside the gates of Stormont, blown up under supervision in a country field or handed in at a police station on either side of the Border. But what was really required, according to republicans, was movement all across the board. Republican activists had what one source called a 'show me the money' attitude. The major institution set up under the agreement so far was the Northern Ireland Assembly, which was seen by republicans as a concession to unionists. Until republicans saw the establishment of the North–South bodies with Sinn Féin ministers taking part, as well as the implementation of other aspects of the Agreement, there was little hope they would even start to consider disposing of arms. At the end of the day one was left with the impression of republicans giving nothing of real and immediate substance to unionists who wanted more than they could ever deliver. Adams had a point when he said at this time that a phrase used by the South African journalist Allister Sparks could also be applied to Northern Ireland: 'Two minds, two worlds, one country.'

Chapter 8

THE SWORD OF DAMOCLES

Decommissioning was a Sword of Damocles hanging over the peace process: it had wrecked the first IRA ceasefire and could now destroy the second. Like swans which appear to be proceeding serenely on their way but are paddling furiously beneath the surface, the two governments were working flat-out to resolve the problem. Despite its length – about 75 minutes – another meeting between Trimble and Adams at Stormont on 1 October came across as a dialogue of the deaf. Nevertheless, Trimble was relaxed, almost chirpy, afterwards and his aides spoke in soothing tones to the reporters: this is not a crisis, we have surmounted bigger problems in the past, this difficulty was always going to arise but it can be overcome. Trimble said there was a failure on the part of Sinn Féin to realise that decommissioning was a 'very clear obligation'. Sinn Féin sources responded that if David Trimble was demanding an IRA surrender, republicans would reply: 'Who the hell does he think he is?'

With stasis and stalemate the order of the day, General de Chastelain seemed the only hope. Political sources said that in his meeting with Martin McGuinness the previous week the General had presented up to a dozen questions for the republican movement. Other groups were presented with the same questions, which related to the 'modalities' (i.e. methods and procedures) by which they proposed to decommission, and whether they believed explosives should be decommissioned before guns. They were being asked to try on the suit of clothes without committing themselves to buy it.

The Blair camp was said to be quite depressed at the trend of events and now there were suggestions that the formal transfer of powers to the new institutions might not take place until April, instead of February as originally hoped. Hume told a youth conference of his party that the decommissioning issue had been exaggerated. Several years of ceasefires had proven the paramilitaries were serious about the peace process, he argued. Besides, when the Executive was formed, ministers were obliged to pledge themselves to observe the Mitchell principles of non-violence.

Trimble was having none of it. Addressing the Young Unionists on the same day but in a different part of Belfast he said: 'If Sinn Féin is allowed to hold on to its weaponry it will destroy the process.' The 'baby barristers' – as their opponents snidely described the youth wing of the party – had done no favours to their leader by inviting him to speak at the end of their debate on 'constitutional affairs'. Peter Weir, an Assembly Member for North Down, set out a series of stiff conditions for Sinn Féin membership of the Executive including, not just decommissioning but IRA disbandment. Other contributions were almost unremittingly hard-line and, as the discussion wore on, his few friends in the room must have worried for Trimble. Yet when he arrived, the leader seemed relaxed. He may have reflected that this would be an easier ride than his last public outing in Portadown where, judging from television coverage, the hostile crowd nearly did for him.

As a speaker Trimble was normally in combative mode, denouncing the republican movement and all its works and pomps, or else having a go at Paisley. He is an excellent debater who thinks on his feet and, because he has done his homework, frequently catches opponents out on points of detail. However, this time he was reflective, considered, almost philosophical. Like a father who catches his young son smoking and proceeds to give him a long lecture about the dangers of lung cancer, he told his fresh-faced listeners the facts of political life. Not widely noticed at the time, his remarks provided a revealing insight into the strategic outlook of the UUP leader and the direction in which he sought to lead his party and indeed his community.[1]

Trimble recalled the words of the late Harold Macmillan, when asked what was the greatest challenge a Prime Minister faced: 'Events, dear boy, events.' Developing his point, Trimble reminded his audience that no one in the position of Prime Minister (or, by implication, First Minister-designate) was totally in control of events: 'Nor can we at any time choose the situation that we are dealing with. We have to at all points respond to the actual situation which we are in.' Recalling the maxim of the

Prussian general, Moltke,[2] that no strategy survives engagement with the enemy, Trimble said: 'You can't start from an imagined or idealised position. You have to start from where you are, in terms of reality.' It had been simple enough to deal with the situation when the republican movement was engaged solely in terrorism. Now republicans had opted for a different approach, and responding to this posed a challenge for unionists. Faced with the slow decline of its campaign the republican movement decided, in Trimble's words, to 'try and cash it in for some political advantage'. How, then, to respond to this challenge? What he termed 'another unionist party' (clearly the DUP) would merely posture and set out 'idealist, impossibilist, fundamentalist positions'. That was withdrawing from reality to become a party of permanent opposition. The strategy of presenting a 'stone face' (a phrase attributed to the anti-Agreement MP Willie Ross) and saying 'No' all the time was adopted in the past and it led to the Anglo-Irish Agreement. 'It's not good enough simply to be passive,' Trimble said. He argued that, at the end of the day, 'the only sensible thing is to be seriously engaged in the situation that you are in'.

Although Trimble inevitably reiterated his stance on decommissioning, the broad thrust of his contribution left one with the feeling that this obstacle, like others in the peace process, would be overcome in due course. Although he did not use the phrase, in essence he was telling his young troops that the Siege Mentality was no longer appropriate. Some of his remarks may have gone over the heads of the youthful audience, e.g., he recalled that his decision to join the ultra-unionist Vanguard organisation, which flourished in the early 1970s, was made after he had read Karl Popper's book *The Poverty of Historicism*[3] – no wonder a friendly commentator called him 'the intellectuals' intellectual'.

There were very few media people present but the speech made a strong impression on those who were. It was a good example of Trimble's ability to be frank and to the point – perhaps unwisely so, in terms of his political welfare – when you least expected it. I often thought about it afterwards when trying to figure out what would happen next and what Trimble would do. He had no love for republicans or the peace process but he found himself in a position where he had no alternative but to deal with what another political leader, Charles J. Haughey, liked to call 'the situation that exists'.

Now there was talk of a fresh initiative to break the decommissioning deadlock ahead of the UUP conference on 25 October. 'Lots of ideas are being bounced around,' an official said. Other sources said a more measured and considered statement of its position was being sought from the IRA. The key point would be that it did not contain the word 'never' but offered the possibility of eventual decommissioning if, in the view of the republican movement, the causes of the current conflict had been removed. However, any prospect of a specific timetable committing the IRA to dispose of weapons and explosives over the coming months was flatly ruled out. Republican sources believed the pressure on the IRA had been eased considerably by comments made at the conference of the Progressive Unionist Party, clearly indicating that the UVF was not planning to dispose of its weapons even if the IRA decommissioned.

There was good news in store for the two main party leaders. Trimble was visiting Denver, Colorado as part of a trade mission with Mallon, when he received word that he had been jointly chosen with John Hume for that year's Nobel Peace Prize. The UUP leader was more measured in his response than his SDLP counterpart – perhaps Trimble was influenced by the imminence of his party conference where such trophies were regarded with suspicion. Sceptical as always, the *Daily Telegraph* asked: What does it profit a man to gain the Nobel Peace Prize if he loses his own party?

Bono of U2 invited Hume and his wife, Pat, to a celebration champagne 'brunch' at the singer's home in fashionable south Dublin the following weekend. Hume said: 'Most people think that pop stars and bands do not live in the real world – well, Bono, you and your band U2 live in the real world. You made the difference, in the referendum, between success and failure.'[4]

The Trimble camp detected a change of tone by UUP dissidents in the week prior to the conference, as though they sensed the need to avoid being portrayed as a divisive force in a party which placed such a high premium on unity. One Trimble supporter remarked that the hard liners had made a tactical error by seeking, not just decommissioning by instalments, but a whole series of measures including the disbandment of the IRA, before Sinn Féin could be admitted to government. 'If they positioned themselves an inch to the right of David, they would get a lot of support, but they are six miles to the right of him.'

Inevitably, the Derry gathering resounded with tough talk on the weapons issue – although dissidents claimed the party had adopted six different stances on decommissioning in three years. The main talking point outside the conference hall was a statement by Jim Wilson, the party's chief whip in the Assembly and long-time general secretary, who told BBC Radio 4: 'It just may be that on decommissioning a mistake has been made in regard to being so firm.' Wilson later reiterated the official party position of no guns, no government, but the hare he started kept running. A cautious and careful man, he would easily have won any contest for Person Least Likely to Talk out of Turn. Certainly his words indicated that thinking at the highest level of the UUP was by no means monolithic on the decommissioning issue. Well-placed sources said that, privately, central elements in the UUP leadership 'couldn't give tuppence' about decommissioning, but it had to be highlighted because of internal unionist politics. The hostility towards the Union First dissident grouping at the conference was very striking. The need for unity was a constant theme in speeches which was regularly applauded from the floor, in what seemed to be a spontaneous reaction from delegates. This no doubt helped strengthen Trimble's position, although there had been reports of discontented unionists meeting in private to discuss the future of the party and its leadership. Plots, it was said, were being hatched, but the plotters were having difficulty deciding on a credible alternative. The most popular choice for the moment was, perhaps surprisingly, not Jeffrey Donaldson but John Taylor. A reluctant rebel, Donaldson was seen to have alienated both the Trimbleistas and their opponents. If Taylor could be tempted to come out against Trimble he might be a better bet, according to dissidents.

Dublin's broadly sympathetic approach to Trimble's internal difficulties had caused some rumblings on the republican side. Senior republicans worried that there had been a shift in Dublin from an essentially nationalist approach to one of pragmatic deal-making, the trademark of the Taoiseach's political career. They said they had made clear to both Ahern and Blair that there would be no decommissioning until what they regarded as the causes of the conflict had been removed. They were somewhat puzzled therefore when Dublin, in particular, continued to put pressure on to obtain the unobtainable. One senior republican reflected rather ruefully that 'the Brits' were behaving better than Dublin from a republican point of view. How ironic that, fifteen months earlier, republicans had helped to install the current Dublin administration.

Mallon now told the Assembly it was probable the 31 October deadline would pass without the formation of the Executive and the inaugural meetings of the North–South and British–Irish Councils. The agreement had listed 12 'sample' areas for North–South co-operation and implementation and, while the politicians wrangled over decommissioning, civil servants on both sides had been preparing papers on areas where (1) co-operation could take place through existing bodies and (2) new cross-Border bodies could be established. It was understood there was a fair amount of agreement between the officials on both sides, although the Irish papers were believed to be somewhat broader in their sweep: probably too broad for unionists.

The Taoiseach came to Belfast on 2 November for discussions on North–South relationships, giving the occasion a significance that went beyond the nuts and bolts of cross-Border co-operation. In a way, the two governments were going along with the UUP strategy of playing a long game, by agreeing to 'park' the decommissioning issue until the time of the transfer of power. There was also a sense in which Ahern, for one, was trying to get around the decommissioning problem by attempting to generate some momentum on the cross-Border elements of the Agreement. The size of the Irish delegation, which also included David Andrews and Liz O'Donnell as well as senior civil servants, was an indication of the serious intent behind the visit. Sources on the Irish side said it marked the beginning of the process of implementing the North–South aspects whether elements hostile to such a development 'liked it or not'. There were echoes of the 1965 Stormont visit by the late Seán Lemass[5] as Ahern and his colleagues arrived at the door of Parliament Buildings to be greeted by the First and Deputy First Ministers-designate.

There was tension between his hosts. Ulster Unionist sources claimed Mallon had rejected a proposal from them for a private three-handed meeting with Ahern and Trimble prior to the round-table session. 'That's not true,' Mallon told *The Irish Times*. Far from excluding the possibility, such a meeting had in fact taken place, as himself and Trimble had spent fifteen minutes over a 'cup of tea' with the Taoiseach in the First Minister's office, discussing the agenda for the round-table meeting. UUP sources commented drily: 'A cup of tea was not what we envisaged.' Had Mallon gone along with the notion of a formal meeting, he would have been roundly denounced by Sinn Féin and probably some in his own party. SDLP sources said the unionists were again trying to negotiate and establish the North–South bodies without Sinn Féin involvement.

Later that week, the Assembly Members decamped to Brussels for three days' induction into the complexities of the European Union. The first night was marred by a furious row between a senior European official and Sinn Féin. The Assembly members – numbering approximately 100 out of a total 108 – were greeted at a special dinner in the Hilton Hotel by the Secretary-General to the European Commission, Carlo Trojan. After his speech, Trojan invited questions from the audience. Barry McElduff, a Sinn Féin assembly member for West Tyrone, asked a question, partly in Irish, about the parallels between the Basque and Northern Ireland situations. Trojan said: 'I didn't understand a word you said.' This brought prolonged and hearty guffaws from unionists, savouring the discomfort of their republican foe. The Dutchman had stumbled into a minefield. Order was restored but Sinn Féin members were fuming. The Mid-Ulster assembly member Francie Molloy said: 'If there was another flight tonight I would take it home.' A conversation afterwards between the Secretary-General and the two Tyrone men failed to ease tensions. Molloy and McElduff alleged that Trojan had played into the hands of unionists; Trojan protested that this was unfair, and adverted to his efforts on behalf of the peace process.[6] The former journalist, now EU official, Jim Dougal helped calm tempers. While Trojan would have won no prizes for linguistic courtesy, it was Sinn Féin who lost out over this episode. It was an unfortunate incident: while his response to McElduff was thoughtless, and lacking in tact, Trojan had a reputation as a helpful official when it came to Northern Ireland and it was generally considered that Sinn Féin should have kept their cool. The most senior member of the Sinn Féin delegation was Mitchel McLaughlin, who was not involved in the exchanges. Surprisingly for such an important event as the Brussels visit, the party at its very highest level was not represented.

The Brussels outing – the first time an entire parliament went to the European capital – underlined the message that the sky was the limit if the arms impasse could be broken and the show got on the road at last. Insiders said they had rarely seen such an impressive and high-powered programme prepared for a visiting group. The President of the Commission, Jacques Santer, led the welcoming party. American involvement had received the bulk of the publicity up to now, but the European commitment was also very substantial – the Yankee razzmatazz was lacking. It was a hopeful sign that mainstream unionists were able to see the funny side of Sinn Féin members trooping into the sumptuous residence of the British Ambassador in Brussels for dinner. One top unionist quipped that they were 'casing the joint'.

Back home, the waters were muddied by mysterious reports that the IRA was planning a convention to decide on a gesture of token decommissioning so that Sinn Féin could get into cabinet. Usually reliable sources, both inside and outside the republican movement, dismissed the stories, which appeared in different quarters of the media. The unionists had persuaded many people, including – most of the time – the two governments, that they had less room to manoeuvre than Sinn Féin. In reality, the opposition in both the UUP and republican camps to the Agreement at this stage was about one-third. Both leaderships had taken risks. UUP dissidents had threatened that the moment their party leaders sat around the cabinet table with Sinn Féin a special meeting of the Ulster Unionist Council would be convened. However, there was a serious question mark over the ability of the dissidents to secure a higher percentage of votes against the leadership than they did in the Europa Hotel ballot on the Agreement the previous April.

The SDLP conference was coming up but among the many motions there was not a single one on the topic that had convulsed the peace process for the previous six months – decommissioning. A party spokesman said no motions had been submitted on the subject! Still the issue surfaced in quite a dramatic way when Mallon unveiled a plan to resolve the dispute which was to have a lengthy shelf-life. Addressing the opening night in Newry, he pledged that the SDLP would support the exclusion of Sinn Féin ministers from government in the North if the republicans failed to meet their decommissioning obligations. Acknowledging unionist fears that Sinn Féin would 'pocket' concessions, such as the release of prisoners, but fail to honour the Agreement's terms on decommissioning within the specified two-year period, Mallon said: 'I believe that this will not occur, and that it is not intended. But no one should have any doubt that if it did happen the SDLP would rigorously enforce the terms of the Agreement and remove from office those who had so blatantly dishonoured their obligations.'[7] This key passage in his speech appeared under the heading 'Solemn Guarantees from the SDLP'.

No comment was made on the Mallon plan by John Hume and the text of the speech had come from Mallon's office, not from SDLP headquarters, arousing speculation that the old Hume-Mallon faultline was still in existence. The sceptics recalled the low profile of the SDLP when Sinn Féin was removed from the multi-party talks at Dublin Castle in February because of two killings attributed to the IRA. It would be very difficult, if not impossible, for the SDLP to move against Sinn Féin because of the high level of support the republicans enjoyed in the nationalist community. However, the two governments could move against Sinn Féin again, as they had the previous February. That was the real danger of the Mallon plan from the republicans' point of view. Some of them were both surprised and immensely relieved when Trimble failed to grasp the opportunity presented to him at the time.

There was a buzz in the air at the SDLP gathering. After 30 years spent mostly in the wilderness, the party was on the threshold of office. There was also deep anxiety, reminiscent of a theatre company that was delighted to be opening on Broadway, but unsure how long the show would run.

Privately, senior SDLP figures on the Hume wing of the party were bitter about the way the weapons controversy had come back to life, like some inextinguishable political vampire. The gist of their sentiments was as follows: 'Don't the unionists and their fellow-travellers understand the mindset of the IRA? The ceasefire is genuine but anything that smacks of surrender just isn't on. This is not the way to handle the issue. Look at the

South – where are the Fianna Fáil guns? What did those new-found friends of the unionists, the "Stickies",[8] do with their guns? You don't need decommissioning to have a properly-functioning democracy.'

Peace process insiders were saying that senior republican spokesmen – whose 'courage and leadership' received surprisingly warm praise from a key Dublin figure – wanted to see decommissioning but couldn't sell the idea to their hard men and women. One suggestion was that it might happen further down the road: perhaps if the Patten Commission[9] proposed an unarmed police force.

Meanwhile, there were indications that the cross-Border issue was coming to a head. A meeting of senior unionists was held at John Taylor's home in Armagh, on 14 November. It took place against a background of reports that agreement with Dublin was imminent. In what was described as an uncomfortable session, trenchant views were expressed to Trimble by leading party colleagues on the need to take a firm stance, otherwise his leadership would be in jeopardy. There was said to be anger at senior UUP level that Dublin was taking concessions on cross-Border matters for granted and this had caused a chill in relations between the UUP and civil servants from the Republic. Although UUP leaders were said to be willing to accept cross-Border bodies in non-controversial areas such as inland waterways, sources said they could not 'buy into' North–South institutions on more substantive areas like tourism at this stage. Relations between the UUP and SDLP were also said to be at a low ebb, with a meeting between the two parties the previous week described as 'the worst they have ever had'. The Ulster Unionists were said to be unhappy with an SDLP proposal for a cross-Border institution to promote industrial development on the entire island. A senior UUP source told me: 'We can't stomach the idea.' However, Mallon had made clear in a meeting at Newry in early November with Dublin civil servants that he wanted strong North–South bodies which would have to include trade and business development.

There was said to be a tacit cross-party alliance between the Ulster Unionists and the SDLP on one key issue, namely the idea that equality and all it entailed should be the responsibility of the First and Deputy First Ministers, and there should not be a separate Department of Equality. The rationale for this was as follows: under the d'Hondt system of allocating ministries, the Democratic Unionist Party would quite possibly be able to take the equality portfolio if it so desired. That wouldn't suit the SDLP. Alternatively, the prospect of a Sinn Féin Minister for Equality was enough to give unionists the heebie-jeebies and would not necessarily delight the SDLP either.

Senior political sources were very confident that agreement would be finalised within two weeks on ten new ministerial posts at Stormont in place of the current six, and at least six new cross-Border implementation bodies. When the continuing programme of prisoner releases, the reductions in patrolling and troop levels and the closure of security installations were also taken into consideration one senior official said there would then be 'a big deficit on the republican side'. This would bring renewed pressure, especially from Dublin, for the IRA to make a substantive gesture on decommissioning. Dublin sources said that in the absence of anything else, the unionist leadership was even 'willing to take detonators'. In Dublin's view, a minimal gesture would remove the obstacles to republican membership of a new Northern Executive and consequently the North–South Ministerial Council. However, reports of an IRA convention the previous weekend to discuss softening the movement's stance on decommissioning had been sharply denied by republicans. The best information available on the republican stance suggested they might be willing to provide flexible and soothing language, but not one bomb, not one bullet, not one ounce of Semtex at this point in time.

It was now taken for granted that North–South bodies would be established in six relatively non-controversial areas. Different lists were circulating, e.g. inland waterways, food safety, aquaculture, marine research, tourist promotion, and transport planning. There was believed to be a strong possibility of agreement on an additional North–South body to promote the Irish language. The SDLP wanted strategic transport planning, with its potential to organise future North–South road, rail and air links, and was irritated when Dublin let this one go, in favour of Irish. 'Dublin wanted to keep Trimble on board at all costs,' SDLP sources said later. 'Sinn Féin fell into a unionist trap when they were looking for Irish; the unionists were always ready to buy

Irish as a lightweight body. Dublin lost its nerve and put the pressure on a reluctant Mallon to accept Irish instead of strategic transport planning or tourism.' The unionists did not feel threatened by Irish and insisted on adding the little-known Ulster-Scots dialect as a responsibility of the new language body, which SDLP sources regarded as ludicrous. Meanwhile, the SDLP continued to push hard to secure agreement for a cross-Border organisation to promote industrial development. There was also speculation about new bodies to oversee economic development and the disposal of European funds.

The Prime Minister flew in on 2 December to give the negotiators a gee-up. He went from room to room, negotiating between the parties, until a deal was almost in place. Blair left Parliament Buildings by a side door in the early hours of the morning, avoiding the media. He must have been feeling well-pleased with himself, convinced he had virtually brokered a deal between the parties over North–South bodies after a gruelling seven hours of talks. A British Government spokesman said there had been 'significant progress' and it was now between the parties. 'We're not there yet but we're getting there.' The SDLP – most sociable of all the parties – was having what one member called 'a muted celebration' with a few drinks in Seamus Mallon's office.

The deal – not signed and sealed quite yet – involved a compromise on the key issue of the powers and functions of a North–South body for the promotion of trade and economic development. Nationalists wanted the new body to have a major role in attracting foreign investment to both parts of the island but, following unionist objections, this aspect was scaled-down. However, it was understood the Ulster Unionists had, as anticipated, come around to the view held by most of the other parties that the six government departments in Northern Ireland should be reconfigured as ten. It was also believed at this stage that there were to be seven or eight cross-Border bodies. The new bodies would deal with such areas as inland waterways, limited aspects of tourism, aquaculture and European funding programmes. The new government portfolios included culture and environmental protection.

In the emotional rollercoaster ride that the process had become, the morning of 3 December was a time for some participants, at least, to wake up in a cheerful frame of mind, confident in the belief that Tony had once more fixed it. Bertie Ahern had stayed away, partly at the behest of the unionist leadership, it was said, who did not want him frightening their nervous supporters by his presence. Now, however, he was gearing up for a triumphant visit North and an even more triumphant return to the annual dinner of Cairde Fáil (roughly translated as 'Friends of Destiny'), his party's fund-raising group.[10]

In the end, the deal was aborted. A leading unionist from the Trimble camp, unable to sleep that night, was said to have switched on the television at 4 am only to see a bulletin on Ceefax that the bodies had already been agreed. That afternoon, John Taylor emerged from a reportedly fraught meeting of the Ulster Unionist assembly group to advise the media to take a week's holiday because nothing would be settled before then. Word got back quickly to the SDLP and, in just over an hour, a grim-faced Seamus Mallon was reading out a statement detailing what he had agreed with Blair the previous night. This included North–South bodies for trade and business development, tourism, strategic transport planning and European Union programmes. He added: 'There will be ten departments with a stand-alone department of finance and personnel.' In a clear challenge to the unionists, he added: 'That is the deal that has been done and I stand by it. It is now for the other parties to confirm their participation in the agreement brokered by the Prime Minister.'

The atmosphere was electric. Rumours were spreading that Blair was on the phone, presumably demanding to know what had happened to the air of compromise he created the night before. Taylor appeared on television to deny that the UUP had retreated from its commitments. They had discussed only two North–South bodies with the Prime Minister, namely EU programmes and 'trade within the island of Ireland'. He taunted Mallon over rejecting a body for the promotion of the Irish language.

Nationalists were putting it about that Blair, who was at an Anglo-French summit in St Malo, was 'spitting blood'. There was never a round-table session and this may have been his mistake. There was even some suggestion that news of the SDLP celebration had reached unionist ears and set the alarm bells ringing. What's good for the nationalists must be bad for unionists.

SDLP sources were claiming Mowlam was upset too. It was unclear whether unionists had reneged on the deal or nationalists had 'blown it' by premature self-congratulation. Trimble was due to leave that morning for the US. He was to receive a peace award in Washington DC, then fly direct to Oslo for the Nobel ceremony. He would not be back until 14 December and what chance, then, of a deal before Christmas?

The Taoiseach cancelled plans to come to Stormont. Arriving at the Cairde Fáil dinner in Dublin, Ahern said it had been 'a bad day'. What was most disappointing was that 'when we packed up last night at 3 am, things were almost there'. The hope had been that agreement could have been wrapped up by the following lunchtime.

While students of the peace process were mulling over the breakdown in communications between the main constitutional parties, there was a renewed blitz of media reports that the IRA leadership was considering prior decommissioning of weapons in order to facilitate Sinn Féin's entry into an Assembly executive. While my own republican sources were not prepared to confirm or deny reports that an IRA convention had indeed taken place at the weekend, they firmly rejected suggestions that the organisation was likely to engage in even a partial handover or destruction of arms or explosives. According to security and other sources the IRA leadership did meet, possibly at a location just south of the Border, to discuss current political developments including the deadlock over decommissioning. The convention, according to the sources, took place over two days, possibly in County Cavan.

The UUP was holding firm to its position that there could be only six cross-Border bodies, which would include the 'subject areas' of inland waterways, aquaculture and food safety. There was said to be a view in Dublin that failure to tie up these negotiations meant inward investment was now 'back on the table'.

Mallon said the UUP was adopting a 'ludicrous approach'. The leadership should have kept Assembly members informed of proceedings, rather than making an agreement with Blair on Wednesday night and only then consulting the Assembly team. A different view came from Reg Empey, who said there had been 'massive hype' that a deal was going to be done on Wednesday night. He insisted that his party had informed Blair before he left London that a deal could not be signed that night as the party leaders would have to consult with the rest of their Assembly colleagues the following day. One of his party colleagues told me: 'The UUP view was that the SDLP took discussion of a cross-Border body to be acceptance of it. That is why they ended up with eight or nine bodies. Our position was always six.'

Trimble and Hume looked rested and relaxed when they arrived in Oslo, despite having flown across the Atlantic. They travelled in a private jet laid on by the Irish industrial and newspaper magnate Dr Tony O'Reilly. Trimble, who tended to take an upbeat approach when he was out of the country, told reporters he firmly expected the formal transfer of powers to the Assembly and other institutions to take place in the spring.

Millions of television viewers and approximately 1,000 invited guests watched the ceremony in Oslo City Hall next day as Trimble and Hume accepted the Peace Prize. The chairman of the Nobel Committee, Professor Francis Sejersted presented a gold medal, diploma and cheque worth approximately £344,000 to each recipient. Many days of misery and tears but very few grand occasions, that had been the history of Northern Ireland for the previous 30 years. Now, at last, it was time for a celebration. There were fanfares by cockaded soldiers in fairytale uniforms who blew silver trumpets. There was a King and a Queen, and they looked the part too. There was snow on the streets, with Christmas just around the corner, and there were children in bright clothes who cheered and sang about peace as they lit eternal flames. There were glamorous people, camera crews that for once focused on smiling faces and not twisted wreckage, and politicians who wore broad grins and dropped tantalising hints about a compromise on difficult issues. There was champagne on ice, there was a banquet ... there was even a little hope if you dropped your guard long enough. Some had argued that the award should be presented to all the pro-Agreement parties, but it was too late now for that debate. Adams, Reynolds, Mowlam, Ahern, Blair, Spring, Clinton, Father Alec Reid ... all would have been entitled to consideration, not to mention many other people in and out of the public eye. Trimble's award was criticised as premature but the Nobel was meant as much to encourage future contributions as to reward past efforts.

Trimble's acceptance speech contained a wide range of intellectual references, from Edmund Burke through Plato and Rousseau to Samuel Beckett and John Bunyan. The Nobel Prize had barely rated a mention at his recent party conference and the early part of the speech seemed to reflect that offhand attitude. On the gold medal and the cheque: 'The people of Northern Ireland are not a people to look a gift horse in the mouth.' He struck perhaps an unduly cynical note when he told the audience: 'The way politics work in Northern Ireland – if John Hume has a medal, it is important that I have one too.' But if the Norwegians took offence, they did not show it.

Then Trimble got into his stride. Burke, hero to conservatives and liberals alike, pragmatic progressive and progressive pragmatist, emerged as the chief intellectual beacon of his approach to Northern Ireland. As the son of a Protestant father and Catholic mother, Burke was deemed particularly appropriate. Some observers detected a slight 'dig' at his co-recipient when Trimble declared he would not be indulging in 'vague and visionary statements'. He made a pointed quip about a politician who talked about his vision and was promptly sent to an optician. He rejected the notion of the North as 'a model for the study, never mind the solution, of other conflicts'.

Trimble also cited Amos Oz, 'the distinguished Israeli writer who has reached out to the Arab tradition'. He admired such men because they held out against fanaticism and could therefore be role models in the Northern conflict, where fanatics on both sides sought to lead their respective communities into an ideological and political cul-de-sac. The UUP leader said it was necessary for democrats to engage in 'what the Irish writer, Eoghan Harris, calls acts of good authority' by dealing with the fanatics on their own side of the fence.

There was an exciting hint of new flexibility on the weapons issue when he said: 'I have not insisted on precise dates, quantities and manner of decommissioning. All I have asked for is a credible beginning. All I have asked for is that they say that the "war" is over.' He acknowledged unionism's failings in the past when it 'built a solid house, but it was a cold house for Catholics'. He added however that 'nationalists, although they had a roof over their heads, seemed to us as if they meant to burn the house down'.

He ended his revealing, provocative and uncompromisingly highbrow oration on a proud note. Referring to the events of Good Friday when, in the view of some commentators at least, David Trimble led his people out of the political wilderness, he said: 'The Agreement showed that the people of Northern Ireland are no petty people. They did good work that day.'

Unionist sources insisted Trimble had written the text of his speech in the US four weeks before, although they confirmed that the broadcaster, playwright and columnist with the Irish editions of *The Sunday Times*, Eoghan Harris, had a very substantial involvement. Commentators and journalists parsed and analysed his comments on decommissioning. A senior unionist almost pleaded with the media not to probe too deeply. One got a sense of differences being narrowed on both sides, but still the glue for a durable solution had not been found.

Not for Hume the austere philosophers Burke, Plato and Rousseau: he preferred to strike a poetic note, quoting Yeats, Louis MacNeice and the idealistic vision of Martin Luther King. Hume's text fitted into the mould of traditional Nobel Prize orations, idealistic, aspirational and visionary. He told the now-familiar story of how he stood between Strasbourg and Kehl, France and Germany, in 1979: 'I stopped in the middle of the bridge and I meditated.' His thoughts centred on how these two countries, forever at war, were now working constructively together on the European project, providing a model for conflict resolution. Sounding yet again the clarion call of his political career, he added that 'they spilt their sweat and not their blood'. He held up the Good Friday Agreement as a similar co-operative venture.

After the ceremony, the prizewinners, their families and guests adjourned to the Grand Hotel in downtown Oslo. There were famous faces: Mrs Jean Kennedy Smith, US Senator Chris Dodd, Bishop Edward Daly – grey now, but he would always be the dark-haired priest waving the white handkerchief on Bloody Sunday.[11] Trimble looked happy and relaxed. He posed for pictures with his wife, Daphne, their two sons and two daughters. 'Does he really have so many children?' a local journalist asked. I said Yes and wondered what the average was in Norway: 'One point one, I think.' It was a tradition after every year's Nobel ceremony that the winners appeared on the balcony of the Grand

Hotel to wave to a torchlight procession below. Trimble and Hume appeared in their evening suits, the 'odd couple', awkward but amiable. They didn't know what to do with their hands, whether to wave or give a thumbs-up sign.

Tensions between the North's two major parties were put on hold. The Ulster Unionists and the SDLP might be at loggerheads back home on cross-Border bodies, but this did not prevent leading members from fraternising in the convivial surroundings of downtown Oslo. At a social gathering in another city hotel, Hume and the UUP treasurer, Jack Allen, paid musical tribute to their native city when they sang 'The Town I Loved So Well' together. They were accompanied on the piano by Phil Coulter, the musician and composer from Derry who wrote the song. The audience joined in, with the SDLP leader conducting and laying particular emphasis on the word 'peace' in the lyrics:

> *We will not forget*
> *But our hearts they are set*
> *On the time we'll have PEACE once again*
> *For what's done is done*
> *And what's won is won*
> *And what's lost is lost and gone forever;*
> *I can only pray*
> *For a bright, brand new day*
> *In the town that I loved so well.*

Trimble was present at the time, but unfortunately for the watching media he was engaged in conversation with a Belfast journalist and did not have an opportunity to take part in the singing. Hume also made a fraternal gesture to the majority tradition in Northern Ireland by singing *The Sash*. The Ulster Unionist MEP, Jim Nicholson, later regaled the crowd with a rendition of *The Boys from the County Armagh*, made famous in the past by recording star Bridie Gallagher.

Earlier in the evening, John Foley of the Waterford Wedgwood company had presented Trimble and Hume with a pair of glass crystal 'Doves of Peace'. In an atmosphere of high good humour, Hume told the group of nationalists and unionists they had all now become Derry people, because the city was founded by St Colum whose name meant 'dove'. He struck a serious note: 'I look forward to the spirit of this evening being developed very strongly by us back at home as we work together.'

There was another remarkable and moving event in Stockholm the following weekend. Trimble and Hume were guest speakers at a peace seminar organised by the Olof Palme Centre, named after the murdered Swedish social democratic leader and prime minister. The discussions took place in a chamber of the Swedish parliament. The usual issues got an airing, but in a more relaxed way than was perhaps the norm. Near the end, singing could be heard and the chairman, political writer Sten Andersson, dimmed the lights. Seven little 'angels' came in, the leader wearing a crown of lighted candles, and sang hymns in heavenly voices. It happens every year, when the peace prize winners come to Sweden. And not once but several times, including early in the morning, which may not have been fully appreciated by the now-exhausted laureates! It happens also, of course, all over Sweden, as a gentle, spiritual introduction to the Christmas season.

Predictably, the decommissioning issue reared its head in the discussion. Trimble reiterated his well-known opposition to Sinn Féin membership of an executive without a gesture on arms. He said this must take place in front of television cameras, a condition reporters had not heard him spell out before, although the First Minister insisted he had articulated it, if not in such blunt terms. It was an 'absolute and irreducible' requirement: 'Whatever is done, there's got to be a television camera there.' He dwelt at length on the recent episode of an aborted soccer fixture between Donegal Celtic, a team from nationalist West Belfast, and the Royal Ulster Constabulary. Republicans were widely accused of having engaged in outright intimidation of the Celtic players to stop the game, because a match between nationalist soccer players and members of the reviled RUC would be in conflict with the republican agenda. Trimble cited it as evidence that Sinn Féin's commitment to democracy was only 'skin deep'.[12] The SDLP leader took a different approach: it was a 'distraction' to seek decommissioning in advance of the implementation of the Belfast Agreement. 'The real issue about weapons is, have they stopped being used?' In conversation later, it was clear the SDLP leader was becoming more and more concerned that the decommissioning issue could derail the entire process.

A few days afterwards, we were back at Stormont where – surprise, surprise – talks aimed at resolving the differences over cross-Border bodies were reported to be at a difficult and delicate stage. The day of 15 December started with optimism but this ebbed considerably as time went on. An initial meeting between the SDLP and the Unionists (the latter still refusing to meet Sinn Féin) around noon was said to have been positive. Reports of internal party difficulties for Robert McCartney boosted UUP morale and increased the party's appetite for a deal with the SDLP. In the early afternoon the talks seemed set fair at last for a package comprising six fairly worthwhile cross-Border bodies and ten ministries. Ironically, the UUP was pleased that Hume had taken a more active role. While unionists much preferred dealing with Mallon in the pre-Good Friday talks, they now professed to find Hume more 'malleable'. A top-level UUP figure was said to have told Blair: 'Bring back John Hume, all is forgiven.' It was understood Hume and Trimble took their visit to Oslo as an opportunity to discuss some of the difficulties between their two parties.

However, morale on both sides took a tumble in the afternoon. Trimble and Taylor attended a meeting with Mallon at 3 pm but, according to UUP sources, they were slightly taken aback when the Deputy First Minister brought the discussions to a close after five minutes: 'He said that we must talk to the governments, he wasn't going to negotiate with us, and he walked out.' SDLP sources conceded that the meeting had 'not been a long one' but complained that the Ulster Unionists had done an about-face on the relationship between cross-Border bodies and government ministries. However, discussions were resumed for about 30 minutes later in the afternoon. Sources confirmed the SDLP had been persuaded to drop its demand for a separate body on strategic transport planning, although the party was expecting a reciprocal gesture from Trimble. Previously, the UUP had insisted the cross-Border bodies could not be agreed until the ministries had been settled, but now the party was taking the opposite stance.

Next day, hopes of a deal rose again. With Trimble and Taylor away on political business in London, Empey led the party in discussions with Mallon. It now seemed virtually certain that the Irish language and Ulster-Scots would be the subject of a cross-Border implementation body. Although this was seen primarily as a gesture to Sinn Féin, republicans were thought to have an even greater interest in the number and designation of government departments.

The main outstanding difficulty was said to be the SDLP's insistence that an implementation body be established in the area of tourism. This would have brought the total number of implementation bodies to seven, a development strongly opposed by the unionists. At least one senior unionist was said to be particularly opposed to an implementation body on tourism as he did not want his constituents confronted by the politically unsettling sight of all-Ireland maps promoting holidays and sightseeing; he was less concerned by the prospect of a body on EU programmes, which might have more substance but would be less threatening symbolically. However, it was reported that the proposed EU body was meeting opposition from Northern civil servants who argued that sharing information with the Republic could compromise the United Kingdom's negotiating position with Brussels. There was expected to be a compromise on tourism, whereby a 'co-ordinating body', possibly established as a private corporation, would be agreed, if the two governments found such a format acceptable.

There were indications that the SDLP, in particular, was 'talking down' the prospects of a deal, for fear any agreement might unravel, as it did after the visit by the Prime Minister. Mallon would not be available next day, associates said, as he had to undergo a minor operation for gallstones.

There were indications of concern in Dublin that the cross-Border bodies would be so weak as to make it impossible to persuade the IRA to make a gesture on decommissioning. Trimble met Blair in London and there were reports that members of the UUP Assembly team were 'jittery' about any cross-Border body which had the word 'Trade' in its title. Trimble's position had been strengthened by the more active involvement of Taylor on the domestic political scene in recent weeks. Dissidents had lost hope in him as a possible 'white knight' and his role could be decisive in persuading the Assembly team to accept the forthcoming deal. While there might be defections to the anti-Agreement side of the House, they were unlikely to be sufficient to undermine Trimble politically.

The last remaining difference over the status and composition of a cross-Border body on tourism was overcome. There would be six officially designated implementation bodies with a North–South responsibility for specific matters. These included the three proposed all along by the Ulster Unionists – inland waterways, aquaculture and food safety. The other three were trade and business development, special European programmes and languages (Irish and Ulster-Scots). On tourism, it was proposed that an all-Ireland private company dealing with policy co-operation be set up instead of an official implementation body. This would allow unionists to claim they had kept the number of such bodies to six while nationalists could make a virtue of necessity by arguing that the tourism body would be the most effective cross-Border institution of the lot because it would be untrammelled by state bureaucracy. This proposal was also said to have particular appeal for the unionists because in strict legal terms it would not be a cross-Border implementation body as outlined in the Belfast Agreement. It was understood negotiations had become quite heated on this topic with Seamus Mallon adopting a direct and robust stance. Even as the differences narrowed, unionists were extremely concerned that it should not be possible for nationalists to present this as a seventh cross-Border body.

Next day, 17 December, began for reporters with a tip-off that a joint statement by Trimble and Mallon was to be made about 2.30 pm. Journalists headed for Stormont: cameras were primed and the hacks hovered with their notebooks and tape-recorders in the Central Hall, under a spectacular chandelier which was a gift from Germany's Kaiser Wilhelm to his cousin, King Edward VII. Far from a joint announcement, the startling news emerged that Mallon had left the building by a side door. He was heading home to Markethill, County Armagh, to fast in preparation for his gallstones operation the following morning. There were further reports of sharp exchanges over the cross-Border body on tourism.

Mallon kept in touch by phone and fax from his home. The old familiar gloom and despair which tended to cloud the penultimate stage of a peace process negotiation took over. The SDLP was saying relatively little, but Sinn Féin launched a major media onslaught, claiming the unionists were once again playing their old game of passive resistance. Martin McGuinness, angrier than many had seen him before, termed the UUP's conduct 'absolutely disgraceful'. Later, as prospects for a deal grew brighter, Sinn Féin claimed it had played a crucial role in putting pressure on the UUP. However, the republicans were not involved in face-to-face talks with the unionists and SDLP sources dismissed claims of republican influence: 'Sinn Féin relied on the SDLP for any information they got. They sat upstairs in a room and were kept abreast by the SDLP.'

UUP spokesmen maintained an upbeat note for much of the day, insisting as they had done for some days previously that a deal was 'tantalisingly close'. This provoked the memorable question from a BBC journalist: 'How long can you be tantalisingly close?' There was bitter resentment in the unionist camp at any suggestion they were acting in bad faith, and when this was echoed by the media, it led to sharp exchanges with one or two journalists. Just before 7 pm the situation took a turn for the better. The positive tone coming from the UUP began to be echoed by key figures in the main nationalist party. As one SDLP source put it: 'For the first time in history, we have all the cards on the table and all the unionists in the building.' This was said in conversation between myself and two SDLP members in the Stormont canteen. Taylor swept past and, glowering at the SDLP people said: 'Don't be gossiping'.

Details of the departmental re-organisation were still being worked on at a very late stage. Sources said there would be two departments of education instead of one, as at present. The Department of the Environment would also be divided in two, one for environmental planning, the second having a watchdog role (these eventually saw the light of day as the Department of Regional Development and the Department of the Environment, respectively). Other departments on the list included four existing ones – finance, economic development, health and agriculture, and two new departments. One of these would deal with culture, leisure, arts and possibly tourism, the other probably with housing and social inclusion.

A meeting of the all-important UUP Assembly team shortly after 7 pm went well for the party leadership. There was talk of a joint statement by the two parties at 9.15 pm, but there's many a slip 'twixt cup and lip. A mild panic broke out when the UUP was given to understand the other side was briefing the media that the tourism company would be a seventh cross-Border body in all but name. This was certainly the Sinn Féin position, but it was not the message coming from SDLP sources, at least not to the present writer.

There was a tug-of-war between the two main parties as to which government department would have authority over tourism. The unionists wanted it to remain with the Department of Economic Development, now apparently to be renamed Enterprise, Trade and Investment. Nationalists said it should be under the new Department of Culture, Arts and Leisure.

Taylor said at one stage a deal was almost agreed with only 'two and a half per cent' of the package outstanding. About 2 am he appeared in the Central Hall. Was everything all right? 'No, it's not,' he replied. 'The two-and-a-half per cent proved impossible.' The politics of the dispute was that a unionist would probably get the Enterprise portfolio and use the position to prevent tourism from developing into a full-blooded cross-Border body. That's why nationalists wanted tourism to go under Culture, Arts and Leisure, one of the ministries thought likely to go to the SDLP or Sinn Féin. At one stage, Trimble came to the SDLP 'war-room' and in deadly serious tones ('He eyeballed us,' said a party source), announced that his party could not live with tourism moving to the Department of Culture. The SDLP gave way, although it claimed to have extracted concessions in other respects. Sinn Féin was extremely angry and accused its fellow-nationalists of letting the side down, but it was 4 am and no one wanted to drag out the proceedings any longer. The gloomy demeanour of Sinn Féin at the end of the night was distinctly ominous, but everyone would have time to reflect on the deal and work out its implications before the Assembly debate in mid-January.

In Mallon's absence, the SDLP team had been led by South Down MP, Eddie McGrady. For the first time ever, unionists and nationalists agreed a carve-up of political power in Northern Ireland. Despite the lateness of the hour and the marathon he had just completed, the First Minister-designate was in high good humour. When asked if he was looking forward to coalition with the SDLP, he quipped: 'We are fast becoming inseparable – look at the hours we're keeping.'

The year 1998, arguably as dramatic as any in the Irish story since 1798, was drawing to a close and the images crowded in. Some were hopeful, some ambiguous, some deeply tragic. Good Friday was the high point of hope: complete strangers hugging each other in the streets of Belfast – we have peace! Mostly, however, the images were ambivalent and uncertain. The endless obfuscation as well as the overuse of diplomatic and political code-words in documents, press statements and answers to reporters' questions. Is there anyone here who doesn't speak with forked tongue? Most powerful of all perhaps were the tragic images, especially that terrible week after Omagh when the funerals culminated in that dignified but emotionally searing memorial service in the town centre.

Then there was the Agreement. As a dissident unionist reminded me, the document was a fudge in many respects. There was a cabinet that wasn't a cabinet – at least not in the normal sense. There was a police commission that might give nationalists what they want – but perhaps only if it could do so without taking what unionists held dear. And then there was decommissioning – which wasn't so much fudged as long-fingered, like a disease that could never be quite killed off, only held at bay. A senior figure on the security side told me privately he regarded the word itself as a kind of joke. 'What does it mean?' he mused over lunch. Certainly, he continued, decommissioning had limited security value – it was more important to remove the will to use weapons than the weapons themselves.

A senior Irish official said the Washington Three precondition of partial decommissioning of March 1995 was devised by 'securocrats' in the previous Tory administration, seeking to use it as a device for squeezing the IRA out of existence. In his autobiography, though, John Major quotes prior statements from Irish politicians to support his contention that they 'made the running' on the issue. People might argue about the cause of the disease, it was another thing to find a cure.

The optimists said the referendum vote marked a fundamental shift, a watershed in the history of the whole island and that, try as they might, the naysayers could not turn the clock back. The pessimists saw David Trimble being gradually marginalised into irrelevance by his dissidents. The political process would collapse and the IRA and the loyalists go back on a full-time war footing. Probably the truth was that the North would continue to muddle its way through to some kind of conclusion to the conflict, messy and untidy and possibly with considerable violence along the way. Nobody would get everything they wanted but the will to fight for more was gradually ebbing away. In that sense, 1998 marked the beginning of the end of the war.

The Assembly was scheduled to meet again on 18 January, with Trimble and Mallon reporting on the cross-Border deal concluded the month before. The Ulster Unionists were said to be anxious to avoid a formal vote on adopting the report because of legal advice that this would remove the barriers to Sinn Féin participation in an executive. They were thought likely to recommend instead that the Assembly 'take note' of the Trimble–Mallon report, not only to avoid triggering the mechanism for Sinn Féin's accession but also for fear of highlighting differences within the UUP Assembly team. The possibility of defections was an ever-present nightmare.

However, Mallon threw down the gauntlet when he said there would be 'an air of unreality' about 'taking note' of something which had already been agreed. He recalled that the first meeting of the Assembly in July had passed a resolution requiring himself and the First Minister-designate to make proposals for new government structures. Senior UUP sources sniffed that Mallon's comments were unhelpful.

A crisis was averted by last-minute compromise. Whereas the 'approval' of a majority of members would be sought when a report was presented to the Assembly, this would not be sufficient in procedural terms to trigger the establishment of the shadow Executive. However, there was now agreement that a formal determination on the report, fully endorsing it under the rules of the Assembly for cross-community voting, would be made on 15 February. This, according to most analysts, would allow the Secretary of State to trigger the appointment of ministers and the establishment of the Executive in shadow form, if she chose to do so.

There was angry reaction to this deal from anti-Agreement unionists. Peter Robinson said if Assembly members approved the report, 'they will be signing a post-dated cheque which effectively will be cashed when it comes to the 15th of February'. Meanwhile Adams accused the UUP leadership of 'delaying the inevitable'.

What was supposed to change between 18 January and 15 February? Senior unionists said there was still quite a lot of work to be done to complete the arrangements for the various institutions that were about to be born. 'Bugger-all has been done about the Civic Forum[13] for example.' One could not avoid the feeling that, like Mister Micawber, they were waiting for something to turn up on decommissioning. The republican answer here was monotonously familiar: there would be no decommissioning to get Sinn Féin into the Executive, no decommissioning to ensure a favourable report from the Patten Commission, no gestures, no puffs of smoke in fields, no big bang in the woods. Decommissioning would only take place when the IRA decided the causes of the conflict had been removed, and we were an enormous distance from that now.

Tell all that to unionists and they lapsed into their mantra that, without decommissioning, there would be no seats on the Executive for Sinn Féin. Options under consideration included a vote in the Assembly to exclude the 'Shinners'. Since that would not get SDLP support, the course of action most often mentioned in senior unionist circles was the possibility of invoking the review clause in the Agreement. This could be their strongest card, especially if there was an outcry among the public over decommissioning, the continuing barbaric practice of paramilitary beatings and mutilations which were also being carried out by loyalists, and perhaps some unforeseen republican 'own goal' along the lines of the Donegal Celtic debacle.

The deepest worry for republicans in the event that the unionists made a determined effort to keep Sinn Féin out of the Executive was, what line would Dublin take? What they saw as conflicting signals on decommissioning from that quarter had caused considerable unease. 'Dublin is giving way too much succour to the unionist position,' sources close to republican thinking said. The party in the least enviable position in many ways was the SDLP, torn as it was between two intransigents. It was said to have been told in extremely trenchant terms by the unionists that, if Sinn Féin was allowed into an Executive, the UUP would walk out. Despite being somewhat shaken by the encounter, senior SDLP people were reported to be holding firm to the view that a UUP–SDLP executive with Sinn Féin in opposition was not acceptable.

The pace of the peace process was stepped up when Mowlam published her detailed legislative programme for devolution by a target-date of 10 March. She pointed out that the new government departments had to be created, North–South institutions formally established and arrangements finalised for the British–Irish Council, and that the Assembly needed to agree its standing orders. The move fuelled speculation she might unilaterally convene the shadow Executive, but that prospect was immediately rejected in a sharply worded statement from the Ulster Unionists.

Relations between the unionist leadership and the Northern Secretary were not showing any improvement. Senior sources said there were 'hot words' between them after Mowlam refused to give a guarantee that she would not 'trigger' the formation of the Executive in the event of a cross-community vote endorsing the package of new departments and North–South bodies. Trimble reportedly 'stormed off' to London to see Blair.

On the other side of the fence, the greater the hue and cry over decommissioning, the more the IRA's back stiffened. Sympathy for Trimble's internal party difficulties was hard to come by in republican circles. Rather, there was considerable scepticism about the extent to which his leadership was really in danger and republicans pointed out that he generally won the key votes in his party by a two-thirds majority or greater. Allied to this, there was a strong conviction among republicans that any move to decommission would make a present of key sections of the grassroots to the Real IRA.

All the time the UUP was carefully watching its rightward flank where the DUP stood, ever ready to pounce. The debate which began in the Assembly on 18 January was meant to last three days but the UUP, with SDLP help, brought in a surprise guillotine motion which shut down the discussion after the first day. In a vote to approve a report on the UUP–SDLP deal on new government departments and North–South bodies, the only UUP member who broke ranks was Peter Weir from North Down, well-known for his anti-Agreement stance. Questioned about Weir's dissenting vote, Trimble said: 'That is not a major problem. That is a minor problem. It will shortly disappear.' Weir lost the party whip next day. Trimble managed to keep his other mavericks in check: sources said he had 'read the Riot Act' in advance to potential dissidents. There was outrage over the guillotine and the DUP subsequently tabled a motion of No Confidence in Alderdice as Initial Presiding Officer which was overwhelmingly defeated.

There was a smack of firm and decisive leadership about Trimble's conduct that even his admirers – a select but enthusiastic band – had not been accustomed to seeing in the past. He took his party by the scruff of the neck, beginning with a meeting of the Assembly team on the morning of the guillotine. 'The implication was fairly strong that anyone abstaining or voting against would lose the whip,' sources in the Assembly party said. There were warnings but there was a fair amount of cajoling as well. Trimble supporters assured the doubters there was no question of going into government with Sinn Féin unless there was IRA decommissioning and that a veto could be exercised over any such development. People were asked to vote Yes for the party's sake and on the basis that the motion was not of any great significance anyway. There was a high loyalty factor in the UUP. 'We're a way of life – like Fianna Fáil,' quipped one senior member.

The Democratic Unionists alleged bully-boy tactics, with Ian Paisley Jnr, for example, claiming he saw one UUP waverer being 'cornered like a rat' and told 'what way he would f***ing vote'. John Taylor snorted that these allegations were typical of the DUP's form. One leading dissident was understood to have received the stark message that his political life was over and his career dead. It certainly seems the atmosphere became somewhat heated, as evidenced by the subsequent resignation of young, liberal South Antrim Assembly member Duncan Shipley Dalton from the post of deputy chief whip, on the grounds that Peter Weir should not just have lost the whip but his party membership as well.

Other potential dissidents toed the line. One of these was Billy Armstrong, who was not prepared to say afterwards whether he would do the same in the next vote on 15 February. 'Things could change,' he said. Likewise Taylor, with his flair for political theatre, refused to give a guarantee that he would vote the same way on 15 February. The pro- and anti-Agreement camps in the Assembly were now equally balanced at 29 members each. Trimble could lose five more votes and still secure the minimum

40 per cent of unionists required under the Assembly's rules for cross-community voting on major decisions. There was the further possibility that the Women's Coalition, say, could come to his aid by changing their designation to unionist, although such stratagems would make him a lame duck in unionist circles.

The official UUP line remained very firmly one of refusing to sit down at the cabinet table with republicans unless there had been at least a symbolic destruction of weapons by the IRA. 'We are not bellying-up on this one,' I was told. Hope that the Provisionals would 'do the decent thing', fuelled by dubious media articles and reports, had not entirely evaporated in the unionist camp. A senior peace process insider said the continuing paramilitary beatings and shootings were doing 'enormous damage' to mainstream republicans and loyalists by undermining the claim of their political associates to be committed to the democratic process. Adams told me in an interview that he was against the attacks but he did not take up my invitation to venture into the territory of outright condemnation. On decommissioning, he rejected the conventional wisdom that it had to take place to save Trimble's leadership: 'Does anybody think there's any logic in anyone going to the IRA and saying, would you decommission to save David Trimble? The whole thing is just totally irrational and illogical, and I'm part of the tragedy of it, maybe.'

The republicans were taking a lot of 'hits' publicity-wise on the beatings.[14] Trimble now requested Amnesty International and the New York-based Human Rights Watch to send teams to Northern Ireland to observe and report on paramilitary shootings and beatings carried out since the Agreement was signed.

The so-called 'punishment' beatings were only one manifestation of the barbarism that came to infect life in Northern Ireland during the Troubles. Dehumanised is the only word one can apply to those who attacked the author and former IRA activist Eamon Collins (44) in Newry on 27 January. As an IRA intelligence officer from the late 1970s to the mid-1980s he was apparently involved in at least five and perhaps as many as fifteen killings: he used his job as a Border customs officer to gather information on potential targets and set them up to be killed. In 1985, Collins broke under RUC questioning and was charged with five murders; he also initially agreed to testify as a 'supergrass' against alleged former associates. He subsequently disowned his statements and a judge acquitted him because of the circumstances of his interrogation. Later, in 1998, Eamon Collins appeared as a paid witness for *The Sunday Times* in a libel case in Dublin where he testified that Thomas 'Slab' Murphy of Ballybinaby, Hackballscross, County Louth, was a senior member of the IRA. Murphy lost the case.

In his 1997 book, *Killing Rage*,[15] Collins gave a vivid, disturbing and brutally honest account of his years in the IRA. He spared nobody, least of all himself. But his literary talent got little chance to develop much further. Regarded as a traitor by his former associates, Collins nevertheless insisted on residing in a staunchly republican district of Newry, and ignored numerous threats to his life. He was savagely beaten and stabbed to death as he took his two dogs for an early-morning walk at Doran's Hill, a country road near his home. Multiple head injuries made it difficult to identify the victim, indeed for several hours it was thought he might have been run over by a car. An RUC officer said: 'It's more akin to a crime carried out by primitive cavemen than it is of a country entering the twenty-first century.' In time, most observers came to believe the murder was carried out by the Provisional IRA but could not be sure if it was done with approval from the top.

UUP sources said they detected a shift in opinion, both public and official, in the Republic in favour of the unionist stance on weapons. Senior unionists claimed the South was returning to the mindset of the mid-1920s and after, when the State set its face against private armies. Certainly unionists had been courting Southern public opinion for some time now, as if they sensed, or even knew, that republicans saw Dublin as the weakest element of the pan-nationalist consensus. A prominent unionist recalled wistfully in a conversation with me on 3 February how even Eamon de Valera had been forced to crack down very hard on the IRA because he felt it was jeopardising the safety of the State.

The only actual hardware the decommissioning body had received so far had come from the Loyalist Volunteer Force just before Christmas. While it was generally accepted that Sinn Féin had been punctilious in its dealings with the decommissioning body, the fact remained that no 'product' had been forthcoming. Even a telephone call to the Commission indicating where arms might be found would be considered a valid gesture and a verifiable start to decommissioning, sources familiar with de Chastelain's thinking said. There was considerable interest in remarks by Martin McGuinness to the *Belfast Telegraph*. He said that, had the power-sharing executive and the North–South council been established last year, 'it is my view that we could have considerably advanced that (decommissioning) agenda'.

I had a break from covering the peace process when I got to interview the former South African president F.W. de Klerk, who had come to Dublin to promote his autobiography. A critical figure in his own country's transition, he was wary of direct comparisons between the Irish peace process and the democratic transformation of South Africa. He recalled that decommissioning never took place as fully or comprehensively in his country as had been agreed, but that the issue was not permitted to derail the process. 'We had to face up to the fact that, while we continued to work at it, we could not allow the lack of diligent compliance to really stop the wagon.' Chainsmoking Peter Stuyvesant cigarettes in the Grace Kelly suite of Dublin's Shelbourne Hotel he added: 'Somehow or another, however difficult the intermediate deadlock or crisis might be, you've got to go beyond it, you've got to move forward, you've got to take the bull by the horns and keep pushing forward.'

Chapter 9

THE FAMOUS DECLARATION

They called it the Valentine's Day Massacre. It was the day Bertie Ahern seemed – the qualification is important – to stop trying to be all things to all men and come down on the unionist side of the decommissioning argument. In tones of ironic tribute, former Taoiseach Charles J. Haughey, had once said of Bertie that he was 'the most skilful, the most devious and the most cunning' of them all. With little apparent effort, Ahern had been keeping both the Ulster Unionists and Sinn Féin more or less happy and content almost from the time he took office. I later discovered, though, that he had put quite a lot of work into developing his relationship with Trimble, with regular meetings and phone calls, even on Sunday mornings, the traditional day off for politicians.[1]

After their 'bad marriage' with Bruton, the republican movement welcomed Ahern's accession to power in mid-1997 and could even be said to have facilitated it. With Tony Blair in power in London, Bertie Ahern in Dublin and Bill Clinton in the White House, all the pieces seemed to be in place for rapid movement on the republican/nationalist agenda. A ceasefire followed in short order.

True, there had been sour notes from time to time. After the Omagh bomb, Ahern beat the law-and-order drum much louder than Sinn Féin would have wished and considerably louder than Tony Blair. However, reports that mainstream republicans were paying 'visits' to dissidents, to remind them where their original loyalties lay, took some of the force out of Sinn Féin's civil libertarian objections.

Privately, republicans were genuinely worried that Dublin could prove to be the 'weakest link in the chain'. The events of St Valentine's Day 1999 seemed to confirm their worst fears. On that date, the *Sunday Times*, long a bête noire of republicanism, trumpeted the headline across the top of Page One: 'No power-sharing before arms handover, Ahern tells Sinn Féin.' Based on a lengthy interview with the Taoiseach, the *Sunday Times* began its Page One report as follows: 'Bertie Ahern has said that Sinn Féin should be barred from the new Northern Ireland government unless the IRA starts to decommission its weapons.'

Some observers, myself among them, felt a more complex reading of an interview which contained considerable ambiguity was in order and that the Page One headline and introductory paragraph were unduly stark. Not everyone agreed, although the Taoiseach subsequently pointed out in the Dáil that he had 'never used the word barred'. I had known and reported on Ahern at close quarters for over a decade and was well acquainted with his ability to bob and weave between different positions, like a soccer-player probing for goal. However, the subtleties in the interview took some time to emerge, e.g. Ahern spoke of decommissioning 'in one form or another' and a 'commencement' of decommissioning, which was reminiscent of the unionist phrase about 'a credible start to the process of decommissioning'. He spoke later in the Dáil of the need for 'an understanding of how the implementation of the decommissioning part of the Agreement would be taken forward'. However, as so often happens, it was the dramatic headline which attracted most attention that Sunday morning.

While the Ulster Unionists knew it was coming, for once the republicans' intelligence network let them down. Mitchel McLaughlin was clearly unprepared when asked about the interview on television. He had obvious problems accepting that the Taoiseach would pull the rug on Sinn Féin in this way. Martin McGuinness phoned Ahern almost immediately and shortly issued a statement to the effect that the Taoiseach had assured him the Dublin administration's line was unchanged. It is, of course, a long-established political ploy to say something controversial and then retreat before the inevitable irate reaction, issuing a denial by way of covering fire. That was the interpretation most in line with the Haughey analysis of Ahern. The Taoiseach would hardly be naive enough to expect the *Sunday Times* to break bad news gently to the republican movement. Government sources in Dublin admitted to me soon afterwards the fact that Fine Gael, the main opposition party in the South, was holding its annual conference that weekend was a prime consideration

in the timing of the interview. The *Sunday Times* had been looking for an Ahern interview since before Christmas.

With the interview, Ahern seemed to be killing not one or
two, but several birds with the same stone. He was using language palatable to his coalition partners, the Progressive
Democrats, whose leader, Mary Harney, Ahern's deputy prime
minister, had complained shortly beforehand about the IRA's
obduracy on weapons. He was 'zilching' Bruton, who would
otherwise have been striding across the front pages with an
ardfheis indictment of the government. And he was doing his
new-found friend David Trimble a big favour. The day after the
interview appeared, I met one of Trimble's chief lieutenants outside Stormont. 'What do you think of Bertie?' I asked. The unionist, in a Mo Mowlam 'touchy-feely' type moment, put his arm
around my shoulder and, with a broad and knowing grin,
replied: 'He's a great guy.'

Trimble was facing a critical Stormont vote two days after
the interview and one of his Assembly Members, Roy Beggs Jr,
had signalled his intention to vote against proposals on North–
South bodies. Ahern's intervention might tip the balance. Yet
while the timing and general tendency of the interview may
have been aimed at helping Trimble, it hardly needs saying that
this did not excuse its content in the eyes of Sinn Féin leaders. In
a lengthy question-and-answer session in the basement press
room at Stormont, where he was pressed particularly hard by
the indefatigable Eamonn Mallie, McGuinness held to the line
that, whatever might have appeared in the *Sunday Times*, Dublin
had never told the republican movement it had to decommission
as the price of entry to the North's government. It was clear from
his demeanour that the normally equable McGuinness was
deeply concerned. Another very high-level republican told me
privately that the interview had been an 'earthquake for us'. A
senior Sinn Féin strategist said later it was the worst moment of
all in the entire peace process – which indicates the scale of reaction in Provisional ranks.

There were ambiguities in the Ahern interview and, in truth,
the Taoiseach had for some time been facing different ways on
the weapons issue – a senior SDLP member aptly described him
as 'playing hopscotch' because he had taken, not one, but a variety of positions. Nevertheless, the *Sunday Times* text provided

such a degree of comfort to unionists that republican despair was very understandable. While McGuinness was no doubt accurate in stating that Dublin had not told him or his colleagues that decommissioning was a precondition, they were busy telling just about everyone else around this time. The present writer was the recipient of a highly emphatic briefing from a key figure in the Dublin apparatus, two months before, at a pre-Christmas function in the 'Bunker' – the headquarters of the Anglo-Irish Secretariat[2] just outside Belfast. I was told in no uncertain terms about the Taoiseach's view that there could be no executive which included Sinn Féin unless IRA weapons were 'rendered inoperational'. Other journalists were being briefed in similarly strong terms. The wonder is, then, that it should have come as such a surprise to Sinn Féin when Ahern decided to 'go public'. There was an argument that such hard-line pronouncements from a Fianna Fáil Taoiseach helped the 'peaceniks' in Sinn Féin, but the same peaceniks showed little public sign that they appreciated the gesture. Dublin sources said that when Rita O'Hare was switched from liaison with Dublin to the demanding task of looking after the Irish republican interest in Washington and the US generally, Sinn Féin no longer had its finger on the pulse to the same extent in the South. Dublin was left with more room to manoeuvre by republicans just at the point where the unionists were stepping-up their propaganda in the Republic. It is difficult to imagine the 'Valentine's Day Massacre' taking place if the formidable O'Hare were still in town.

Insiders said later that Ahern was always keen to maintain good relations with the unionists and show some understanding of their position. 'He felt at times republicans were trying to get off the hook on this [issue] and treat decommissioning as a complete dead letter instead of doing something about it.' I was told that Ahern considered he had put himself out to an extraordinary extent for republicans at various times and perhaps did not always feel that he received an adequate return. In some ways, Ahern had a stronger conviction than most of the Dublin officials that decommissioning could not be pushed into the middle distance and that some resolution had to be found, through a combination of putting pressure on republicans and whittling-down the unionists' demands. For their part, republicans wondered later if their former associates, now leading the Real IRA, had somehow persuaded Fianna Fáil that the Provisional main-stream was intent on decommissioning.

As was his wont, Adams looked at the bigger picture and decided to put the episode behind him, at least in public. By Monday he was telling the media, 'That's yesterday's news'. And while the memory of Bertie's démarche lingered on, most attention now focused on Trimble's surprise victory in the Assembly when he retained the support of Roy Beggs Jr in the critical vote on cross-Border bodies. The ghost of Brian Faulkner was driven from his door – for the time being anyway.

In the never-ending internal squabble that was modern unionism, this was a signal triumph for the UUP leader. It was said that anti-Agreement forces had press releases in readiness to crow about Beggs' defection but these had to be binned when he toed the line. Instead it was the UUP who got to issue a press release in Beggs' name. Clearly prepared some time in advance, this well-manicured statement outlined the reasons Beggs voted the way he did, including Ahern's strong line on IRA weapons.[3] The Assembly Member said he had received 'concrete assurances' from his party leader. It was said Beggs had received a letter from Trimble promising to resign if Sinn Féin received ministries without a disposal of IRA weapons. There was no confirmation of this from any quarter but a UUP spokesman pointed out that this commitment was in the party's election manifesto in any case.[4] Later, in an interview with myself, Trimble asserted that Beggs was a 'party man' who would not lightly go against his colleagues.

The next big deadline was 10 March, set by the British as the 'Appointed Day' for devolution: it was fascinating how these phrases, concocted by some civil servant or other backroom person, gained immediate and widespread currency and became a type of rhetorical peg on which everything else could be hung. The unionists laid considerable emphasis on this day, stressing that all other elements were in place and it only remained for the IRA to make a gesture so that the Executive could get up and running. For the next two to three weeks it was business as usual: statement, counter-statement, charge and denial. Meetings continued at Downing Street and Stormont, but to no apparent effect. Ahern was busy mending his fences with Sinn Féin and, in early March, gave a speech which could have been written by Gerry Adams, it contained so many comfort-phrases for republicans. All the right buttons were pressed: Ahern noted that the 'guns were silent' (a phrase used by the republicans themselves); he glided over decommissioning as though it were some minor wrinkle that needed ironing-out; he employed high-flown rhetoric about the failure of the partition settlement. It was all music to Provo ears, although they doubtless realised by now that he could be playing a unionist tune next day. It was Ahern's way of moving people out of entrenched positions.

As the deadline inched closer it became obvious there would be no devolution, at least not on the Appointed Day. The focus shifted to the US, with the now-traditional exodus of Northern political leaders to Washington and New York for the pro-gramme of events around St Patrick's Day. Ahern and the Northern party leaders had already arrived in the US and were settling into the round of receptions, dinners and other func-tions, when a great gloomy shadow was suddenly cast over the jamboree. Having made the transatlantic trek myself, I was in a hotel room working on an article about the latest twist in the decommissioning saga when a contact telephoned with shock news from the North. Rosemary Nelson, the high-profile lawyer for the Garvaghy Road residents and several leading Armagh republicans, had been the victim of a car bomb attack and was badly injured.

Mrs Nelson had been in the US the previous September where she told a sub-committee on Capitol Hill of loyalist death threats against her; she also claimed to have been physically and verbally abused by the RUC. It was alleged that a client of hers was told during a police interrogation: 'You're dead. Tell Rosemary she's going to die too.' A birthmark which disfigured one side of her face was attributed in loyalist folklore to the pre-mature explosion of a bomb she was preparing in her imagined role as an IRA activist: no story was too far-fetched to be believed. 'She was frightened,' one of her close friends told me on the day of the attack.

Mrs Nelson had returned to her home in Lurgan, County Armagh, on the evening of 14 March, after a weekend break in Donegal. During the night an explosive device was attached to the underside of her silver BMW car. After midday she set out for her office but, when she braked the car at an intersection, it blew up underneath her. The explosion took place close to a primary school where her eight-year-old daughter was a pupil. Mrs Nelson lost both legs and suffered serious abdominal injuries. She was taken to Craigavon Area Hospital and died shortly afterwards.

The gruesome killing sent shockwaves through the nationalist community. There were inevitable implications for the peace process, because it would now be ten times more difficult to achieve decommissioning. Whatever limited openness to at least discussing the idea of weapons disposal might have existed on the republican side quickly evaporated. Although the killing was claimed by a dissident loyalist group, the Red Hand Defenders, experienced observers felt the level of technical sophistication suggested the real culprits were elements from the Ulster Defence Association (UDA), which was the largest of the mainstream loyalist paramilitary groups and was officially on ceasefire. Most disturbing of all, perhaps, was the nagging suspicion among nationalists and republicans that the killing might have been carried out with the participation, co-operation, or at least tacit approval, of elements in the security forces. A colleague of mine said bleakly that the killing was a case of 'the Orange state striking back'.

The Nelson murder heightened the drama of events in Washington. The leaders of the main pro-Agreement parties were all on site, along with the affable Cedric Wilson of the newly formed Northern Ireland Unionist Party, which had emerged from a split in Robert McCartney's UKUP. At the Plaza Hotel in Manhattan, George Mitchell received the award for Irish-American of the Year from Niall O'Dowd's *Irish America* magazine. I could never enter the Plaza without thinking of that bored, sultry and ultimately menacing scene from Scott Fitzgerald's *The Great Gatsby* – another Irish-American, of course! In his acceptance speech, Mitchell pressed the Northern politicians to reach agreement, warning that history would not forgive them if they failed. Two nights later, the annual dinner of the American Irish Fund took place in the spectacular setting of the National Building Museum in downtown Washington. At one time the only representative from the unionist side who would attend this event was Gary McMichael, but by 1999 the balance had greatly changed and the UUP's newly knighted Sir

Reg Empey boasted proudly that 'there's more unionists here tonight than Shinners'. Their anti-Agreement colleagues would say they were being lured deeper into Irish America's web.

Next day at the White House there were so many guests that a tent had to be erected to accommodate them. Everyone who was anyone in Irish America was on hand and Clinton conducted operations personally from the platform. I noticed him make a 'cut-throat' sign to his staff to indicate that a noisy air-conditioning system be shut down. I was surprised how much he was involved in the nuts and bolts. Sitting beside me was Edna O'Brien, novelist and free-speech heroine of my youth. Hollywood star Aidan Quinn was leading the entertainment. A senior official left halfway, excusing himself with the whispered word, 'Kosovo'.

Mitchell was receiving another award, this time the Presidential Medal of Freedom, which Clinton personally draped around the Senator's neck. Adams and Trimble sat in the same row, indeed Adams stood up to allow Trimble to take his seat. The UUP leader had a prior engagement it was reported and had to leave shortly after his arrival – Adams again standing to let him out. I wondered what Gerry was saying – he always had a phrase for such occasions. No doubt Trimble's excuse for leaving was genuine but his early exit was widely remarked upon afterwards.[5]

Mitchell reiterated his Plaza Hotel plea for peace. He asked the party leaders to stand up, praised them for their efforts up to that time and went on to stress the heavy responsibility on them to continue to a successful conclusion. It was at odds with his deft handling of the Stormont talks and smacked of the Great White Chief telling the 'Injuns' what to do. Clinton too was in schoolmaster mode, looking over in the direction of Adams as he stressed the need to pay back debts previously incurred – presumably a reference to the US visa he had 'swung' for Gerry in 1994. There was also an element of good old-fashioned Democratic Party politics about the occasion. Hillary Rodham Clinton introduced the proceedings and although she made no mention of her latest ambition – to be a member of the US Senate for New York – Mitchell made a semi-humorous allusion to it, evoking huge applause from the crowd and a discreet smile from the First Lady.[6]

Clinton had earlier made a room available at the White House for an unscheduled half-hour meeting between Adams and Trimble, reportedly held at the President's request. The unionist leader spelt out, in the clearest terms yet, what precisely he meant by decommissioning and what he wanted from the IRA. Next morning at a press conference on Capitol Hill, Adams told the media in tones of some disbelief about Trimble's demands. He wanted, not one, but several 'events', Adams reported, in which substantial and gradually increasing amounts of rifles, handguns, detonators and explosives would be destroyed. Adams reiterated in the strongest possible terms that he could not 'deliver' on this and that Trimble knew he could not deliver. Flanking the Sinn Féin president were the Congressmen Peter King (Republican), Richie Neal and Joseph Crowley (both Democrats).

But at the same time that he rejected Trimble's material demands out of hand, Adams also used striking new language which served to inject fresh life into the peace process and keep it going politically for several months. He said he and his colleagues were prepared to 'stretch the republican constituency' provided David Trimble was 'in the loop'. Adams held out the prospect that himself and Trimble would 'jump together'.

One observer said cynically that by stretching the republican constituency, Adams merely meant yet again stretching the resources and ambiguities of the English language; he was just responding rhetorically to the pressure from the White House and others to move on decommissioning but, no matter what Adams said, the IRA would never hand over their guns. Be that as it may, Trimble and his associates seized on the 'jump together' line and threw it back at Adams every chance they got over the succeeding months. Their message was, We have always been prepared to form an inclusive executive Gerry, let's see you 'jump' on weapons. Yet even changes of rhetoric by the Sinn Féin leadership had to be taken seriously as they might presage significant action. As they pointed out themselves, Adams and his friends had already secured two IRA ceasefires, despite the fact that many observers regarded the prospect as unthinkable and dismissed the possibility until it actually happened.

The previous day, Trimble had given his regular US news conference at the National Press Club in Washington, where he spoke in unusual terms, for a unionist leader, about the history of Northern Ireland. He said there had been a problem in the half-century after 1921 because one party, namely his own, had won all the elections, which was 'fine for us, but not so fine for other people'. This was an echo of his remark in the Nobel Prize speech that the North had been 'a cold house for Catholics'. How much this was the real Trimble and how much a public relations gesture was still unclear.

Trimble returned to the North to face a minor but not insignificant setback at his party's annual general meeting. The dissidents had regrouped and successfully fought off attempts to remove their representatives from the officer board. Trimble's people were badly organised, with the result that all four honorary secretary posts were won by anti-Agreement candidates. The meeting ended on a difficult note with the chair appearing to close off debate after two delegates challenged Trimble on the precise meaning of his much-used phrase, 'a credible start to decommissioning'. When Trimble said 'credible' meant 'significant', he was greeted by shouts of 'fudge' and 'shame'. The UUP leader, who had just finished a speech appealing for party unity, was clearly taken aback by the heckling.

The next stage of the drama was the expected arrival of the two prime ministers in the North for talks aimed at breaking the arms deadlock in time for the first anniversary of the Agreement. In the interim, rumours began to circulate that the IRA was at last about to yield up the 'disappeared', i.e. those of its victims whose bodies were never recovered. Most were Catholics who had been shot in the 1970s for the alleged provision of information or other assistance to the security forces or allegedly stealing IRA weapons. Their bodies were buried at undisclosed locations, leaving their families without even a graveside at which they could mourn. Subsequently, IRA policy in this morbid area of activity was changed, so that when alleged informers were 'executed', their bodies were left for discovery, usually on some lonely Border roadside.

There was also much speculation at this time about the intentions of Mo Mowlam on the political front: if agreement were not reached on decommissioning, would she still insist on triggering the d'Hondt procedure for nominating ministers? The main effect of this uncertainty was to increase the pressure on unionists to make a deal with Sinn Féin. Talks between the two parties began mid-morning on 29 March and continued until late in the afternoon. Afterwards, UUP sources refused even to say when the meeting had ended and merely commented that it was 'very businesslike'. It was considered encouraging that the participants were so tight-lipped. A previous meeting between the two parties before the weekend was said to have gone well.

That evening, just as Blair and Ahern were due to arrive, the IRA gave briefings to a number of journalists, myself included, to inform them that the locations of nine 'bodies of the disappeared' had been found. The names of the dead and the alleged acts for which they had been shot were provided. While the IRA representative denied the move had anything to do with the talks going on at Hillsborough, it was widely seen as an attempt to influence the negotiations. The organisation had been accused of dragging its feet on this issue and showing a lack of consideration for the bereaved families, so the latest move struck some observers as cynical. Whatever the short-term considerations, republican insiders said it was a significant development in the movement's psychology, an attempt to draw a line under an unhappy episode, or series of episodes, in the past.

Next day, 30 March, was being widely billed as 'D-Day'. The 'hand of history' may not have been on Blair's shoulder this time but he pledged: 'I will not stop or rest until this thing is done.' Another soundbite of course but, in fairness to the man, he never stinted on time or energy when it came to Northern Ireland. He and Ahern were heckled by loyalists during a visit to Stormont, before they adjourned to the safe haven of Hillsborough Castle, south of Belfast, to meet the main Northern parties. Sinn Féin was first into the Castle's 'Lady Gray Room', for a two-hour meeting with Blair which the Taoiseach also attended for twenty minutes. There was a first for the talks when the Ulster Unionists and Sinn Féin met Ahern and Blair in a four-hander. The choreography was in place but, when the music started up, would everybody dance?

Rumour and counter-rumour had been floating about all day. The Sinn Féin stance was, Set up the institutions, then we can resolve decommissioning. The UUP position: Hold on, let's see some guns first, then we can have a devolution of powers. Officials from both governments, particularly Dublin, were attempting to resolve the conundrum in the usual way by developing a position that would accommodate both unionist and republican demands.

Against this background, there were intriguing comments on television from the UUP chief negotiator, Reg Empey. In one of those interviews that looked more like a political ploy than a casual response to a series of questions, Empey outlined for the UTV evening news what his party needed from the republican side. 'First of all, an IRA statement that says they accept the principle of disarmament and that they are prepared to enter into negotiations with General de Chastelain about the modalities of commencing a credible process of decommissioning.' Empey continued: 'That allows us then to work out the details of how the Executive is formed, the timing and all of these other matters. But unless we have that understanding, then it's impossible to get the process of negotiation started.'

Around 7 pm, Trimble left the talks to give a half-hour briefing to his Assembly party at a nearby hotel. Reporters swooped down on the building but it was clear from the downbeat mood of Assembly members coming out that speculation about a deal was premature. The hopes raised by Empey's interview were dashed by Taylor, who reiterated in very strong terms that it would not be possible to form an Executive with Sinn Féin unless there was a prior handover of IRA weapons.

Before the talks adjourned for the night, Blair's spokesman, Alastair Campbell, said that agreement was 'difficult but doable'. However, unionist sources laughed when told of Campbell's claim that 'real progress' had been made in the talks. At the gates of Hillsborough a group of loyalist protesters jeered 'Traitor Trimble' and sang *The Sash My Father Wore*. Inside, officials from the two governments had been asked to prepare a position paper for presentation to the Taoiseach and the Prime Minister at 9 am next day, reflecting some movement which they believed took place 'on the margins' of the main issue of decommissioning. The Hillsborough Declaration was gestating.

The traditional IRA Easter statement marking the anniversary of the 1916 Rising was issued next day, reiterating the organisation's desire for a 'permanent peace' but making no mention of decommissioning. That in itself was possible grounds for encouragement because in the past the IRA had mentioned the issue only to rule it out forever and for aye. The two prime ministers left around mid-morning with Ahern making a tantalising throwaway comment which echoed some of what Empey said in his UTV interview: 'Surely we should not lose out because two of the parties could not agree on times and dates.' This caused some annoyance in republican circles as it was open to the interpretation that 'product' might be forthcoming in advance of the formation of an Executive. A spokesman for the Ulster Unionists indicated that the talks were adjourned for a week and announced they were decamping to Stormont. The UUP appeared to be trying to adjourn the talks unilaterally but this move was quickly slapped down by Blair's people who signalled that the Prime Minister would be returning later in the day: 'The talks are continuing. There is no adjournment.'

Blair and Ahern returned for the 'big push' negotiations that evening. The entire UUP Assembly team was at Hillsborough Castle. So, too, were many leading Sinn Féin members, the entire *ardchomhairle* (executive council) it was said. There were the usual rumours about Provisional Army Council members hovering around the negotiations. It never rose above the level of media chit-chat although there was no denying that many present had a long record of involvement with the republican movement.

We seemed to be re-running the long-drawn-out events of the previous Good Friday. There was the same exhaustion but not quite the same sense of drama. The media, kept in the dark and fed contrasting spins, lingered outside and chatted quietly among themselves or made an occasional strategic call on their mobile phones. Inside, Sinn Féin delegates were having trouble using their own mobiles. From time to time, leading republicans went out on to the front lawn to get a better signal. The loyalists chanted: 'If you hate [named Sinn Féin member] clap your hands.' The Sinn Féin group, inured to loyalist hatred, amused itself by watching to see who got the most abuse. Suddenly there was a massive outpouring of contempt and derision – but with no Sinn Féin member in evidence. It turned out that Trimble had been spotted at an upstairs window making a call on his mobile: obviously his signal wasn't the best either. He was caught in a television spotlight and, when they saw him, the loyalists went crazy. No Sinn Féin delegate reached that decibel level all night.

Sources inside the talks later described it as a hectic night of 'rolling meetings'. Every nook and cranny, even the photocopy room was taken up with groups of one sort or another discussing issues, documents and ways around the current problem. Senior unionists contrived a situation whereby Blair 'accidentally' met about a dozen members of the party's Assembly team at the bottom of the stairs at around 4.30 am, including the potential dissident, Billy Armstrong. The stratagem allowed the Prime Minister to exercise his persuasive powers on this critical group without being obliged to hold formal meetings with all the other parties.

There was a free bar for delegates but nobody overindulged. Most of the social side took place in the throne room but some tactful Northern Ireland Office type had draped the seats reserved for Her Majesty and Prince Philip so as not to offend republican and nationalist sensibilities. Nevertheless, there were reports of well-known republicans posing irreverently for photographs while sitting on the throne. Observers were impressed by Blair's staying-power: 'The man's stamina is something to be seen. He just kept going through the night.' It was just as well he didn't need any sleep because Ken Maginnis was ensconced in the Prime Minister's bed while Taylor slept in the bed intended for Alastair Campbell.

It was not a happy night for Sinn Féin. About 10 pm, the atmosphere had seemed quite positive, and both unionists and SDLP members sensed a deal was attainable. Fairly quickly, though, the Sinn Féin mood seemed to darken. After all the toing and froing on decommissioning and the taking of contrasting positions by Bertie Ahern in particular, at long last the strategy of the two governments was becoming clear. Get the IRA to decommission some weapons in as 'detoxified' and innocent a context as possible, so that the Executive can finally 'go live'. Mark Durkan of the SDLP crystallised it afterwards, in one of his inimitable phrases, when he said decommissioning had become a 'genetically modified precondition'.

Sinn Féin had been saying to the media all along that it could not deliver IRA weapons in advance of an executive with devolved powers – and maybe not even then. If that were the case, then republicans were in grave danger of political isolation. If Trimble agreed to risk joining an executive with Sinn Féin ministers on the understanding that decommissioning would happen in a number of weeks, and there was no IRA gesture forthcoming, Adams and his friends would be saddled with the blame. The UUP leader could say he had tried: he had made the leap of faith but Sinn Féin let him down. In this scenario, the Prime Minister, the Taoiseach, the SDLP and the entire establishment would be ranged against the republicans, who would then be faced with the choice of decommissioning and facing a damaging split, or holding on to the guns and becoming political pariahs once more.

There were unconfirmed reports of shouting matches between Sinn Féin delegates and representatives of the Irish Government. While that did not sound like the usual Adams way of doing business, it was entirely plausible that there was tension, especially between the Government and the republicans.

Shortly before 1 am, Campbell said the situation was 'far better than we left it earlier today'. Not for the last time, however, this upbeat reading was contradicted by a Sinn Féin representative who said that as far as his party was concerned there had been no movement and no progress and the situation was still deadlocked. He said Blair's spokesman had a tendency to put a 'gloss' on the situation.

The message from the unionists and Sinn Féin was relentlessly downbeat. Reporters had the difficult task of divining which was the correct 'spin'. The message from the Blair camp at 6 am was that the two prime ministers believed key elements of a deal were falling into place. What was 'real progress' at 1 am had now become 'substantial progress'. There were indications afterwards that rooms at Hillsborough were bugged: a very senior British representative let slip to a third party that he knew the contents of Sinn Féin's internal discussions.

April First was a day of glorious sunshine and the village of Hillsborough had never looked prettier. The media were there in their hordes, held back by crash barriers. Word filtered through that unanimous agreement had not been reached. Sinn Féin was still holding out on decommissioning and the talks would be adjourned for about ten days, but what was initially called a 'communiqué' would be issued by the two governments.

There was apparently some debate about the wisdom of releasing this document, with unionists taking the view that it would be used against Trimble by his enemies in the party, but the two governments arguing that its contents would be leaked in any case. Trimble brought the document to a meeting of his Assembly team at lunchtime to 'talk them through it' and was greeted with a round of applause. Taylor quipped that asking the IRA to decommission its weapons at Easter was a bit like the UUP's best-known Catholic member, the much-decorated former soldier Sir John Gorman, inviting him to attend Mass on the Eleventh Night, the eve of the Twelfth of July celebrations. His witty comment brought the house down, with the amiable Sir John, famed for his exploits in the Second World War, joining in the merriment.

The first to appear with the text in public was Monica McWilliams of the Women's Coalition, who came outside for an interview in a Radio Ulster caravan at 3 pm. She initially came across as positive and upbeat in her attitude to the document – now being called a 'declaration' rather than a communiqué – but her tone changed after further reflection next day. I was a guest on the same radio programme and she generously allowed me a quick perusal of the text. Key phrases jumped out: the IRA would put a quantity of weapons 'beyond use' in an all-island 'collective act of reconciliation', in which the security forces would also be involved. There would be a simultaneous transfer of powers to a northern executive which would already be in place in shadow form. However, it seemed as if it might be a 'pre-shadow' or 'shadow of a shadow' executive, which would be named but not actually meet.

Finally, like naughty children released into the playground, the media were permitted to enter the well-manicured grounds of Hillsborough. The Prime Minister read the document to the press and television crews. Unlike the Good Friday Agreement it was a draft proposal: the parties had not agreed to it. It was clear that the people having most teeth pulled under the plan in the short term were the republicans, although there was some pain for unionists too.

The 'collective act of reconciliation' was suggested by Tim Dalton, civil service head of the South's Department of Justice and a member of the Dublin negotiating team. It was reportedly developed from a theme previously explored by the head of the Catholic Church in Ireland, Archbishop Sean Brady, as a means of breaking the impasse in the peace process. There would be collective acts of remembrance, some of them possibly of a religious nature. *Roget's Thesaurus* must have been consulted because decommissioning was now being described as an 'obligation' rather than a 'precondition'. An unspecified quantity of paramilitary weapons would be voluntarily put 'beyond use', which was taken to mean destroyed or placed in deep storage under the watchful eye of General de Chastelain. The British Army and the RUC would also engage in acts of reconciliation of an unspecified nature. One presumed – there was a lot of presuming with the Hillsborough Declaration – this meant closing police barracks and security installations.

First of all, though, the ministers would be nominated to their posts. They would not take office, nor would the Executive meet, even in shadow form. The safety-net for Trimble was that, without weapons, the Executive would not 'go live'. The 'sweetener' for the Provos was less obvious. True, as a prominent republican pointed out to me the following evening in a surprise telephone call to my flat, British Army, RUC and IRA weapons were implicitly placed on an equal footing. There was a grey area over the guns-and-government issue. The Declaration said that ministerial appointments would 'fall to be confirmed by the Assembly'. If this meant an Assembly veto over cabinet posts, this was not in line with the Agreement, where the only qualification for getting a ministerial position was the number of seats your party won in the elections, and the Assembly had no say in the matter.

The mood among the parties was reflected in a report that there was an attempt by the British to get Trimble, Hume and Adams to hold their press conferences at the far end of the garden from where the two prime ministers had spoken. There was immediate cross-party agreement that this wasn't on. Gerry Adams sat on the steps beside where the two prime ministers were standing, as though re-enacting the old civil rights sit-down days with its anthem, *We Shall Not Be Moved*. Despite having been 'shafted', the Sinn Féin group retained its composure and Adams even made a jocular reference to the fact that Martin McGuinness had just become a grandfather. Their faces told a different story and, behind the scenes, senior republicans were mad as hell. A senior SDLP figure commented that the republicans thought they would be able to get into government without disposing of a single weapon or pound of Semtex, but that there was a general feeling now that Sinn Féin was having to face political reality. Privately, unionists were feeling very pleased with the result on the day but managed to maintain some reserve in public. There was some unionist concern that the remembrance ceremonies envisaged in the document appeared to raise the prospect of IRA dead being included in semi-official ceremonies honouring the victims of the Troubles.

Trimble was being offered a post-dated cheque on decommissioning but, if the cheque bounced, Sinn Féin would be bounced from the list of ministerial nominees. The UUP leader was seen laughing and joking, although some of the journalists wondered if the unionists had read the small print with sufficient care.

It emerged that President Clinton had made several interventions during the night, despite the simultaneous pressures of the Kosovo[7] crisis. He made at least three telephone calls, the first at 8.45 pm and the other two later in the night.[8] It was established that he spoke to Blair and Adams and presumably other key participants. Sources said that Clinton's interventions may have helped to ensure Sinn Féin was comparatively restrained in its public criticisms of the document.

Privately, there was deep anger in Sinn Féin at the perceived support for the unionist position on decommissioning by the Taoiseach. Dublin sources acknowledged there had been a 'clear-the-air session' with Ahern, with Sinn Féin leaders explaining their objections in precise detail. Bertie made clear that he felt their pain but was not about to change course. Indeed, while remaining deeply dissatisfied, some republicans initially thought they could see 'wriggle room' in the document on such issues as decommissioning: they did not interpret the text as providing for a handover of IRA guns. Dublin's assessment afterwards was that the political side of republicanism might have been open to further negotiation on the basis of the document at the very least but the military people had turned it down.

At least one senior Sinn Féin member received a 7 am phone call next day from a person on the military side who wanted to know what the hell was going on. There was said to have been a lengthy meeting of the IRA leadership to discuss the issue. One senior republican was described as speechless with anger over the Day of Reconciliation proposal, while others in the leadership were quite interested in the idea. A top Irish official later acknowledged that the 'Army' (the IRA) had rejected the Hillsborough Draft. There were still some in the SDLP and elsewhere who insisted that, with a little more time and work, the Hillsborough initiative might have worked: the draft was released prematurely.

The Hillsborough talks were set to resume two weeks later, on 13 April, with a view to agreeing a final draft. However, there was a sea-change in the interim. There was considerable media focus on an Easter commemoration address by leading Belfast republican and former prisoner Brian Keenan, characterised in the media as a hard-liner, who stated in emphatic terms that there would be no IRA decommissioning in advance of the establishment of new institutions, even if this meant the collapse of the Good Friday Agreement. 'If it falls, it falls,' he told a crowd at Inniskeen, County Monaghan.

The speech prepared for delivery by Adams to a Dublin crowd at Glasnevin cemetery was more measured in tone. 'The way forward proposed in the governments' declaration, as explained to me, may have merit, but it may also be counter-productive if it amounts to an ultimatum to armed groups,' he said. Such 'difficulties' could only be resolved within the context of the Agreement. Observers took this to mean that only the establishment of the North–South Ministerial Council with Sinn Féin ministers participating could offer any chance of solving the decommissioning dilemma. Adams was keen to stress that his private and public positions on the Hillsborough Declaration were one and the same, an indication that the whispers about a Sinn Féin 'secret deal' had reached his ears.

The UVF was not happy either and its political wing, the Progressive Unionist Party, also rejected Hillsborough. The Alliance Party and the Women's Coalition both took their distance from the document, much to the annoyance of Seamus Mallon. The house of cards constructed at Hillsborough was collapsing. The IRA was holding onto its weapons and it was the Hillsborough Declaration that was being put 'beyond use'.

Chapter 10

'Seismic Shifts'

It came as no great surprise to most people when Sinn Féin formally and publicly rejected the Hillsborough Declaration on 13 April, which was the day designated for a resumption of discussions on this Blair–Ahern text. The key factor for the republicans was their inability to secure prior decommissioning from the IRA but there was also some marginal annoyance with the 'spin' coming from Dublin, to the effect that the 'Shinners' didn't really mean it about decommissioning, they would come round. Mitchel McLaughlin said he had read in some newspapers that 'Dublin government sources' were claiming his party had not rejected the document.

Some future student of the media could get a workmanlike Ph.D. thesis out of following the twists and turns of reporting on the decommissioning issue, especially in the lead-up to Hillsborough. Most reports indicated the IRA would in fact dispose of weapons in advance of Sinn Féin's admission to high office. It was also stated from time to time by people who purported to be in the peace process 'loop' that senior Sinn Féin members privately conceded there would have to be prior decommissioning. The present writer was never told any such thing by Sinn Féin either privately or publicly.

The mood was gloomier than it had been for a very long time. Asked to paint the picture as they saw it, contacts in the Dublin administration responded plaintively: 'There is no picture at the moment. All we have is canvas.' However, when I met Seamus Mallon in the basement canteen at Stormont and asked him for his assessment, he conducted a upward, then downward motion with his hand, so much as to say: It's a Bad Hair Day, not Armageddon. At a press conference upstairs, Reg Empey revealed an interesting nugget of information when he called for clarification of 'What is meant by this day of reconciliation'. He added: 'We had had no advance notice of it before it was published.' Apparently republicans and the security forces had no inkling of the Day of Reconciliation scheme either. Some observers felt it was yet another reflection of the gimmicky nature of the Hillsborough plan.

There was also the problem of prime ministerial 'hype'. Launching the Declaration on 1 April, Blair described it as 'another huge and significant milestone'. On the same occasion Ahern said, with a combination of inaccuracy and exaggeration: 'We have now succeeded in overcoming the last difficult hurdles that are standing in the way of the implementation of the Good Friday Agreement.' Even in official circles in Dublin there was unease over the heavy emphasis on decommissioning, to such an extent that one middle-ranking bureaucrat was said to have broken down in tears at the manner in which he felt the Taoiseach was being misled about the IRA's true intentions.

Hillsborough might be dead but some of the ideas within it still had a shelf-life. Liz O'Donnell told reporters at Stormont that an 'inclusive' set of institutions was not going to be established on the basis of the Declaration: 'But it might be on a combination of other forms of the Declaration.' Someone was being very clever.

The fact that decommissioning had been adjudged an obligation rather than a precondition in the Hillsborough draft had a lingering appeal for some nationalists because it gave greater flexibility on timing. The unionists continued to hanker after the Declaration because it was still based in essence on the idea of prior decommissioning. In a phrase made famous by the Irish television personality, Gay Byrne, when he was distributing gifts on his show, there was 'something for everybody in the audience'.

The reaction in republican circles showed that prior disposal of weapons wasn't going to happen – at least not at this stage. Ever the pragmatists, Blair and Ahern began to look for other solutions. However, any notion that the SDLP could go it alone, forming an executive with the unionists but minus Sinn Féin, was knocked smartly on the head by British government sources. 'Let's deal with political reality,' they said.

A series of meetings in Downing Street was co-chaired by the two prime ministers. They spent just short of an hour with the UUP delegation but about two hours with Sinn Féin. At the Sinn Féin meeting the hapless government leaders had to endure almost 45 minutes on the failings and mistakes of the two regimes – especially London – from different mid-level Sinn Féin representatives before the room was cleared, leaving the two men alone with Adams and McGuinness for the rest of the time. The game was on again.

There was encouragement from an opinion poll commissioned by *The Irish Times* and conducted by Ulster Marketing Surveys who interviewed 1,000 people from both communities in Northern Ireland on 22 and 23 April. The main thrust of the questioning was on decommissioning and, as the journalist detailed to report the results in the paper, I naturally intended to focus on this aspect. The real news story of the day, however, turned out to be the fact that support for Good Friday had not only held up, but increased slightly. A total 73 per cent of respondents said they would still support the Agreement, compared with 71.12 per cent in the referendum the previous May. London, in particular, was said to be encouraged.

A proposal from John Hume that Sinn Féin commit itself to a 'self-expulsion' clause, to be activated if the party were in government and its friends in the IRA returned to violence, was considered helpful in nationalist quarters but caused annoyance to unionists as it took the focus off decommissioning. Always much sought-after on the world stage, Hume was even more in demand now that he had become a Nobel laureate. His relatively low profile at home began to excite some comment but he came back with a bang when a dinner attended by hundreds of friends and admirers as well as invited media people was held in Belfast's Europa Hotel to celebrate the SDLP leader's 30 years in politics. The event was remarkable and revealing in many ways, not least for the number of past and present Irish civil servants in attendance who were publicly thanked from the platform for their work to resolve the northern conflict over the years. When Hume began his crusade to remedy the grievances of nationalists by peaceful means, there was in most cases only a token interest in Northern Ireland among the Dublin bureaucracy (Dr T.K. Whitaker was a notable exception). Much of the credit was due to Hume for the fact that there was now a substantial network of officials, especially in the Departments of Foreign Affairs, the Taoiseach and Justice, who devoted a substantial amount of their time – in some cases all of it – to the northern issue.

A round of meetings now began in Downing Street. Normally some would have taken place in Dublin but the demands of the Kosovan war made it difficult for Blair to leave London. Speculation in the British media about a 'transitional' executive which would be given full powers within six months if the IRA decommissioned was quickly discounted. The cartoonist Ian Knox in the *Irish News*, with his knack for catching the mood, portrayed an elderly nationalist complaining to his wife: 'A six-month transitional statelet is what they told us back in 1920.' This time the idea was put forward by the Women's Coalition but, though they had a good rapport with Mo Mowlam, the Northern Ireland Office said it was 'one of a range of options' and had not come from the two governments. The Taoiseach rejected the plan outright, telling reporters it was 'not our preferred option or on the agenda'. Having been highly critical of the Taoiseach in the run-up to Hillsborough, republicans now spoke with something close to warmth about his firm stance against attempts to 'park' the process for the summer.

It was understood one of the formulae under discussion at this time involved solemn assurances of peaceful intent by the republican movement. 'If they can say decommissioning is going to happen, then Trimble might have some room to manoeuvre,' one source said. Careful note was being taken of comments made by McGuinness during a visit to the US in early May but persistent reports that he had said Sinn Féin accepted decommissioning must be completed by May 2000 were strongly denied by the party. He flew from Washington direct to the talks in London and observers reported seeing himself and Adams conversing in the garden of Downing Street near a wall which still bore the scars of the notorious IRA mortar attack on the British cabinet eight years before.

At the Sinn Féin *ardfheis* in Dublin on the weekend of 8 and 9 May there was prolonged applause for a delegate who said, in reference to decommissioning, 'We were prepared to bite the bullet, not give it away'. There was a telling signal from Downing Street the same weekend in the form of comments attributed to Blair on the weapons dilemma, which he said was 'an issue more of symbolism and trust than it is to do with the foundations of the Agreement'. The timing of his remarks was doubtless intended to send a signal to the Sinn Féin leaders among others. Senior sources in Dublin said Blair's words were 'a very public soften-ing of his line'. However, Dublin believed Trimble had to get 'something' from the republicans which he could 'sell' to his party. Words from Sinn Féin could be important, depending on 'how good those words are'. In fact it was Dublin's line rather than Blair's that needed softening, according to some.

Adams gave a briefing to the media in a private room at the Royal Dublin Society premises in Ballsbridge, location for the *ardfheis*. As we sat around on armchairs and sofas, in a setting far removed from Belfast's Conway Mill, he said Sinn Féin had put forward proposals for resolving the impasse over weapons but he refused to spell these out in any detail. I was able to ascertain later in the day that they envisaged a wider role for General de Chastelain than had hitherto been the case. Indeed, nationalists had been discreetly critical for some time over the prevailing narrow interpretation of the General's role under the Agreement. They felt he should be seen to be more independent of the governments and the parties, since in their view the Agreement gave him the same level of independence as the chairman of the policing commission, Chris Patten, or the head of the new Human Rights Commission in the North, Professor Brice Dickson. Republicans did not envisage that the General would be in a position in the short term to report that IRA weapons had been decommissioned. They felt, however, that having been in cordial consultation with Martin McGuinness over a considerable period, de Chastelain should be able to report, for example, that Sinn Féin was fulfilling its obligation under the terms of the Agreement to 'work constructively and in good faith' with him. Republican sources said that Sinn Féin was prepared to offer significant forms of words on decommission-ing by way of reassurance to Trimble and the unionists.

Adams had said in an interview shortly before the *ardfheis* that the IRA probably would have disappeared by now if the 1994 ceasefire had been properly welcomed by London and the unionists. He now indicated in conversation that he regretted the comments because of the fuss being made about them. Meanwhile, Sinn Féin confirmed what had been common knowl-edge in media circles for some time, that its ministerial nominees for the new executive would be Martin McGuinness and Bairbre de Brún. Previously, McLaughlin's name had been in circulation and it was regarded as a significant move when McGuinness, with his formidable reputation as a republican chieftain, came to the fore instead. It was seen as the more militant element in the movement asserting itself.

Whether the pair would ever take up office was a moot point. Republicans were trying to generate a greater sense of urgency, claiming that if Blair failed to pressurise Trimble within two or three weeks into forming a cabinet that included Sinn Féin, loyalist attacks could wreck the process. There was a certain sense of urgency on the British side also because, with Scotland and Wales about to have devolved government, the third leg of the stool was still not in place.

The two governments had by now accepted that there would be no decommissioning in the immediate future and their thinking was focused on devising some other type of concession to offer Trimble. There was little indication of impending drama as Blair and Ahern arrived for another session of talks with the parties in Downing Street on Friday 14 May. Indeed there had been indications during the week of a lack of enthusiasm on Downing Street's part for further futile discussions and it was noteworthy that the announcement of the Friday session came via Dublin. The mood ahead of the talks was generally glum. Despite having put forward a plan of his own just recently, Adams was particularly gloomy, declaring that the UDA and LVF ceasefires were over. The mood behind the scenes in Sinn Féin was equally bleak and there was even a slight question mark at one stage over their attendance. It was also reported that Trimble had no wish to return for further negotiations. Sometimes a downbeat mood is created ahead of a meeting on the basis that, the lower the expectations, the greater the prospects for success. Was this synchronised gloom or genuine pessimism? There was no knowing for sure.

The document produced from these talks, which went on for ten hours, was on two A4 sheets of paper. It was never officially made public, despite or perhaps because of challenges to Trimble from Paisley and McCartney to 'lay it on the table'. There were leaks of its contents and I subsequently obtained a copy for my files. The Downing Street Draft, as it became known, was reportedly written by the Prime Minister himself. It began with the usual motherhood and apple pie but quickly got to the main point: 'All parties agree to the full implementation of all aspects of the Agreement, including the objective of achieving total disarmament and the complete withdrawal of all weapons from politics in Ireland. They accept that the issue of arms must be finally and satisfactorily settled and will do what they can to achieve the decommissioning of all paramilitary arms within the time-frame set down in the Agreement, in the context of the implementation of the overall settlement. The Independent International Commission on Decommissioning will now begin a period of intensive discussions with all parties and report back on progress before 30 June. In light of that report, all parties anticipate, without prejudice to their clear positions on this issue, devolution of power by June 30th.'

In view of these commitments, the Assembly parties intended to proceed to the appointment of 'ministers-designate', under the d'Hondt procedure, during the following week. 'Such ministers will take up office on devolution on or before June 30th.' The document added: 'The two governments will carry on doing all they can to give effect to the will of the people to see the Good Friday Agreement implemented in all its aspects, including institutions operating in shadow form, and for their part have made it clear that June 30th is the final date by which devolution must take place.'

The pivotal element in Blair's document was the General's report, in the light of which, devolution was supposed to take place. With qualifications, it had a strong similarity to the Sinn Féin plan, but nobody would admit this of course.

When Trimble brought the draft to a meeting of his Assembly team in Stormont at noon the next day, it did not go down well. In a vivid account of the proceedings, a dissident source said there was consternation: heads in their hands, Assembly members wondered what their leader had done. On the face of it, at least, the document was effectively saying that the republicans would 'do what they can' to achieve decommissioning (to most unionist ears this came across as 'nothing'); the d'Hondt procedure would be triggered during the coming week, with Martin McGuinness, of all people, as Minister-designate; the General would issue some sort of report, and then the Executive would 'go live'. Where was prior decommissioning? What about 'no guns, no government'?[1] Where was the guarantee of any decommissioning, any time, ever? Only two of the more intellectual members of the party found merit in the document. It was understood that at least eight of the 27 Assembly Members spoke against accepting it despite Trimble's insistence that actual decommissioning ahead of formation of an executive was in fact envisaged. Significantly, sources said Trimble made no serious attempt to 'sell' the draft and that the new plan failed to convince Empey, seen as the critical 'persuader' in the Assembly team. The consensus was that Empey's influence would be crucial in swaying the middle ground of unionist politics. 'Empey is the key man,' a top Dublin official said. Liberal unionist sources gave a more benign and low-key report of the meeting. The mood was that 'Somebody had better tell Tony there is an election on' (there were European Parliament elections the following month). It was not a case of people rejecting it outright, so much as saying, 'Where's the rest of it?' The theory and principles weren't in the document, an explanatory appendix was needed. The Assembly party members did not have a sense of what was in the Prime Minister's mind when he wrote the draft.

The fact of the matter was that, after all the talk, the guarantees, the *Sunday Times* interview and so on, prior decommissioning was gone and the unionists didn't like it. There was also a reluctance to take any major risks in advance of the European elections on 10 June especially since the UUP candidate, Jim Nicholson, was getting a hard time in the tabloid press and from opponents about his private life.[2] Unionists pointed out that there was a significant space between the 10 June poll and the 30 June deadline: three weeks was a long time in politics.

Had the unionist Assembly team 'bought' the Downing Street paper, it is understood there would have been a major statement from the two prime ministers announcing that the d'Hondt system would be triggered the following week. It seems Downing Street had briefed the Sunday papers on the outline of the proposals on Saturday morning, the day after the talks, and later primed them to expect a significant announcement at 5 pm. When it became clear that the unionists were holding back, it was thought there would be no statement at all from Downing Street and it came as a surprise when Blair named 30 June as the 'absolute' deadline for devolution (Scottish and Welsh devolution were set for 1 July.) Unionists had been used to a more compliant posture on London's part, with the usual understanding and sympathy for Trimble's internal difficulties, but it seemed Blair was determined to get all his devolution ducks in a row. Blair's decision was said to be in line with advice he received from the NIO Political Development Minister, Paul Murphy. Unionist nerves, at least at senior party level, were not good that weekend. Discontent with the document grew, rather than abating.

Trimble acknowledged later that 'Downing Street had reason to believe that I was going to recommend it', but he said that was on the assumption that all the detail would be worked out on Friday evening. 'What I left with was not complete,' he said.

If this were the case, why did Downing Street not issue some anodyne statement to the effect that 'progress' had been made but work was continuing? Why the need for an emergency meeting of UUP Assembly members and why the tip-off to the media to expect a significant announcement? Some nationalists felt in retrospect that Blair should have marched Trimble out to the waiting media to say, 'Look what we have just agreed'. Taylor had left Downing Street, but not by the media-guarded front entrance, at around 4 pm and had not reappeared. Perhaps if he had been there he would have counselled Trimble against giving Blair 'reason to believe' he would recommend the document.

While 14 May was rapidly becoming a day of ill-fame in unionist mythology, when London allegedly came close to selling Ulster down the river, reports of Trimble's demeanour as he emerged that Friday evening did not suggest a man bullied into submission. One theory, propounded by a nationalist and therefore not fully impartial, was that he fell victim to the seductive atmosphere of Downing Street and the flattering attentions of the Prime Minister.

At last Blair seemed to be biting the bullet. 'This could not have gone on indefinitely,' senior sources in Dublin said. Despite the interpretation on the part of many unionists that the 14 May document had sold the pass on decommissioning, some Dublin sources said decommissioning was still in there, not explicitly, but in a more insidious way than at Hillsborough. The 1 April text had only envisaged partial decommissioning but despite a claim by the chief of staff in Blair's office, Jonathan Powell, that this document had a 'far more modest' aim, it was in fact going for total disarmament, admittedly after the Executive was set up rather than before. This point was made by Blair himself in an article published later in *The Times*.[3]

These subtleties were not apparent, or not significant, to the UUP assembly team. The rejection of the document would normally have meant a return to Downing Street for further negotiations but Blair had upped the ante by announcing his 'absolute' deadline. He did not spell out publicly what the consequences would be if the deadline were missed but it was put about privately from unspecified, probably British Government, sources that the Assembly would be suspended, along with the generous salaries of its members – not to mention the expenses available to them.

A UUP statement on Monday 17 May reiterated the party position on the need for 'a credible and verifiable start to a process of decommissioning, before Sinn Féin can participate in government'. There was an ambiguity in the phrase 'start to a process'. Did it mean guns on the table or just preliminary steps towards that objective? In the last paragraph, the UUP repeated the line that Trimble 'did not present the [British] government's proposal as a final or agreed text to the Assembly members on Saturday. The proposal was incomplete and clearly insufficient in terms of clarity or substance'. This seemed to come as a surprise to Gerry Adams who called on Trimble 'to make his position clear'. He added: 'If this statement is an accurate account of what happened, then Trimble needs to explain why.' Seamus Mallon sounded a similar note, expressing surprise at the outcome of the UUP meeting because Trimble's reaction to the document in London 'seemed fairly positive'. Mallon claimed the arrangement was for each party to telephone Downing Street to confirm its acceptance of the text.

Blair's determination to secure devolution by the end of the month for Northern Ireland, in parallel with Scotland and Wales, had made a strong impression on the participants in the 14 May talks. He transformed what was forecast as a routine occasion by his insistence that progress must be made. Insiders got a sense that Dublin, which had been the driving force at Hillsborough, was now in the back seat. Republicans were initially much encouraged by the events of the weekend, not least Blair's decision to 'name the day' despite – or perhaps because of – the negative outcome of the unionist deliberations at Stormont. Yet as so often, worries began to accumulate afterwards. As republicans saw it, Trimble was trying to get off the hook once more and there were signs of equivocation from the governments. For their part, unionists were reportedly encouraged by the Taoiseach's statement in the Dáil that Dublin and London would have to 'reflect and assess' the situation if the 30 June deadline was not met. Reflection and assessment sounded remarkably like a review to some unionist ears and did not please Northern nationalists. Ahern hinted that he did not think the deadline such a great idea, stressing the difficulties for unionist parties of setting up an executive with Sinn Féin, less than a week before Drumcree Sunday. Yes, it was that time of year again.

It was not public knowledge at that stage that, in the aftermath of the UUP meeting, the Prime Minister's chief of staff, Jonathan Powell, sent Trimble a letter which was reportedly written in very close telephone consultation with Blair, who had left for the Balkans. This latest in the series of 'letters of comfort' came in response to a submission earlier in the day from Trimble and appeared at first glance to offer the UUP leader a pledge that Assembly standing orders would be changed so that, after the d'Hondt nominating formula had been applied, those chosen for ministerial posts would not even have 'shadow' status and their nominations would automatically lapse if devolution failed to occur by the 30 June deadline. The contents of the letter were leaked to the media by pro-Trimble sources but the version they released omitted the important qualification by Powell that any such change in standing orders would be 'subject to the views of other Assembly parties'.[4] Despite the qualifier, republicans were alarmed by some of the letter's implications. As they saw it, only two days after Blair had laid down an 'absolute' deadline for devolution, a letter in the name of his chief of staff was engaging in verbal acrobatics in order to appease the unionists. Interestingly, the letter referred rather pointedly to 'the text we agreed on Friday'.

Trimble's leadership style was unorthodox to say the least and he had puzzled many by flying off to the US and Canada as the European election campaign was gathering steam. On his return he was due to visit Israel for a few days to receive an honorary doctorate in Tel Aviv but a sectarian murder carried out in his constituency by loyalists led him to call off the trip.[5]

In parallel with the political stasis there was widespread dismay that continuing excavations for the remains of the 'disappeared' at locations identified by the IRA had so far failed to uncover any bodies. In time, some of the victims would be found, but the surprising thing about this episode was how little electoral damage it caused Sinn Féin in the European poll on both sides of the Border and in the local elections in the South: the republicans increased their vote significantly in both jurisdictions and the number of Sinn Féin local councillors in the Republic rose from 28 to 62.

The pessimists notwithstanding, Nicholson held the European seat for the unionists although his vote was reduced and he was almost 'caught' by McLaughlin of Sinn Féin, who was less than 2,000 votes behind him. Paisley held off Hume to top the poll for the fifth time in a row. He immediately claimed the result showed that 'a majority of the majority' was opposed to the Agreement and called for an immediate review. His assertive anti-Agreement approach had paid more dividends than the half-hearted stance of the UUP. Martin McGuinness drew my attention to the fact that the nationalist vote was the highest in the history of the North at over 300,000.

Blair moved quickly to promote the peace agenda, arriving in Belfast the day after the election count to kick-start the latest critical stage with an address to students at Stranmillis College. 'The alarm bells are ringing,' he told them. There was positive Sinn Féin reaction to the speech because of Blair's insistence that, 'We must return to the Good Friday Agreement', and his clear acknowledgment that 'Decommissioning is not a prior precondition of the Executive'. This marked the definitive end of the Hillsborough approach.

Blair's strategy was to address the ordinary people, over the heads of the politicians, no doubt hoping this would generate pressure for compromise. Instead of meeting party leaders, he took telephone calls from members of the public on Radio Ulster's popular *Talkback* programme. Admitting to some exasperation at the pace of progress he said: 'I have had talks and talks and talks and talks. I've had days and days and days of it and at some point people have got to come to a decision.'

The Taoiseach, who had previously spoken of the difficulties for unionists in meeting the deadline because it was so close to

Drumcree, had made an apparent U-turn and was now talking tough in the Dáil, warning that the Agreement would be 'set aside' and the Assembly might be suspended. He made clear that the idea of a shadow or 'pre-shadow' executive did not appeal to him. 'That makes no logical sense to me whatsoever.'

While talks and meetings continued, most people were holding their breath for the revival of the 'Tony and Bertie' show back in Northern Ireland. They were the only ones who had the clout with the republicans and the unionists to move them to a compromise position. Everyone knew from the beginning that it would go down to the wire: negotiations in this process were imbued with the psychology of the last-minute deal. A political symmetry had developed between Sinn Féin and the Unionists whereby movement from one side had become conditional on a cast-iron guarantee of reciprocal movement from the other. The Adams phrase about Trimble and himself 'jumping together' had become a central feature in strategic thinking on how to break the impasse. The UUP was harping on the 'no guns, no government' slogan although there was also a fair emphasis on the alternative phrase about 'a credible and verifiable start to a process of decommissioning'. Suggestions that the latter was a more flexible formula would not be entertained by the UUP leadership but some of their dissidents had cottoned onto the fact that it did contain loopholes. On the face of it, however, the gap between the two sides seemed as wide as ever and the challenge facing Blair and Ahern was to find imaginative ways of bridging that divide.

One of the unionist Assembly Members with a military background was reported to have said at Hillsborough that he did not want to talk to Sinn Féin, but to 'soldiers'. There was a certain irony here, in view of the UUP's famed reluctance to talk to Sinn Féin. He must also have forgotten the formidable history of some of the Sinn Féin representatives present, not to mention the constant reports, citing security sources, that there was a significant overlap between the upper echelons of Sinn Féin and the IRA Army Council. But he was reflecting a feeling, which was not confined to unionists, that an undertaking from the political wing of the movement was insufficient: they wanted words from the IRA itself. Throughout this phase of the process there were continuous calls for an IRA statement, either announcing that the 'war' was over or accepting that decommissioning was an 'obligation' – or both. Republican sources kept playing down the possibility of any such statement. The IRA had already ruled out decommissioning three times and it was suggested that any statement from that quarter might not be 'helpful'.

As part of his strategy of reaching out to the people, especially the younger generation, Blair did a one-hour special on UTV with a group of young people from different political and religious backgrounds. It was a minor disaster for the Prime Minister, with youthful unionist hardliners dominating the proceedings. Blair was told to his face that he was 'damaged goods'[6] because he had allegedly failed to keep his pledge to unionists on decommissioning. The PM looked like a man at the end of his tether with Northern Ireland and echoing his *Talkback* comment said: 'We have gone on talking and talking and talking. At some time people have got to make up their minds.'

The prime ministers came to Belfast on 25 June and settled into talks at Castle Buildings. Prior to their arrival, the main parties were giving non-committal reactions to an article by Blair in *The Times* in which he suggested republicans could be admitted to government without weapons up front, provided there was 'a clear guarantee of decommissioning by Sinn Féin *(sic)*' under a ten-month timetable laid down by General de Chastelain. In a key phrase, Blair added that there should be 'a cast-iron, fail-safe device' that if it didn't happen according to the timetable, that executive couldn't continue.[7] Leading unionists privately compared the Prime Minister's remarks favourably with his Stranmillis College speech, which was felt to be unduly close to the Sinn Féin position. Grave doubt still remained about the ability of the UUP leadership to sell any compromise to its Assembly team, many of whom were only interested in prior disposal of guns. Blair appeared to be trying to provide Trimble with a shield against his internal party critics by attaching conditions to the existence of any executive formed in the absence of decommissioning.

Following a series of meetings between the two prime ministers and the parties at Castle Buildings, Blair announced that agreement had been reached on the following three principles: (1) An inclusive executive exercising devolved powers; (2) Decommissioning of all paramilitary arms by May 2000; (3)

Decommissioning to be carried out in a manner determined by the International Commission. During their brief appearance to announce the agreement on principles, Blair and Ahern allowed no questions. Shortly afterwards Pat Doherty read a prepared statement from Sinn Féin, which welcomed the assertion from the two prime ministers that the Good Friday Agreement was 'binding' and 'the context for moving forward'. In what was seen as a significant passage, Doherty said: 'The three principles that they put forward, firmly bedded in the terms of the Good Friday Agreement, can resolve the impasse if there is the political will.' Trimble later expressed the hope that republicans were 'making their own Damascus road conversion by accepting their obligation to decommission'.

The choice of Doherty to read the statement was seen as significant, given his status in the pecking order. Official sources claimed an important step had now been taken. At the very least in the coming week there would be clarity: here are the principles, now let's see how we implement them. The unionists accepted – in principle – there should be an executive which included Sinn Féin. The republicans agreed – in principle – there should be total decommissioning by May 2000. And all parties agreed – in principle – decommissioning must be 'carried out in a manner determined by the Independent Commission on Decommissioning'. None of the parties shifted from their fundamental position, but there was an important reformulation of their views. Republicans correctly pointed out that there was nothing in the three principles which conflicted with the terms of the Good Friday pact. However, we were not used to hearing it stated in such stark terms that Sinn Féin, along with the other parties, was committed to the principle of total paramilitary decommissioning within ten months. Small wonder some elements in the media became very excited when they saw this written in black and white. The statement read by Doherty – a reassuring figure to militants – had to have been prepared more or less simultaneously with the Blair–Ahern text. Observers felt a definite sense of the republican constituency being stretched, in the now-famous Adams phrase, and of a leadership intent on ensuring the stretch did not reach breaking-point. Sinn Féin had made its heaviest verbal commitment so far to the principle of decommissioning, with the usual conditions and riders. The promise was there, the headline was in type – the rest was negotiations. The Ulster Unionists, too, had taken a risk. They had effectively handed the weapons issue over to General de Chastelain.

In an interview with myself at the time, Martin McGuinness outlined his perspective on the weapons issue: 'The challenge is to, first of all, set up the institutions, to inject dynamic into the process, to bring about the implementation of all aspects of the Agreement dealing with equality, injustice, human rights, policing, prisoners, and to effectively make that the engine of the process so that, once you effectively remove the reasons why people feel the need to rise up in arms, then the issue of how you remove all the guns from Irish politics becomes very straightforward.' He revealed that Sinn Féin had not formally asked the IRA to decommission: 'From our point of view in Sinn Féin, we – and maybe people think this is a fault – only like to ask the question when we have a fair idea of what the answer is going to be. The danger is that asking the question and getting a negative could actually be detrimental to the type of work which we are involved in.' There was only one question in the interview that seemed to cause the Mid-Ulster MP some momentary hesitation. Did he think the British and Irish governments knew what they were doing? 'I would like to think that the two governments know what they are doing,' he replied.[8]

As Monday 28 June dawned it seemed a critical day in the talks process was about to unfold, but instead it turned into a minor farce. The two prime ministers spent most of their time in an unsuccessful last-ditch effort to resolve the Drumcree stand-off, now drearily looming again. Round-table sessions on the decommissioning issue were postponed and finally cancelled. Nationalist parties ended up cooling their heels most of the day at Castle Buildings as Blair and Ahern held discussions with the Orange Order and the Garvaghy Road residents, to no avail.

There were alarming reports that two Provisional IRA members had been arrested transporting a bomb which, some versions held, was for the purpose of attacking Protestants participating in the 'Long March', a protest demonstration for 'Protestant civil rights' which was progressing through a number of towns in the North before finishing up at Drumcree. There was sharp Ulster Unionist reaction to reports immediately afterwards that two remand prisoners in Portlaoise had been accepted onto the

Provisional IRA wing, apparently arising out of the same incident. The UUP leadership was threatening to call for a determination by Mowlam as to whether the Provisional IRA and other ceasefires still held. Martin McGuinness insisted the ceasefire was 'rock solid'. It looked for a moment as if the process could be in serious trouble. Then, just as quickly, the problem evaporated. Claims by republican sources that the bomb-making equipment was simply being moved to a safer place, perhaps to keep it away from dissidents, and that no attack on the Long March was intended were apparently given credence in official quarters.

The incident showed how jumpy everyone was, especially the UUP, but it also suggested the process was acquiring greater resilience. In the US, Clinton said there was a 'good chance' the parties could reach agreement. Addressing unionist concerns on decommissioning, he pointed out that they could bring down the Executive at any time if commitments weren't kept. Clinton's remark epitomised the new approach by the governments since Hillsborough.

There was a rare outbreak of optimism among the media who were enclosed in a huge tent at Castle Buildings. This was probably based on the suggestion that the Provisionals had shifted their position and were subscribing to much milder rhetoric than heretofore on decommissioning. There were still those inside the talks who warned against complacency. There had been progress all right, but it was still a toss-up between breakthrough and breakdown. Sure, Sinn Féin was stretching as far as it could within its own interpretation of the Agreement, but there was still no guarantee that the deal would be good enough for Trimble to sell to his party. Special legislation to impose sanctions on Sinn Féin if the IRA failed to decommission was said to be among the ideas under consideration, although this notion was vehemently opposed by the republicans on the basis that it was outside the terms of the Agreement.

Blair had promised a report from de Chastelain 'before June 30th' and it was expected the previous afternoon. Word filtered out around lunchtime that it would be delayed. Blair's spin-doctors, making one of their regular visitations to the media tent, confirmed that the two prime ministers had held a half-hour meeting with the General and the other members of the decommissioning body. Although de Chastelain was ready to deliver, he agreed to delay presentation until next day to take account of progress which Blair and Ahern told him would be 'relevant to his report'. Fuller information on the prospects for the future was apparently being incorporated into the final text. Suggestions from sceptical elements in the media that the two governments would write the report, with the General simply putting his name to it, were firmly rejected as unfair. But even members of the Commission were reportedly amused by an Ian Knox cartoon in the *Irish News* which showed a stubble-cheeked Blair tossing a coin and saying to Ahern: 'Heads you write the de Chastelain report and I'll get the coffee.'

Provided with very little in the way of concrete information, the media were treated to a curious political dumb-show involving Trimble and Mallon. The pair, whose relationship was as chequered in its way as the one between Iran and Iraq, strolled together into the press tent to have some coffee. They refused to answer any serious questions, in an exercise clearly intended to be 'for the optics'. A show of unity, but did it have any substance?

As so often for reporters, it was a case of mooching around, trying to pick up odd scraps of information. SDLP sources said they were impressed by Blair's demeanour, describing it as 'steely'. The Prime Minister was determined not to leave empty-handed, as at Hillsborough. There was pain for all sides. 'Every party has to take its turn in the dentist's chair,' was how an Iveagh House official put it. There was considerable media interest in the presence of well-known republicans like Martin Ferris and the veteran Joe Cahill. A South Armagh man thought to be the head of the movement's 'unparliamentary side' was said to be in the vicinity, but nobody was sure what he looked like since he was rarely photographed. This report was later firmly denied by usually reliable republican sources. One of the wilder rumours was that Blair had sent Sinn Féin away and demanded, in effect, 'Bring me the head of the IRA Army Council'. The London-based *Independent on Sunday* paper later reported that Blair had in fact met the Army Council, but this was denied by Downing Street.[9] The reality was that there were so many seasoned republicans in Castle Buildings, it probably mattered little what hat they were wearing.

Republican sources poured scorn on the notion that their

movement was about to 'roll over' on weapons to get into government. They would go as far as they could in terms of language, but nothing was possible which went outside the Good Friday document. While republicans felt Trimble was inching towards a deal, there was an abiding fear that he would allow the prime ministers to squeeze every last drop of compromise out of Sinn Féin and then walk away.

Alastair Campbell was reassuring the media on Blair's behalf: 'Today has been better than yesterday and tomorrow will be better than today.' However, Sinn Féin sources warned repeatedly against an over-optimistic reading of the situation and described the 'spin' emanating from this quarter as excessively positive. Remember how you got burnt at Hillsborough, they told reporters.[10]

The morning of 30 June began with renewed expectation of the decommissioning report; not so much *Waiting for Godot* as Waiting for de Chastelain. Ignoring the smirks of some journalists, the Blair camp insisted it had not seen the text. The possibility was also mooted of a separate document from the governments and the parties, dealing with non-decommissioning matters. Spokesmen for both Ahern and Blair gave upbeat reports on the negotiations. Sinn Féin admitted some progress was made, but again warned against excessive optimism. Trimble said flatly: 'Little actual progress has been made.'

It was ascertained, however, that there had been significant progress in talks with Sinn Féin. Political sources said the party had hardened its verbal commitment to the principle of decommissioning and to using its influence to persuade the IRA to dispose of weapons, accompanied by the usual mantra that this must be done within the Agreement.

Official sources denied a timetable for decommissioning was envisaged. It was more a question of de Chastelain outlining a series of stages, intermediate and final, for fulfilling the decommissioning requirement in tandem with the rest of the Agreement. 'Most of the day was spent on Sinn Féin. The governments think they have a deal on that side and they are trying to sell it to Trimble.' The UUP leader's demeanour was encouraging; his bottom-line position still unclear. There was concern that he might have fallen back to his original demand for prior decommissioning but the governments were said to be holding

256

firm to the view that this was not contained in the Agreement. Sources close to republican thinking claimed the UUP leadership was engaged in 'a major poor-mouth exercise', highlighting the difficulties of selling any agreement to the party's members. The Taoiseach was seeking the maximum clarity on the positions of both Sinn Féin and the UUP. The key issue was what the unionists meant when they sought a credible start to the process of decommissioning – that phrase again – and whether this necessitated guns in advance of government. It emerged that the previous Friday's meeting between the UUP and the two prime ministers had been an intensely heated affair despite the claim by Blair and Ahern in their joint statement that all the talks were 'good-natured'.

The General's report was delayed yet again. Dame Rumour said it might only be his inaugural report, with another one to come later, 'when the IRA decommissioned'. Republicans continued to deny that short-term decommissioning was a 'runner'. Even a leading unionist said flatly: 'There might be some hope of Sinn Féin saying the war is over, but there's nothing to indicate decommissioning will happen by May 2000.' The swirl of rumour and counter-rumour was said to be having an unsettling effect on the republican movement and making life difficult for their negotiators.

The disposal of weapons might not be about to happen – indeed might never happen – but the issue had to be addressed. A form of words, an undertaking from republicans which would ensure that David Trimble did not have to face his party empty-handed, this was one of the focus points in negotiation. Five days earlier, the prime ministers had succeeded in pruning all excess verbiage from the republican stance on weapons, leaving only the bald declaration that, along with the other parties, Sinn Féin was committed in principle to the decommissioning of all paramilitary arms by May 2000. The next step was to harden this up to a point where unionists could have grounds for confidence that the principle would be translated into practice. There was room for creative diplomacy here because Sinn Féin had never ruled out the possibility of decommissioning as part of the Agreement. There had been indications late on the night of 29 June that this commitment to theoretical decommissioning might even extend to a notional calendar. Some journalists were calling it 'shadow decommissioning'. Sinn Féin was certainly winning 'brownie points' with the two governments, but the sceptics wanted to read the small print.

On the evening of 30 June, Blair's spokesman came out to tell reporters about the huge amount of time the Prime Minister and the Taoiseach were putting into the talks. 'There certainly can be a deal by midnight,' he said. 'If he didn't think he could do a deal he wouldn't stay here.' The spokesman everyone wanted to hear, though, was not Alastair Campbell but 'P. O'Neill', the pseudonymous signatory of IRA statements, who could perhaps play the role of *deus ex machina,* making the critical intervention that would clinch the deal. Undoubtedly, the two governments would have liked to hear him soften his hardline stance on decommissioning but the hours passed by and still nothing was heard from that quarter. If you heard it from P. O'Neill you were hearing it from the horse's mouth. In the absence of such a development, Dublin was said to be 'working on' Sinn Féin for a statement along such lines as, 'We believe we can successfully persuade the IRA to play its part in removing the guns from Irish politics.'

Word came through that Clinton[11] was calling the Prime Minister, and presumably everyone else. Blair and Trimble were due to attend the formal opening of the Scottish parliament in Edinburgh next morning, but now that looked problematic. The unionist mood was pessimistic: 'We had a meeting with the Irish Government and made it clear that sitting in a devolved executive without guns was not acceptable.' A great deal depended on John Taylor. The Strangford Showman's words contained little space for compromise but old hands said that if he saw an opening he would go for it. An academic unionist declared that Sinn Féin's language might get a D instead of an F from examiners but it was 'still not fit for unionist consumption'. Blair's 'absolute' deadline was 30 June but now there was talk of extending it and it was clear tough negotiations were still taking place. The missing ingredient had yet to be found.

After all the difficult and tortuous work with the republicans, the two governments felt they had probably come up with as strong a commitment on weapons as they were ever likely to get. True, it was only words, but words could lead to action and under the right circumstances there was meant to be virtual certainty of seeing guns on the table. Political insiders claimed the

Provisional Army Council was 'on side' for the new, improved Sinn Féin language; Blair grabbed headlines by talking-up the 'historic, seismic shifts' by both republicans and unionists, in a phrase which some felt was over the top.[12] If at the end of the day the republicans failed to deliver, then it was understood the Prime Minister would have legislation in place to ensure, so to speak, that no undecommissioned weapon went unpunished. This would be the 'cast-iron, fail-safe device' he had spoken about in his article for *The Times*. But the air turned blue when I mentioned this to a prominent republican. Yet while there would be no Sinn Féin welcome for a legislative mechanism, it seemed difficult to avoid under the prevailing 'equal gain, equal pain' principle. If all other aspects of the Agreement except decommissioning had been implemented, the institutions – Assembly, Executive, North–South Council – would go into suspended animation and a review of the whole process begin.

There was an unconfirmed report later that a senior republican made a dramatic dash to see the General at 11.30 pm, but Blair's 'absolute' deadline of 30 June still passed without devolution. The Prime Minister's spokesman was unfazed. What happens now? he was asked. 'What happens now is what's happening now.' This was presumably a reference to the continuing negotiations. Had the governments started work on Plan B? 'We're still working on Plan A.' The Prime Minister had been in bilateral meetings with the Taoiseach, David Trimble, Sinn Féin and the SDLP. There had been a phone conversation with President Clinton. Now he and the Taoiseach were chairing another round-table meeting of the parties where he would make clear there had been 'huge progress'.

There had been a lot of talk about the Prime Minister being exasperated, but now it was the turn of the nationalists and republicans. 'Ludicrous' was one SDLP negotiator's description of the latest turn of events. It was now the First of July: so much for deadlines. Instead of showing the unionists he meant business, Blair had turned around and asked everyone from the UUP to the Women's Coalition to submit position papers. What was he up to? Didn't he realise Sinn Féin wouldn't want anything specific on paper unless they knew they had a deal with Trimble and, even then, the words would be filtered through de Chastelain. John Major had to indulge David Trimble because of the parliamentary arithmetic, but New Labour had no such difficulty. Ahern had delivered Sinn Féin, now it was up to Blair to deliver the unionists. The lapsed deadline was a threat to his credibility. Had he known what he was about when he set 30 June as the outer limit of his patience?

It was reported that the Taoiseach was asked to go back to Sinn Féin to seek further improvements in their position but that this move met with polite disbelief, given how far the republicans felt they had come already. It appeared as if the republicans had moved, or at least reformulated their position, and the pressure was now on Trimble. The request for papers sounded like a way of buying time.

Adams stressed the fateful nature of the proceedings. 'What people in the building have to decide is whether they want this process to collapse; whether in particular they want to hand the initiative, which is still the best opportunity for peace this century, back to those who are against change.' Asked if Sinn Féin had changed its position on decommissioning during the day, Adams replied simply: 'Yes.' He did not elaborate.

Trimble countered that he had no concrete proposals from Sinn Féin. He had seen press reports that the IRA might give an undertaking to abide by a decommissioning timetable: 'No such precise undertaking has been offered to us, nor have we seen any details about a timetable or schedule.' Suggestions that an executive could be formed, with decommissioning starting in three to six months, were 'simply not in the real world at all'. There was a need for 'concrete confidence-building measures' in the same time-frame as the formation of the Executive. Clearly he wanted at least simultaneous decommissioning.

Talks dragged on through the day and into the early hours. The de Chastelain report was finally delivered to the two governments but there was some doubt as to whether it would be given any wider circulation. Its release was said to be 'conditional to some extent' on agreement being secured with the Ulster Unionists. If the deal fell through, there would be an official reluctance to reveal how far Sinn Féin had been persuaded to go on the arms issue, under specified conditions, lest it jeopardise future peace efforts.

The hope of the two governments was said to be that the General's assessment of the decommissioning issue would persuade the UUP to agree the immediate formation of an executive, including Sinn Féin ministers, in the expectation that arms disposal would begin by the end of the year. Advance indications of the report's contents said the General would give it as his opinion that, in the context of full implementation of the Agreement, Sinn Féin would be in a much stronger position to persuade the IRA to begin decommissioning by the end of the year. It was a subtle distinction.

The UUP Assembly team met at Castle Buildings and it was reported Blair had offered to address them. Sinn Féin spokesmen refused to comment on a report that Blair had suggested Adams should also address the unionists. An SDLP source said privately that Sinn Féin had the UUP 'on the hop' because the republicans had held out the possibility of a start to IRA decommissioning by the end of the year provided there was immediate formation of an inclusive executive. Instead of accepting this offer, Trimble was isolating himself by insisting on weapons being destroyed right away.

A late-night meeting between Sinn Féin and the unionists went badly. Without taking the time to put on their ties, the normally dapper Adams and McGuinness emerged spitting fire. The media had umbrellas or raincoats, but the Sinn Féin group stood bareheaded and unflinching in their jackets, shoulders back like soldiers in a barracks square, hardly noticing the rain that fell on them as Adams execrated the unionists. I watched the drops form on the greying head of Martin Ferris and wondered what was going on in the mind of this classic republican who was jailed for ten years in 1984 for his part in trying to import six tons of arms from the US and was perhaps the most prominent republican south of the Border. Adams declared that his party's initiative had 'failed' because of unionist intransigence. He released the text of a Sinn Féin declaration which stated that as part of the overall implementation of the Good Friday Agreement and with the formation of an inclusive executive, 'we believe that all of us … could succeed in persuading those with arms to decommission them in accordance with the Agreement'.

Yet even as Sinn Féin indicated the negotiations were doomed, word was also coming through that all was not lost. A deal could still be on the cards: the unionists were nibbling. They were comfortable with the assurance that if Sinn Féin went back on its word, there would be sanctions. There could still be a breakthrough, based on joint proposals from Ahern and Blair to be made to the parties after everyone had a night's sleep. Talks participants said Blair had scored a major negotiating success with the unionists by persuading them to give due weight to his legislative proposals to provide for penalties in the event that decommissioning failed to take place. The Prime Minister had met the UUP Assembly team for over half-an-hour in a question-and-answer session. The legislative guarantee was a key ingredient in what was described as a very successful meeting; Blair told them that they would have sight of the Bill within a week. A formula put forward face-to-face by Sinn Féin to the unionists had been rejected, but the de Chastelain report could have a different reception. The two governments were convinced that the republican movement was serious about decommissioning. This view would also be propounded by de Chastelain in his report. It would be a good deal easier for the unionists to accept a recommendation from the General and the two governments than directly from Sinn Féin. The next stage of the process was to persuade the unionists to accept the de Chastelain text. If the unionists were satisfied, a meeting of the Ulster Unionist Council could take place within ten days to approve participation in an inclusive executive.

Republicans were privately very dismissive of suggestions that the unionists would accept from de Chastelain what they would not buy directly from Sinn Féin. It was just a case of the prime ministers seeking a 'soft landing' for a failed negotiation.

Friday 2 July was a slow day with little indication of what, if anything, was going on inside Castle Buildings. Rumours swept the media village: one of the first to be knocked on the head was the idea of Sinn Féin being expelled from the Executive if decommissioning failed to take place. This elicited a dismissive eight-letter Anglo-Saxon expletive from a normally reserved Irish government official. There was a review clause in the Agreement which could be invoked if there were problems with Sinn Féin or any other party for that matter. It turned out later that suspension of the whole thing, not expulsion of one party, was what was envisaged.

Papers were flying around the interior of Castle Buildings like confetti. There was greater calm in the UUP's Assembly team than previously: they were described as 'reasonably stable' and in fact somewhat more relaxed than their leader at the prospect of a deal. It was Trimble's call: the people around him were looking to the leader.

There was concern in the Sinn Féin constituency. Although it was sneered at by some, their language on decommissioning was stronger than many had expected. 'Some of the rank and file are certainly not happy,' informed sources said. Sinn Féin's leaders were also upset. Was Tony Blair going to lay it on the line to Trimble? There had been enough pussyfooting. Sinn Féin wanted this prime minister to keep his date with history. As for the unionists, republicans were wondering if anything was acceptable to them. And no paper on exclusion clauses had been put to Sinn Féin, sources said. The party would not sign it. Republicans had their own internal tensions and reports from Castle Buildings indicated robust discussions inside their delegation – Sinn Féin only being a monolith on the outside. One republican member of the Assembly was heard to moan in the corridor, in mild exasperation, 'F*** this for a game of cowboys. Up the 'Ra[IRA].'

There were lively discussions, too, between members of the UUP Assembly team and the many anti-Agreement unionists who hung about Castle Buildings all week, with Robert McCartney and his former party colleague Cedric Wilson well to the fore. A fair amount of finger-wagging was done by the No camp, and a hapless Trimble aide was greeted by a chorus of tut-tuts from DUP members whenever he entered the canteen. It was said that one of the NIO ministers kept a UUP dissident talking for an hour to prevent the latter from lobbying pro-Agreement colleagues.

De Chastelain's report was finally released. Sinn Féin had already revealed the party's hand on decommissioning the night before and now the General said there was 'the basis for believing that decommissioning can be completed in the time prescribed by the Good Friday Agreement'. There was comparatively little of a concrete nature in the report on the latest developments and no detailed timetable was set down – that would await discussions with the paramilitary groups. In truth and after all the negotiations, it was thin enough gruel: 'The Sinn Féin statement of 1 July offers promise that decommissioning by all paramilitary groups may now begin.' Significantly and fatefully, the UUP's Security Spokesman and one of the party's chief risk-takers for peace, Ken Maginnis, made the damaging point that the document failed to confirm 'the absolute commitment of paramilitary organisations to disarm within the time-scale as required'.

Then, suddenly, there seemed to be white smoke. At around 5.20 pm I received a phone call from a prominent nationalist who told me: 'There's going to be a deal.' Another well-placed contact on the British side said, with no hint of irony, 'Hold the front page'. The torpor in the press tent began to be disturbed as news seeped in that business was being done on the other side of the barrier, inside Castle Buildings. Tony and Bertie had done it, we were told. The initial reaction was sceptical. There had been too many false dawns since we gathered in the media village five days before.[13]

The shape of the 'deal' began to leak out. There would be an agreed sequencing plan. The ministers would be nominated; devolution would follow in short order; the General would get into high gear on decommissioning and there would be a failsafe mechanism in case it didn't take place. However, the parties, especially the UUP, would not have to sign up to the package right away. It was all very upbeat. There was confidence that the Ulster Unionist Council (UUC) could be delivered. Some Dublin officials were confident there would be total decommissioning by the IRA and colleagues of theirs who had expressed scepticism were subjected to some gentle ribbing.

It was raining as Blair and Ahern emerged from Castle Buildings at about 7.30 pm to announce their initiative in a two-page document entitled *The Way Forward*. The plan was aimed at ensuring the full implementation of the Agreement, with the establishment of new institutions including a devolved government. It proposed the nomination of ministers on 15 July, with a devolution order laid before parliament at Westminster next day. In the meantime, the decommissioning body would have urgent discussions with 'points of contact' agreed by paramilitary groups. Decommissioning would start 'within a specified time' set by de Chastelain and there would be three progress reports, in September, December and the following May. If commitments on decommissioning or a devolved executive were not met, the governments undertook to suspend the operation of the institutions set up under the Agreement, principally the Executive.

The UUP leaders were happy, it was said, but would imitate Gerry Adams on Good Friday by saying they had to consult their party. That could be fraught: there would be dissidents, secret meetings and cabals, with politicians from both factions engaging in operatics, all the drama and emotion that accompany those moments when an attempt is made to shift a political movement on its axis.

The governments were prepared to accept Sinn Féin's good faith on the weapons issue, but would that, allied to the General's document, be enough for Trimble and his people? The word coming out from a meeting of the Ulster Unionist Assembly group was that no decision had been taken. No news was good news, perhaps, but the coming fortnight would be a long one. The Assembly would be suspended if the joint Irish–British plan was not accepted within a fortnight, the Taoiseach said.

Dissident unionists said they would be watching carefully for any shift by Trimble from the official party policy of 'no guns, no government'. Should the UUP leadership advocate acceptance of the Blair–Ahern document, which contradicted the party manifesto, dissidents said the required 60 signatures would be produced so that the issue could be thrashed out at the UUC. This would be 'the last great debate of this process' within the UUP and would end up in a split or a change of leadership.

Meanwhile, a senior IRA figure was expected to be nominated to discuss the modalities of weapons disposal with the General. Sources close to republican thinking said there was a 'definite commitment' to decommissioning but, inevitably, this statement was accompanied by the proviso that all the aspects of the Agreement were being implemented.

Contrary to widespread speculation, a Trimble aide and a number of his parliamentary and Assembly colleagues insisted that he would not call a special meeting of the UUC. Ominously, it was said a number of those closest to him in the party cautioned against this late on Friday afternoon on the grounds that it could split the party.

Two days later I was at Drumcree, sitting in the lunchtime sun behind police and army lines. Across a tiny river, Orangemen and their supporters stood, again asserting their right to march down the Garvaghy Road, which had again been barred against them. The crowds were not as big as previous years: the steam had gone out of it, at least for the time being. A massive display of force by the authorities and the reluctance of middle-ground, law-abiding Orangemen to become involved in confrontation had served to weaken a protest which in the past had threatened to spark off civil war. The British Government was taking the kind of stance on the security front that republicans and some nationalists wanted them to adopt politically. On a transistor radio, I listened to Ahern give a feisty interview to RTE's *This Week*, where he outlined the merits of the new initiative and appealed to the IRA to make a statement to ease unionist fears. Contacts in republican circles again poured cold water on any prospect of comforting words from the IRA. One of the ironies of the process was that the weaker and more divided Ulster Unionists appeared to be, the greater their influence over political developments. Like worried relatives standing around the bed of a hospital patient, the governments and parties wrung their hands and wondered what remedies could be applied to effect a miracle cure. 'The UUP is in such a desperate state that everybody that can help them should do so,' said one worried SDLP figure.

However, the IRA would not help; the SDLP might provide tea and sympathy but, in view of political realities, the party could hardly give a cast-iron guarantee to form an executive without Sinn Féin if the IRA failed to decommission. Sinn Féin meanwhile complained it was being given far less leeway than the Ulster Unionists.

The unionists continued their deliberations. 'Controlled fury' was the reaction of anti-Agreement party officers at their meeting in Glengall Street the morning after the joint initiative was launched. Friends said the leader's mood had often been better. With the Prime Minister pushing him one way and party dissidents the other, perhaps this was understandable.

The conciliatory noises from Blair to the unionists were making Sinn Féin distinctly nervous. British government sources shrugged their shoulders, saying in effect that *realpolitik* required the PM to send signals to the unionists that he understood their fears and the unavoidable side-effect of this was republicans becoming twitchy. What else was new?

I was struck by how little faith either nationalists – including both the SDLP and elements in Dublin – or republicans still had, despite all his efforts, that Tony Blair was 'for real'. The old ingrained suspicion of Perfidious Albion survived. The Prime Minister called off a trip to Poland so he could be on hand over the weekend. His work in other areas must have been suffering because of the prolonged focus on Northern Ireland. All that would be forgotten of course if the power-sharing inclusive government could be established.

Unionist sources said their decision would be made at 'five minutes to midnight'. The fact that the 'Twelfth' parades were looming did little to improve the atmosphere for unionist compromise. Having for years insisted that Sinn Féin was just the IRA without a mask, the Unionists still wanted the IRA to echo and confirm Sinn Féin's commitment to the principle of decommissioning. This implied that they regarded the two organisations as separate, but when the Taoiseach declared his belief around this time that, yes, they were distinct entities, Unionists rejected this outright. Republican insiders insisted the best way to obtain a statement from the IRA was to ask for it privately rather than publicly. Sinn Féin was pleased with Ahern's distinction between the two organisations. The unionist argument was that if they sought a guarantee of decommissioning from Sinn Féin, they would be told that Sinn Féin could not speak for the IRA.

The process had survived on what an academic observer called 'constructive ambiguities'. The resources of the English language had been stretched almost to breaking-point to devise formulae which allowed both sides to claim victory. The shooting had stopped, apart from occasional incidents, but the argument over who was right and who was wrong had still not been settled. Time and again the decommissioning obstacle was overcome by constructively ambiguous language. Even now it was clear the IRA would only contemplate a plan to destroy or abandon its guns if it did not amount to saying, 'We were wrong'.

In the various government departments, the offices for the new ministers were ready, civil service advisers and backup teams had been assigned and the official cars waited in their garages. All aspects of Northern Ireland devolution were in place and had been for some time: all that remained was for Trimble and his Assembly team to throw the switch and the machinery of the inclusive power-sharing administration would come into operation.

McGuinness returned to the US, meeting representatives of the National Security Council in Washington on 12 July. Although the Castle Buildings negotiations had been held in private, it was understood McGuinness and his colleagues – principally Adams, Ferris and Gerry Kelly[14] – had impressed their interlocutors in the two governments with their genuineness. The scepticism in the media and elsewhere about Sinn Féin's intentions was not shared by senior figures on the official side in the negotiations from Dublin, who praised what they describe as the 'courage' of Adams and McGuinness and their commitment to the new institutions with all their 'prizes and pain'. They also spoke very favourably of Trimble and what they saw as his courageous stance against the rejectionists in his party.

While there was undoubtedly a considerable amount of unease in republican ranks, fuelled by a lack of clarity on the commitments given by their political leaders in the talks, reports from different quarters said there was no sign of mutiny or a split. McGuinness had been reassuring activists in New York on 11 July. A meeting in the city the previous week was addressed by Rita O'Hare and sources described it as lively but not fractious. The audience included some notable 'hard men' but no significant expressions of dissent were reported.

There was growing speculation about Mowlam's future. A Cabinet reshuffle was widely expected by the end of the month, and there had been suggestions she was likely to be 'sacrificed' as a gesture to the unionists. Neither Dublin nor the SDLP would wish to see her badly treated. 'There would not have been a Good Friday agreement without her,' Dublin sources maintained. The fact that she was as popular as Blair – if not more so – in the Labour Party was not considered advantageous in the circumstances. In the end, she 'cheeked' the Prime Minister by declaring publicly that she was not ready to leave.[15] Blair left her where she was – for the time being.

A meeting of the Ulster Unionist executive on 9 July carried a motion rejecting the Blair–Ahern document and was then adjourned until 14 July, just before the day for the nomination of ministers. There was also the delicate matter of a DUP motion at the Assembly to exclude Sinn Féin from office. This had 29 signatures – including the UUP Assembly Member who lost the whip, Peter Weir – but one more was required, under Assembly rules, before it could be debated. It seemed clear that the UUP leadership would like to oblige the Prime Minister and form the power-sharing Executive but not at the expense of their own skins. Trimble went to Dublin at short notice on 11 July to see Ahern and made clear that it was virtually impossible for him to back the deal. The same message was getting through to Blair because, as the week wore on, the Prime Minister publicly indicated that he knew Trimble's position was impossible.

When Blair's 'failsafe' legislation was published, Sinn Féin sent out Alex Maskey to say republicans and nationalists were 'furious' over its contents. Trimble's response in the Commons to the legislation disappointed the British, who had gone to enormous trouble and postponed other measures before the Commons in order to facilitate him. The amendments he proposed were politically difficult. If 'softer' amendments had been put forward, London could presumably have made a great show of accepting them. Trimble's approach doubtless reflected the UUP leader's assessment of his political position: he had obviously decided to let the hardliners rule for now. Reports from London indicated that the British were resigning themselves to the idea that Trimble could not deliver his party at this stage. Sources close to the UUP leader had been saying for some time that he personally wanted to see the Executive formed, but was deeply uncertain about which way the party would jump.

There was some excitement at Stormont when news came through that the Secretary of State had finally 'triggered' d'Hondt. At least the procedure would now have to be gone through. The indications were that Trimble would not be nominating anyone for the three ministerial posts to which the UUP was entitled. The resumed meeting of the Ulster Unionist executive on 14 July came to an abrupt end after fifteen minutes. Trimble read the policy motion carried five days earlier, rejecting the *Way Forward* document and said that, on the basis of what he had heard since, he was not recommending any change. There was applause and members sang *God Save the Queen*.

Unionists were remarkably tight-lipped about their next move. In the morning, the media were contacted to say that the Assembly team would be holding a news conference outside Glengall Street at 10 am. A heavy downpour forced reporters to seek shelter in doorways as they waited for the unionists to appear. First out was prodigal son Peter Weir. This meant the DUP motion would now have only 28 signatories. A triumph for Trimble in the narrow context of unionist infighting, but at what cost to the process in general? All the Assembly team finally emerged and there was good-humoured jostling as media and politicians sought to keep a foothold on the narrow pavement, with the usual motor traffic in the background. Trimble announced what had been strongly signalled the night before: he would not be nominating unionist ministers. The additional twist was that he was not even attending at Stormont, nor were his colleagues from the Assembly team. Clearly his objective was to avoid a situation where UUP members were placed under moral pressure by the DUP and others to back the exclusion motion directed against Sinn Féin. Thus Trimble was closing one door but leaving another ajar. Had he wholeheartedly gone over to the No camp, he would have backed the DUP move.

The Assembly proceedings were reduced to farce by the absence of the largest party. The Speaker, Lord Alderdice, called for nominations from the UUP but was confronted by empty chairs. The DUP appeared somewhat nonplussed at the turn of events and, when asked to bring forward nominations, Paisley sought and was given a recess of fifteen minutes. Back in Glengall Street, the UUP were watching on television and they roared with laughter at the sight of Paisley wrongfooted.[16]

On his return to the chamber, Paisley told the Speaker his party would not be proposing anyone for ministerial posts. The SDLP and Sinn Féin went ahead, however. There was some embarrassment for the SDLP when, after John Hume had proposed Eddie McGrady for a ministry, the South Down MP stood up to say he did not want his name to go forward. Under Mowlam's standing orders, the Executive could only be established on a cross-community basis, i.e. with unionist participation, which meant that in any cabinet likely to be given power, the main nationalist party would have three ministers apart from Seamus Mallon. However, McGrady was the fourth name put forward, which indicated that he would probably not get a portfolio in the 'real' government. A full list of ten ministers was completed, composed of the SDLP, Sinn Féin and Alliance. Since the unionists were not on the list, Alderdice had to declare that the Executive could not be formed. Afterwards Mark Durkan, when asked what he had been minister for, replied: 'About ten minutes.'

If there was farce, there was high drama too. Seamus Mallon stood up, more ashen-faced than usual, to announce that he was resigning as Deputy First Minister-designate. His speech was a very pointed attack on Trimble who, despite the concessions from London, still had not been able to do the business. Never a man to mince his words, Mallon accused the unionists of attempting to 'bleed this very process dry' by seeking more and more concessions from the two governments. 'They are dishonouring the Agreement. They are insulting its principles.' Stark charges, but it was clear the Newry–Armagh MP's patience was at an end.

The balance-sheet at the end of the day was grim, from a pro-Agreement point of view. Trimble had blocked Sinn Féin entering government but at the expense of becoming a prisoner – for the time being at least – of his own right wing. He had achieved a united party but on a basis of implicit rejection of the Good Friday Agreement. He had delighted his most bitter opponents in the unionist camp and dismayed those who thought he could move towards his self-proclaimed goal of a pluralist parliament for a pluralist people.

However, if there were pluses and minuses for the UUP leader, it seemed almost entirely negative for Tony Blair. He certainly deserved full marks for trying, but there were doubts over the political wisdom of throwing every concession within his power at Trimble when he was almost inevitably going to be spurned in the end.

Looked at in a certain light, Sinn Féin might have seemed clear winners. The argument that the whole decommissioning issue was a unionist smokescreen for atavistic opposition to power-sharing with 'the other side' could now get a much wider hearing. The Ides of July was not a good day for the leadership, however, who now faced more questioning and criticism from sceptical followers, along the lines of: 'You made concessions to the unionists and they threw them back in your face; you put your faith in the British and they let you down.'

The main winner, on the face of it, was the No camp in the UUP; to retain his leadership, Trimble was forced to sing from their hymnsheet. It was too early to say the rejectionist unionists had scored a permanent victory: Trimble had not disavowed the entire process, nor had he walked away from the table. But whatever trust he enjoyed among nationalists had largely evaporated and would be very difficult to restore.

The biggest loser was the SDLP. This, after all, had been John Hume's game-plan for at least a quarter of a century. Out of many bitter and disappointing days for the SDLP leader, 15 July, 1999, must have been among the worst. The strain on the man was visible but his quest for peace would continue and, like Sisyphus, he would roll the stone back up the hill no matter how many times it rolled down. It was a bitter day too for Seamus Mallon and, although doubts would grow about the wisdom of his decision to step down, he had emerged with more credit than most. It was not every day a politician quit a £62,556-a-year position on a point of principle.

Sadness was the main emotion around Stormont among those who believed the future of the two communities depended on the historic compromise of Good Friday. There was a smell of political death about the place: staff worried about their jobs and visitors crowded into the gift-shop to buy souvenirs as though collecting the last remaining pieces of the Berlin Wall. Even reporters who had waited outside Glengall Street for Trimble's announcement found it a slight shock to come into the Assembly chamber and see the UUP benches deserted. The majority party on one side of the community had adopted an abstentionist tactic while, in the topsy-turvy scheme of things, Irish republicans were being nominated to become, in theory anyway, ministers of the Crown. There was no more fragile plant than democracy in Northern Ireland and these events were the equivalent of a sharp frost from which it would be extremely difficult to recover. In any normal society, a 71 per cent vote of approval for a new political dispensation would see the people's will being implemented with haste. Since the end of May 1998, it could be argued that there had been the equivalent of a creeping constitutional coup which scored a triumph in the rain that morning outside Glengall Street.

The Mallon resignation came as a surprise to the UUP leadership, and indeed to everyone else at Stormont, despite the fact that he had hinted publicly at such a move. UUP sources said party strategy was to seek to have a Deputy First Minister, preferably Mallon, back in place within a short period and they complained that Mallon had stepped down in a 'fit of pique'.

Professor Paul Bew, a close associate of the UUP leader's, wrote later in *The Irish Times* that the First Minister was tempted to follow Mallon's example: 'Trimble is a proud man. It was difficult work behind the scenes to persuade him not to resign as First Minister ... even though that might have finished the Agreement there and then, as it was unlikely there were enough unionist Assembly votes to place him back in office.'[17]

While the UUP leader was muted in his public reaction to Mallon's criticisms, some of his party colleagues were less reticent. Relations had never been great, they said, but had turned decidedly icy the previous December in the negotiations on cross-Border bodies. The fierce tension during that long-drawn-out saga had been forgotten by the general public, but politicians have longer memories, and unionists recalled how 'Mallon led a vicious attack on us'. Criticism of Trimble by his ministerial colleague in a Channel Four documentary did not go down well either.[18] There was also constant UUP irritation with Mallon's characterisation of the unionist stance on disarmament as absolutist. The party had moved from decommissioning before the formation of an executive to simultaneous delivery of 'guns and government' and complained that it never got credit for this from Mallon.

The focus on blaming the UUP rather than Sinn Féin in Mallon's Assembly speech was also bitterly resented by the unionists. It put the spotlight on Trimble. UTV interviewer Mike Nesbitt wanted to know, not just how long Trimble would stay on as First Minister but whether he would now be returning his Nobel Peace Prize. 'No, because I earned it and I am continuing to earn it,' was his reply.

However, it would be a mistake to narrow the causes of the crisis down to a personality clash between two politicians. The roots of the problem went much deeper. The approach and technique of the two prime ministers may have had more to do with the breakdown than the fact that neither David Trimble nor Seamus Mallon suffered fools gladly. Nobody could dispute the commitment of Blair and Ahern to the process which was such as to silence the cynics with their charges of self-seeking and opportunism. The question was, however, did they go about it the right way? Ahern helped to entrench the UUP in their 'no guns, no government' stance by appearing to take a similarly hard line in his *Sunday Times* interview of 14 February. For a period the 'spin' from Dublin was, if anything, harder than anything emanating from Glengall Street. Unionists were merely saying the IRA must carry out prior decommissioning, but Dublin was going one further by adding a forecast that this would in fact take place. This provided the basis for the abortive Hillsborough Declaration.

Republicans were adamant that they never gave any indication to the two governments that prior decommissioning was on the cards. When the 1 April document was released, the republican hard men and women hit the roof. The uncharitable thought occurred that the need for Blair, in particular, to look good might have had more to do with the publication of the Hillsborough text than any likelihood of political success.

Having failed to 'bounce' the IRA into prior decommissioning, the two governments seemed to reel back to a position of bringing unionism round. Certainly there was more 'give' on that side of the house, but Trimble had painted himself into such a corner on the issue that it was incumbent on Sinn Féin to try and help him out. Again the 'spin' that was put on events served the peace process badly. Blair's talk of a seismic shift in the republican stance on arms oversold the position. There certainly was a change in Sinn Féin rhetoric which, in a movement where words can be a matter of life and death, signalled a deeply underlying change of outlook. The people who had brought about two republican ceasefires were now pledging to use their best efforts to achieve total IRA decommissioning as part of the full implementation of the Agreement.

Turning republicanism eventually on to the constitutional road was on offer. Unionists and others were suspicious: beware the Greeks bearing gifts. However, there was certainly a compelling argument for the short-term formation of an executive to see whether the IRA was bluffing. Instead of refusing to come to Stormont on 15 July, Trimble could have stayed away in a few weeks' time. Pragmatic realists might argue it was an offer worth taking, but long-standing suspicion and fear of the enemy meant that, for unionists, it was a bridge too far.

Chapter 11

'WE'LL BURN THAT BRIDGE WHEN WE COME TO IT'

Now it was time to activate Plan B. The rumour mill had mythologised this into an elaborate counter-strategy devised by the two governments but instead it turned out to be, 'If at first you don't succeed, try, try again'. No suspensions, no punishments, just further talks. It would be known as 'a review into the implementation of the Agreement'. George Mitchell had pulled it off before, why not give him another try? Almost immediately, the Senator was invited to meet Blair and Ahern in London 'to discuss what role he might play to take the parties forward'. The long arm of the peace process was reaching out to bring him back to chair the Review. For all his celebrated fortitude and public stoicism, Mitchell would have been less than human had he not felt a certain weariness of spirit as he returned to reconcile the warring factions again in early September.

There was a near-total media blackout this time: where once there was a tent of Barnum and Bailey proportions and you could hobnob with some of the most famous faces of the small screen – Jeremy Paxman here, Jon Snow over there – now there were only two tiny prefabs, provided after intense lobbying; four telephones; and a row of portable toilets without any lighting. Supporters of the blackout, which was in line with Mitchell's overall approach to the Review, acknowledged it did not make journalists' lives any easier, but claimed it was contributing to the most serious engagement so far between the Ulster Unionists and Sinn Féin.

Whatever the cause, there was no denying that the relationship underwent a transformation. The talks were very tough until the venue moved briefly across the water on 13 October to the US Ambassador's residence in London, Winfield House. The media were not told about it, but enterprising BBC journalist Mark Simpson got a tip-off and managed to secure some footage, through a hole in the back fence, of Adams and McGuinness looking out a window and the UUP's Reg Empey and Dermot Nesbitt walking in the commodious gardens. Mitchell later revealed that he banned political discussion at mealtimes and insisted on other topics of conversation so that participants could come to view each other, not as opponents but as people. McGuinness was said to have discussed his favourite hobby, fly-fishing.

Reporters gleaned that David and Martin (it was first-name terms we heard) were generally getting on well but that the Adams–Trimble relationship still had rocky moments. The unionists defrosted and Sinn Féin also 'lightened up', treating their old adversaries as political leaders in their own right rather than lackeys of British imperialism. Two years earlier, in September 1997, McGuinness gave an intriguing interview to the *Observer* in which he spoke of the 'love' that developed between the two sides in the South African conflict once they entered into serious negotiations – it was unusual language for a man with his reputation as a militant.[1] It was possible now to discern the growth of something not unlike friendship in the contacts between republicans and unionists and one even heard the surprising news that, after all their criticism of Trimble's refusal to 'face down his rejectionists', republicans had come to admire and respect his courage.

There was no love in the peace process yet, though, and it needed more than sociability to succeed. The deal still had to be struck, the risks taken, the rank-and-file on both sides persuaded, placated and cajoled. The biggest risk, initially, was for Trimble to take. He had to make the first move: allowing an executive to be formed with Sinn Féin in the absence of 'product', as the long sought-after consignment of Semtex and rifles was called. Although John Taylor had refused to take a direct part in the negotiations after the discovery of an apparent IRA gun-smuggling operation in Florida,[2] he wrote in the *News Letter* that any agreement in the Review must be 'underwritten and guaranteed by Provisional IRA'.

The Dublin-based commentator Eoghan Harris, credited with the bulk of Trimble's Nobel Prize acceptance speech, had given an impassioned address to the UUP annual conference at Enniskillen on 9 October, urging delegates to set up the executive with Sinn Féin without prior decommissioning. 'Where do you get the arrogance to think it was your job to disarm the IRA? It is the job of the [British] Government to disarm the IRA,' he said. Harris had been a leading republican intellectual in the past and was now one of the IRA's harshest critics; his views were taken seriously by unionists. 'Look,' he said. 'Sinn Féin fought for 30 years. It's like a kid wanting a bike for Christmas. The bike they wanted was a united Ireland. They didn't get the bike. Please give them a few stickers.' Trimble was observed watching the speech from the press room 'with obvious pleasure'.[3]

The publication the previous month of the Patten Report on policing, proposing a root-and-branch revamp of the RUC, had generated ill-feeling in the unionist community but the 'feelgood factor' was restored to some extent with the replacement of Mowlam as Secretary of State by Peter Mandelson[4] in a cabinet reshuffle, a move already signalled in a press briefing by David Trimble.

Mowlam's role in helping to conclude the Good Friday Agreement would guarantee her a place in the history books, and her personal courage in carrying out her duties, despite having to undergo radiotherapy for a brain tumour,[5] was widely admired. She was initially in bad odour with nationalists after the Orange parade was forced down the Garvaghy Road in 1997, but quickly made up lost ground. Her efforts to be even-handed lost her friends in the unionist community who felt someone in her position should be solidly and assertively on their side. Her last major decision as Secretary of State was her ruling that the IRA ceasefire had not been breached by the murder of Charles 'Chucky' Bennett in Belfast during the summer. The body of the 22-year-old Catholic taxi driver had been discovered on waste ground off the Falls Road on 29 July. He was blindfolded, his hands were tied behind his back and he had been shot in the head. He was reported to have had close links with the republican movement and to have supplied information to the RUC since the 1994 ceasefire, when he was only seventeen, but his family denied claims that he was an informer.

Now the situation required someone who could persuade the unionists to go into the Executive in advance of decommissioning. Mowlam's contribution to the success of Good Friday helped ensure that she could not be that person and the UUP tended to bypass her and go directly to Downing Street. The job now passed to Mandelson, the legendary 'Sultan of Spin', who was credited with masterminding Labour's landslide in the 1997 general election. The fact that the Prime Minister's 'favourite son' was coming to Hillsborough Castle meant that the North was still very high on Blair's list of priorities. Although unionists welcomed the appointment, old hands remembered that they were generally quick to find fault with new secretaries of state.

The Review dragged on and finally, as it entered the tenth week in early November, Mitchell was reported to be 'taking the temperature' of the parties and assessing their willingness and capacity to strike a deal. A further report on decommissioning from de Chastelain was thought to be in preparation: it would hopefully have the effect of bolstering confidence that the para-militaries were serious about dealing with the weapons issue, pro-vided the 'context' (the latest buzz-word) was right and the other parties accepted their responsibility to create such a context. I had taken some time off to work on this book and returned to my duties on 8 November. For once, my timing was right: meetings at Castle Buildings that day were described as the most critical so far. These exchanges could shape the outcome of the Review – whether it would lead to the establishment of the Executive, or a 'soft landing' that would effectively amount to failure.

Contacts in the know whispered, 'The deal is there, but nobody is prepared to say it is set in stone.' The elements of a compromise were in place, but it could slip away at any time. Republicans emphasised that this was the critical week and Trimble would have to decide one way or the other. Mitchell was said to be gauging his own next step: he had travelled to meet Clinton, Blair and Ahern the previous week and it was highly unlikely that making those visits to three busy political leaders was for the purpose of reporting failure. The strict and, in terms of the peace process, unprecedented confidentiality imposed on the talks ensured few details were available outside. However, the notion of the IRA nominating an 'interlocutor' – some preferred the French *interlocuteur* – who would work with de Chastelain was widely mentioned. Describing his own phi-losophy of the talks, a high-level Dublin official said: 'In this thing you take one day at a time.' Newspaper reports that some form of IRA decommissioning was imminent gained consider-able currency with a news-starved media, but were sharply dismissed by republicans and greeted with scepticism in the Trimble camp. 'We'll believe it when we see it,' said Trimble's people. 'Or rather when General de Chastelain sees it.'

Insofar as the shape of the deal could be discerned, it was that Sinn Féin would use its best efforts to bring about total decommissioning by the agreed deadline of May 2000, provided this was done within the terms of the Agreement. However, any notion of IRA members hoisting the white flag and handing over their Kalashnikovs and Armalites had to be dismissed right away. Other approaches would be used: there was some life still in the idea for a collective act of reconciliation. The critical need at the moment was to create the environment in which decommissioning, or whatever it was ultimately called, could take place. That meant setting up the Executive and, most important-ly, the North–South bodies. These were the shield behind which republican leaders could take the risks that unionists and arm-chair pundits had demanded of them for the past four years and more. When a new day dawned in Northern Ireland, with union-ists and nationalists working together in a spirit of compromise and respect for each other's identities, then the paramilitaries would be obliged to ask themselves: 'What are we here for? What is our function?'

As the days passed, and despite the media clampdown, it emerged that a planned series of statements which could unlock the door to progress lay at the heart of the crisis talks. Statements would be separately issued by Mitchell, de Chastelain, Trimble, Adams and probably others. The hope was that the combined set of statements would create the conditions for implementation of the Agreement. A number of 'incremental' and 'reciprocal' steps would be taken, e.g. appointment of the IRA interlocutor would be accompanied by the establishment of the Executive, although this might be in shadow form. There would be no dramatic overnight moves, rather a gradual progression or 'sequencing' – the word had become very fashionable – towards a fully-func-tioning executive and a solution to the decommissioning prob-lem. Meanwhile, de Chastelain's paper would contain recom-mendations on how decommissioning could be achieved.

It was said certain assurances were offered to the unionists on decommissioning at the start of the week and, although Trimble had reportedly rejected them in emphatic and even heated terms, discussions continued, and there was a feeling that gradual progress was being made. On the evening of 9 November, however, it appeared that the unionists were still having very considerable difficulties with the deal on offer; Sinn Féin, on the other hand, was described as 'ready to brief its people on the ground that the deal was done'. The offer was on the unionists' plate, but they had not picked it up as yet. As the evening progressed, optimism that unionists would take the required political risk – government before guns – began to wane slightly. The talks broke up at about 9.30 pm.

By 10 November, it was emerging that a Sinn Féin statement against violence was another key element, along with the appointment of the IRA intermediary. Trimble was briefing his Assembly party on the package. 'The genuine sense is that he's going for it,' insiders said. It remained unclear whether he could win the support of his colleagues though. Discussions with them on the evening of 10 November did not go terribly well, by all accounts. Nevertheless, renegotiating current proposals was ruled out by informed sources. Trimble had convened a further meeting of his Assembly party next day, where he was expected to deliver his verdict on the proposed deal. There were suggestions he was close to gambling his political career on the quality of a republican commitment to a decommissioning process which would follow the creation of a power-sharing executive. Nationalist sources said there were fears Trimble might lose his nerve.

An IRA statement appointing its interlocutor was on the horizon and, almost inevitably, there was a build-up of expectation and speculation over what else it might contain. High-level republican sources were emphatic that it would not include any declaration that the 'war' was over, nor any guarantees of decommissioning either, although it would be broadly supportive of the peace process. Indeed, any prospect of decommissioning in the short term was very firmly rejected by authoritative republican contacts. When my report of this assessment appeared on 11 November it apparently created ripples in the unionist camp and not all republicans appreciated it either. 'Whoever told you that should be shot,' a prominent republican told me – but I don't think he meant it literally! A close observer of the scene laughed when I reported the unionist reaction – did they want republicans to tell lies?

While the appointment of an interlocutor would be a significant departure for the IRA, unionists would have to decide whether or not it represented the beginning of the long-sought 'credible process of decommissioning'. Trimble disclosed some months later that around this time he had offered to meet the IRA face to face, although the only topic he wished to discuss was decommissioning.[6]

While there were some loose ends of the package to be tied up, these were said to be of little significance compared with the 'huge issues' that had allegedly been surmounted. Sinn Féin's statement against violence would include opposition to the so-called 'punishment beatings' carried out by paramilitaries. If the compromise came off, further fragmentation in unionist and republican ranks was expected as a result. This would cause problems for the pro-Agreement parties at Stormont, as Trimble might well lose a number of Assembly members to his political opponents. The nationalist side was hoping for a quick decision by the unionists but a well-placed source said, 'They can't make up their mind'.

Depending on the outcome of unionist deliberations, the series of statements was expected before the end of the week. Unlike the events of Good Friday, the culmination of the Review was likely to be low-key. Meanwhile, in an unusual and somewhat risible show of solidarity, Sinn Féin and the Ulster Unionists issued virtually identical statements criticising press speculation, but without stating that the 'speculation' was inaccurate.

Crisis erupted on the evening of 11 November with reports that the UUP had rejected the settlement package. While sources close to the UUP leadership still insisted all was not lost, Adams announced that Sinn Féin had been told the unionists had said No to the deal. It was the first test for the new Secretary of State and he led an intense effort during the evening to persuade the unionists the risk was worth taking.

There were sharply-conflicting accounts emerging from meetings held by the UUP Assembly team at Parliament Buildings throughout the day. First, a report received widespread circulation that the deal had been rejected in a vote taken early in the afternoon. Figures of fourteen against and thirteen in favour were quoted by some elements of the media.

Doubt was subsequently cast on the status of this vote, which was variously described as a show of hands and a rough assessment of the mood of the meeting.

Later in the day, probably around 7 pm, a majority of UUP Assembly members reportedly backed Trimble's proposal to refer the deal to a special meeting of the Ulster Unionist Council. Again there was confusion: the vote was described as a secret one with the result known only to Trimble, but at the same time figures of nineteen for and seven against were being quoted. There were unconfirmed reports that Taylor was among the opposition. In terms of political professionalism, it was not unionism's finest hour.

The loss of five Assembly members would be enough to give the anti-Agreement group in the Assembly the requisite 60 per cent share of the unionist vote needed to block Assembly business. As the talks closed down that night, a UUP spokesman said: 'It would be wrong to write this off. We will be back here tomorrow. The party leader is determined to try and make this work.' There was a note of urgency coming from the republican side. In statements and briefings they again sought to convey the message that the deal had to be done within the week.

Despite the news blackout, it had been possible to glean that Sinn Féin was prepared to promise a great deal in terms of seeking an end to violence. The IRA, on the other hand, was promising nothing but was giving Sinn Féin the all-important seal of approval, the republican quality-mark. Most members of the IRA, it had been authoritatively learnt, did not want to go back to the armed struggle. The leadership could not say this, however, without risking a major split leading to a bloodbath.

Mandelson, only a month in his new job and already facing disaster, was said to be engaged in a major drive to shore up Trimble, who did not have a great history of enthusiastic salesmanship. The main task in hand was to persuade doubters in the UUP to see the merits of the deal. The package on offer could deliver IRA guns in due course, unionists were being told. While the UUP leadership had been afforded ten weeks 'up close and personal' to gauge Sinn Féin's sincerity and seriousness of purpose, the same opportunity was not available to the lower ranks of the party. Unionists were reassured, first of all, that the deal was a good one and, secondly, that they would not suffer any adverse consequences if the republican movement failed to keep its promises. Television cameras caught Mandelson, ostensibly in an unguarded moment, arguing that if there was no decommissioning, unionists could always walk away.

No decisions were taken at a meeting of UUP officers at Glengall Street the following night, which heard a report from Trimble on the situation. However, it was understood he gave notice that the officer team might have to reconvene shortly to consider calling a special meeting of the UUC, should there be a successful conclusion to the Mitchell Review. Negotiations with Sinn Féin had officially concluded, but Trimble was understood to be pressing for further clarity on the timetabling of the envisaged decommissioning process.

Unionist nerves having apparently been steadied, it was decided to initiate the sequencing process. The improved relationship between the UUP and Sinn Féin was reflected in a near-simultaneous release of statements from their party leaders on the morning of 16 November. Trimble indicated he would support the establishment of the Executive, once the IRA's decision to appoint an interlocutor had been announced. It was a breathtaking political risk as there had not been so much as a rusty peashooter from the IRA. I remember reading it again and again: he had finally done it.

In the Sinn Féin statement, Adams said his party accepted that decommissioning was 'an essential part of the peace process'. It was understood Trimble had rejected suggestions from Sinn Féin that, as a gesture to nationalists, he should acknowledge the failings of 50 years of Stormont rule. Senior UUP sources claimed the Mitchell deal was much more difficult for Sinn Féin but, if they really believed that, they did not understand the risk Trimble was taking this time.

The happiest man at Castle Buildings was John Hume. Battered but unbowed after recent serious health problems, which necessitated emergency surgery when he collapsed during a visit to Vienna, the SDLP leader had a smile on his face as he read the UUP and Sinn Féin statements. Adams spoke of 'transforming the existing situation through constructive and dynamic political development' and Trimble declared his party's fealty to 'the principles of inclusivity, equality and mutual respect'. However, a senior Sinn Féin member expressed his displeasure to me when I wrote that the statements were permeated by 'Humespeak'. I was aware, of course, that the deal had been done by Trimble and Adams under the tutelage of Mitchell, but for decades Hume had been creating the atmosphere.

One reason for staggering the announcements was to ensure that each day there was something new, some positive development to maintain the momentum and focus interest on the parties which were trying to implement the Good Friday pact rather than those who sought to wreck it. With the UUP and Sinn Féin statements out in the open, the pace of developments was set to shift up yet another gear with the release of the IRA statement and Mitchell's return to Stormont after a brief visit home to the US.

The Review was expected to conclude on 17 November, with Mitchell delivering his final report. However, if the Executive collapsed in the New Year over decommissioning, the Assembly could be closed down with the parties presumably going into Review again. Officers of the UUP were due to meet at 7.30 pm that evening and convene a UUC meeting in Belfast for 27 November, where the package would be debated by delegates. As speculation developed about Taylor's attitude, it emerged that he had left on 15 November for Tehran as part of the first British parliamentary delegation to visit Iran since the fall of the Shah. The mullahs would hardly pester him about his voting intentions at the UUC.

Should the 860-strong Council[7] approve the leader's approach, a meeting of the Assembly was likely to be convened within days. Move on, was the watchword, why give the naysayers time to organise their forces? The position of Seamus Mallon following his resignation as Deputy First Minister was a cause of quiet concern. Restoring him to the post without a vote of the Assembly was a conundrum puzzling senior figures in the process. Assuming this difficulty could be overcome, the d'Hondt mechanism for the appointment of ministers would be applied, rapidly followed by the first meeting of the new Executive. At last we would see that first photograph, presumably minus the two DUP ministers.

So far so good, then, until we came to the real crunch further down the road. General de Chastelain would then be expected to answer the question: has the IRA done the business at last? Speculation that rapid decommissioning was on the cards was described by republican sources as a rather liberal interpretation of the deal on offer. The climate in the republican movement was not conducive as yet to such an action. There was no explicit public statement anywhere which guaranteed that guns would be disposed of at such an early stage. However, there was a belief in republican circles that, once the movement had gone finally and definitively political, the weaponry would have to be put beyond the reach of those who might want to continue the armed campaign, not to mention other, more venal, elements which might want to use the guns for criminal activities.

A brief IRA statement was issued before lunchtime on 17 November. Its content did not match some of the more dramatic forecasts. An interlocutor would be appointed to meet the decommissioning body, but this would only be done after the new institutions were established. Mandelson said the statement marked 'a very significant step forward'.

Tensions were rising in the Ulster Unionist camp and that evening Trimble moved quickly to disown a statement issued from Westminster by five members of his parliamentary party, rejecting the package agreed in the Mitchell Review and dismissing the IRA statement as 'totally inadequate'. Released after the weekly meeting of the parliamentary party, the statement said the IRA had offered 'no certainty or clarity' on decommissioning. It was faxed out at 7.35 pm but only nine minutes later there was a response from Trimble dissociating himself from the text which, he added, had received the endorsement of only five out of the ten UUP MPs at Westminster. It was understood there was an attendance of six at the meeting, with Trimble in a minority of one. The MPs who rejected the package and the IRA statement were: William Ross, William Thompson, Rev Martin Smyth, Clifford Forsythe and Roy Beggs Snr. John Taylor was still in Iran and it was reported that Donaldson had to return to Northern Ireland for an urgent meeting, although he later declared 'full support' for the statement. Cecil Walker and Ken Maginnis were also absent.

Meanwhile, there were congratulations all round for Mitchell's role in the Review. Whereas he had in the past taken considerable guidance from the two governments, this time it seemed he was much more his own man while still receiving advice from London and Dublin. His own deepening experience doubtless contributed to this, but there was also the fact that the trick of bringing in the two prime ministers, which worked so well on Good Friday, began to lose its lustre at Hillsborough. Its credibility declined still further in July when Tony Blair claimed there were 'seismic shifts' but the ground failed to move. Historians may also decide that the hype which tended to accompany all prime ministerial visits ultimately damaged the process. On Good Friday, rosy reports of progress may have helped to push the unionists towards a deal. At Hillsborough and in July there was a sense the republicans were getting the 'treatment' but that it was having the opposite effect to what was intended. The hardened veterans of Castlereagh detention centre did not wilt easily.

Perhaps now the decommissioning issue would be dealt with and put to one side. The international media, in particular, had come under its spell. Unversed in the complexities of Irish history in general and republicanism in particular, they could not see the problem in handing over a few pistols and maybe a wee bit of Semtex. Look at the political gains for Sinn Féin if it would only decide to do the decent thing at last? However, it was not that easy or simple. The need to retain weapons to defend the nationalist population against possible loyalist pogroms was what anthropologists would call a 'foundation myth' of the Provisional IRA. No working-class nationalist had forgotten 1969: the story of how the leadership of the republican movement went overboard on politics and left the Catholics in the Belfast ghettos defenceless was being passed on from generation to generation. While this version of events had been challenged, it still retained tremendous potency.

The nomination of ministers was now expected on 29 November, two days after the UUC meeting. This would be followed by the formal devolution of powers, the first meeting of the new Executive and the appointment of paramilitary representatives to meet the decommissioning body. All these actions would take place the same day and be quickly followed by the first meeting of the North–South Ministerial Council in Armagh (Mallon had ensured his city would be the headquarters) and the inaugural session of the British–Irish Council, probably in London. The IRA interlocutor would be appointed and begin meeting the decommissioning body. The conditions for a new 'context' and atmosphere would be created. For the first time, republicans and unionists would be working together in government. The republican and nationalist hope was that decommissioning would be greatly diminished against the background of historic change and today's impasse become tomorrow's distraction. Perhaps the General could come up with some umbrella of ambiguity to shelter everyone from the storm.

A news conference called by Trimble to announce the forthcoming UUC meeting turned into an embarrassing wrangle when a leading opponent of the deal, David Brewster, interrupted the proceedings to challenge the veracity of Trimble's account of a party officers' meeting which they had both just attended. Later, the two opponents issued a joint statement expressing regret over the incident and asking the media to 'disregard the unfortunate exchange of comments'. There was further embarrassment for the leader when one of the two deputy whips in his Assembly party, Derek Hussey, asked to be relieved of his duties on the grounds of opposition to the deal. There was a still further setback when one of Trimble's closest allies, the director of the party's information office in London, David Burnside, indicated he might vote against the proposals.

Opponents of the deal inside the UUP had already begun organising against what they regarded as a 'sell-out'. They estimated each side in the debate had the support of about 40 per cent of delegates, with slightly fewer than 200 still undecided. While senior unionists supporting Trimble expected him to win the UUC vote, they said he must do so by a significant margin. Observers agreed the vote in favour of the package would have to be at least 60 per cent to be convincing.

On 23 November, Mandelson pulled off a minor public-relations coup when it was announced that the RUC was being awarded the George Cross for gallantry. The move had been in preparation for some time but, with only five days to the UUC meeting, it was easy to believe it was a ploy to appease critics of the Patten report on policing and bolster Trimble's position. On the other hand, unionists had always insisted their loyalty was to the Crown, not to Downing Street, and here was the Crown bestowing the most prestigious award next to the Victoria Cross. There should now be no political necessity for the Northern Secretary to stir up a hornet's nest among nationalists by defaulting on the recommendations of the Patten Report and indeed there was no indication, at this stage anyway, that he intended to do so. The hurt and grief suffered by the bereaved relatives of RUC members who had died could never be healed – any more than the hurt of other bereaved people in Northern Ireland – but it was now being recognised and honoured in a solemn way.

The Trimble camp suffered a fierce blow to the solar plexus with reports from the US about comments made by Sinn Féin's Pat Doherty and Martin Ferris, suggesting that when the institutions were up and running there would be no stomach on the part of the political establishment to bring them down for the want of decommissioning.[8] Informed sources said the reports gave 'serious ammunition' to the No lobby, on a par with the release of the Balcombe Street Gang during the referendum campaign.

Nobody in either camp of unionism was taking anything for granted at this stage. The view in the pro-Trimble group was that a 60 per cent vote for the leader's approach was achievable but not certain. The No camp insisted it had 300-odd votes out of approximately 860 in the bag already and great hopes rested on the 120 Orange representatives who had been invited to discuss the issue at the Order's headquarters in Belfast on the eve of the meeting at Belfast's Waterfront Hall. While the No people conceded that Trimble was still ahead, they claimed they could overtake him or at least take the shine off his victory. 'What kind of a win is 55 per cent?' asked one prominent No campaigner.

The No lobby held private meetings throughout Northern Ireland the week prior to the meeting. An office with eight telephone lines was set up in Belfast and opponents of the deal – mostly younger party members – canvassed for as long as eight hours a day. Trimble won the media battle, as the establishment side usually does, but the real campaign was waged in the background, away from the spotlight. The No people hired a marketing research company to set up 'focus groups', mainly composed of UUC delegates, to tease out the issues. From these sessions, the No camp was able to identify the subjects that should be avoided and those which ought to be highlighted. The sturdy Ulster folk who made up the bulk of UUC members did not like public attacks on the leader; they were uncomfortable with expressions like 'stalking horse' and found the word 'split' highly repellent. At the same time there was uncertainty about the small print of the deal on offer.

A number of young UUP members had previously been brought to the US – ironically, as part of the peace process – to attend courses in political leadership and technique. They were particularly impressed by the methods of the Democratic Party and took to heart the concept that voters could be broken down into 'six categories of persuadability'. District councillors, for example, who made up a significant proportion of UUC membership, were urged to reject the deal because it would affect their chances of re-election.

While it was hard to believe that an experienced politician like Trimble would have gone ahead with the UUC meeting unless confident of victory, there were signs that canvassing by the No lobby was narrowing the gap. Estimates of Trimble's likely margin of victory were being gradually revised downwards. Although he was still thought likely to win, sources close to the leadership reported 'nerves' and 'a lot of worry'.

Reports suggested many delegates were still undecided. It was much easier to be hard-line in public and the No camp had more people willing to testify aloud. The Yes camp was quieter and more reserved: no point in drawing fire on yourself. It could even be dangerous, as the Secretary of State found out at Portadown when he and Trimble had to be given police protection from protesting loyalists. A 'dirty tricks' letter forged on Sinn Féin notepaper emerged, which called on delegates to support Trimble.

Interviewed in the *Daily Mail* the day before the vote, Daphne Trimble was in no doubt as to the consequences of failure for her husband: 'If the vote goes against him, that would be it for David. We've discussed it absolutely calmly, and we know it would be the end of his political career.' In his speech to the previous month's UUP conference in Enniskillen, Trimble recalled how, two years earlier, he and his wife had discussed the 'possible outcomes' of the multi-party talks at Stormont. 'She predicted that I would probably obtain just enough support at each stage to go on, but that it would be a constant uphill struggle.'

There was a note of anxiety, even near-panic, among some of Trimble's well-wishers just prior to the Waterfront meeting. On a happier note for them, there were indications Taylor would give his support to the leader. Trimble supporters were also encouraged by reports that only 35 out of 120 Orange delegates turned up to hear a hard-line message at the Order's headquarters in Belfast. Still, the overall picture was gloomy, not to say alarming. Something would have to be crafted to stave off disaster.

From Clinton down, political leaders had been telling Trimble: go into the Executive and, if you're not happy over weapons, you can always walk away. He now proceeded to offer UUC delegates a similar option. He told them at the meeting that he had lodged a letter with the UUC President, Sir Josias Cunningham. While he was not specific about the letter's contents it was understood to be a post-dated resignation, although the date was not revealed. Similar letters were to be requested from other UUP ministerial nominees. He also proposed a motion for conditional entry to the Executive which instructed Cunningham 'to reconvene the Council in February 2000 to take a final decision'.

Always best with his back to the wall, Trimble closed the meeting with an impassioned speech. In what even leading opponents described as a 'bravura performance', sources inside the meeting said he hit back at speakers who had suggested his strategy was a betrayal of the victims of the IRA. As at the opening of the Assembly, he invoked the memory of Edgar Graham, a law lecturer and unionist politician shot dead by the IRA in 1983. If Graham were still alive, Trimble said, he would be backing the leader. Indeed, he would probably *be* the leader: 'I would not have been standing here today, Edgar Graham would be standing here today.' He also recalled the late Rev Robert Bradford, MP for South Belfast, who died in an IRA gun attack in 1981. The UUP leader quoted a letter from Rev Bradford's widow, Norah, pledging her full support and urging him to keep at the difficult job.

The motion to reconvene the Council in February was carried by 480 to 349 votes, or 58 to 42 per cent. It was a disturbingly narrow margin and, without the estimated seven per cent thought to take its lead from Taylor, he would have been hovering around the 50 per cent mark. At his press conference Trimble sent a blunt, dramatic message on decommissioning to Adams: 'We have jumped, now it's over to you.'

The effect was immediate: Adams was in bed with 'flu but was so alarmed by the February reconvening that he called

Radio Ulster and said on air that Trimble had stepped outside the Mitchell Review and the Belfast Agreement by unilaterally introducing a new decommissioning deadline. I have established that the NIO had no forewarning of the move either.

Unionists could argue, with considerable plausibility, that the crucial vote would have been lost if some device had not been found to reassure the doubting middle ground. It was clear from the expression on Daphne's face and, indeed, from Trimble's own demeanour that it had been the closest shave so far.

A leading No campaigner observed that Trimble had been obliged to make significant concessions to 'squeak' through. Yet there was a grudging admiration for the leader's 'bareknuckle' closing speech. 'It was the first time he has really seemed to me to be impassioned,' the unionist dissident said, 'but what troubles will it store up for him at the end of January?' There was considerable comment after the meeting about the fact that Taylor had not spoken. A spokesman for the Strangford MP said the deputy leader had applied to speak but was not called. Taylor walked swiftly away from the Waterfront after the vote, without speaking to the press. As he did so, elderly loyalist women heckled him from behind a barrier and one opposition delegate commented angrily: 'He's got his knighthood now.'[9] Another predicted the DUP's Iris Robinson would have no difficulty taking the Westminster seat for Strangford next time.

While there was much talk of 'Northern Ireland's future' and laying the groundwork for the next generation, the fact remained that the younger element in the UUP was in large number opposed to the Agreement and all that flowed from it. One No lobbyist said he felt like the eldest son on a very good farm watching the parents squander his inheritance. You got the feeling that unionists, especially the younger ones, hankered for the days of Carson and Craig and leaders with passion and gravitas. The impassioned tone of Trimble's final oration may have swung more support his way than the pledges that he offered. 'Trimble doesn't *do* passion,' was how one of his opponents put it, with reluctant admiration. It seemed the more Trimble showed he meant business about implementing the Good Friday Agreement, the more likely he was to rally the party behind him. If it came to another vote in February, the First Minister would need to put himself about more in the constituencies, sip more cups of tea in Orange halls and attend more cake sales and rugby dinners. Many UUC delegates were elderly and did not belong to the media generation; they responded better to one-to-one contact and reassurances. Empey had played a useful background role in this regard over recent weeks and one No lobbyist grudgingly admitted he was 'a class act'.

By all accounts, Trimble's démarche took Dublin by surprise too. It was a departure from the deal agreed in the Review, but clearly the UUP leader felt it necessary if he was to win maximum support among UUC delegates. It had created serious problems for the Sinn Féin leadership at a very delicate and sensitive time when it was seen as essential to lead the republican movement into the new political era without a split. While a case could be made that nationalism had gained more than unionism out of the Agreement – the near-unanimous level of support among nationalist voters tended to confirm that view – there were still a lot of very jumpy people on the republican side, awed by the magnitude of what they were doing and susceptible to claims that the new order was merely a copperfastened version of partition. The IRA could, in theory at least, take the heat out of the situation by unilaterally destroying a quantity of arms and explosives before the end of January but, despite media claims, there were no reliable indications that this was likely to happen. The Trimble deadline and the reports of post-dated resignation letters from himself and other UUP ministers had also strengthened the suspicion which still lingered in some republican minds that the peace process was not – to borrow a phrase from the South African context – a 'negotiated revolution' but the working-out of a counter-insurgency strategy using decommissioning as a device to divide, demoralise and destroy the republican movement.

With the UUC vote barely digested, the issue of Seamus Mallon's resignation had to be dealt with in the Assembly, due to sit in two days' time. It was most helpful to the two governments when an Alliance Party motion was tabled which essentially sought to airbrush it from history: the resignation had never been formally accepted, therefore it was not valid. The DUP's Nigel Dodds quipped that it reminded him of the demise of Bobby Ewing in the television soap opera *Dallas* – he was actually in the shower all the time!

It was a tricky situation: on 15 July, with all the sense of drama he could command, Mallon had told the Assembly: 'I offer my resignation with immediate effect.' An impressive act of defiance at the time, it was now beginning to appear counter-productive. Alliance was proposing, 'That this Assembly wishes, notwithstanding his offer of resignation as Deputy First Minister (designate), that Seamus Mallon MP hold office as Deputy First Minister (designate).' This motion would only require the support of 40 per cent of unionists, provided there was backing from 40 per cent of nationalists and an overall 60 per cent majority in the Assembly. Were Mallon's resignation to remain in force, he would require a majority of nationalists and unionists to be re-elected under the Parallel Consent rule which applied to the election of First and Deputy First Ministers. The Agreement specified that Trimble would have to offer himself for re-election at the same time, and his prospects of securing a majority of unionists were probably less than Mallon's.

A change in Standing Orders from the Secretary of State was required, to facilitate the implementation of the Alliance motion. Pending devolution, the British Government was responsible for the day-to-day rules governing the Assembly. There was little doubt, in terms of common sense, that Mallon quit his job the previous July. Yet when the question came up on 29 November, the Speaker declared: 'It is a question of law, not of common sense.' By all accounts a great deal of work went into the preparation of the new standing order, presented just an hour before the Assembly convened in the afternoon. There must have been a fair amount of nail-biting, since the prospect of Paisley or McCartney rushing off to get a judge to press the pause-button on the well-planned sequence of events seemed quite real. There was the usual procedural wrangle that accompanied almost every step forward in Northern Ireland. The mild-mannered Mandelson was accused of carrying out a 'dictatorial act' and even compared to Mussolini. While peace process insiders had been reasonably confident over the weekend that the move would succeed, there must have been a large sigh of relief when McCartney indicated he was not considering court action, because it would be locking the stable door after the horse had bolted. Paisley said he was seeking legal advice, although nothing came of this. It was not parliamentary democracy's finest hour, but in the end the pro-Agreement parties held their noses and voted the Alliance Party motion through by 71 votes to 28. Resignation – what resignation?

It was time to move on to the formation of the Executive. The most dramatic event of the day, even though it had been widely forecast, came at 5.47 pm (I checked my watch) when Martin McGuinness accepted the nomination by Gerry Adams to the post of Minister of Education. Something that was unthinkable even a few years before had now come to pass. The classic republican had become a key player in a daring and difficult political experiment. Cedric Wilson of the Northern Ireland Unionist Party walked out and a seething loyalist in the Gallery yielded up his lunch, to the discomfort and inconvenience of some SDLP visitors. It was not too much to say that Northern Ireland, the republican movement and British–Irish relations would never be quite the same again. McGuinness was leading everyone across the Rubicon and past the point of no return. The rumours had been that he would take the Agriculture portfolio, with Bairbre de Brún going for Education. In the event, de Brún became Minister of Health with Agriculture going to the SDLP. There would doubtless be shock waves in sectors of the education system over McGuinness' nomination, and a feeling that the Goths had taken over the Colosseum. However, the Derry republican had won respect in the peace process and officials had praised his conduct in the Mitchell Review, where he had particular rapport with Empey. The militant firebrand had reinvented himself as a skilful politician.

In short order, the full Executive was nominated: three UUP, three SDLP, two Sinn Féin and two DUP. On the UUP side, Reg Empey was an expected choice as Minister of Enterprise, Trade and Investment. Michael McGimpsey, who took over the Culture, Arts and Leisure portfolio, had also begun to emerge as a key Trimble lieutenant over the past year and was frequently sent out to bat at difficult moments during the Mitchell Review. But the plan to have greatness thrust upon Sam Foster, one of two UUP Assembly members for Fermanagh–South Tyrone, was kept a closely guarded secret. Sources reported that Belfast voted overwhelmingly against Trimble at the UUC the previous weekend, but that he had scored well west of the River Bann, and Foster's loyalty was now to get its reward.

Journalists recalled video footage of Foster helping to pull the victims from the rubble after the 1987 Enniskillen bombing in which eleven people died. The scale of what was taking place was exemplified by the fact that Foster, who had been a member of the B-Specials, the locally-based constabulary which was hated by nationalists and had been disbanded early in the Troubles, was now about to sit at the same cabinet table as Martin McGuinness, perhaps the most prominent republican militant of his generation. There was some surprise when Foster was named, rather than Taylor. The Strangford MP, who previously served in a Stormont government put a positive construction on things, 'I don't want to do what I did 30 years ago. I am so involved with Westminster, I would rather concentrate on that.' The SDLP ministers were all well-known and highly experienced politicians. Bríd Rodgers had been forecast to go to the Department of Culture, Arts and Leisure but ended up in Agriculture; Mark Durkan in Finance and Seán Farren in Higher and Further Education were not major surprises. The DUP's Peter Robinson, as Minister-designate for Regional Development, made a positive initial impression by his undertaking, without prejudice to his anti-Agreement convictions, to be 'scrupulously fair' to all, regardless of creed or political belief. His party colleague Nigel Dodds took the Social Development portfolio.

The uncertainty which had characterised the peace process in general now became evident with regard to the operation of the new Northern Executive in particular. One of the initial difficulties concerned the position of Robinson and Dodds. DUP sources said their two ministers would operate their departments and keep in regular contact with the First and Deputy First Ministers and the Minister for Finance and Personnel. There would also be meetings on matters of mutual interest with other ministers, except for McGuinness and de Brún, who would be treated 'as if they were not there', and this implied non-attendance at meetings of the Executive. They would not become involved in the cross-Border implementation bodies. Regarding attendance at the North–South Ministerial Council, the DUP pointed out that there was provision in the Agreement for the First and Deputy First Ministers to 'make alternative arrangements' where a minister refused to participate.

One wondered how long the DUP could keep the Executive at arm's length. The pledge of office committed each minister 'to participate with colleagues in the preparation of a programme for government'. The Good Friday pact laid down that the Executive would seek to agree this programme on an annual basis and, if the DUP failed to attend Executive meetings, it could be found in breach of the pledge of office. Indeed, a strict policy of abstention could prove to be self-defeating politically: the other parties would approve the programme anyway, although there would obviously have to be consultation with the DUP departments.

UUP sources made it their business to tell reporters, almost immediately after the Executive was appointed at Stormont, that Sinn Féin had only one implementation body even partly under the auspices of its two ministers, namely Food Safety Promotion,[10] which was thought, at least at that time, to be mainly an Agriculture matter, but had a peripheral bearing on de Brún's Department of Health. Sinn Féin responded that Health and Martin McGuinness' portfolio of Education were among the six areas specified for North–South co-operation. It became clear also that Sinn Féin ministers would have substantial budgets under their control; almost £2 billion in de Brun's case, and £1 billion for schools. More than half the discretionary, i.e. non-security, budget would be at the disposal of the Sinn Féin ministers. The bulk of the celebrated 'block grant'[11] from Westminster was in republican hands!

The formal devolution of powers took place at midnight on 1 December. The North took the event in its stride: it was history in the making, but more Holywood, County Down, than Hollywood, Los Angeles. Besides, what right had we to expect that a squalid war would come to a conditional end with fanfares, glorious sunsets and dancing in the street? If there was little sense of occasion in Belfast, outside the confines of Stormont, the television pictures from Dublin suggested that the much-heralded dropping of the territorial claim to the North had left the populace neither shaken nor stirred.

David Andrews made a thoughtful speech at a joint ceremony in Iveagh House with Mandelson to mark the entry into force of the British–Irish Agreement. He gave the best definition to date of the developing relationship between nationalists and

unionists who were 'on a continuing voyage of mutual self-dis-
covery'. Cynics could dismiss it as an Iveagh House chat-up line
but it was an accurate description of what might happen if the
dynamic inherent in the Belfast Agreement came properly into
play. Andrews also gave a useful definition of the Agreement
itself when he said it was 'not a blueprint but a framework – a
framework for co-operation and common action, for reconciliation, for mutual respect and for partnership'.

The sense that the reality of what was going on had still not
bitten into the Republic's psyche continued with the low-key,
almost apologetic, manner in which the Taoiseach announced
the demise of the old Articles 2 and 3, especially since, without
his drive, ambition and daring we would not have arrived at this
juncture.

Unionists were entitled to some satisfaction over what they
saw as the detoxification of Articles 2 and 3. It was an issue
which concerned few of them until it was drawn to their attention. Then it became a shibboleth, not unlike decommissioning
in the current phase. If they had been told in the early stages that
the offending Articles would be traded for cross-Border bodies
with a multi-million pound budget and a small army of bureau-
crats beavering away at their tasks, it might have given them
pause for thought.

On the afternoon of Devolution Day, attention shifted to
Room 21 at Parliament Buildings, location for the first meeting of
the devolved Executive – Robinson and Dodds were not there, of
course, and held a news conference at the same time. Apparently
after some hesitation, it was decided to admit the cameras briefly
to film the ministers sitting at their round table. Although the 75-
minute meeting was later described as businesslike, it took place
against a backdrop of anxiety, with some political insiders even
worrying if David Trimble would turn up: he had pulled surprises in the past. The agenda included detailed discussion of
public service finances as well as the preparation of a programme of government, a draft ministerial code and the initial
legislative programme. Mallon was disarmingly honest when he
spoke of his fears entering his new post – or rather the old one
he had supposedly never left!

The fate of the new administration would depend, not on the
ministers, but on General de Chastelain and his colleagues. The

Commission's skill and adroitness, and the quality of any advice it might get from the two governments, would be tested to the limit in the coming months. The dream that the General would emerge sooty-faced from some paramilitary bunker at the start of the New Year, to report that the IRA had done the business, still looked problematic. Indeed, the best reported comment of the day came from a republican who said, in the course of a conversation about decommissioning: 'We'll burn that bridge when we come to it.'

At 8.30 pm the IRA made the long-awaited announcement that it was nominating a representative to enter into discussions with the decommissioning body. Instead of the expected brief notification, the statement went on to reiterate the IRA's 'concern', previously expressed at the end of November, over the UUC decision to impose, in effect, a three-month deadline for the start of decommissioning. The IRA did not name the interlocutor and republican sources said the identity of the individual in question would not be officially released for security reasons. This did not stop the media in general from speculating about a variety of named republicans as the go-between.

Historic events were coming thick and fast: the next one would be the inaugural meeting of the North–South Ministerial Council at Armagh on 13 December. Leading unionists downplayed it as a 'necessary nonsense' and insisted their eyes were fixed instead on the British–Irish Council meeting, a few days later. The significance of the NSMC for the mainstream republican movement could not be underestimated. For this unprecedented political link between the two parts of the island, they had entered a six-county Assembly at Stormont and conditionally accepted the existence, for the time being, of the Northern state which they spent nearly 30 years trying, with bomb and bullet, to destroy. Trimble might have had considerable success – both on Good Friday and subsequently – in minimising both the number and responsibilities of the cross-Border bodies but, as republicans saw it, the principle of policy implementation on a North–South basis had been established and, out of this acorn, they believed a mighty oak could grow. Leading republicans conceded there would be a lot more symbolism than substance in the day's events, but substance could develop out of symbolism.

The Taoiseach had been made fully aware of the potential difficulties which the inaugural meeting could cause for the UUP leadership. There was some concern in UUP circles at the prospect of its four ministers being outnumbered by over twenty nationalists. However, at the inaugural session of the British–Irish Council, United Kingdom ministers would form a majority.

The NSMC was a good news story for a change: so many times in the previous few years one had traversed the same road, stopping short of Armagh to veer into Portadown for the latest instalment in the long-running saga of tension, nerves and occasional violence at Drumcree and the Garvaghy Road. This time it was on to the 'Cathedral City' and, for a change, a positive atmosphere. Nationalists and republicans looked happy, unionists were at least relaxed. McGuinness called it a joyous day, Trimble adopted a cooler tone. Rejecting the notion that the Armagh council was the ante-room to a united Ireland, he suggested the body to be set up in London would mark the re-entry of the Republic to the British–Irish family of nations.

The sight of twelve ministerial cars from Dublin appearing on the brow of the hill above Armagh's Palace Demesne, with a Fianna Fáil cabinet member in each, became the media highlight of the day. A colleague made the cruel but apt observation that it was like a Mafia wedding: the image stuck and was repeated continuously. Nevertheless, to many northern nationalists who had spent all their lives under an administration they regarded as alien, it was a heartening sight. When the arrival of the cars was followed by the thunder of an Air Corps helicopter with Irish tricolour insignia, carrying the Taoiseach, the Tánaiste (deputy prime minister) and Minister for Foreign Affairs, you felt things would never be quite the same again between North and South. More than the winter leaves on the ground were being scattered by Bertie Ahern's whirring blades as he hove to outside the Armagh council offices in the Palace Demesne at 10.55 am.

There was an air of civility about the event, due not least to Trimble himself, who maintained an unfailing good humour and conducted the four-handed news conference of the main leaders afterwards with aplomb. The last thing supporters of the peace process needed on the day was a surly unionist who looked as if he was heading towards his own execution.

Sinn Féin was not troubling to hide its agenda for the new

body. Speaking in Irish, Bairbre de Brún said its importance could not be overestimated. The new Health Minister and her Sinn Féin colleague made it clear that the project of achieving Irish unity would proceed apace. This was not what Trimble signed on for, however, and, as the Taoiseach warned, there would be difficult days in the future and 'many tough debates'.

However modest their remit, the new implementation bodies would have offices throughout the island, from Enniskillen to Cork, from Monaghan to Belfast. A joint secretariat had been set up in Armagh, and the various boards and officials would be working away at their tasks from now on. Twice before in the twentieth century unsuccessful attempts had been made to set up a body with a North–South political and administrative remit. A Council of Ireland was provided for in the Government of Ireland Act 1920, but failed to come into operation. The idea was revived in the 1973 Sunningdale Agreement but never took effect.

The fact that Empey was the first of the Northern ministers afterwards to go south under the new arrangements, rather than, say, an eager member of Sinn Féin, was seen as helpful in allaying the fears of the majority community in Northern Ireland and it also reassured nationalists that the UUP would play its part. Dublin sent its Minister for Education, Micheál Martin, northwards to meet McGuinness, in line with SDLP advice that a unionist minister should be first to go south of the Border.

The British–Irish Council inaugural in London four days later, on 17 December, was one of the last 'defining moments' in that stage of the peace process. An exotic touch was lent by the presence of political representatives from the Channel Islands. Their titles were unusual, at least in the British and Irish contexts: Senator Pierre Horsfall represented the Bailiwick of Jersey, and Conseillor Laurie Morgan spoke on behalf of the Bailiwick of Guernsey. Little did John Hume and Gerry Adams know, when they started their discreet series of conversations in early 1988, how far-reaching the political and constitutional effects would be. The Isle of Man's Chief Minister, Donald Gelling, pointed out that his homeland had experienced more than 1,000 years of continuous parliamentary government. On a day when little or no Irish was heard (although there were generous dollops of Welsh from First Secretary Alun Michael), Gelling broke into Manx to pray *Dy bannee Jee ny eabyn ain* (May God bless our endeavours). Now all these places, which had been at peace for so long, were united in the same body as storm-tossed Northern Ireland. It all added up to what Trimble called 'the charm of this occasion', but although the word 'historic' appeared in the text of Trimble's speech, he refrained from actually saying it.

The various representatives were greeted personally at the front door by the Prime Minister. There was a handshake for Bairbre de Brún – the first time in public for Downing Street and Sinn Féin. Blair looked towards the cameras, as though anxious to have it recorded, but not entirely sure he was doing the right thing.

With the British–Irish Council duly inaugurated, the two prime ministers adjourned to Downing Street for the first meeting of the new British–Irish Intergovernmental Conference, another part of the Good Friday 'architecture'. At a news conference held inside the building, the Taoiseach brought the first touch of real politics to a largely ceremonial day when he was asked if he had a message for the paramilitaries on the decommissioning of weapons. In a tantalising reply, Ahern said: 'They should assist us in decommissioning the word decommissioning. Get rid of it.' This was classic Ahern, who seemed to be saying, in effect, you have got your institutions, boys, now do something on the weapons.

It was my first time inside No. 10. As we waited for Blair and Ahern to give their press conference, some of us looked out the window at the garden and wondered where the IRA mortar bombs had landed in 1991. Like everyone else, the journalists were having trouble shaking off the relics of the old era and getting into the spirit of the new. Outside the front door, instead of the traditional ornaments and decorations, the Christmas tree had been festooned with imitation white doves of peace against a background of cotton-wool snow. From mortars to cotton-wool: things had come a long way.

Chapter 12

No Hat, No Rabbits

The moment of reckoning was fast approaching. Sinn Féin was hanging tough. 'Anyone that jumps ship at this time is going to drown,' Adams said as he left for the US on 11 January. It was the Last Hurrah for Castle Buildings because, no matter what happened politically, there was a widespread feeling that it wouldn't happen there. Although it was impossible to regret leaving such a dismal place, I nevertheless felt a certain sadness that this chapter in my life was over. I had spent perhaps more time than any other journalist in the prefabs and tents, but the surroundings never took from my feeling of privilege at covering such significant events.

As the last of the politicians were clearing their desks, a senior republican told me of his hopes that the 'air' might go out of the decommissioning issue when the Executive and other institutions were up and running. When I asked him who would end up with egg on their faces, those who were confidently predicting the decommissioning of weapons in January or the smaller number, such as myself and a few other journalists, who could find no evidence that this was about to happen, he replied with a meaningful look, 'I think you will be vindicated'. Security sources at the highest level confirmed this: contrary to reports that the republican leadership was preparing its grass roots for a handover, the exact opposite appeared to be happening with the 'base' being assured there would be no gestures.

The White House explored the various possibilities on weapons, among other issues, in its 45-minute meeting with Adams. Unionists might have wished Clinton to put him under pressure but when he emerged the Sinn Féin leader looked quite relaxed. There were heads of state who would have difficulty getting to see the President but not the former political pariah who could not even get into the country until 1994; Secretary of State Madeleine Albright and National Security Adviser Sandy

Berger were there for good measure.

While most observers accepted that Trimble had to propose a reconvened meeting of the UUC to save his political skin, republicans, who had other priorities, regarded the move as a breach of faith. The implication from what the IRA said subsequently was that the agreement reached in the Mitchell review almost came off the table. Happily for the peace process, the IRA interlocutor was not withdrawn; such a move could have precipitated a major crisis. We will never know for certain what would have happened had Trimble not set an implicit deadline for the IRA, which could never allow itself to be seen as dancing to a unionist tune. There are still those who believe something imaginative could have been done on weapons.

As the days passed various solutions, some plausible, others verging on the absurd, were floated in political circles. The idea of a 'dummy run', or simulated decommissioning, under the gaze of the de Chastelain commission, was greeted with incredulity by my republican contacts. There was also much talk about ways and means of fulfilling the legal stipulation that arms be made 'permanently inaccessible or unusable'. Both the Irish and British legislation included this formula as part of their definition of the 'destruction of arms'. There were suggestions about arms being buried under several tons of concrete, with alarms that would go off in the General's office if anyone tried to break through. The idea of verifiable dumping was in circulation – I first heard the phrase from my fellow-journalist Eamonn Mallie. It raised constitutional issues: could the authorities in, say, the Republic, tolerate a situation where the locations of arms dumps had been notified to an official body and no further action was taken? The legislation already provided that persons who handed over weapons would not be subject to prosecution. Republicans carefully replied that the issue was academic because the notification of arms dump locations to the decommissioning body was not under consideration at this time. They did point out, however, that the 'gear' had been in the ground and the guns silent for most of the previous six years. This was not enough to keep the unionists happy, but it seemed to be all that was on offer – for the time being.

Much would depend on General de Chastelain's next report, due by the end of January. While he might not come up with the words the unionists wanted to hear, perhaps he could provide sufficient reassurance for them to consider staying in the Executive, at least until May. If the General reported that the republicans had defaulted on their obligations, the institutions were likely to be suspended and the Executive to lose its powers, perhaps continuing in shadow form while a further review was conducted. Moderates would find this a wearisome prospect: the Executive had been 'doing the business' and, broadly speaking, Northern Ireland was a society at peace.

Over lunch in Belfast, a colleague from a unionist back-ground predicted there would be another fudge, remarking that there was a time we would not have got from soup to coffee without the sound of an explosion from the city centre. People were getting on with their lives: did they need another shock to the political system? But it was ominous when liberal unionist Duncan Shipley Dalton told the Assembly on 17 January that he would not support his party remaining in government unless there was decommissioning by the end of the month.

That same week, it was reported that the British Cabinet had been considering the Patten Report on policing and had decided, on the recommendation of Peter Mandelson, to rename the RUC as the Police Service of Northern Ireland. As for the police badge, London was reportedly keen on the idea of having the crown beside the harp, instead of on top. There was also a sprig of shamrock on the RUC badge, and some versions of the story had all three symbols side by side. Dublin lobbied hard for imple-mentation of the precise terms of Recommendation 151 of the Patten Report, which urged that the police service 'should adopt a new badge and symbols which are entirely free from any asso-ciation with either the British or Irish states'. Dublin could point to the particular emphasis in the use of the word 'entirely'. The discussion, some sources called it 'haggling', continued until quite a late stage. Finally, Mandelson announced that the matter would be addressed by the new policing board. This increased the chances that the symbol eventually agreed would be apoliti-cal. That was the case in the Assembly, which employed the innocuous but pleasant emblem of the flax plant, with which Northern Ireland was traditionally associated; the Women's Coalition claimed credit for the original idea.

Mandelson revealed his approach on the badge issue in the

course of a general statement to the Commons announcing that he was accepting the main recommendations of Patten. It was a difficult day for unionist leaders, perhaps the most painful yet in the process of adjustment to the new political realities. Nationalists, and probably even most republicans, had long since passed through the pain barrier of realising and accepting that partition would stay as long as a northern majority so desired. Part of the price they exacted was equality within a new dispensation: the changes in policing were arguably the most important element in the package.

Naturally, the UUP dissidents seized on the police issue to stoke-up their campaign against the Agreement and, by implication, Trimble's leadership. Signatures were being sent to party chairman Dennis, now Lord, Rogan, requesting a special meeting of the 110-member executive to discuss the policing issue. Dangerous times for the UUP leader and consequently for the peace process, although dissident sources commented with wry resignation: 'The only thing David Trimble will defend to the hilt is his own position.' The timing of the announcement on Patten did not help Trimble in a situation where the IRA was showing no signs of handing over guns or Semtex.

It was now axiomatic on the part of senior unionist sources that Trimble could not continue as First Minister without a decommissioning 'event' in January. However, the view at the highest level in the NIO was that, if he resigned, he would have great difficulty getting re-elected under Assembly rules. To avoid a repetition of the farce over Seamus Mallon's position as Deputy First Minister, it would be necessary to suspend the institutions. Once the review was successfully completed, the light-switch could be thrown again and Trimble resume his position without a vote. All very neat and tidy until you considered the state of feeling on the republican side. A suspension of the institutions, with McGuinness and de Brún losing their newly acquired portfolios and, in particular, the removal of powers from the North–South Ministerial Council, would provoke widespread anger. Pleas from the establishment, that republicans had gained a lot and decommissioning was the payback, fell on deaf ears.

Republican sources were categorical that there would be no handover of IRA weapons by the end of the month, nor in the immediate future. Since the only deadline set for decommissioning in the

Agreement was the following May, it now seemed unlikely the General would be able to report a default on the terms of the Agreement. Nevertheless, a decision to suspend the Executive, resume direct rule and institute another review process was still believed to be a serious possibility. A high-level NIO figure had told me in very strong terms as long ago as November that this was likely to happen.

Describing the latest developments as bizarre, senior republicans said the prospect of the institutions being put on hold defied all logic. Claiming that the British Government was trying to put pressure on the IRA by making preparations for suspension, they were adamant this strategy was not going to work. Suspension after only eight weeks would 'pull the rug' from under those elements of the movement which were arguing for a political way forward. On the other hand, if the Executive was allowed to function successfully for two years, there would be very few people in republican circles supporting the resumption of armed struggle.

There was now a growing suspicion among republicans that the Ulster Unionists were more interested in isolating them politically than in making the new institutions work. The sense of frustration among republicans would be all the greater, in the event of suspension, because the Executive at Stormont had been allowed to get off the ground in the first place. Republican sources also revealed that they had 'very deliberately' adopted a low-key approach and curtailed their public comments on the political situation. They did not want to 'push Trimble further into the corner that he is in'. Their message to unionists was: 'This thing is working, give it a chance.'

Nerves were fraught on the unionist side in the aftermath of Mandelson's initial response to Patten and a review was seen as a means of buying time for Trimble. In his previous report the General said, 'the Commission is prepared, if necessary, to state that actual decommissioning is to start within a specified period'. While there was a possibility he could set out his own timetable for the achievement of total decommissioning by May, it was not clear how this would assist Trimble whereas it would certainly arouse adverse reaction from the republican side. If the General were able to announce that the IRA had agreed the 'modalities' (methods and procedures) of decommissioning, this would be seen as a step in the right direction, but as the republican movement believed Trimble had in effect delivered an ultimatum on weapons, an agreement on modalities would prove difficult to secure at this stage. A Women's Coalition supporter said, only half in jest, that the stand-off was all about 'male pride'.

Efforts to resolve the impasse were being hindered by the tabling of an Ulster Unionist motion at the Assembly, calling on members 'to take note of reports from the Independent International Commission on Decommissioning'. The motion was down for discussion the day after the General's report was due. It had originally been tabled in the name of the party chief whip, Jim Wilson, but now appeared on the order paper in Trimble's name. Despite the innocuous wording, nationalists were fearful of how a debate on weapons would go at such a time: 'The place will explode.' Republicans were said to be taking the motion as a step towards a unionist withdrawal from the Executive and wondering what was the point of making even verbal concessions in that context. There were signs of intense diplomatic activity on the part of Dublin, London and Washington. Dublin, in particular, was reported to be 'twisting Sinn Féin's arm'.

It was thought the General might be in contact with the IRA interlocutor over the last weekend in January. Contacts up to now had produced little and usually well-informed sources said if the General's report were being produced immediately it would be negative in tone. Sources on the Dublin side said they had been urging caution on the British over the suspension. Mandelson said that if the General reported decommissioning was still 'on track', he would be guided by that conclusion, but British sources explained that 'on track' had to mean more than 'warm words'.

Another aspect of the unfolding political tragedy was that both unionists and republicans were enjoying their ministerial posts: not so much the plush offices and accoutrements as the opportunity to put their policies into practice and make a difference to the lives of ordinary people. Unionists took satisfaction from having demolished a number of myths during the Executive's eight-week existence. The taunt could no longer be made with conviction that – to paraphrase a former unionist leader's infamous remark about Catholics – they wouldn't have 'one' about the place.[1] All external appearances suggested the mainstream unionist leadership had entered the power-sharing arrangement willingly and in some cases with gusto. The myth that they would try to undermine the North–South bodies from the first day had also been scotched, as nobody had been more enthusiastic or high profile in this respect than Empey, in his role as Minister of Enterprise.

In an interview with Radio Ulster's *Inside Politics* on 29 January, Adams warned that, if the institutions were suspended, the IRA would probably withdraw from talks with de Chastelain. Republican sources confirmed privately that the channel between the General and the 'Army' would indeed be closed down if the Executive fell.

A major political and diplomatic effort was under way the night before delivery to ensure de Chastelain was in a position to give a positive report. Officially due by 31 January, at a late stage the night before it had still not been written. Senior officials from Dublin were spearheading the diplomatic push, with the active encouragement of the new Minister for Foreign Affairs, Brian Cowen, who had succeeded David Andrews when the latter announced his retirement. While it was broadly accepted that there was no possibility the General could report an actual decommissioning gesture, political and diplomatic efforts were reportedly aimed at securing a convincing undertaking from the IRA that it would use its best efforts to meet the May target for total disarmament – an implicit deadline. It was clear from the protracted nature of the negotiations that the two governments were experiencing very considerable difficulty in getting the IRA to move. Mitchell's book had shown how the governments' role could even extend to writing a whole section of a draft docu-ment. The General might not want for anonymous would-be scriptwriters but he would have to stand over what appeared in his name.

The de Chastelain eagle finally landed with British officials at Stormont around midnight. The Irish side, which was based downtown, received a copy at 1.30 am on 1 February, 90 minutes past the deadline. It was said that the IRA was in contact with the General late the previous night with 'a form of words'.

Cowen and Mandelson were to meet that afternoon in Dublin: it was stated later that the Irish had put off the meeting from Friday. We were told that the report would not be made public until afterwards – maybe long afterwards. This was not a healthy sign: Dublin was believed to have asked for it to be withheld. The sceptics were strengthened in their view that suspension and the consequent withdrawal of the IRA interlocutor could not now be avoided.

When the text was finally released almost two weeks later, it confirmed the widespread belief that the IRA had given little or no ground. The Commission recalled its own December declaration that there was a basis for an assessment that decommissioning would happen. Now it was saying, 'While we believe that conclusion was well-founded, we await further evidence to substantiate it.' There were continuing ceasefires and positive IRA language, but no sign of any guns: 'Our sole task is decommissioning and to date we have received no information from the IRA as to when decommissioning will start.' The report ended on an ominous note: 'If it becomes clear to us that decommissioning is not to happen, the Commission will recommend to the governments that it be disbanded.'

While the text was not immediately released to the media, there were no prizes for guessing that the report was fairly thin gruel. It was now clear that the Mitchell Review had been a very uneasy compromise indeed. Trimble had agreed to buy a fudge on decommissioning before, and got away with it, but this time he was caught. There was a tetchy dispute now over what was actually agreed in the Review. The unionists were adamant that Sinn Féin had indicated there would be a practical gesture on weapons by the end of January. There were claims that George Mitchell expected this to happen, but the Review chairman kept his counsel. SDLP sources went out of their way to point out that setting the end of January for delivery of the General's report implied that there would be decommissioning by that date.

Republicans flatly rejected these suggestions, claiming to have supporting correspondence and other written evidence. The unspoken implication from the republican side was that the UUP leadership had said one thing in private in the Review and was now saying something different in public. There were hints from the Sinn Féin camp that in the event of suspension the 'smoking gun' correspondence would be produced. On the one hand, their restraint was in line with speculation that they had been asked to take a low-key approach in public at this time, resisting the temptation to hit Trimble as hard as he was hitting them. But if they possessed documentation to discredit Trimble's claims, the republicans lost out heavily in the short term by with-holding it, giving rise to doubts in Dublin and SDLP circles that they indeed possessed such evidence. There was charge and counter-charge and, given the inherent establishment bias against republicans and any group linked with unofficial vio-lence and changes in the status quo, Sinn Féin sustained serious damage in the media battle.

Judging from the UUP leader's tone, the 24 hours after deliv-ery of the report were not one of his better days. Clearly a man under pressure, he told a crowded news conference at Parlia-ment Buildings in Stormont that suspension was 'regrettable but inevitable' because Sinn Féin had defaulted on its obligations. The calling of the news conference at such short notice to under-line the necessity for suspension suggested the unionists were worried about what might emerge from the Cowen–Mandelson meeting later in the day and that suspension might not be announced immediately afterwards.

When Sinn Féin addressed the media afterwards, Martin McGuinness spoke in quite emotional terms about the compro-mises he had made to advance the peace process. The seasoned republican seemed on the verge of tears. As he and Adams stood before the assembled reporters and camera crews in the main hall at Stormont, DUP members gazed down from the balconies at each side, although they did not heckle. The young DUP Assembly Member, Paul Berry[2] was smiling from ear to ear.

Cowen and Mandelson were walking up the stairs to their meeting in Iveagh House, Dublin, at around 4 pm when RTE's Chief News Correspondent, Charlie Bird received a phone call from an IRA source. Bird took down a statement made on behalf of the IRA which pointed out that the organisation had met the de Chastelain commission three times – 'and as late as last night we were in contact'. The purpose of the meetings, the statement said, was to stress that the cessation was being maintained, the guns were silent and the IRA was no threat to the peace process. Bird immediately passed on the statement to officials, who brought it into the ministerial meeting. There had also been con-tact earlier between Dublin and Sinn Féin, where the republicans were reportedly told in blunt terms that the IRA had clearly not engaged seriously with the General.

Although couched in the usual 'Provo-speak', great significance was being read into the latest IRA text by republicans and their sympathisers, who maintained that it was a roundabout way of saying the 'war' was over. At worst it was a signal the republican paramilitaries were still 'in play'. Sources close to the unionist leadership said privately that if the statement had been issued after the first ceasefire in 1994 it could have allayed fears which then prevailed about the permanence of that cessation. It might also have halted moves to introduce the decommissioning issue – brought in, according to these sources, as a means of testing the IRA's commitment to peace.

Unionists had expected swift action from Mandelson to suspend the institutions but Cowen managed – with some difficulty, according to the Irish side – to persuade the British to defer the deadline by 48 hours until Thursday, the day before Trimble's resignation was expected to take effect. The faces of Cowen and Mandelson afterwards showed the strain of a tough meeting. The extra time – Mandelson called it a 'breathing space' – was given in the hope that the IRA could be pressured into giving the General grounds for believing that decommissioning would take place by 22 May. Close observers of the republican scene believed this was a bridge too far. Republicans did not see much difference, if any, between a start-date for decommissioning and the real thing.

Dublin officials and Sinn Féin negotiators worked on new drafts of a stronger commitment on weapons, which were in turn shown to senior IRA figures for their comments. The Sinn Féin filter was essential: persistent suggestions that Dublin was directly involved face-to-face with the IRA were strongly denied. Dublin's thinking was revealed to me by a senior source who pointed out that republicans had always said the decommissioning issue should be left exclusively to de Chastelain and his people. In the esoteric discourse on decommissioning, disposing of weapons in consultation with the General would, in theory at least, be different in republican eyes from a weapons gesture carried out at the behest of the Ulster Unionists. It looked like a clever attempt to trap republicans in their own logic.

The Agreement provided for the parties to use their best

efforts to bring about total decommissioning within a two-year period, but republicans always argued the clock should only start ticking with the appointment of ministers to the Executive, which did not take place until December 1999. As a compromise, a possible eighteen-month period was in the air, which would be subject to the full and wholehearted implementation of the other aspects of the Agreement. There was an additional complication arising from the fact that an IRA convention would reportedly have to approve any major initiative on the weapons issue.

The prospect of a straight weapons handover was as usual being ruled out, but the possibility of a move to disable explosives was mooted, apparently by Dublin. Republicans were coming under pressure to be more specific about 'modalities'. For their part they continued to complain about what they called the 'anaemic' manner in which the decommissioning body carried out its business. They felt it should be more pro-active and less reliant on the advice of the two governments, taking its lead rather from the Patten Commission, which was seen as an example of robust autonomy. Dublin's frantic activity was calculated on persuading the republicans to express their position in a new way so that a more positive de Chastelain report could be compiled, which London in its turn could cajole the unionists to accept. Ambiguity and fudge had brought the process a long way – even as far as setting up a power-sharing executive – but the options were narrowing at this stage and the famed creativity and linguistic flexibility of the Irish civil servants were facing their greatest test yet.

Rarely had one seen Adams and McGuinness look as tired as they did on emerging from their 2 February meeting with the Taoiseach at Government Buildings in Dublin. Word had it that the encounter was unsatisfactory from Dublin's viewpoint because of the size of the Sinn Féin delegation. Taoisigh and prime ministers liked to deal with Gerry and Martin alone, it appeared. A senior member of the republican delegation told me he was impressed with Cowen but he also stressed that the basic republican stance on weapons was firm: echoing loyalist and unionist rhetoric, he said they were the real 'no-surrenderers'.

The republican mindset on decommissioning at this stage had been accurately conveyed by Sinn Féin vice-president and Assembly Member, Pat Doherty, to the *Boston Herald* in

November. Asked if he could say that the IRA would disarm, he replied: 'No, no, no.' He added: 'Do you think it is conceivable that if the institutions are working and if the ceasefire is holding and that arms are not being used that the whole thing would be collapsed? That would just be lunacy.'

The plan nearly worked. Had Trimble emerged untrammelled from his UUC meeting on 27 November, Mandelson would not have been under anything like the same pressure subsequently to suspend the institutions. There would have been no gun to the Secretary of State's head, in the form of a resignation letter signed by Trimble and wielded by Sir Josias Cunningham. The Executive would then have continued in existence at least until 22 May, with a fighting chance it could survive even beyond that. 'Doherty's remarks helped create the situation he [Mandelson] was trying to avoid,' British sources told me later.

A meeting between Ahern and Blair was expected on 3 February but the Prime Minister had embarked on a tour of England's West Country. A group of Irish journalists pursued a will-o'-the-wisp Blair from Exeter to Plymouth, finding themselves at one stage subject to questioning by the police. The posse intercepted Blair as he was about to board a train at Exeter. 'I'm sorry guys,' he told them. 'I can't answer questions on Northern Ireland at the minute, honestly.' Downing Street did not seem to want to know too much about the North that day and there was considerable doubt whether the meeting with Ahern would actually take place.

Trimble was said to be playing solitaire on his computer in the House of Commons while the governments tried to sort things out. Associates said it was a habit of the UUP leader, when he needed time to think. By early evening the shape of things to come had begun to emerge. Mandelson would make an announcement on legislation to suspend the institutions, but the British Government intended to hasten slowly and the royal assent would not be given until well into the following week. If the decommissioning difficulty had been resolved by that time, then the new law need never be used. It was also understood that Trimble's resignation would be put on hold until the legislation went through. The IRA had been given an extra week.

'Clarity' was now the watchword. It was used by the Taoiseach, who said 'clarity' and not 'product' was the issue. The word was a euphemism for a timetable and it appeared in the Mandelson statement to the Commons: he told MPs that definite information was needed as to when the disposal of weapons would begin. He greatly annoyed republicans when he described the lack of adequate engagement with de Chastelain as a betrayal of the entire community in Northern Ireland. However Mallon made the most pointed contribution of the debate when he said there were two questions for the Provisionals: 'One: Will you decommission? Two, if Yes, when will you decommission?'[3] This stark formulation became the template for subsequent events and even though Mallon himself pleaded that there be no suspension, his words were adopted as a refrain by critics of the republican stance. Republicans felt Mallon should have considered the likely consequences of his words more carefully.

There had been speculation that Mandelson would make a holding statement rather than announce the start of the legislative process. Republicans claimed this was their understanding and it was believed Dublin neither expected nor wished the Secretary of State to go as far as he did. However, under London's logic, anything less would not have preserved Trimble and this was the overriding factor.

Further words, it appears, were secured – not without difficulty – by the Taoiseach in his contacts with republicans and this enabled him to fly to England for his meeting with Blair, which had been pencilled-in for lunchtime in Exeter and then moved to Plymouth in the late afternoon, before it finally took place at 9 pm at a cliff-top hotel in St Austell, Cornwall. For the Irish side, top civil servant Paddy Teahon asserted strongly that more time was needed to resolve the weapons issue.

The *Observer* reported later that Adams was on the phone to complain to the Secretary of State within twenty minutes of his Commons statement and that an exhausted Mandelson had tried to calm him down. Next day, 4 February, the Sinn Féin president sounded like a man preparing public opinion for the worst when he accused Mandelson of undermining his efforts by charging republicans with betrayal. There was concern in the republican camp about the consequences, in the likely eventuality that the pressure on the IRA did not work. 'What are we left to deal with if the institutions collapse?' republicans asked privately. Adams and McGuinness would start to lose the argument inside republicanism, and there was no knowing the end-result.

A hard-line tone was set by the UUP with a statement issued on the morning of 4 February in the name of Sir Josias Cunningham. The UUC president said he was 'seeking confirmation' from Mandelson on the timing of the suspension of the institutions. 'It is clear that these institutions cannot continue in the absence of actual decommissioning by paramilitaries,' he said. The pressure was on, but Mandelson bought some time with a speech in Liverpool that evening: 'If there are no clear changes for the better to give confidence that decommissioning will happen, I will put on hold the operation of the institutions in seven days' time.'

A fifteen-minute meeting next day between Adams and Trimble yielded little. There was a further IRA statement – they were coming thick and fast these days – recognising that 'the issue of arms needs to be dealt with in an acceptable way'. As usual, one's interpretation depended on one's point of view: the IRA was coming to terms with reality or just serving up further palaver. Dublin officials took part in intensive discussions with Sinn Féin over the weekend in Belfast while, on the security front, a small bomb planted by the Continuity IRA at a hotel in Irvinestown, County Fermanagh, contributed to the fraught atmosphere.

A high-level NIO source told journalists in a private briefing in Belfast that the British Government would stand by Trimble, who was a good and courageous man. Leaving him high and dry would be altogether unthinkable. If Trimble resigned it would probably mean fresh elections to the Assembly within six weeks, with moderate unionism and nationalism losing out heavily, given the current climate. The senior NIO source did not see the latest IRA pronouncements as progress: he was hoping for a further statement, on which a decision to suspend or not could be based. It was unclear whether the source believed Trimble could go back to the UUC without 'product'. The NIO man seemed pleasantly surprised at the spontaneous consensus against Sinn Féin and its paramilitary friends on the decommissioning issue, which had included John Hume and major US newspapers, but he had no wish to see the republicans isolated or ostracised.

Adams, McGuinness and de Brún travelled to London on 8

February where they met Blair just as the debate on the suspension legislation was about to start in the Commons. Most unusually for Sinn Féin, they went in by a back door to No. 10, avoiding camera crews and journalists. The London visit came amid reports of growing pressure on the IRA to issue yet another statement, the third in a fortnight, aimed at easing the difficulties in the peace process. There was talk of a republican offer to stand down the IRA over an eighteen-month period: Downing Street was said to be interested, with unionists cool towards the idea. Another suggestion in circulation at this stage, with covert encouragement from London, was a redefinition of decommissioning. This might involve a change in the legislation passed in Dublin and London, seen by some as being unduly restrictive and leaving little scope for exploring that area between what would satisfy unionists and what would leave republican pride intact. The desired situation was one where 'guns in the ground' or an order to dump arms constituted decommissioning if the IICD said so, but the IICD was constrained by the definitions laid down in law which specified that the weapons must either be destroyed or otherwise rendered permanently unusable.

Considerable interest was aroused by a proposal in an editorial in the *Guardian* on 8 February for a Day of Reconciliation, as previously suggested at Hillsborough. This would involve British demilitarisation, accompanied by decommissioning of weapons on the part of republican and loyalist paramilitaries. There were even suggestions of US interest in the plan: it was thought to have come up in a telephone conversation between the Taoiseach and Clinton that evening but it might all be too late. Even if republicans 'bought into' the day of reconciliation, would it be acceptable to unionists? One imagined, though, that the ceremonial aspects of an event signalling a new era in relations between the two communities, and, indeed, between Britain and Ireland, might have a certain appeal for New Labour, not to mention 'New Sinn Féin'.

By all accounts, the White House was watching events very closely. Clinton was thought to be ready to do anything he could to save the process. 'There's probably one roll of the dice left,' US sources said. Dublin and London were meant to be working on a formula.

The mood in the Trimble camp was fatalistic. When republicans spoke of a unionist game-plan to undermine the institutions and bring about a return to direct rule they might well have been overestimating the strategic capacity of the UUP. Unionist ministers were enjoying their new jobs and would almost certainly wish to avoid suspension if a plausible alternative could be found. The peace process was a nationalist invention and unionists were initially reluctant to participate in it but now it had drawn in just about everybody: even the DUP had, with inevitable qualifications and disclaimers, taken up its ministries in the power-sharing administration.

After a day of intense political and diplomatic activity on 9 February, the shape of a possible compromise began to emerge. The plan being worked on by Dublin with London had a familiar ring to it: parallel moves towards the decommissioning of weapons and a scaled-down British military presence in the North (the proliferation of British Army installations in South Armagh was a particularly sore point for republicans). The suggested inter-governmental proposals would be based on contrasting the alleged certainty of achieving decommissioning in the longer term with the equal alleged certainty that decommissioning would never take place while the institutions were suspended. The view in political and diplomatic circles was that the Ulster Unionists would have to look seriously at these proposals for fear of losing the moral high ground attained in recent weeks and becoming politically isolated. Broad consensus was said to be emerging between the two governments, the White House and Sinn Féin on the shape of a compromise package. The question remained as to whether the Ulster Unionists could accept proposals which one Dublin official said were 'pregnant with decommissioning', or choose to bring the Agreement down and risk a return to conflict.

The IRA was expected to clarify its stance over the next two days but it might be 'filtered' through a third report from de Chastelain. The strongest language so far on the weapons issue was predicted. As of the evening of Wednesday 9 February, no meeting had been arranged between the Taoiseach and the Prime Minister, but it was believed that if the IRA statement was strong enough they would meet within 36 hours and might make a joint recommendation to the Ulster Unionists to accept. A variety of sources in the peace process said an idea put forward by the Bishop of Derry, Dr Hegarty, to take arms into his care for a year would not form part of any package recommended by the two governments, although the emergence of the Hegarty proposal was a telling indication of the Church's concern. Nationalists were looking on the bright side but reliable sources on the British side cautioned against undue optimism. London seemed to have learnt the lesson of Hillsborough: don't let the expectations get ahead of the game.

Cowen met Mandelson at 5 pm on 9 February for 75 minutes in London but the Irish minister's demeanour afterwards did not suggest significant progress. It was reported later that, on hearing Cowen's report of the discussions with Sinn Féin, Mandelson had said there was still not enough to save Trimble and the institutions. Trimble travelled to Dublin on Thursday morning for a meeting with Ahern who apparently told him that the latest response from the republican movement might not be available until Friday morning. This was cutting it very fine.

The first essential to be borne in mind was that the IRA was not about to decommission at the behest of David Trimble or the Ulster Unionist Council. The second was that the republican movement was prepared to say and do a great deal in the context of the Agreement, but it must be voluntary and it would take time. Interviewed by Emily O'Reilly in the *Observer* on 6 February, Martin McGuinness had made a statement which crystallised the philosophy of the 'peace process' wing of republicanism on the weapons question. Asked whether the IRA would continue to exist if the decommissioning issue was resolved and the political institutions continued to operate, McGuinness replied: 'That's a matter for the IRA. The Old IRA existed in the South for years. They attended commemorations, they buried their own comrades, and they did so peacefully. It's an odd question in my opinion. Why should we worry about it?'

Some observers were inclined to ask questions about Dublin's role. How did the myth of achievable short-term IRA decommissioning persist? After all, any number of republican spokesmen were telling everyone who would listen that (a) the IRA was not going to decommission in the near future; (b) the IRA would never hand over guns to an authority it did not recognise, in any context that had the remotest connotations of surrender; (c) the IRA would probably never do anything that unionists would define as decommissioning but, in the fullness of time, might well decide to dispose of weapons in its own way. This information was freely available and was almost certainly conveyed to the authorities in Dublin at the highest level. There was clearly a reluctance to accept it at face value, as evidenced almost exactly a year before, despite a certain amount of ambiguity, in the Taoiseach's *Sunday Times* interview.

There was a view that it would have been more honest and ultimately more fruitful to spell out the realities to the unionist community. Decommissioning in short order was not going to take place and, even if it did, it would have no value in security terms, as was shown by the LVF decommissioning gesture in December 1998[4] and as John Hume and senior security figures had pointed out. Defending their approach afterwards Dublin sources said it was necessary to reassure the unionists at all times, taking them through a series of 'staging-posts' on the road to an honourable compromise over weapons.

Pragmatism ruled at this stage and as yet little thought had been given to the constitutional implications of what Mandelson was proposing to do. Professor Brendan O'Leary wrote in *The Irish Times* that, following the repeal of the Government of Ireland Act as part of the Belfast Agreement, Westminster had no right unilaterally to suspend the institutions without the consent of the devolved Assembly. He also argued that suspension was not necessary to save Trimble's political position: although the UUP leader would probably not be re-elected first minister under current procedures, there was provision in the Agreement for changing the rules to ensure Trimble was returned to office.[5] Although it was not a point made by O'Leary, Mandelson had dispensed with the niceties when restoring Seamus Mallon to office became the overriding imperative the previous November.

Well-placed sources were reporting on the evening of 10 February that the situation was 'pretty bleak'. An IRA statement in conciliatory language had been on offer, but the republicans wanted to know in advance that the two governments would accept it and then put pressure on Trimble to compromise. Unless there was an improvement in the republican position, suspension would go ahead; worse than that, it would be suspension without a time-limit. Blair was reported to hold the view that Trimble had taken enough punishment. In a few weeks, when the media and propaganda ripples had died away, there could be another attempt at squaring the circle.

A four-point plan was floated in the media, based on the by now well-worn idea of decommissioning in parallel with demilitarisation: it had Dublin's fingerprints on it but insiders said the situation had moved beyond that. At this very point in time, senior Dublin civil servants were in Belfast talking to Sinn Féin and the leak, if it came from Dublin sources, may have been an attempt to influence those negotiations. Republicans were said to be extremely wary of a direct link between their weapons and, say, the closure of British army bases. The IRA apparently took the view that demilitarisation was helpful in creating the right context for dealing with the weapons issue but there was no question of a straight and simple trade-off between, say, the closure of a few army installations and an actual handover of guns and explosives. The issue was not what the IRA would do on a small scale this week but what spectacular gesture of reconciliation it might be persuaded to make in a year or two.

There had been a last consultation with Bertie Ahern and Brian Cowen on Thursday before the group of top Dublin officials headed North. The trio were, Paddy Teahon from the Department of the Taoiseach, Dermot Gallagher from Foreign Affairs and Tim Dalton from the Department of Justice. Since the autumn of 1998 they had comprised, with Martin Mansergh, a special 'directorate' of four to co-ordinate northern policy and try to find a solution to the problems, especially decommissioning. The work often involved very long hours and difficult meetings but, as one source put it, 'They just kept at it and didn't give up.' Dublin's negotiating technique was described to me as follows: (i) have your draft in first – so both sides work from that; (ii) have the ability to listen; (iii) know more about the subject than anyone else; (iv) remember that everyone has to get up from the table with something to sell to their constituency; (v) be prepared tactically to 'lose your temper'.[6]

Discussions between the three Dublin officials and the republicans continued in Belfast until 4.30 am on 11 February when they were finally given the text of a statement the IRA was prepared to make to the de Chastelain commission under certain conditions, including the continuation of the institutions. They drove back to Dublin and briefed the Taoiseach on the statement at 10 am. The Dublin version was that Ahern, in turn, had the statement faxed to Blair and also informed Mandelson of its contents.

Mandelson said afterwards he had planned to sign the suspension order at midday but was told at 11 am by Irish officials about overnight developments 'including a proposal on the latest IRA position'. He put back the suspension, first until 2.30 and then until five o'clock. He said he asked Adams to see Trimble and tell him what was on offer. However, instead of Adams, McGuinness went to the meeting, gave Trimble no details of the latest IRA proposal and simply demanded that he withdraw his resignation letter and call off the following morning's UUC meeting. Mandelson later said he even suggested post-dating the suspension until 14 February to allow for clarification of the IRA's position – nobody was interested. He regarded the new IRA position as a significant move but added that it was 'unclear and undefinitive' and should have been put forward two weeks earlier than it was.

The lean figure of Sir Josias hovered over everything and the spectre of the UUC president striding towards the office of the Assembly Speaker, Lord Alderdice, to present Trimble's letter of resignation was unionism's not-so-secret weapon throughout the proceedings. Ironically, for someone who was now demanding decommissioning, the UUC president was a grandson of Samuel Cunningham, who signed the cheques that paid for 50,000 German rifles landed at Bangor and Larne in 1914 by Sir Edward Carson's Ulster Volunteer Force to resist the imposition of Irish Home Rule.[7] Mandelson was said to have persuaded Cunningham to postpone delivery of the letter from 2.30 to 4.30 pm while the Secretary of State phoned de Chastelain for reports of movement. Mid-afternoon seems to have been the decisive time. British Government sources said that by 4 pm Mandelson was 'completely in the dark' as to the IRA's position and Trimble was 'bemused'. Mallon met Mandelson and advised him against taking an action that would effectively be in the interest of one party alone.

Reporters struggled to keep up with the fast-developing sequence of events. First the statement of suspension from Mandelson was said to be coming at 5 pm (sources called it the 'death certificate'). As the minutes ticked away, a statement came, but from Sinn Féin, not the Secretary of State. Adams was heralding a fresh breakthrough but, according to London sources, the order to suspend had already been signed at 5.03 pm. Details of the Adams breakthrough were not immediately clear and, shortly before 6 pm, the Mandelson statement finally came out. The reimposition of direct rule was to take effect from midnight and the Executive, Assembly, North–South Ministerial Council and British–Irish Council would all be put on hold indefinitely. Now details of the 31 January de Chastelain report began to emerge and republicans immediately accused the Northern Ireland Secretary of leaking it as cover for his actions. British Government sources strongly rejected this. Eventually the text of this report was officially released.[8]

Responding to republican claims that the Northern Secretary was aware of significant moves on decommissioning by the IRA before he took the decision to suspend, London was adamant that Mandelson had already signed the ministerial order before Adams announced that a new proposition was on the way. Adams said the two governments had been kept abreast of developments leading to what he insisted was a major break-through on weapons: 'There is no question about them being surprised by this or this coming too late.' Trimble told reporters about his meeting with McGuinness during the afternoon and a subsequent telephone conversation with Adams: 'No information was available to me, and they had nothing for me, and con-sequently suspension became inevitable.'

Fevered activity continued that evening, but did not seem to be achieving much. It emerged that a further de Chastelain report might be on the way which could change the complexion of events. A nationalist source said Mandelson had moved too soon: 'He could look awfully foolish.' The second de Chastelain report began to leak, with initial reports ranging from 'nothing sensa-tional' to potentially seismic. This text, when it was released around 9.30 pm, indicated for the first time that the IRA was pre-pared to put its weapons 'beyond use'. De Chastelain said there had been 'several contacts' with IRA and loyalist representatives in the previous eleven days, since the delivery of his earlier report. The IRA had engaged 'frankly and helpfully' and had given an undertaking that it would consider how to put arms and explosives beyond use, as part of the full implementation of the

Good Friday Agreement and in the context of the removal of the causes of conflict. The Commission described this undertaking as 'particularly significant' and viewed it as 'valuable progress'. It said that, earlier in the day, the interlocutor had indicated to the Commission the context in which the IRA would initiate a comprehensive process to put arms beyond use, in a manner calculated to ensure maximum public confidence. The report concluded: 'The Commission believes that this commitment, on the basis described above, holds out the real prospect of an agreement which would enable it to fulfil the substance of its mandate.'

This was much more positive language from the Commission than the previous report. A prominent republican struck an apocalyptic note in conversation: 'If Mandelson is suspending in the face of us getting that from the IRA, the whole thing is finished.' However, a leading unionist of pragmatic inclination told me next day that the report would not have been sufficient to get Trimble through the UUC. This man said he was reading and re-reading the IICD report to divine its exact meaning. He was concerned about the phrase 'in the context of the removal of the causes of conflict'. This was more ambiguous than 'the full implementation of the Good Friday Agreement' and he wondered if the IRA was, in fact, hardening up its position. However, he said he would read the report again.

One of the difficulties in interpreting the report was that the public was not privy to the actual IRA statement made to the General and had to depend on his second-hand account. It was unclear whether the expression 'beyond use' was employed by the IRA or was inserted by the de Chastelain commission. The Taoiseach later said that having received the IRA statement in confidence he could not make it public. He did confirm, however, that the statement (known to insiders as 'Angel Two')[9] had been given to his officials at 4.30 am in Belfast on the day of suspension. While Dublin said it was faxed to Downing Street after a 10 am conversation between Ahern and Blair, Downing Street said the British Government had nothing on paper until after the suspension order was signed.

There was a protracted dispute over the time when Mandelson became aware of the contents of the second de Chastelain report. The strongest indictment came from the BBC

Northern Ireland *Spotlight* programme broadcast on 22 February, in which Political Editor Stephen Grimason said he had seen the Secretary of State receiving the document at approximately 6.25 pm, but that Mandelson had gone on to give the impression in subsequent television interviews that he had not seen it. The Northern Ireland Office sharply rejected this version of events, adding that the document was a note from a civil servant, not a copy of the report.

A joint communiqué from Dublin and London was expected, but with Dublin reported to be upset that Mandelson had moved without waiting for the second de Chastelain text, the communiqué never came. Dublin had been working flat-out for a solution even at the last minute, had argued against suspension on political and legal grounds and was deeply disappointed when Mandelson proceeded with the collapse of the institutions. It was reported that the Irish Attorney General, Michael McDowell, had advised Dublin that the British could not unilaterally suspend the institutions, which were set up under the terms of an international treaty, the British–Irish Agreement.[10]

London believed the suspension move may have jolted the IRA into its first significant initiative on decommissioning, replacing fancy footwork with meaningful action. Previously there had been 'a lot of words, a lot of pieces of paper', but there had been doubts about the seriousness of Sinn Féin's negotiations with the movement's paramilitary wing. Angry republicans completely rejected this scenario and also expressed disappointment with Dublin's stance, which they claimed had been insufficiently firm.

It was understood that the UUP leadership was anxious to have the suspension order announced in time for the six o'clock news on 11 February so that UUC delegates would know what was going on. There was concern lest they arrive at the Waterfront next morning in a grumpy and confused state. A journalistic colleague put it in graphic if quite disparaging terms: the unionist leadership were 'so panicky about getting screwed in the middle of the night that they want it on the six o'clock news for their rednecks'. Given the reports of continuing activity after the Mandelson statement and the difficulty even seasoned observers were having 'reading' the game, the sturdy farmers and shopkeepers might have been, if not confused, certainly bemused as they took their seats.

The reconvened UUC meeting was marked at times by heated debate, although it did not reach the level of tension and drama of 27 November. When Trimble first got up to speak, there was a surprise interruption from Ms Michelle Williamson, both of whose parents had been killed by the IRA bomb on Belfast's Shankill Road in October 1993. She was neither a delegate nor a party member and was said to have been brought into the hall by a leading campaigner against the Agreement. As soon as he recognised her, the leader courteously yielded the platform to the visitor, who spoke for about two minutes. She held Trimble personally responsible for the UUP's entry to government with Sinn Féin/IRA and called for his resignation. There were shouts of approval from younger delegates and some rose to their feet to applaud. However, a Trimble associate later dismissed the intervention as a 'f***ing stunt'.

Trimble put forward a motion: 'In the event of any proposal by the Secretary of State to revoke the suspension of the Assembly and executive, before any UUP participation the leader will make a further report to this council.' He claimed the British Government would not have moved the suspension legislation and signed the subsequent order had it not been for his resignation letter. An amendment to Trimble's motion was proposed by David Burnside from the Unionist Information Office in London, linking future participation in the Executive with the retention of the 'proud name' of the RUC. Trimble spoke again, pleading with the party not to adopt the amendment but to take on board a less-restrictive resolution passed a meeting of the Executive six days before. Burnside said he was putting his trust in the leader: he would withdraw the amendment as requested but, if sufficient progress were not made in the meantime, the amendment would be re-submitted. The motion was passed by a show of hands, with Cunningham estimating later that only about fifteen out of some 760 delegates had opposed it.

Meanwhile, the Sinn Féin fightback was beginning. They weren't taking events lying down. At a news conference in West Belfast that afternoon, Adams went into considerable detail in an effort to repudiate suggestions that Mandelson had not known what was on offer from the IRA when he signed the suspension order. Recalling events in the early hours of 11 February, Adams said: 'As part of very intense shuttle diplomacy an advanced IRA position was secured.' Sinn Féin gave this to the Irish Government in the marathon meeting that ended at 4.30 am. This position was subsequently passed to the British Government and Adams spoke to Blair about it by phone around noon; he also spoke to the Taoiseach and Mandelson in the course of the afternoon. He had intended to meet Trimble but when, for unspecified reasons, this was not possible he asked McGuinness to do so and that meeting took place at 2 pm. The IICD had also received the IRA's position; McGuinness discussed the issues briefly with them and phoned Adams afterwards.

'Martin and I formed a clear view that the second report would be positive and was imminent.' Adams spoke to Mandelson and, on the basis of the new initiative, urged him not to collapse the institutions: 'It was obvious that he was intent on proceeding with suspension.' The Sinn Féin leader spoke to Trimble by telephone and asked him, also on the basis of the new initiative, to withdraw his resignation but, according to Adams, Trimble said it was not enough. In this context, Adams decided to go public in the hope of forestalling suspension. 'I issued a statement at 5.10 pm outlining the initiative. The rest is history.'

The deed was done and now there was likely to be a cooling-off period of at least a couple of weeks. No format for the expected review of the Agreement had yet been drawn up, but there was speculation that a 'low-profile international figure' might be asked to chair it. John Major's name, which seemed to fit this description, came and went in speculation. British sources said that while the latest de Chastelain report was welcome and constituted progress, further clarification was needed. Although it had opened a path which might eventually lead to a lifting of the suspension, this was not just a matter for the two governments. For their part, republican sources were muttering about conspiracy: the old alliance of unionists and Britain had connived to bring down the institutions.

It was not advisable at this stage to mention Dublin to certain Sinn Féin members unless you were prepared to withstand a stream of invective about double-crossing weaklings who could and should have used their clout to stay Mandelson's hand. This anger inevitably modified over time as Dublin sought to inject fresh momentum into the process. There would probably never be an agreed version of the 11 February events between the Secretary of State and Sinn Féin. No public, agreed record was available of what Adams and McGuinness told Mandelson and Trimble that day. Perhaps republicans did not really believe the suspension would go ahead, which may explain why the Adams statement heralding an IRA breakthrough was issued so late, after Mandelson had already signed the suspension order. It must have been particularly wounding for republicans when Bill Clinton, who had so often been a dream president from their point of view, publicly criticised their timing: 'I regret that the IRA did not give the de Chastelain commission a more timely commitment on arms decommissioning to maintain the momentum toward full implementation of the accord.' It was probably true that if the second de Chastelain report was ready to be made public in, say, the early afternoon, Dublin would have pulled out all the stops and might well have halted the suspension.

Republican brinkmanship or London–Glengall Street conspiracy? The correct analysis was not immediately clear. However, as in the past, the pieces had to be picked up and some effort made to get the show back on the road. Writing in *The Irish Times* on 14 February, the Taoiseach said the formulations in the latest de Chastelain report had 'deep significance'. He argued that the Commission was saying, in effect, that it had a commitment from the IRA that decommissioning would happen. Later that Monday, Mandelson conceded the possibility in a speech that the latest de Chastelain report 'may be the first sign that the IRA are, after all, prepared to give up their arms once and for all'. British Government sources insisted there was no British–Irish rift, merely 'differences of emphasis'.

Sinn Féin sources were extremely sceptical about the prospects of an imminent rescindment of the suspension order, as suggested by the SDLP. Republicans argued privately: 'The Irish Government should have said, "We are not going to tolerate this being suspended over our heads and we are publicly going to say this is a breach of international law".' There was a question mark over Sinn Féin's participation in a review if the conditions appeared to allow for any re-negotiation of the Good Friday Agreement.

The following day, 15 February, the IRA announced the withdrawal of its interlocutor from the decommissioning body along with the proposals it had put to de Chastelain. Although it was an inevitable consequence of Friday's events, it still came as a nasty jolt. It was a significant political setback, since it was probably the first time in its history that the movement had discussed the issue of voluntary disarmament with an official body. There had been speculation that, if Mandelson was prepared to reinstate the institutions in short order, the new IRA proposals would remain on the table. The immediate result of the IRA announcement would be to render a meeting scheduled the next day between the Taoiseach and the Prime Minister a fairly hollow affair. While Dublin insisted the announcement had been anticipated, nevertheless the Taoiseach seemed to be thrown off balance when the text was given to him while he was on his feet in the Dáil chamber.

The question that no doubt exercised the minds of the two leaders meeting in London was whether the IRA offer could be restored and clarified – or if it had gone for good. Initial indications were contradictory and not always encouraging. Long-time Provo-watchers believed the debate on decommissioning would have to shift to new ground. The element within the republican movement which favoured a straightforward and blunt rejection of decommissioning demands seemed to have won a debating point with the 'fancy footwork but still no handover' wing. The right-wing *Daily Telegraph* put it in melodramatic terms: 'The wolves are in charge; the serpents have lost out.'

An alternative analysis of the impasse held out greater hope. The IRA move was tactical and some creative 'thinking outside the box' could move the situation forward. Political sources were still hopeful that the IRA was playing a tactical game rather than taking an irrevocable step on the weapons issue: 'It's quite a calculated upping of the ante.'

Mandelson needed to mend some fences with the republican side. It appeared a meeting he had with republicans on 15 February was as bad as it gets, but accounts differed as to who patronised whom. Nevertheless, observers found it hard to argue with the logic of 'No David Trimble, no peace process'. No nationalist or republican wanted Peter Robinson, say, as First Minister. There were signs that the Irish Government was seeking to avoid 'taking the rap' for the whole debacle with a report in the *Irish Independent*, on the day of Ahern's London summit with Blair, that Dublin was blaming Mandelson for the disaster.

Since the IRA statement to de Chastelain had not been published, there was inevitably considerable interest in what it might contain. A report in a Dublin-based Sunday newspaper, for example, said that the IRA, in its 'private note' to de Chastelain, had agreed (i) to take part in a day of reconciliation where republican, loyalist and British Army weapons would be disposed of as a signal that the conflict was ended; (ii) to state within three months that the war was over, and (iii) to put its weapons beyond use in a series of choreographed steps over an eighteen-month period in parallel with demilitarisation by the British Army, including the dismantling of Border posts.[11]

It was relatively unusual for the republican paramilitaries to respond directly to media reports, but in a briefing to selected journalists on 22 February, an IRA representative said the organisation had not made any proposal for decommissioning in parallel with demilitarisation; that no time-frame for weapons disposal had been offered to General de Chastelain; and that no gesture on decommissioning was envisaged. The IRA source said it was 'totally wrong' to make a linkage between decommissioning and demilitarisation.

The IRA briefing did not halt the speculation as to what had been on offer to de Chastelain. Sources said that republicans held out the possibility of a permanent end to the organisation's 30-year campaign of violence. However, it was believed republicans were not prepared to take any definitive steps by the 22 May deadline because the institutions had only started in early December. The IRA could not give a pot of jam today but could apparently wind down the factory tomorrow.

Sinn Féin sources thought they had convinced unionists in the Mitchell Review that the logical result of developing the peace process would be a voluntary IRA decision to 'end in a permanent way the physical force tradition of republicanism on this island'. Unionist scepticism when presented with such a scenario was understandable, not least against a background of gunrunning and unclaimed killings, but it was a prize of such proportions that the possibilities had to be worth exploring.

The paperback edition of Donald MacIntyre's *Mandelson and the Making of New Labour*, published the following year,[12] would provide fresh detail on the events surrounding suspension and publish the draft text from the IRA leadership for the first time. The IRA statement speaks of initiating an 'internal' process to put arms 'beyond use'. The organisation would 'facilitate verification' of this but, critically, the IRA would not permit de Chastelain to refer directly to this undertaking in his report. MacIntyre also writes that, in a phone call with Blair, a top Irish civil servant angrily condemned Mandelson for signing the suspension order, unaware that the Secretary of State was plugged into the conversation on an extension line.

Decommissioning was now engraved so firmly on the process that it would be well-nigh impossible to remove it as an issue. In an ideal world it could be put to one side, and leading republicans rued the day they agreed to entertain the subject in the first place. The radical commentator Eamonn McCann described Sinn Féin's policy as, 'Fudge your way to freedom'.

The Day of Reconciliation still survived as a possible way out·of the maze. There was a strong adverse reaction from sections of the British media and unnamed military sources to the notion of 'equivalence' between the security forces and the IRA. Nevertheless, the idea would probably be pursued and probed a little further. One of the weaknesses of the peace process was that it had not made the feelings and concerns of the bereaved and the wounded a more central issue. The Troubles would not be resolved by giving ex-paramilitaries a new suit and £38,000 a year but by achieving some form of closure on the suffering and the pain, clearing away a patch of neutral ground where former foes could say: 'We inflicted much; we endured much; now it's over.'

It had been suggested that the Northern parties should be brought to the US for concentrated discussions, along the lines of the Dayton talks in 1995 about the Bosnian conflict, possibly with George Mitchell in the chair. The Senator had rejected the prospect of returning to the North, but if George would not come to the mountain, then the mountain might come to George.

Sinn Féin wanted the institutions reinstated, but a high-level Dublin government source said this was unlikely without movement on the weapons issue. While the latest efforts to resolve the impasse had been unsuccessful, the source said, 'the package will be much the same'. Most of the sessions at a Sinn Féin conference in Dublin City University on 27 February were closed to the media, but there were few external indications of serious criticism of the leadership. The speech from Adams was interrupted by applause from time to time, and he was given a standing ovation by delegates at the end. He was clapped when he said the Sinn Féin leadership could not be expected to secure an IRA surrender where the British Army had failed.

Queuing for soup and sandwiches at the college canteen, I asked Adams what he saw as the way forward. He told me he would need a week off, doing nothing except thinking and hanging about, before he could provide an answer. I noticed he was taking Rescue Remedy, a herbal product widely used for relaxation purposes. There was some banter with Gerry Kelly, who turned down a good-humoured offer to take some too. But if Adams had a 'rescue remedy' for the peace process he was keeping it to himself.

Chapter 13

TRIMBLE'S RISK FOR PEACE

David Trimble was early. Pottering about, he waited with his usual air of mild amusement for the journalists and camera crews to settle around the table and in the corners of the small, overcrowded room. He had arrived even before the American journalist who was to introduce him and chair the press conference. When Peter Hickman turned up at the set time, he found the Trimbleistas already clustered around the podium.

The location was the National Press Club in downtown Washington. Every year on St Patrick's Day, jetlagged and lamenting my lack of sleep, I took a taxi from the hotel to attend Trimble's traditional early-morning encounter with the media. The Club had the air of a university common room rather than the usual seedy retreat for hacks. I recall adverts for bursaries, scholarships and awards; well-taken black-and-white photographs of silver-haired media veterans beside their inspirational mottoes; and notices for other events in the afternoon or next day, that I would love to attend if I had more time. One of these years I am going to spend a few days there, sitting in on all the press conferences, studying the memorabilia, and hearing the old hands tell their tales of the Nixon campaign trail or the travails of working in the Saigon bureau in 1969.

John F. Kennedy and Fidel Castro had spoken there, as well as every other mover and shaker over the years. Politically speaking, Trimble performed on a narrower stage than Kennedy or Castro and had been seen up to now as a reactor, an accommodater, a coper, someone who would come to terms with the new dispensation on behalf of the unionist community, but generally not a mover and shaker. Today would change that.

He had a startling announcement to make. After all the fuss and heartache of suspension five weeks earlier, he revealed he was still prepared to go into government without guns in advance from the IRA. 'We are prepared to be involved in a fresh sequence which will probably not involve arms up front but it has to involve the issue being dealt with,' he said. There was a sting in the tail for the republicans, because honeyed words were not enough, they had to be given concrete expression: 'A mere assertion which isn't reflected in terms of people's actions isn't going to carry credibility.'

Trimble was vague about the details. In the past he had spoken in very specific terms about what he required on this issue. I could still remember the shock on the faces of senior republicans, exactly one year earlier, when he told Adams at an unscheduled White House meeting that he wanted not one, but several, decommissioning 'events' in which substantial and gradually-increasing amounts of rifles, handguns, detonators and explosives would be destroyed. Try selling that to the IRA.

The new Trimble demand was nothing like as specific. He had already gone into the Executive without any explicit undertaking on the public record that the IRA would do more than engage in formal discussions with the de Chastelain commission. It hadn't been enough; his followers could not stomach it; hence the pledge to reconvene the UUC. He needed something more now, not specifically guns or explosives, but a visible and convincing sign from republicans that 'people who hitherto have been involved in paramilitarism and terrorism are going to put that behind them on a permanent basis'.[1]

When the press conference was over and we were still trying to absorb the message, Martina Purdy of the BBC remarked to me that we were dealing here with a pretty big story. I hung about afterwards to get a quiet word with Trimble and maybe some clarification, but could not get near him. As so often, short-term breaking news was distracting from the bigger picture. Word had come from Belfast that the Craigavon councillor, Jonathan Bell, who had been mentioned as a possible 'stalking horse'[2] challenger for the leadership, had instead decided to resign from the party. The UUP leader was being asked for his reaction. Sir Reg Empey pointed to Trimble in wonderment, marvelling at his leader's seemingly endless supply of luck.

When I went back to my hotel room I phoned the *Irish Times* newsdesk in Dublin to ask for generous space to give a full account of Trimble's words. Nevertheless, I still had some lingering doubts. There had been many false dawns and failed initiatives and I was afraid this was another decoy, an empty gesture to make an opponent look bad without giving anything meaningful away. That was not a reflection on Trimble's character but on the gamesmanship of politics, in Northern Ireland as in other places. In the end, I took the same view as my BBC colleague and wrote as an introductory paragraph: 'In a significant initiative, the Ulster Unionist leader, Mr David Trimble, has held out the prospect of restoring the Executive in the North, provided the IRA convincingly demonstrated its commitment to exclusively peaceful and democratic means.'

Generally speaking, and especially when he is prepared in advance, Trimble says exactly what he wants to say, neither more nor less, and no amount of probing from reporters will make him go further. It can be frustrating for journalists, but it's his God-given right. Thus, as my report notes, he refused to go into detail about his offer to rejoin the Executive with Sinn Féin. Speaking later by telephone to the *News Letter* in Belfast he was able to claim, with some plausibility, actually to have hardened his stance, since he had gone into the Executive last time on a promise but was now looking for 'action'. His comments were so vague and ambiguous – the *Belfast Telegraph* called them 'enigmatic' – that Jeffrey Donaldson said he did not know if the leader had softened his line or not. We were all having this problem.

Along with another leading dissident, Arlene Foster, Donaldson was a member of the working group on party strategy set up after the last UUC vote. This body, which was meant to produce a report, had met for two hours on 10 March; Trimble was present but gave no hint of his pending démarche. It was hard to avoid the suspicion that setting up the group with dissident members on board was another manoeuvre, like sending Donaldson to that meeting with the Irish Attorney-General at a critical moment on Good Friday. Had the Lagan Valley MP been outfoxed again?

Trimble's initiative caught Sinn Féin on the hop. Having called on him to show leadership and 'face down his rejectionists', the republicans were nonplussed when he took precisely this course of action; indeed the UUP leader boasted afterwards of having 'ambushed' them. Republicans initially said it was all just for show, fine words on a foreign field that would not be reflected in Trimble's actions back home. Adams was meeting Clinton at the White House and in a waffly exchange with the press he challenged Trimble, in effect, to repeat his National Press Club remarks in Belfast. Pressure was coming on the republicans from Ahern who commented that there were aspects of what Trimble said, including the weapons issue, on which 'others' must declare. Up to now, Sinn Féin had been relying on soundbites to get them through the week: a travel-weary Adams said on arrival that the North had seen '50 years of apartheid, 30 years of war and eight weeks of inclusive government'. In a far cry from the days of the visa controversy, he said he was going to Washington 'out of a sense of duty'.

Some of Trimble's closest supporters were astonished by his remarks and it appears the British Government was not expecting them either. Many observers wondered about his political wisdom and timing. True, the Americans appeared to be putting on the pressure, judging from a two-day visit to Belfast by Deputy National Security Adviser, James Steinberg, on 7–8 March, to meet the political parties. When it was put to the US delegation at a press briefing on 8 March that there was no chance of movement in the immediate future, possibly not before the next Westminster elections, one of them replied in can-do terms, 'We're Americans'. Certainly Clinton and his colleagues could have few complaints about Trimble's brave, even foolhardy, initiative. The conventional wisdom had been that Trimble could no nothing before the annual general meeting of the UUC on 25 March. At this event every twelve months the party leader had to submit his name for re-election. Win the vote before you take the risks, that was how most politicians would have approached it. But Trimble wasn't 'most politicians'.

Trimble's Washington words had rapid political consequences when, two days before the AGM, the Rev Martin Smyth, Chief Whip of the UUP in the Commons and a former Grand Master of the Orange Order, announced he was making a bid for the leadership. Donaldson argued against a challenge and, by all the laws of politics in the age of the spin-doctor, the 68-year-old Presbyterian minister and serving MP for South Belfast should have been laughed off the stage. However, the affable clergyman was well liked and respected in the party and had the support of the young hard-liners, the Orange Order leadership and most of

335

the party's Westminster MPs.

The result of the vote was a shock to Trimble's allies, who predicted an hour beforehand that Smyth would poll well below 40 per cent. One senior unionist had joked, 'Stalking-horse? Oh no, Martin's a cart-horse' and *The Times* of London dubbed him a 'decent dinosaur'. Smyth caused a major surprise and startled even some of his own supporters by securing 43 per cent of the vote to 57 per cent for Trimble. Half the delegates gave the leader a standing ovation; the others remained seated, although some threw aside traditional unionist restraint, punching their fists in the air and shouting 'Resign! Resign!'

As if the Smyth vote wasn't bad enough, David Burnside, a Trimble ally who had been making hard-line noises, re-submitted his motion from the last UUC meeting, linking participation in government with the retention of the RUC name. This was endorsed after a stormy debate in which a less-explicit amendment from the leadership was rejected. Again the conventional wisdom was that Trimble's room for manoeuvre was now so restricted that 'government before guns' was unlikely if not impossible. The Chief Whip of the Irish government, Seamus Brennan, had a different 'take' on the result, insisting that, despite the slim margin, the victory was still decisive, particularly in light of Trimble's Washington statement. Making a visit to the North, Brennan said: 'If you stand right back from it, what he was saying was quite breathtaking, and he got a decision today in his favour. For a unionist leader to come through, even narrowly, given that kind of announcement, will be seen in time to come as courageous.'

Brennan was virtually a lone voice, but he had a point: Trimble had given no hostages to fortune, there was no postdated letter of resignation and no pledge to reconvene the UUC. The Burnside motion was awkward but, since the precise form in which the RUC name should be retained was not spelt out, there might still be room for manoeuvre. Seen in that light, and in view of the fact that only about eight more delegates had turned against him since November, perhaps the result was not as bad as it seemed. Trimble was safe for another year, unless a group of 60 UUC delegates requisitioned an emergency meeting to vote on the leadership. But how eager would, say, Jeffrey Donaldson be to take over a deeply divided party when the leadership could well fall into his lap in due course anyway? Writing in the *Andersonstown News*, former Sinn Féin publicity director Danny Morrison highlighted the irony, 'that the UUP who remained fairly united during the armed struggle are tearing themselves apart in response to a republican peace strategy and the pressure to compromise'.

When the Sinn Féin conference at Letterkenny in July 1994 rejected the Downing Street Declaration, virtually everyone except Albert Reynolds took it as the end of all hope of an IRA ceasefire. There was a sense in which the King's Hall AGM was the unionists' Letterkenny. In the background, senior Dublin sources were saying the suspension and its aftermath had proven that no initiative could ever succeed unless taken jointly by the two governments. The sources spoke in vague but tantalising terms about the need to 'broaden' the decommissioning issue. This was a curious echo of suggestions from other quarters that the definition of decommissioning could be softened and made more flexible. The sexy diplomatic and political phrase of the day was the 'alternative context' needed for the decommissioning issue to be addressed.

It was clear Dublin would not be repeating the scenario where three of the highest civil servants in the land were meeting intermediaries for the IRA at 4.30 am in West Belfast. Not everyone in Dublin was impressed by Sinn Féin's negotiating skills either: why had the 11 February 'Angel Two' paper from the IRA not been produced at the end of January, when there would have been time to build on it and tease out some of the detail? Dublin was aware of the importance the republicans attached to their two ministries, which opened the door to so many political opportunities in North–South terms and within the North itself. As regards disposal of the guns, Dublin was flexible about the method. 'They can throw them out in the f***ing street', was how one Southern politician colourfully put it. Meanwhile, Mandelson used the Alliance Party conference on 8 April to send a message to republicans: 'An unmistakable signal of their peaceful intentions would be worth a lot more than a one-off gesture of token decommissioning.' Whatever this was, it wasn't the Washington Three precondition.

The pattern in the peace process was always one of refusing to dwell on apparent setbacks but to move on, so with Trimble's re-election out of the way a new push to break the deadlock began. The public and media perception was one of a near-disastrous situation, but officials from both governments still spoke and acted as if it were a question of finding the correct route to the finishing-line. The source of this confidence was not always apparent: Trimble even told a church service in Lisburn, the day after the Smyth vote, of his sense that a higher power might be involved and that he was merely carrying out a predetermined plan without knowing the final outcome.[3]

At this time, senior republicans were privately musing over the prospects of winning enough seats south of the Border to be eligible for membership of a future coalition government in Dublin. The issue was the subject of heated debate at the Sinn Féin *ardfheis* on the weekend of 8–9 April. A majority of speakers favoured a rejection of coalition or even further debate about it but, in an unexpected and revealing intervention, Adams successfully urged the conference to defer the decision to a special delegate meeting after the next general election. Meanwhile, north of the Border the republicans got a boost from a by-election to Omagh District Council in which their candidate, Barry McElduff, won the seat and doubled the republican vote despite a great deal of unfavourable publicity about Sinn Féin's political activities in the area.[4]

As in the lead-up to Good Friday, sources said Dublin and London could agree more or less instantly on a joint formula but that the problem was 'bridging that gap' between the Ulster Unionists and the republican movement. The challenge lay in what insiders called 'making that very fine judgment'. Even the thorny issue of demilitarisation, especially the elaborate British Army network on the hills over South Armagh, would not be allowed to stand in the way if a breakthrough were in sight. While there might be resistance from 'securocrats', pragmatism would be the order of the day if a deal were achievable. Pro-Agreement unionism seemed in a sorry state, but even here the perennial optimists found sources of comfort in the comparative success of Trimbleistas in elections to officer posts at the UUC meeting. The argument continued that, if Trimble had not given his Washington press conference, he would have secured another 50 votes in the leadership contest.

The two prime ministers were as always ready to come to

Belfast, but official sources reiterated that there had to be a solid basis on which to proceed: there was no question of flying in on a wing and a prayer, or of raising expectations without good reason. Despite the continuing criticism of Mandelson's decision to suspend the institutions London remained unapologetic, because Trimble was still a better bet than any of the likely alternatives when it came to implementing the Agreement.

Officials from the two governments had started working on a formula from the beginning of April. Initially, there were two issues: (i) what would full implementation of the Agreement mean? (ii) what kind of statement could the IRA be persuaded to make? Irish officials, say, would work out a draft and show it to the British and Sinn Féin: 'This might work.' The idea was to get the republicans to state, in effect, that the war was over. The resources of the English language were being tested yet again. Dublin sources say that a third factor came into the equation at the instigation of the British, namely, the concept of a Confidence-Building Measure by the IRA. 'There had to be some dramatic gesture,' a participant recalls.

From the militant end of the Provisional movement, the message was: 'Why should the IRA move on decommissioning when there is no evidence David Trimble can deliver the Executive anyway?' The worry on the republican side was that Dublin might be tempted into another Hillsborough scenario by agreeing a document with London which, despite the urgings of the media and the political establishment, republicans could not accept.

Discussions at Downing Street on 2 May involving the two prime ministers and the main northern parties lasted more than seven hours, two hours longer than expected, and gave rise to fresh speculation about a breakthrough. Trimble and his team left at lunchtime, but Sinn Féin and the SDLP stayed until 6.30 pm. There were unconfirmed reports that Blair and his chief-of-staff Jonathan Powell had met Sinn Féin leaders the previous weekend. It was understood the two governments were seeking to restore the Executive on the basis of a republican pledge to put weapons permanently beyond use, but that the unionists were holding out for a more specific IRA commitment to a verifiable process of actual decommissioning with a timetable. It was taken as a sign of strain between the two governments when a planned phone call from Blair to Ahern at lunchtime next day did not take place.

With less than three weeks to go to the 22 May anniversary of the North–South referendums, the two governments were making a determined push for a deal. There was talk of a fresh sequence of events, starting with the publication of a joint British–Irish 'audit' of the Agreement – what had already been achieved and what remained, such as police reform, demilitarisation and decommissioning, with a programme for full implementation of these aspects. This would be followed by a statement from the IRA providing unionists with the requisite 'clarity and certainty' on weapons. The last move in the sequence was meant to be a promise from the UUP to rejoin the Executive on the basis of assurances given. Prior decommissioning was long gone and the issue now was, what undertakings could be entered into on weapons that would see Trimble through another meeting of the UUC? Officials from the two governments spent 3 May refining a series of draft statements in consultation with Sinn Féin and the UUP.

Blair and Ahern finally arrived in Belfast and set up shop at Hillsborough Castle on the afternoon of 4 May: the DUP claimed that the Prime Minister wanted to be out of London for the result of the city's mayoral election next day, when the Labour candidate, Frank Dobson, was universally expected to be trounced by party maverick Ken Livingstone.

The Ahern government had been accused of briefing against the British in the aftermath of suspension, but now it was Dublin's turn to suffer. The prominent unionist, Chris McGimpsey, said a document was given to him that day in a brown envelope by a British government source who wanted the people of Ulster to know what was going on behind the scenes. The sheet of paper, containing a single paragraph from a longer document, was promptly handed over to the BBC and UTV and inevitably dominated the evening news bulletins.

The latest leak, apparently an internal civil service briefing note, spoke of 'a vigorous exchange' between Mandelson and Cowen over dinner during a visit by Blair to Dublin on 18 April. The subject was obviously police reform and proposed changes in the name and badge of the RUC. The text read: 'Cowen's line appeared to be that, beyond the constitutional acceptance that

Northern Ireland remained part of the UK, there should be no further evidence of Britishness in the governance of Northern Ireland. It was an argument presented with all the subtlety and open-mindedness that one would expect from a member of Sinn Féin. There was no disposition among members of his entourage or indeed by Martin Mansergh, who was also present, to water down this line. It is not one, however, that I would have expected the Taoiseach to put over in such an unvarnished way. It underlined the view which I know the Secretary of State holds that Cowen has no feel for or understanding of Unionist concerns and can usually be reliably counted on to tack to the green at every opportunity.'

The text was less significant than the fact that someone decided to put it out at such a sensitive time. The number of possible authors was limited and Dublin sources were quick to name the memo-writer as a very senior British civil servant,[5] although there was no official confirmation of this on the British side. Dublin sources felt it was sanctioned at a high level by the British and was quite deliberate. Naturally the leak, which was provided without any context, dominated the news of the day but there was an underlying feeling that, while a deal might not actually be cooking, recipes were certainly being exchanged. As usual, Downing Street was talking up the progress made. Dublin was more downbeat but, for once, close observers were giving greater credibility to the London 'spin'.

Distracted by the decommissioning deadline of 22 May, most observers originally thought the key period would be the days leading up to that date. However, the real negotiations and horse-trading had already been taking place in London and insiders hinted that, if the deal wasn't done within days, we could forget about serious progress until the early autumn.

Suggestions that the IRA might declare the 'war' over were dismissed by republican sources and the notion of a timetable for decommissioning had also fallen by the wayside at this stage. However, provided the institutions of government were reinstated, republicans might be prepared to reappoint the interlocutor to the de Chastelain commission and place the assurances of 11 February back on the table. As filtered through the General's report of that date, the IRA appeared to be offering to put its weapons 'beyond use' under certain unspecified conditions. In the past, Sinn Féin had suggested there might be a role for a third party to verify this procedure. This idea had surfaced in a little-known Sinn Féin document from 1995: nothing had been heard of it since and the document itself had become a collector's item.[6]

Senior British sources spoke with grudging admiration of Sinn Féin's skill at the negotiating table. Almost in the same breath they went on to lament the disparate and dissonant nature of unionism. This lack of coherence now appeared to be the major problem from London's point of view.

Mid-morning on Friday 5 May, Blair gave a press conference at Hillsborough. It had not been a great day so far: Livingstone was romping home in the election for Mayor of London and, all the previous night, Labour councils had been falling like skittles in the local elections. The Prime Minister's lips were pursed, teeth slightly on edge, facial expression sombre: nobody told him there'd be days like these. Yet Belfast was not the worst place to be, especially with the makings of a peace deal on the table. He brightened visibly when reporters turned from developments in London to questions about the North. Admitting that expectations had been deliberately played down, he now held out the prospect of developments during the day: 'I hope I will have more to tell you later.' For once 'Hillsborough hype' had failed to take hold and Blair's advisers were remarkably circumspect. 'We sense the makings of a new impetus but it's no more than that,' they said cautiously.

The Prime Minister gave his press conference in one of the outhouses at Hillsborough Castle; some said it was the stables converted to modern use. An Ulster Unionist news conference had to be held outside the gates and I found it a telling illustration of who wielded the power in the North these days.

At this stage there were no republicans in sight. They appeared to be leaving it to Blair to 'sort out' the unionists. Eventually Adams and McGuinness turned up at the head of a sizeable posse just after 4 pm. Their demand was simple: Blair should get the institutions up and running. The word on the grapevine was that Sinn Féin felt the Prime Minister should stay until a deal was made because the negotiations would fall apart, the minute he left for London, as the talks on cross-Border bodies had proved. Senior unionists were speculating that the negotiations could continue into the next day, or alternatively might be adjourned until the start of the following week. As always they were playing for time, going for the 'long game', hoping no doubt that Blair and Ahern would weary of the quest.

If decommissioning was being acknowledged at last as a problem to be got around, rather than confronted, other difficulties were rearing their heads. The Patten Report was described as a 'huge' obstacle for Trimble's people, who were constrained by the Burnside UUC motion on the name. SDLP sources quipped that the unionists were trying to maintain a body called 'The Continuity RUC'. There were also said to be difficulties over partnership boards for local policing: the unionists were worried about Provo 'godfathers' ruling local areas while Sinn Féin was concerned about continuing unionist domination. While not everyone at the table might have been able to articulate the precise relationship between symbols and substance, the unionists knew what they wanted to keep and, for their part, nationalists and republicans knew what they were after. The unionist project of engaging in the peace process only to render it harmless was coming up against the republican programme for 'hollowing out the Union' by denuding it of crown regalia and rendering Northern Ireland a symbolically neutral zone prior to its ultimate absorption into an agreed united Ireland.

As the evening wore on, speculation about a possible deal intensified. The UUP and Sinn Féin were said to be having their most serious engagement since suspension. The size and composition of the Sinn Féin delegation had inevitably led to the usual speculation that both wings of the republican movement, political and military, were represented. It now became known that, in addition to six or seven hours in Downing Street on Tuesday 2 May, Sinn Féin had been involved in further significant contacts on Wednesday 3 and Thursday 4 May. A formula was being refined which Sinn Féin might be willing to present to the IRA, but the republicans needed reassurance that the unionists would reciprocate by forming the Executive.

It later emerged that the UUP and Sinn Féin leaderships had begun a meeting at 6.30 pm which lasted about 50 minutes. It was the first serious bilateral discussion they had undertaken since the suspension. The news of an agreement circulated very rapidly after that meeting broke up about 7.20 pm.

Decommissioning, the besetting problem of the process for the previous five years, was at last apparently on the way to being either resolved, gotten around, long-fingered or shelved. Whatever might happen further down the road, it was no longer an immediate obstacle. However, three to four hours were then taken up with discussion of unionist objections to the Patten Report, especially the recommendation for a name-change. The unionists reportedly wanted the force called 'the Police Service of Northern Ireland (incorporating the RUC)'. There were strong nationalist objections to a 'double-barrelled' name and to the notion of retaining the crown symbol in the badge for the new force. The fear among nationalists was that this would prove to be the 'Derry/Londonderry' option, with Protestants continuing to refer to the force as the RUC while Catholics used the new name. Senior Dublin officials told me that 'you have got to have a police force that can go anywhere in the North and be given a cup of tea'. At any rate the governments could not bridge the gap or, as one insider put it, 'The Brits and the Irish could not agree on Patten, so they just left it'.

Finally, after almost 30 hours of talks, a joint statement from the two prime ministers was issued just before midnight. It set 22 May as the date for restoration of the Assembly, putting the deadline for full implementation of the Agreement back to June 2001. There would also be substantial demilitarisation measures by the British on condition that the paramilitaries 'urgently state that they will put their arms completely and verifiably beyond use'.

It was clear that Adams had a stake in the deal when, instead of his usual downbeat response, he called on all pro-Agreement forces to 'rally behind this initiative'. Trimble was said to be studying the plan but left Hillsborough without speaking to the media. The implication in the joint statement was that, whether or not the unionists allowed the Executive to be reconstituted, the rest of the Agreement would be implemented anyway. It was also possible to interpret it as (a) placing the decommissioning issue once and for all in de Chastelain's care and (b) guaranteeing that in the event of further difficulty a review would be conducted without suspension of the institutions.

A letter was sent next morning to the northern parties, containing further proposals from the two governments for the full implementation of the Agreement. Most attention was drawn by the explicit commitment to have legislation implementing the Patten recommendations on the statute books by November and all eligible paramilitary prisoners released by 28 July.

An IRA statement was also expected, but when it came out around lunchtime it contained a surprise extra ingredient. In addition to a pledge to resume contact with the de Chastelain commission, it included an undertaking to permit outsiders to look at its weapons within an unspecified number of weeks. 'The contents of a number of our arms dumps will be inspected by agreed third parties who will report that they have done so to the IICD [Independent International Commission on Decommissioning]. The dumps will be re-inspected regularly to ensure that the weapons have remained secure.'

This was a sensational development and was understood to have been hammered out in the discussions at Downing Street the previous Tuesday. However, insiders were taken by another paragraph which, despite the usual tortured language, contained a declaration that was unprecedented in republican terms: 'The full implementation, on a progressive and irreversible basis by the two governments, especially the British Government, of what they have agreed, will provide a political context, in an enduring political process, with the potential to remove the causes of conflict, and in which Irish Republicans and Unionists can, as equals, pursue our respective political objectives peacefully.'

Not much was made of this at the time in the media, where the main focus was on the more concrete and dramatic issue of arms inspection and the commitment to 'completely and verifiably put IRA arms beyond use' (the phrase echoed the words of Blair and Ahern). But the new language in relation to unionism was a striking departure with potentially enormous consequences. The number of qualifications suggested that there had been reservations and discomfort within the IRA over the statement, not to mention considerable residual distrust of the British Government in particular. Yet at the same time there were echoes of the famous declaration by Wolfe Tone, founder of Irish republicanism, that the means he would employ to 'break the connection with England, the never-failing source of all our political evils' would be to 'substitute the common name of

Irishman in place of the denominations of Protestant, Catholic and Dissenter'. There were hints now of a new approach by republicans based on winning the progressive elements in the Protestant community around to their vision of a new, inclusive, agreed Ireland. Trimble aide and speechwriter, Steven King said the IRA had accepted the principle of consent: 'Its analysis might still be that Partition is the root cause of division, but the possibility of the Union continuing on a progressive and equal basis has been left open.'[7]

Some commentators, including myself, gave considerable credit to Cowen at the time for his role in the negotiations, where he had built on the rapport that developed between himself and Martin McGuinness. Cowen was a mainstream nationalist and constitutional republican in the pragmatic Fianna Fáil mould. He was close to Reynolds: though not as great a risk-taker he probably possessed more political savvy and resilience. I was surprised when certain media commentators who were always quick in their attempts to squelch any expression of nationalism failed to demonise Cowen from the moment of his appointment. Clearly his enemies did not realise how active he was in trying to move the process forward. However, far from being a republican footstool, informed sources reported that Cowen engaged in 'some of the toughest discussions' with Sinn Féin. 'He told them what was required of them.' The republicans did not like sweet talk and flattery: straight talking was best and Cowen was the all-Ireland champion in this respect. Insiders paid tribute to his mental toughness over the previous difficult months. The leaking of the dinner-party memo was a left-handed tribute to Cowen's skill.

When I wrote favourably of Cowen's performance, Sinn Féin sources contacted me immediately to claim the credit in very emphatic terms for their party leader who, they said, had been working assiduously on the issue almost from the time of suspension onwards, including a visit to the Prime Minister's weekend residence at Chequers. As Sinn Féin sources presented it, Cowen played a fairly minor role compared to Ahern, but especially Adams, who had worked flat out. 'It was largely between us and the British,' Sinn Féin insisted. Later on, republicans expressed some annoyance when the SDLP claimed credit for fresh moves on British Army demilitarisation. Sinn Féin sources claimed this was worked out between Adams and Blair during intensive contacts over previous weeks. Fighting over the spoils of political success was a new development from Sinn Féin but it indicated how rapidly they were becoming a normal democratic party!

The involvement of the Catholic hierarchy in a process to resolve the weapons issue had been under consideration for about a year and there had been an echo of this before now in the offer from the Bishop of Derry, Dr Hegarty, to take arms into his care on a temporary basis. Towards the end of April this idea was dropped in favour of a formula which did not include the bishops. Now, in response to the IRA statement, the two governments announced that the arms inspectors would be former secretary-general of the African National Congress, Cyril Ramaphosa, and former president of Finland, Martti Ahtisaari.

Elements of the latest initiative had been foreshadowed in December 1995, when Sinn Féin told the International Body on Decommissioning, chaired by George Mitchell, that 'the disposal of arms by those in possession of them is a method which may find acceptance'. In language reminiscent of the latest IRA statement, the 1995 submission continued: 'The entire issue of arms will need to be dealt with in a way which imbues and maintains public and political confidence. An independent third party could prove to be of assistance here. This would, of course, have to be agreed by those in possession of weapons. Public safety considerations must be high on the agenda of any process. Adequate safeguards against misappropriation of arms by others is clearly an important matter.' The document also stressed the need for demilitarisation of the British presence.[8] Nationalist sources in the peace process were under the impression that the republicans might have gone further than they intended in the 1995 document, which was why it was now so difficult to lay hands on the text. 'It's a great document,' a Dublin official said.

The military theorist, Karl von Clausewitz, wrote that war was politics by other means: the Provisional republican doctrine was that politics was war by other means. As in war the element of surprise in politics was invaluable, and the démarche by the IRA caught the enemies of the peace process napping. It was a coup for the two governments to secure a major symbolic gesture from the IRA which broke a long-standing taboo. They could have achieved it earlier if they had taken their distance more from the unionist agenda. As one well-informed contact put it: 'When the governments came back to viable territory, the response [from the IRA] was serious.' It was also put to me that, once the emotion had been stripped away from the issue, decommissioning would solve itself, but that Trimble should have declared a victory on 5 May rather than manufacturing fresh shopping lists.

On Sunday 7 May, the day after the IRA statement, the annual commemorative rally for the republican activists who died in the 1981 hunger strike for political prisoner status took place at Dunville Park, off the Falls Road in Belfast. Adams, who was the main speaker, was clearly pleased at the attendance, which was higher than previous years. The crowd of an estimated 10,000 was a useful vote of confidence in the Sinn Féin leadership at this delicate time. These were the dispossessed from Belfast's nationalist ghettos who had supported the Provisionals through thick and thin, regardless of whether their beloved Gerry was a political pariah or an honoured guest at the White House. Their continued wholehearted backing would be crucial. After a poor response in February to an Adams call for a series of protests against suspension, it was important for the Provos to get a good turnout.

While nobody was pointing out individuals, there would have been a substantial number of IRA members present at the event. In his speech Adams referred to 'the Army', which is the shorthand in republican circles for the IRA. He urged republicans to open up a thoughtful debate on the week's developments and 'look at them all in a strategic fashion'. As in the past, he was appealing to his followers to look at the Big Picture.

You cannot have a proper conversation with Adams on these occasions because he is subject to the constant attentions of his admirers. A media colleague even took a photo of her brother standing beside him. I managed only to say, 'Nice one', in reference to the arms move, which was a fairly drastic shorthand version of my professional assessment that he had pulled off a remarkable coup by deflecting the criticism made of republicans for refusal to decommission with a gesture which, though laden with drama and symbolism, did not constitute a weapons handover under the terms of Mayhew's Washington Three precondition. Despite demands from unionists and others, the pseudonymous IRA spokesman P. O'Neill had not declared that the 'war' was over, nor had he given guarantees that the dumps were sealed and the guns would never be used again. The IRA still remained in control of its weapons and, in theory at least, could use them again if the peace process fell apart. I am not sure, however, that my two-word comment to the Sinn Féin leader conveyed all of these subtleties!

While Adams acknowledged in his speech that some members of the audience might be concerned at the content of the latest IRA statement, most observers believed neither he nor the rest of the republican leadership would have contemplated such a move if there was any prospect of serious and sustained dissent. The Provisionals were famous, not to say notorious, for keeping in contact with what they called their 'base' and ensuring no gap developed. No doubt questions were being asked in places like South Armagh and Tyrone, but if there was any danger of a split the IRA would never have taken this latest initiative. Whatever about Martti Ahtisaari, the notion of Cyril Ramaphosa viewing arms dumps was unlikely to discommode republicans, given the very close relationship between Sinn Féin and the African National Congress over many years.

The early summer weather for the rally was bright and warm. The music was too loud and it was impossible to stand and chat afterwards. The crowd melted away fairly quickly. An RUC Land Rover which appeared to be filming the proceedings pulled away. Large screens had been placed around the platform, which cannot have made the police camera operator's task any easier. Press photographers were there too and, next day, Adams and McGuinness appeared on the front page of *The Irish Times* eating ice-cream cones. War – what war?

The ball was now at the unionists' feet. Trimble gave a qualified welcome to the IRA move: 'I have to say the statement is very interesting; it does appear to break new ground.' But he was still not letting go of the decommissioning bone and wanted to be sure that arms inspection was a prelude to arms destruction. There were suggestions from some quarters that the UUP leadership had not expected the IRA to go as far as it did. Meanwhile, the dissident West Tyrone MP, William Thompson posed some hard questions: 'They are not actually going to give up any arms. And they're only talking about a number of dumps, not all. These are illegal weapons and should be completely destroyed. Somewhere down the line what's going to stop Sinn Féin/IRA deciding they don't like what's happening and getting them out and using them again?'[9]

Taylor gave the republican initiative a cautious welcome on the basis that there was now an IRA statement, which was worth more in the present context than one from Sinn Féin. Taylor had a point, because one of the difficulties in the peace process – particularly though not exclusively from a unionist point of view – was the dual identity of the republican movement. Sinn Féin was committed under the Agreement to use its influence to bring about decommissioning. However, when the heat became too intense Sinn Féin could always respond: 'We are not the IRA.' No matter how much Downing Street and everyone else insisted that the political and military wings of republicanism were inextricably linked and two sides of the same coin (some said they were the same side of the same coin), it was still very difficult to pin the republicans down. Now, Trimble's supporters could claim to have stripped away the seven veils of Sinn Féin and drawn the IRA definitively into the political process.

Once again, though, Trimble was fighting for his political life. Had he got the passion and commitment to win over the UUC or would he allow the naysayers to have their way? And what would the two governments do if the UUC failed to endorse the Hillsborough package? If Northern nationalists were not allowed a share in government, Dublin's role might have to change from oversight to some form of incipient joint administration. Unionism was therefore caught in a cleft stick: go into government with the republican movement or face the prospect of creeping joint sovereignty with the Republic.

The initial reaction in dissident unionist circles to the latest events was bleak and demoralised. One high-level contact, who had predicted the Executive would be suspended for a long time, was now gloomily comparing Trimble to the French collaborationist leader, Marshal Pétain, with the qualification that at least the ruler of Vichy France had retained his gendarmerie. With commendable honesty, activists in the anti-Agreement camp now confessed to doubts over their ability to win a majority at the UUC. They said they were spending a lot of time these days persuading their friends and political contacts not to give

up: stand your ground, and less of that defeatist talk about moving to Scotland.

Trimble announced a meeting of the UUC for 20 May but
cautioned that this did not mean 'that we have committed ourselves to endorse any set of proposals'. Adams spoke for more
than republicans when he expressed concern that the UUP
leader had 'not fully embraced the opportunity which now
exists'. Taylor relapsed into his usual ambivalence. 'Taylor is like
the wind,' moaned a friend of Trimble's. Iris Robinson of the
DUP, who was challenging for the Strangford seat at
Westminster, said Taylor was trying to 'distance himself from
himself'. Other senior UUP figures were curiously muted.

A new note of optimism now began to be heard from the No
camp. Rumours began to circulate that if Trimble put the deal to
a vote he would lose, 60–40, or even, according to some extrava-
gant estimates, 70–30 ('Would that it were so,' sighed a No lobbyist.) Against this background and after consultation with the
Assembly party at Stormont on the morning of 18 May, Trimble
decided to postpone the UUC meeting by a week, although he
indicated he would positively recommend rejoining the
Executive. 'He is actually prepared to stand up and sell the deal:
he looks like a man with a mission,' someone close to him said.
There were immediate concerns that the republican movement
would withdraw its 6 May statement, but McGuinness set minds
at rest with some upbeat comments. Sources said the republicans
were told about the postponement in advance of Trimble's
announcement. It was said that, 'Sinn Féin will hold for a week
as long as there are no more concessions.'

On 17 May, Mandelson told the Commons he believed the
Police Bill should include a 'legal description' to incorporate the
name of the RUC in the 'title deeds' of the new service. Adams
warned that Sinn Féin could not recommend its supporters to
join the revamped force on the basis of the new legislation.
Privately, republicans were hinting that, with police reform
being watered down, the basis on which the IRA initiative was
achieved might be lost: the issue was causing 'ructions' in the
republican camp. There were reports of intense lobbying by the
British in Washington to secure the 'double-barrelled name', but
this would not wash with republicans. It looked as if the deal
could be lost over a subtitle. In private conversation, senior

republicans seemed badly torn between allaying the anxieties of their followers on decommissioning and a desire to avoid creating difficulties for Trimble. There was an increasingly hard-line tone from Trimble's internal opponents on this issue: 'RUC must be the working name, we will not be bought off with subtitles', was the cry of a prominent No campaigner. Whatever emerged must pass 'the side of the Land Rover test', in other words the RUC letters must be displayed on police jeeps. For their part, supporters of the Agreement envisaged a situation where the police would travel about in cars and no longer have need of Land Rovers. It was a telling difference in perspective.

Writing in the Irish editions of the *Sunday Times* on 21 May, Trimble said his understanding was that the arms inspection would involve three substantial dumps. Commenting on the IRA declaration that the potential now existed for both unionists and republicans to pursue their objectives peacefully, he said: 'It means to me that the IRA campaign is finally over.' It looked as if the question Trimble posed on the evening of Good Friday 1998 had now been answered.

A debate on UTV on the night of 22 May between Yes and No panels from the UUP – one led by Trimble, the other by Donaldson – turned out well from the party leader's viewpoint. There was an eloquent performance from a Fermanagh stalwart, Bertie Kerr – father of Trimble's press officer, David Kerr – who argued in realistic, common sense tones that the IRA offer should not be turned down. The No camp had borrowed the Madison Avenue device of the 'focus group' where a sample gathering of the type of people you wish to influence is exposed to your product and perhaps those of your competitors. One of these groups was watching the UTV *Insight* programme and saw Donaldson and his fellow No man, Peter King, being taunted with the allegation that they had come up with no alternative to the policy and programme of the party leader. The focus viewers felt Trimble had the better of the exchange on that particular point. 'David Trimble threw down the gauntlet', a senior No campaigner said. 'It was felt prudent to pick it up.'

Taylor was reported to be in 'the Far East somewhere'. He had been in Taiwan, but even close associates were unsure if he had gone on to Singapore or Japan. He was a member of a Westminster parliamentary delegation which also included

Martin Smyth. Someone made the point that by their joint absence they cancelled each other out – but only if Taylor remained a Yes. Tracked down by an enterprising radio journalist, Taylor said he would resign as deputy leader of the UUP at Westminster if he found himself opposing the Hillsborough package. Taylor's remarks were played down by Empey at a hastily-arranged news conference in Stormont: 'He is making his contribution in his fashion and in his style.' Behind the scenes, however, some normally sanguine Yes people were turning the air blue with their views on these interminable ambiguities. A No campaigner made the understatement of the week when he remarked that Taylor was 'not a team player'. The No people were busy in the background, however. A Trimble activist told me on 23 May that no less than nine separate pieces urging him to vote No had arrived through the front door. Seven of the nine appeals were anonymous and there were many cuttings from the newspapers: 'They are quoting Eoghan Harris but you couldn't ask for a more pro-Agreement, pro-Trimble person than Eoghan Harris.'

By the evening of Wednesday 24 May, with three days to go, it was a vote-by-vote battle between the two sides. Party sources said the middle ground had narrowed to between 45 and 70 delegates. The undecided ones were described as 'people who don't like voting against their leader but have deep and real concerns and are very, very confused'. There was said to be a growing reluctance on the part of the average UUC delegate to prompt a bitter and divisive leadership contest, which would be a likely consequence of defeat for Trimble's approach. 'It's probably the last thing they want,' members of the No lobby conceded. It now seemed that considerations of solidarity might override misgivings about Trimble's tactics. Trimble made a series of discreet visits to different parts of the North to address groups of delegates. The venues were not announced in advance, for fear of DUP protests. The UUP leader had been criticised in the past for failing to sell the Agreement pro-actively to his party, but now he was doing exactly that.

Although both Downing Street and the White House rubbished reports which claimed that Blair had made two unsuccessful attempts by telephone on 10 May to persuade Clinton to put pressure on Dublin and Sinn Féin to soften their stance over dropping the RUC title, both republican and Irish-American sources maintained there had indeed been an intense lobby by the Prime Minister and others on the issue. Although one British politician reportedly told his US counterparts that the concession to unionists was only 'smoke and mirrors', republican sources were now indicating very strongly that the 'double-barrelled' name would result in the withdrawal of the IRA statement. A source close to republican thinking said wearily, 'The feeling you get from Blair is that everything is negotiable.' However, it was believed that if Trimble lost the vote, the two governments would jointly move forward with the implementation of all the non-institutional aspects of the Agreement in the expectation that the IRA would not withdraw its offer to put arms beyond use.

In a clever article for the *Belfast Telegraph* on 24 May, Mandelson said that, although the IRA had not surrendered, under the right conditions it would fade and wither away. This echoed previous comments from Martin McGuinness and marked the public death-knell of Washington Three at long last. No better man than Mandelson, who had slaughtered so many sacred cows in the Labour Party, to dispense with a failed and discredited policy without much sentiment. The Secretary of State was very active at this time but, ironically, a leading No campaigner confided to me that he felt Mowlam would have been more persuasive because, despite her poor relations with the UUP leadership, she had the grassroots 'eating out of her hand' whenever she toured Northern Ireland.

There had been some delay in producing a Donaldson counterproposal and on 26 May, four days after the UTV programme, it was presented in the form of a letter to UUC delegates. Donaldson's key requirement was partial IRA decommissioning in advance of unionist participation in the Executive. There would also be a timetable for complete disarmament, an effective exclusion mechanism in case of default, restoration of the Assembly with or without the Executive, and the retention of the RUC name and insignia.

Cleverly worded, the letter echoed the demands coming from the likes of Mandelson and Mallon the previous January for clarity and certainty from the IRA. The right buttons were pressed by stressing the 'twin objectives' of devolution and disarmament along with the need to preserve party unity. Whereas the No lobby had been inclined to alienate the middle ground with hard-line demands, the clever marketing strategy in the Donaldson plan was to attract the broadest possible constituency on a moderate-sounding basis similar to Washington Three.

The divisions in the No lobby were unhelpful to their cause. Their best bet would have been to rally around the most moderate anti-Trimble position rather than espousing a variety of stances from right-of-centre to extreme hard-line. The hard right should have been told to quieten down on the basis that a moderate approach was the best way to ensure Trimble's undoing. There was a feeling with this last-minute proposal that the correct tactics were beginning to dawn on them, but too late.

Trimble met Donaldson at the latter's request for about an hour, but there was no agreement on the way forward. At a news conference in Glengall Street immediately afterwards, the party leader dismissed the proposals as 'out of date'. If the UUP were to revive these ideas now it would be regarded by the other parties as moving backwards and as a unionist wish-list. With only 24 hours to go, Trimble looked pale and must at this stage have been tired, but he was resolutely good-humoured and there was the usual quota of banter.

During the day, Trimble supporters canvassed heavily to ensure that any drift to Donaldson on the basis of his new plan would be firmly halted. Late estimates suggested the fate of the deal was in the hands of about 50 delegates, described by a prominent No campaigner as, 'People who don't like voting against their leader but still have real and deep concerns'. This source admitted frankly that the No people were 'trying to scare the bejabers' out of these 'very, very confused' delegates. Some delegates were wailing: 'I am so confused I am not even going to bother going.' A leading No lobbyist confided: 'I suspect that David Trimble might squeak it ... the party will not desert its leader.' Over on the nationalist side, there was continuing apprehension about what one of my contacts called 'a muddy outcome', e.g. a fresh timetable for decommissioning or some other hostage to fortune that could unsettle the Hillsborough deal. The situation had its lighter moments: No lobbyists told how one of their number asked a well-known party waverer to declare his position. 'I'm neutered – no, neutral,' he stuttered. The No campaigner laughed, 'You were right the first time.'

Next morning was bright and clear as delegates made their way into the Waterfront once more. There was a frantic media scrum when Taylor arrived, waving and laughing. He said airily that he had been in touch with Trimble 'by telephone, Internet and all that'. There was a set of bronze sculptures outside the building depicting a shepherd and his sheep, so anti-Agreement protesters hung a placard around the shepherd's neck which read, 'IRA/Sinn Féin' and placed name-tags on the sheep for Trimble, Empey, Maginnis and Taylor. That evening, the Polish State Opera was scheduled to perform Verdi's *Aida*, which the Waterfront publicity material aptly described as 'a compelling story of jealousy, treachery and divided loyalties'. Some said the description was more appropriate to the morning show being staged by the unionists.

Inside the hall, Trimble spoke against an incongruous backdrop of Egyptian mummies from the Verdi stage set, plus the Union Jack. Journalists were excluded from the debate but it emerged that, in a passionate opening speech, the leader had told delegates rejection would 'leave nationalists radicalised and unionists demoralised'. Donaldson made an impassioned plea for the other side, the speech of his life it was said. He had 'lain in ditches defending Ulster' when he was a member of the Ulster Defence Regiment.[10] There was hushed silence for Daphne Kinghan whose father, Sir Norman Stronge, and brother, James Stronge, were murdered in 1981 by the IRA, which called them at the time 'symbols of hated unionism'. In a short but powerful contribution she said she was backing the Trimble approach because it was the only way forward. Then Taylor, ignoring the catcalls and jeers from the floor with his usual regal disdain, announced he would be voting Yes. He said he had a letter from Mandelson offering concessions on policing, but did not take up an invitation from Donaldson to reveal the text.

When the votes were counted, Trimble scored a narrow victory, with 459 votes (53 per cent) for rejoining the Executive to 403 (47 per cent) against, and one spoilt vote. Even in the leadership contest against Smyth he had secured 57 per cent. At the same time, this was a victory without strings. A source in the Trimble camp described the vote as 'nerve-wracking' but said their tally beforehand was 53.7 per cent compared with the eventual result of 53.2 per cent.

Trimble had taken to mentioning Sinn Féin in canine terms and, at the press conference in the Waterfront after the vote, he said: 'As far as democracy is concerned, these folk ain't house trained yet ... we do actually need to see the Assembly running so the checks and balances that are there eventually bring them to heel.' This was about the third time Trimble had made such a comment and, earlier that morning, it had come up during a radio discussion in which I was a participant. I felt a question was in order but, before I could get in, there was an incongruous but entertaining interlude where the UUP leader was badgered by a socialist activist with a broad Dublin accent about his position on the minimum wage. When Trimble was finally able to take my question, I asked him if implying that Sinn Féin were dogs was an inclusive sentiment. He responded rather sharply and tried to turn the tables: 'One uses these phrases from time to time. I wouldn't have used the words that you used – it's your language, not mine.' It was later reported that the 'house-trained' comment gave great offence in republican and wider nationalist circles, where it was seen as an indication that, despite his protestations about pluralism, Trimble had still not got into the spirit of the new dispensation.

After such a narrow vote, the party seemed hopelessly divided. 'One party, two leaders' was how a delegate described the situation. The No people had brought their level of support up four per cent and the obvious temptation was to keep pushing: Trimble had to win all the time, but his opponents needed to win only once. There was little joy on the faces of the delegates from either camp though. 'There's two parties here under this roof,' a leading No lobbyist remarked as he left the Waterfront Hall. Another noted that Trimble's 'comfort zone' was now very slim indeed but added, 'There is just a sense that he might have got away with it.' The No people would retreat temporarily to the long grass and wait for an issue to arise which they could use to unhorse their leader. However, it would be much harder to bring down an executive than to block its formation. It was reported that two delegates from opposing sides came close to blows, with the pro-Agreement member being warned: 'Keep your nose out of Newtownabbey' – a reference to a forthcoming council by-election.[11]

Mandelson wasted no time and that Saturday afternoon

signed the order providing for restoration of devolved powers by midnight the following Monday. 'The cars should be there to pick them [the ministers] up on Tuesday morning,' a source in the SDLP told me. There had been some speculation about a legal challenge in the event of a narrow Trimble victory, but now the deed was done.

Italian coalitions used to last less than a year on average, but this one could be more rocky still, so numerous were the fault-lines. Pro-Agreement unionists were often simply going along with the new dispensation rather than embracing it wholeheart-edly. A senior party figure predicted that the restored executive would be chaotic. 'Every time Sinn Féin do something, there will be a crisis.'

It seemed premature to speak about a watershed at the Waterfront, but Trimble was untrammelled by formal conditions other than a commission of party elders which would monitor progress on weapons and other issues. The proposed reform of the UUC could generate a considerably larger majority for him in the future. The Young Unionist delegation was expected to have its wings clipped and a review of the relationship with the Orange Order would also have voting implications (although 40 per cent of the Orange delegation was believed to have support-ed Trimble this time).

Some commentators sensed that the Trimble era might be foreshortened and that the shadow of Brian Faulkner was final-ly closing over him. But there was general acknowledgement that he had fought his corner hard. As one observer put it: 'He really earned his Nobel Prize money.' Deric Henderson of the Press Association, one of the North's most experienced journal-ists, summarised the UUP leader's contradictory personality well: 'Trimble, the intellectual who persuaded unionists to make a massive emotional shift, is a principled pragmatist, a detail addict with both eyes on the big picture and a shy man whose dogged determination won through again today.'[12] Meanwhile, the ever-attentive Clinton made a courtesy call to Mallon and presumably other leaders, a few hours after the Waterfront vote. The possibility of a presidential visit was mentioned. 'Bring your golf-clubs,' Mallon quipped.

It was time to take stock: decommissioning might have receded as an issue but there were continuing rows about the refusal of the two republican ministers to fly the Union Flag over their departments on any of the twenty officially designated days – mainly the birthdays of the Royal Family – unless the Irish tricolour was flown alongside. Outside the political process, dissident republicans and loyalists remained active. However, there was an upbeat tone from Trimble who said he would be 'very surprised' if republicans failed the weapons test, because they knew what was at stake. Sources close to the Trimble camp were pessimistic about the longer term and felt there would be major problems ahead, probably in the autumn: 'It might disintegrate one more time, there's probably one more collapse in it.'

After much internal discussion, the DUP adopted a complicated strategy which led to the temporary resignation of Robinson and Dodds from their ministries, to be replaced by party colleagues who would hold office for short periods before being replaced by others. The strategy would only apply until the Westminster election, which was expected within twelve months. There were charges of cynicism from opponents who pointed out that Robinson and Dodds could then resume their ministerial duties full-time until the end of the Assembly term in 2003. Had the DUP decided to quit the Executive once and for all, their ministries would have devolved to the UUP and Alliance.

The IRA statement had undertaken to permit an inspection of arms dumps 'within weeks' and, as time passed, anxiety began to grow that the republicans – angered at the perceived dilution of Patten – might default on their commitment of 6 May. It was a full seven weeks before Ahtisaari and Ramaphosa announced on 26 June that they had carried out an inspection of 'a number' of dumps (believed to be at least three) which contained 'a substantial amount of military material'. They added: 'We have ensured that the weapons and explosives cannot be used without our detection.' The dumps would be revisited on a regular basis to ensure that the weapons remained secure.

There was a flurry of speculation as to the locations of the dumps. The general view was that they must be in the Republic, probably underground and in remote areas. The Taoiseach said that 'the bunkers will be sealed'; Mandelson said there was a 'device' in place so any unwarranted interference with the arms could be detected and that the inspectors could return 'at a time of their choosing'. Suggestions being put about that this device could be monitored by British Army equipment were angrily rejected by Dublin officials. The *Observer* quoted 'a senior Irish source' who said there was probably a dual-lock system in operation at the dumps, with one key held by the inspectors, the other remaining with the IRA.

Some said the dumps contained older arms from the Libya shipments or the US that the IRA had no intention of using, as they were unsuitable for the type of operations the organisation had engaged in over recent years. Given the secrecy of the republican movement, it was difficult to assess the size of the total IRA arsenal but this did not stop people from guessing. One estimate put it at two tons of Semtex explosive; 600–700 AK47 semi-automatic rifles; twenty heavy calibre machine-guns and at least a dozen general purpose machine-guns; 40 rocket grenade launchers; one SAM (surface-to-air) missile; 100 Webley revolvers.[13]

There were claims that this, at last, was the long-awaited gesture of decommissioning. Blair disagreed: 'The whole process of decommissioning has to be gone through. This is a confidence-building measure. It is not decommissioning itself, it is a step on the way.' Unionists expressed similar sentiments, while Ahern intimated, with his usual ambiguous overtones, that he believed the decommissioning issue had been dealt with, and hoped it would fade from the agenda. Privately, Dublin was cock-a-hoop. Assessing the IRA move, senior officials commented, 'It's their way of saying that the conflict is really at an end'. The inspection constituted a turning-point: 'It sends a hugely positive signal and defuses the decommissioning thing. There is a process now and everyone has confidence. The IRA delivered on its promises within the time-frame.'

Sinn Féin was anxious to have it placed on the record that the idea for a third-party arms inspection had come from Adams, not the British Government. Party sources said Adams had negotiated on an almost daily basis with the two governments and the de Chastelain body, beginning within a few days of the suspension and continuing until late on the night of 25 June, the day before the two inspectors announced that they had carried out their work. The fact that negotiations continued even after the 6

May statement suggests that details of the inspection and how it would be presented afterwards had not been finalised at Hillsborough. Adams said, 'In 200 years there has not been an initiative like this.' He stressed that it had not been easily achieved: 'Let no one think there aren't all sorts of worries opened up within republicanism.' Around this time, an eye-witness described a meeting of Hume and Adams in a corridor at Stormont on their way to a joint radio interview. They shook hands. 'We're getting there,' Hume said. Adams replied: 'We've moved it on another bit. It's a good day.'

Trimble was in the Middle East and television news footage showed him in conversation with the Palestinian leader – formerly reviled as a terrorist – Yasser Arafat. Friends of his were saying the inspection had ensured his political survival until the autumn but that his long-term position remained in doubt: 'He is not a popular leader.' In a thoughtful editorial, the *Belfast Telegraph* welcomed the IRA move. 'The inspection itself left a lot to be desired, and it cannot be construed as actual decommissioning, but that was always going to be the case ... The importance of the exercise is that it was actual and symbolic evidence that the IRA is moving away from its reliance on force. A private army which opens up its arms dumps is sending a message not only to the outside world, but to its own supporters that its war has undergone a fundamental change. It may never be declared 'over', but clearly the chances of the IRA returning to the old, failed methods of bombing and shooting for a united Ireland are greatly diminished ... A first step has been taken, voluntarily, to remove the gun from mainstream republicanism for the first time in history.'

Just over a month later, on 28 July, another chapter in the Troubles closed with the release of the final batch of paramilitary prisoners from the Maze, formerly Long Kesh, which was now scheduled to be shut down. The released prisoners included republican Seán Kelly, serving nine life terms for the Shankill bomb, and loyalist Torrens Knight, a participant in the Greysteel pub massacre in which eight people died. Four members of the IRA sniper team from South Armagh were also freed: their victims included Lance Bombardier Stephen Restorick, whose death is chronicled in the second chapter of this book.

The wheel had come full circle: the guns were silent and

sealed; the prisoners were out; unionists and republicans were in government together; troops were off the streets, most of the time. Although tensions remained, age-old sectarian hatreds continued to flourish and many political problems remained unsolved, it was becoming ever harder to deny that the war, the long, painful, bloody and squalid conflict in which nearly 4,000 people died, was finally approaching its end.

Chapter 14

GROUNDHOG DAY

'Each negotiation in each office or stately home, accompanied by each ritual press conference, has often been Groundhog Day, for you, for me, for all of us.'

Tony Blair, Belfast, 17 October 2002

The Bill Murray film *Groundhog Day*, about a man reliving the same 24-hour period over and over, popularised the phrase on this side of the Atlantic. Whenever the latest in the repetitive series of crises erupted in the peace process, journalists and their contacts in politics and officialdom would joke among themselves: 'It's like *Groundhog Day* but without the same element of surprise' or maybe an old favourite: 'It's déjà vu all over again.'

Republicans worried that the unionists would pocket any concessions on decommissioning and give nothing in return. Unionists were equally wary of the Provos as well as being generally suspicious of the Good Friday Agreement and all its works and pomps. Decommissioning was the political manifestation of this mindset and continued to bedevil the process like some demented virus for which no antidote could be found. A senior British official, Sir John Chilcot, put it well on one occasion when he said that decommissioning 'lay there at the heart of the process like a coiled snake'.[1] Blair's media guru Alastair Campbell correctly identified 'the absolute nub of the problem' which was that, 'neither trusted the other to deliver if they were meant to go second'.[2]

Sooner or later, the IRA would have to deliver, but republicans kept insisting the circumstances had to be right. There could be no whiff of surrender and no sense of a defeated army giving up its weapons: they could never concede anything that would allow unionists to crow in triumph over them. Objects of horror to others, the guns and explosives were the equivalent of the family silver for republicans. They seemed dubious about the wisdom of investing these precious commodities, as they saw them, in the shaky and unstable leadership of David Trimble, whom they regarded as a half-hearted peace processer in any case.

There was another factor not generally understood: the mindset of republicans and the way they look at the world. A senior negotiator with a deep knowledge of republicanism says the IRA was 'obsessed with its word' and fulfilling commitments to the letter. 'Hours and hours would be spent getting the language right.' Like a well-known brand of wood stain, it seems the IRA was determined to 'do exactly what it says on the tin' or, as this source put it, 'If they promised to shoot you, they would.' But at the same time he did not always believe the IRA when it denied responsibility for particular actions.

In a major political surprise, Peter Mandelson resigned as Northern Secretary on 24 January 2001 after it was claimed that he had helped a wealthy Indian businessman to obtain a British passport. It was his second time to lose a cabinet post in the Labour administration. A subsequent inquiry cleared Mandelson's name but he had already been replaced at Stormont by the Scottish Secretary, Dr John Reid, the first person from a Roman Catholic background to hold the job. Campbell records those very confused few days in his diary. There was ambiguity as to whether Mandelson had or had not called the Home Office about the passport and, with a media firestorm developing, Blair sacked Mandelson in advance of the inquiry's findings.[3]

Campbell's account contains nothing to suggest that any disagreement over Northern Ireland policy might have influenced the Prime Minister's decision. But according to the *Guardian*, 'At the time of his departure Alastair Campbell, then the Prime Minister's official spokesman, openly questioned Mr Mandelson's judgment over Northern Ireland on the grounds that he became overly sympathetic to the unionists and too hostile to Sinn Féin.'[4]

Lacking Mowlam's free and easy ways[5] Mandelson could never aspire to her level of popularity with nationalists, especially after the suspension of the Executive in February 2000.

Dublin loved Mowlam (even though one senior minister could not pronounce her name properly, referring to her as 'Mo Moland') but relations with Mandelson could be quite rocky.

Nobody ever owned up to the notorious and extraordinary leak of an internal British memorandum in which Brian Cowen was portrayed as a deep-dyed, knee-jerk nationalist (see pp. 340–41). Clearly the story came from within the British system and Mandelson's reputation as the 'Sultan of Spin' inevitably made him an object of suspicion – even though there was no real evidence he was to blame. The resentment towards him ran deep: nearly three years later I was having dinner with a senior government figure from Dublin when Mandelson's name came up in conversation. My dinner companion angrily pointed to the ceiling, indicating that the 'f***ing light bulb' was more congenial to him than Peter Mandelson.

Mandelson had been instrumental in bringing the unionists into the power-sharing executive in November 1999 and later in May 2000. Mowlam couldn't have done it because her relations with the UUP were so poisonous. There were quiet sniggers when he started bringing a Labrador called 'Bobby' around with him. This led to a minor diplomatic incident at an official dinner when a foreign civil servant of delicate sensibility found Bobby's conduct excessively intrusive, but Mandelson had already retired for the night at that stage. Also on a lighter note, it is understood that Cowen, an accomplished mimic, did a brilliant take-off of 'Mandy'.

Nearly four months later on 8 May, it was Trimble's turn to drop a bombshell. Just hours before Blair was due to call Westminster elections, the UUP leader hurriedly informed the Assembly of his intention to resign as First Minister on 1 July if there was no progress on IRA decommissioning. Much later, Trimble told BBC journalist Martina Purdy that the election strategy was worked out the previous February or March in a café in Massachusetts with close advisers and confidants, including Professor Paul Bew (later Lord Bew) of Queen's University Belfast.[6]

It was a bad election for the middle ground in both communities. The UUP came back with six seats, a net loss of four, while the DUP increased its share of Westminster seats from two to five. Sinn Féin doubled its representation from two to four

MPs (all abstentionist, of course) with the SDLP remaining static at three. West Tyrone had been described as the SDLP's Stalingrad, where a victory for Bríd Rodgers would turn back the Sinn Féin tide. The hype proved hollow when Pat Doherty easily took the seat and the SDLP candidate finished third behind Willie Thompson of the UUP.

When the 1 July deadline came around, Trimble duly stepped down but was replaced by Sir Reg Empey, whom he nominated in a caretaker role for a six-week period. Just over a week later the parties adjourned for talks at a 'secret' location, soon revealed to be Weston Park, ancestral home of the Earls of Bradford on the borders of Shropshire and Staffordshire. The British had a fondness for country-house diplomacy and at the time there was a fair degree of optimism that the problems could be resolved in short order. A high-level source says the Weston Park gathering was convened 'to finalise the outstanding issues – as we thought'. The DUP was not invited and the UVF-linked Progressive Unionist Party walked out in frustration after a few days. A semi-detached Trimble also left before the end but his internal party critic Jeffrey Donaldson took a more serious interest in the talks.[7]

The Weston Park deliberations took place from 9–14 July 2001, a month or so prior to the arrest of three Irish republicans, James Monaghan, Martin McCauley and Niall Connolly (initially thought to be 'David Bracken', the name which appeared on his passport), as they were about to board a flight to Paris at Bogotá's El Dorado airport on 11 August. The three were charged with training Colombia's left-wing FARC guerrillas in IRA bomb-making techniques and with using false passports. The Colombian authorities said later that two other suspected Irish republicans, a man and a woman, were arrested at the same time but then let go for lack of evidence.

The British Government knew about the Colombian escapade at Weston Park. An Irish source says the British always conveyed such information very rapidly to the highest political level: 'Their intelligence system links in with their political system. This place [Ireland] is far more politically-driven than security-driven.' Another Irish source says, 'the British priority was to have a major deal done' back home and the Colombian episode was seen in that context.

Trimble biographer Dean Godson writes that, 'The [British] security services had been on the trail of the three republicans for some time and had informed No. 10 of their movements ... Blair had been briefed on events in Colombia at the time of Weston Park.' Godson also quotes an interview he did with Sir Ronnie Flanagan in which the then-RUC Chief Constable is quoted as saying John Reid told him at the time of the arrests that he believed the three men may have been in Colombia without the knowledge of Adams and McGuinness.[8]

Many observers would be highly sceptical that key republican leaders would not know about the Colombian adventure. But the suggestion that not everyone in the leadership was entirely in the picture derives some support from the embarrassing episode where Adams and Co denied that Connolly was their man in Havana, but were then forced to backtrack after they were contradicted by the Cuban authorities. It is surprising that the Sinn Féin leadership in Belfast would not know the identities of its own representatives abroad, but it appears that in the republican house there are many mansions.

It's an intriguing thought that news of the Colombian venture was in the air at Weston Park, yet Sinn Féin apparently never knew the secret was out. If they had, it is hard to believe they would not have tried to tip off their republican comrades that the 'Brits' were onto them. Although it could not be officially confirmed for this book, the Irish Government delegation almost certainly knew about Colombia as well.

At this time also there was a series of secret engagements 'on and off for at least a month' involving senior Irish and, to a lesser extent, British officials, members of the Decommissioning Body and key Sinn Féin representatives at Clonard Monastery in Belfast, whose Redemptorist community includes peace intermediary Father Alec Reid. Finally on 6 August General de Chastelain stated publicly that the IRA had come up with a plan to put its weapons 'beyond use'. This was confirmed by an IRA statement on 9 August but, in the absence of 'product', Reid suspended the institutions for a single day, a technical device which allowed for another six weeks of pulling and dragging over weapons.

News of the arrest of the 'Colombia Three' was released by the authorities in Bogotá on 13 August. Next day, the IRA issued a statement withdrawing its decommissioning plan, citing British bad faith and unionist rejectionism.

By this stage I had taken up a new position at *The Irish Times* as Foreign Affairs Correspondent, but continued to cover issues related to Northern Ireland as and when appropriate. I was assigned to the Colombia Three story and made several trips to Bogotá to cover the trial, which was poorly prepared on the government side and turned into something of a farce. One had the feeling that the Colombians' hearts weren't in it and that the British and/or Americans had bounced them into the whole affair.

I have always harboured a suspicion that the trio would have been quietly let go were it not for the 9/11 terror attacks, which took place a month to the day after their arrests. The events of 11 September changed everything, most of all the political climate in the US, where there had previously been a certain level of implicit 'understanding' for the factors which led to the IRA campaign.

Sinn Féin's new-found friends on Capitol Hill and in corporate America were not in the mood to make excuses for any departures from conventional politics. It was significant that Republican Congressman Peter King, a long-time friend to Sinn Féin when few other public figures would give them the time of day, became chair of the House Committee on Homeland Security.

By sheer coincidence, at the time of the 9/11 attacks, Adams and McGuinness were in Government Buildings in Dublin for talks with the Taoiseach. So too was President Bush's special envoy on Northern Ireland, Richard Haass, who was scheduled to meet Mr Ahern separately. The Taoiseach met the Sinn Féin leaders at 1.45 pm and was due to receive Dr Haass with the US Ambassador to Ireland, Richard Egan, at 2.15 pm. In between the two meetings, news of the 9/11 attacks emerged.

When Haass and Adams met later that day in Belfast (the more convenient option of meeting in Dublin was obviously deemed inappropriate), the Sinn Féin leader was left in no doubt as to Washington's severe disapproval of the Colombian expedition. Haass said in a media comment that 'any co-operation with people in Colombia who are challenging the law, promoting the sale of drugs, any co-operation with them is to the US extremely,

extremely disturbing. My concerns about those contacts are real.'[9] A security source says US agents knew all about the Colombia venture and had even listened in to phone calls made by the Irish trio.[10] If the republicans lost the American constituency they would be in serious trouble.

In the absence of decommissioning, three senior UUP ministers at Stormont resigned from their positions on 18 October (Trimble having already stepped down on 1 July), to be quickly followed by the DUP. The Executive was teetering on the brink when, at a press conference four days later, Adams said it was time for the IRA to make a 'groundbreaking' move on the arms issue to save the peace process. Within 24 hours, the IRA announced it had begun putting arms beyond use. The great day had dawned, although the long wait and the arm's length nature of the proceedings – the decommissioning was witnessed by General de Chastelain and two IICD colleagues – served to reduce the media and publicity impact. Nevertheless, the resignations of the UUP and DUP ministers were promptly withdrawn.

Meanwhile the SDLP's Mark Durkan became Deputy First Minister, in succession to Seamus Mallon, who had stepped down (Durkan would shortly take over the party leadership also when John Hume stepped down). On 6 November, after they had been voted into office by the Assembly, Trimble and Durkan emerged into the Great Hall of Parliament Buildings for their first joint press conference as First and Deputy First Minister. The UUP leader was immediately greeted with cries of 'Cheat!' and 'Traitor!' by DUP opponents who moved in on the group around Trimble and Durkan.

Someone pushed Ulster Unionist MLA Joan Carson from behind and she pitched forward, creating a domino effect whereby Alasdair McDonnell of the SDLP and Sinn Féin's Mitchel McLaughlin were propelled into a phalanx of DUP hecklers. A general melee ensued, which immediately entered the annals as 'The Brawl in the Hall'. Not for nothing at around this time did a top NIO figure remark, paraphrasing his master Tony Blair, that he felt 'the hand of history' clenching his private parts.

There was a sense at this time that various secret bodies, particularly the IRA and British intelligence entities, were 'tidying-up' as the war came to an end. On St Patrick's Night, 17

March 2002, while the North's main political leaders were on their annual pilgrimage to Washington, a break-in took place at police special branch headquarters at Castlereagh in Belfast where no doubt many sensitive files were kept. Claim and counterclaim ensued, with security sources insisting it was the IRA, while Martin McGuinness blamed those infamous 'securocrats'.[11]

Meanwhile the loveless power-sharing marriage limped on, getting a minor boost when the IRA said on 8 April it had put a second consignment of weapons beyond use, in the presence of the Independent International Commission on Decommissioning (IICD). But the torpor of the peace process was shattered on 4 October when Sinn Féin's offices at Stormont were raided as part of a police investigation into alleged intelligence-gathering by republicans. The sight of PSNI Land Rovers outside Parliament Buildings with armed police officers in flame-retardant overalls and baseball caps making their way up the steps was not a scenario one expects in a normal democracy. The Taoiseach's former special adviser on the North, Martin Mansergh, said it was the sort of thing 'you might associate more with Turkey and President Mugabe'.[12] Chief Constable Hugh (later Sir Hugh) Orde subsequently apologised for the way the operation was handled.

There have been many intriguing episodes in the history of Northern Ireland but this was one of the murkiest of all. There were other police raids in Belfast that day and a woman and three men were arrested, including Denis Donaldson, chief administrator of the Sinn Féin office at Stormont, who had been imprisoned with hunger striker Bobby Sands. At Donaldson's initial hearing, attended by Gerry Adams and Bairbre de Brún, the court was told that police had found a rucksack containing highly sensitive documents at his home. These documents were said to contain personal details of known loyalists and serving police officers and there were other documents of a restricted nature originating from government offices. There was more to Donaldson than met the eye, but it took over three years for a fuller picture of this jovial and apparently irreverent Sinn Féin operative to emerge.

Whether or not the 'Stormontgate' raids were an attempt to recover files stolen from Castlereagh six months beforehand was unclear. A fully-fledged crisis had developed by now and, within ten days, Reid announced the suspension of devolution and the return of direct rule by London ministers from midnight.

With everyone still reeling at the sudden turn of events, Blair came to Belfast on 17 October 2002 to give a speech in which he came up with a new phrase for what the peace process needed: 'acts of completion'. He strongly implied that the standing-down of the IRA was one of these. 'The fork in the road has finally come,' he said, adding that, 'we cannot carry on with the IRA, half-in, half-out of this process.'

The Agreement's fifth anniversary came around on 10 April 2003 but the IRA's 'acts of completion' were still deemed too vague. Blair's Chief of Staff Jonathan Powell came over to Dublin on 13 April, joining the Taoiseach as well as other politicians and civil servants at Bertie Ahern's constituency office, St Luke's in Drumcondra, where the group sat and waited all day for Sinn Féin leaders to arrive with an IRA statement that would hopefully revive the process.

'We had been promised the IRA statement [at] 2.30,' according to a participant. They were still there at 7.30 pm in the small, red-brick detached house beside the busy airport road. It was a difficult weekend for Powell, whose mother was seriously ill and who was himself also quite unwell. In order to pass the time, some of the group adjourned to Fagan's pub across the road, a favourite haunt of the Taoiseach's. 'Adams and McGuinness contacted us [and] with bated breath, said they were on their way down. They were all excited.' It is understood the Sinn Féin leaders had been meeting in the Border area with other senior republicans – Adams liked to call them 'people of substance'.

When the Sinn Féin duo finally arrived, tired out from their exertions, they met with a group that included the Taoiseach, who was chairing, Justice Minister Michael McDowell, Foreign Affairs Minister Brian Cowen, Powell and a number of senior civil servants. Their hosts were distinctly unimpressed with what Adams and McGuinness brought to the table. 'We threw collective cold water on it: not clear enough.' Adams and McGuinness were nonplussed and McGuinness asked, somewhat plaintively, 'Have we no friends here at all?' A source from the other side of the table says: 'We all went home that night crestfallen.' Powell flew back home immediately.

This was just one of many mood swings throughout the peace process. 'Sometimes the governments would be upbeat and Sinn Féin would deflate them, sometimes the other way round,' a senior negotiator recalls. There was even an occasion in Hillsborough Castle where republican negotiators were deflated by their own back-room people.

McGuinness was more popular than Adams with officials and ministers on the other side of the table because of his relaxed, down-to-earth demeanour, but this did not mean he was an easy mark. A top official recalls wearily how a particular, lengthy negotiating session with the Derryman was 'like trying to catch eels by hand'. He continues: 'McGuinness would listen to you for maybe an hour and then respond in four lucid sentences, explaining why "this [proposal or suggestion] is not on".' Dublin sources felt that Adams was not sufficiently respectful of the offices of Prime Minister and Taoiseach, although that disclosure will do him little harm in the republican heartland.

A key factor in advancing the process was the existence of a semi-permanent team of negotiators from the different sides: London, Dublin and Sinn Féin (see also p. 320). This provided an underlying structure for the negotiations, although it meant that sometimes senior civil servants would be brought into meetings ahead of ministers, who would be left waiting outside.

Since IRA statements were so crucially important it was inevitable that the two governments would seek to influence the tone and have particular elements included or even left out. Such statements were generally signed 'P. O'Neill', which had been the traditional pseudonym used by the Provisionals. But P. O'Neill began to widen his cloak and, via Sinn Féin negotiators, accept contributions, suggestions and even drafts from impeccably respectable civil servants on both sides who had never fired a shot in anger in their lives. These officials even became adept at making the usual gestures towards republican core values while at the same time 'trying to get in a couple of things we wanted'.

Some might see this as a corruption of the democratic process, but underlying the whole endeavour was a simple desire, simply expressed: 'stop the killing.' A key player in Dublin describes it as the principal motivating factor. Likewise another senior Irish negotiator says Blair and Powell brought a new note of pragmatism to the British Government's approach: 'Their attitude was, "Let's stop the killing and worry about the detail later".'

Leisure time and family life not infrequently took second place to the peace process. One of the negotiators describes a session in the Prime Minister's country residence at Chequers where 'children's toys were strewn around' (young Leo was still a toddler). At the start of the meeting with British and Irish civil servants and Sinn Féin representatives, Blair announced he had to be 'out of here' by the early afternoon. It was not to be: 'He was still there at 3 a.m. the following morning.' Blair's enthusiasm for getting personally involved in drafting documents and statements, etc., was very striking and seen as unusual for a top politician.

But these late-night sessions could have a lighter side. After one long-drawn-out encounter at Hillsborough Castle, three top Irish civil servants – Paddy Teahon, Tim Dalton and Dermot Gallagher – relaxed in the grounds with an impromptu early-morning game of Gaelic football, presumably the first time the 'catch-and-kick' code was played in such surroundings. Back in Dublin, meetings with Sinn Féin representatives usually took place in out-of-the-way coffee shops or the back room of a pub, away from prying eyes and the gaze of some overzealous junior detective in the Special Branch who might get the wrong idea. For their part, the republicans were always very discreet and, in the words of one official, 'could teach civil servants how to maintain confidentiality'.

Following intense behind-the-scenes contacts, a timetable of events was agreed between the parties and the two governments. Shortly after 7 am, on 21 October 2003, Downing Street announced 26 November as the date for Assembly elections. Regarding a deal as imminent the Prime Minister, despite a recent health scare, flew into Belfast at lunchtime and was later joined at Hillsborough Castle by the Taoiseach. General de Chastelain told a press conference in the Castle's Throne Room that there had been 'a third event in which IRA weapons have been put beyond use'. But although the IRA had begun to move, it still insisted on a very high degree of confidentiality from the General and, when pressed by journalist Eamonn Mallie, he was unable to give precise details about the arms disposal. The press conference rapidly turned into a disaster. Trimble was also very unhappy and put moves towards a pre-election deal on hold.

The elections went ahead in any case, but on the day beforehand, 25 November 2003, a development took place that was to have a significant long-term impact on the peace process. In the resolution of disputes and disagreements, it is often useful to have a source of 'third-party validation' and, in this regard, the signing of a treaty between the British and Irish governments to establish the Independent Monitoring Commission was a positive development. Much as republicans might rail against it, the IMC carries real authority.

The Commission, which commenced operation on 7 January 2004, reports to the governments on activity by paramilitary groups, on the normalisation of security measures in the North, and on claims that ministers or parties in the Assembly are not living up to the standards required of them. The four commissioners at time of writing are: former Assembly presiding officer and Alliance Party leader Lord Alderdice; former secretary-general of the Irish Department of Justice, Joe Brosnan; former head of Scotland Yard's anti-terrorist squad John Grieve; and former CIA deputy director Richard Kerr.

The Assembly elections marked the end of Trimble as a major political force. The DUP and Sinn Féin emerged as the largest parties on either side of the Assembly. The DUP won 30 seats to the UUP's 27 and Sinn Féin came back with 24, compared to 18 for the SDLP. On 18 December 2003, Jeffrey Donaldson quit the UUP along with two other newly elected Assembly members, Arlene Foster and Norah Beare. Within weeks they announced they had joined the DUP, which now had 33 seats to the UUP's 24.

With Trimble and his party effectively out of the equation, the challenge now was to bring the DUP together with Sinn Féin. Three days of intense negotiations at Leeds Castle in Kent ('Home to Royalty, Lords and Ladies for over 1,000 Years') in September 2004 ended without agreement, but there was still a mood of cautious optimism afterwards and, on 17 November, the two governments put their proposals for breaking the stalemate to the two parties.

On 29 November in Downing Street, Adams held his first ever meeting with PSNI Chief Constable Hugh Orde. But the following day, Paisley put the cat among the pigeons when he repeated his call for the IRA to 'wear sackcloth and ashes' and repent its misdeeds. Adams said Paisley's comments were 'offensive'. The DUP leader also wanted photographic proof of decommissioning. However, in a statement to *An Phoblacht* on 9 December, the IRA said it was committed to the peace process but would 'not submit to a process of humiliation'. DUP demands for photographs of decommissioning were 'never possible'.

At least the politicians could look forward to a quiet and uneventful Christmas before returning to the table in January. But every time the North seems to be going into hibernation, there is another sensational development. On 21 December an armed gang stole £26.5 million from the Northern Bank in Belfast city centre. The IRA's denial of involvement in one of the biggest bank robberies in history met with widespread disbelief. Republican protestations notwithstanding, the generally accepted narrative in other quarters is that the Paisley 'sackcloth and ashes' démarche convinced key IRA people that the peace process was going nowhere for the moment, so they might as well take the opportunity of making this unorthodox bank withdrawal. But it seems the IRA never expected such a massive haul. Had it been a 'mere' two or three million, the raid would have been largely forgotten by the New Year. A particularly interesting 'take' on the robbery from a well-placed Dublin source is that the IRA needed money to pay off their members at the end of the lengthy guerrilla campaign. They would have received a modest wage while on active service and this was to be a form of severance or retirement pay, so to speak.

The New Year began with a categoric statement from Chief Constable Hugh Orde on 7 January that the IRA carried out the robbery. But even worse was to come with claims that IRA members were involved in the killing of Robert McCartney, a father of two children, who was stabbed to death near a Belfast bar on 30 January. Over the coming year, Mr McCartney's sisters led a high-profile campaign calling for his killers to be brought to justice. The high point was on St Patrick's Day when President Bush received the McCartneys at the White House whereas, unlike previous years, Northern Ireland's politicians were not invited. This was understandably very much resented by the

SDLP as it was manifestly unfair both to themselves and to the unionists, neither of whose supporters had anything to do with the McCartney killing.

'During all of this time,' according to a high-level source close to the negotiations, 'senior civil servants and politicians on both sides were heavily engaged in efforts to settle the language of peace – words were of central importance throughout the process.' A concept that became the source of major difficulty was that of 'exclusively peaceful means'. For some time, Sinn Féin would not commit unequivocally to the term 'exclusively' because the IRA had not, at that time, decided that 'the war is over'.

In addition, the presence in government of Michael McDowell as Minister for Justice was not a factor likely to make life more comfortable for Sinn Féin and the IRA. This was the man who described the IRA as 'a massive criminal organisation which kills, tortures and plunders' and accused Sinn Féin of 'vomit-making, stomach-turning hypocrisy'. Sinn Féin in turn charged McDowell with putting 'personal ambition and narrow sectional interest' before the peace process and Gerry Adams scornfully declared, 'I wouldn't send him to the shop for a bottle of milk.'

It was against this background that verbal wrangles continued. There was a deep divide between the position jointly held by the two governments, which officially designated all paramilitary activity as criminal, and the republicans, who maintained that the actions of the IRA were justified and legitimate. How can you get an organisation to forswear criminal activity in the future when it doesn't accept anything it did in the past came into that category? The answer was to secure a commitment that the 'war' was over, thereby providing a doctrinal umbrella under which republicans could comfortably condemn acts of violence, etc.

This debate became entangled with a dispute over the continued incarceration of the killers of Garda Jerry McCabe, who had been shot dead by an IRA unit during an attempted robbery of a postal van at Adare, County Limerick on 7 June 1996. There was an outpouring of public sympathy, with up to 40,000 people lining the streets of Limerick for the funeral. Although Sinn Féin consistently demanded the men's release, the Irish Government would not budge. According to a senior negotiator, the controversy 'demonstrated, very clearly, that the vast majority of people in Ireland were not prepared to accept that all of what the IRA had done over the years should be classed as incidents of war, justified by reference to the fight for Irish freedom.'

Some of the more pragmatic government negotiators were taking the view that, 'in the interests of avoiding roadblocks, when the end of the IRA campaign was literally in sight, the better course was to secure a commitment, first, to the ending of politically motivated violence because it was this, rather than purely criminal escapades by individual IRA members that had produced the toll of death and destruction for several decades'.

Against the background of this debate, Adams issued a lengthy statement on 6 April, in which he appealed to the IRA to 'fully embrace and accept' the pursuit of its aims 'by purely political and democratic activity'.

Westminster elections took place on 5 May, with the DUP emerging as the big winner locally, taking nine out of the eighteen Northern Ireland seats at Westminster , while the once-mighty UUP came back with only one MP. Trimble lost out to the DUP's David Simpson in Upper Bann and I can still hear the thunder of Lambeg drums outside the count-centre in Banbridge as Paisley and his followers celebrated their victory. Trimble immediately stepped down as UUP leader, to be succeeded by Sir Reg Empey. On the nationalist side, Sinn Féin went up from four to five seats but the SDLP did better than many expected by winning in three constituencies, including the crucial Foyle seat which Mark Durkan took over from his predecessor as party leader, John Hume.

On 28 July, the IRA said it had formally ordered an end to its armed campaign as of 4 pm that day. The statement, read on DVD by Seanna Walsh, a former cellmate of Bobby Sands, declared: 'All IRA units have been ordered to dump arms. All Volunteers have been instructed to assist the development of purely political and democratic programmes through exclusively peaceful means.'

Here it was at last, the magical three-word phrase, 'exclusively peaceful means'. A senior negotiator comments: 'The insistence by both governments that "peaceful means" meant no less than the absence of criminal activity, however motivated, was quite important. For one thing, it provided assurance to Northern unionists – and to many others besides, north and south of the Border and in the UK – that the Irish Government was not going to settle for a "soft" deal from the IRA.'

The IRA statement added that arrangements were being made to complete the process of decommissioning: 'Our decisions have been taken to advance our republican and democratic objectives, including our goal of a united Ireland. We believe there is now an alternative way to achieve this and to end British rule in our country.'

Speaking in almost biblical tones, Adams said: 'There is a time to resist, to stand up and to confront the enemy by arms if necessary. In other words there is a time for war. There is also a time to engage, to reach out and put war behind us.'[13] As he addressed the press conference in the opulent Martello Room on the seventh floor of Jury's Hotel, Dublin (a far cry from Belfast's Conway Mill), one couldn't help noticing that long-time militants were on the edge of the group around him while the newer recruits with no 'form' were standing close to the leader. The shape of things to come.

Tony Blair said it was a 'step of unparalleled magnitude'. Within days, London was setting out a two-year plan to scale down the British Army's presence in Northern Ireland. All this would have come as music to the ears of Mo Mowlam who sadly died on 19 August.

Developments were coming hot and heavy and, on 26 September, General de Chastelain announced that the IRA had put all of its weapons beyond use. The two churchmen who witnessed the process, Father Alec Reid and ex-Methodist president Rev Harold Good, said they were 'satisfied that the arms decommissioned represent the totality of the IRA's arsenal'.

On 8 December 2005 three Belfast men at the centre of the alleged IRA spying incident at Stormont were acquitted of all charges. At an unlisted hearing in Belfast Crown Court, all charges against Sinn Féin administrator Denis Donaldson and two other men involved in the case were dropped. The prosecution said that, 'in the public interest', no evidence would be offered.

As if the affair wasn't murky enough, Donaldson admitted on 16 December that he had been a paid British agent for two decades. When the news broke, he was immediately expelled from Sinn Féin. It was a major shock: Donaldson had been a key Sinn Féin operative in the US in the early days of the peace process.

A few months later, the *Sunday World* newspaper broke a story that Donaldson was living in a remote cottage near Glenties, County Donegal. Most agents and informers seem to leave Ireland for safer pastures, but not him. Soon afterwards, on 4 April 2006, he was found shot dead at the cottage. At time of writing nobody has been arrested or charged with his murder. It could have been a republican revenge killing – although the IRA denied it – or else a British undercover unit seeking to shut him up. Logic also suggests that whoever decided to arrest Donaldson in the first place did not know he was a British agent. But logic isn't always the best guide to Northern Ireland.

Two days later, Blair and Ahern held a press conference at the historic Navan Fort (*Emain Macha*) outside Armagh to unveil their blueprint for restoring devolution. Assembly members would be given until 24 November to set up a power-sharing executive. If the attempt failed, salaries would stop and the two governments would work on partnership arrangements to implement the Good Friday Agreement. This was the so-called 'Plan B', which was never publicly revealed, although the implicit threat of joint authority was clearly meant to scare unionists. In response to my sceptical questioning, a senior political source told me he had actually seen a Plan B document, although it was not signed by the two governments: 'Plan B was for real.'

On 11 October 2006, three days of intensive multi-party talks began at St Andrews in Scotland. Peter Hain later told the *Guardian* about his lasting memory of the Prime Minister at that time: 'I remember going into Tony's room at about 7 am. He was still in his bare feet and his track suit, unshaven, and he was working away on ideas and so on.'[14] Another negotiator told me: 'We felt we had to get them into a hothouse.' But the talks were 'really fractious' and 'went down to the wire'. On the last day of the talks there was a difficult meeting between Sinn Féin and the two governments with Adams questioning Blair quite sharply.

Eventually the Prime Minister said, 'That's it' and adjourned for the plenary.

'We went into the room where the plenary was to happen,' recalls one participant. 'We didn't know if Sinn Féin would come in, till the last minute. We wondered if Paisley – who was looking cross – would walk out. Sinn Féin weren't overly happy with the thing but came in eventually.'

Paisley wanted to leave early for London as he and his wife Eileen were celebrating their fiftieth wedding anniversary, but he was delayed by several hours. At the end of the plenary, the Taoiseach presented the Paisleys with a bowl carved by Liam O'Neill from the wood of a fallen walnut tree at the site of the Battle of the Boyne, a celebrated event in the unionist tradition.

As one eyewitness puts it, Paisley was 'absolutely chuffed'. The idea came from an Irish civil servant in the Department of Foreign Affairs named Peadar Carpenter. At dinner with the Taoiseach and advisers the night before, Blair had asked Powell what the British side was giving Paisley. Powell replied that it was a photo album – high-quality and purchased at Smythson of Bond Street, a smart stationery outlet whose creative director is Samantha Cameron, wife of the Conservative Party leader.

'Taoiseach, what are you giving?' asked Blair. One of those present reports that, when Ahern told him, Blair responded along the following lines: 'Oh f***! Jesus, Jonathan, how come the Taoiseach can come up with these inspired ideas and all we can present is a f***ing photo album?' (It is only fair to point out that things were going particularly badly for him on Iraq at this time.)

Ahern presented the gift to the Paisleys about noon next day, Friday 13 October. The DUP leader said the bowl was 'coming home' and that he hoped Friday the thirteenth would be a great day 'for all of the people of Ireland' as well as for his and everyone's children and grandchildren. Someone produced a small, personal camera and took a picture as the two men shook hands for the first time.

A senior Dublin figure told me that, before meeting the DUP leader in the Sycamore Room at Government Buildings, ministers would be warned in advance that Paisley 'doesn't want to shake hands' although they would routinely shake hands with Ian Paisley Jr and Peter Robinson at the end of a meeting. Shortly after the St Andrews presentation, Ahern received a handwritten letter from Ian Jr expressing deep appreciation of the gesture on behalf of the family.

After the plenary, Blair and Ahern hosted a press conference against a backdrop with the words 'St Andrews Agreement' emblazoned upon it. A senior member of the Dublin delegation told me they were 'gobsmacked' at this move by the British. 'We felt quite peeved that they already had backdrops. We were a bit worried at the time that, "The Good Friday Agreement is no more".'

The parties were given until 10 November to respond to what the governments somewhat presumptuously called the St Andrews Agreement, which had yet to be formally endorsed by the political parties ('There was a paper called an agreement,' says an official source). Key points included full acceptance of the PSNI by Sinn Féin; restoration of the political institutions; commitment by all parties to power-sharing as well as North–South and East–West arrangements; devolution of criminal policing and justice powers from London by May 2008.[15]

In accordance with this 'road map', the Assembly would meet on 24 November to nominate the First and Deputy First Ministers. The Agreement would be endorsed by the electorate in March 2007, either in an election or a referendum. 'It was very, very clear Paisley wanted an election,' says a source in the talks. The Irish mulled over the issue of whether a referendum was required in the South, similar to the Good Friday vote, but Attorney General Rory Brady advised this was not the case. On 26 March, power would be devolved and the d'Hondt procedure for appointing ministers would operate. 'Failure to agree to establish the Executive will lead to immediate dissolution of the Assembly, as will failure to agree at any stage, and the Governments will take forward new partnership arrangements on the basis previously announced,' the Agreement stated.

But when the 24 November deadline arrived, the DUP were still not ready to deal. Assembly proceedings were interrupted as loyalist killer Michael Stone tried to force his way into Stormont. He was later charged with murder bids on Adams and McGuinness. Unwittingly, Stone created an interlude for the two governments to salvage the Agreement. 'Michael Stone saved the day. He gave us four hours to sort out the mess,' says one official. Paisley confirmed that, when the circumstances were right, he would indeed accept a nomination as First Minister.

On 8 January 2007, Progressive Unionist Party leader David Ervine died after suffering a heart attack and subsequently a stroke and brain haemorrhage. The attendance of Gerry Adams at his funeral was seen as a significant gesture of reconciliation. How sadly ironic that the chatty, amiable, ever-constructive Ervine should pass away as the process entered the home stretch. The journey he had undertaken was a loyalist equivalent of the one Adams and McGuinness had also travelled. In a speech after the successful conclusion of the Mitchell Review in November 1999 he quoted the Van Morrison song, *And the Healing has Begun*, and I have used it as the title for my final chapter in this book.

At a special conference in Dublin on 28 January 2007, following a series of public meetings in different locations, Sinn Féin endorsed participation in the PSNI by an overwhelming majority. The spotlight now turned on Paisley and the DUP: will they, won't they?

Assembly elections followed, confirming the strength of the two parties. I was in Stormont on 26 March 2007, which had been named by Northern Secretary Peter Hain as the deadline for 'devolution or dissolution'. There was no great air of anticipation and the media turnout was modest, but this only compounded the drama when the moment arrived. By prior arrangement between the parties, Paisley and Adams sat on either side of the apex of a diamond-shaped table layout with their respective delegations. When the Big Man began to speak in those booming tones, reminiscent of an Old Testament prophet, it brought home the point that this was indeed a Day of Judgment for Northern Ireland.

You had to pinch yourself to make sure it was real when Paisley announced that a date for restoring the institutions had been agreed with Sinn Féin. The DUP sought the best future for 'all' the people of Northern. There would be 'regular meetings' between himself and Martin McGuinness to prepare for their new roles as first and deputy first minister.

Adams responded in kind, with the usual sprinkling of phrases in the Irish language. But he helpfully translated the sweet and kingly tongue of the Gael for his new partners. '*Tús maith leath na hoibre*,' he said. 'A good start is half the work'. Precisely.

The 26 March deadline had given way to a new date for devolution on 8 May, but nobody cared. Deadline schmedline. There was even talk of 'Paisley: The Movie', with reports that Hollywood was looking at fellow Ballymena man Liam Neeson for the title role. An actor from a Catholic background to play Paisley: why not?

As in April 1998, we were overdosing on historic events and defining moments. The next one was a meeting of the DUP leader with the Taoiseach at Farmleigh House in Dublin on 4 April. The warmth of Paisley's greeting to Ahern took many by surprise. Bounding from his car, the DUP leader and First Minister-in-waiting said in his usual booming tones: 'I have to shake this man's hand! Give him a grip!' It was the first time they shook hands in full public view and under the media glare. The pair adjourned to the Library Room where they ate egg and cress sandwiches and talked for 90 minutes. Describing it as 'one of the most open and frank and incredible meetings' without any 'aggression', a participant pointed out to me that the attendance included 'Two Aherns (Bertie and Dermot), two Paisleys (Ian Sr and Ian Jr), two Johnstons (Government Press Secretary Mandy and DUP press officer Timothy) and one Michael Collins (senior official in Taoiseach's department).'

Paisley told reporters afterwards: 'I am proud to be an Ulsterman, but I am also proud of my Irish roots. My father's birth certificate was lodged here in the courts after he was born. Like many of his generation he fought to see, as a member of Carson's army, Ireland remain within the Union. But that, of course, was not as history planned it ...'

When Devolution Day came around on 8 May, I had the privilege to be in Stormont once again. There were a lot of big names: Tony Blair, Bertie Ahern, Ted Kennedy, Jean Kennedy Smith, Albert Reynolds, John Reid and a panoply of ambassadors and senior civil servants. Notable absentees were David Trimble and Seamus Mallon: Trimble was fixing up his barge in England and Mallon was annoyed that neither himself nor Trimble had received an official invitation from the Office of First and Deputy First Minister.

It was twenty years to the day since the Loughgall ambush in which eight IRA men and an innocent bystander were killed by the SAS, and ten years since the death of a young Portadown Catholic, Robert Hamill, who had been attacked by a loyalist mob. The road had been a long one but now we had Ian Paisley and Martin McGuinness entering government together with their parties. There were so many pictures of them laughing together that they came to be known as 'The Chuckle Brothers'.

Events had gone beyond the 'pinch me, is it real?' stage although it was still amazing to see so many militant republicans sitting in the previously reviled unionist enclave of Stormont, claiming their share of ownership. Across the floor, Paisley sat with both hands spread on the bench in front of him like a gun-slinger in a Wild West saloon showing he was unarmed. There were some real-life former gunslingers on the Sinn Féin benches but they, too, were in conciliatory mode. There had been rivers of blood and torrents of hate between the two sides but hopefully we had now arrived, in Seamus Heaney's phrase, 'on the far side of revenge'. When the newly elected Speaker, William Hay of the DUP, announced after various Assembly decisions, 'I am satisfied that cross-community support has been demonstrated', you knew Northern Ireland was embarking on a new voyage.

A concert was laid on afterwards in the Great Hall where a group of special needs performers appropriately named 'The Sky's the Limit' mimed opera and ballads. 'You Raise Me Up' was the one that struck home. An Assembly official explained that the mime was meant to put across a message 'that this place is open to every section of society'. This was a new Stormont where no one would be left out.

At last the peace process had reached a type of closure. A protracted and tragic drama was ending, with a new and more hopeful one about to begin. Some of those who had set the scene would soon be leaving by the stage door. Whatever failings he had in the eyes of his critics, especially over Iraq, nobody could take Tony Blair's role as a peacemaker away from him. But Blair was about to leave Downing Street and Bertie Ahern was in the last phase of his long political career.[16] Other stalwarts of the peace process were also there but the basic message for Assembly members was: 'Over to you.'

This being Northern Ireland, there had to be a cup of tea for the main players afterwards. The cameras and microphones bore witness as Paisley and McGuinness chatted and joked with Blair and Ahern in what the wags rapidly dubbed 'The Vicar's Tea-Party'. Blair had to undergo some gentle teasing from the 'Doc' about the fact that the prime minister was signing off at 54 years of age while the DUP leader was taking the helm at 81.

Perhaps the final act in the drama came when Ahern was invited to address a joint session of the British houses of parliament at Westminster on 15 May, the first Taoiseach to do so. It was only nine days before a general election in the South and, despite Downing Street's insistence that the event was arranged before the election date was known, critics said Blair was doing a political favour for his old pal. But there was something about the occasion that transcended politics. Ahern's speech ranged widely over previous centuries of Anglo-Irish conflict but looked forward to a bright, peaceful future. He said that although the 'bloodstained chapters' of the past could not be torn out, that did not mean they should be written into 'the story of our future'.

The great and the good came out in force for the occasion and the attendance gave a telling indication of the scope and sweep of the peace process. Among them I noticed ex-prime minister Sir John Major as well as past and present Northern Ireland Secretaries Peter Hain, John Reid, Peter Brooke, Paul Murphy, Tom King and the controversial Roy Mason. Blair paid fulsome tribute to Ahern who returned the compliment in equal measure. But Sinn Féin were unimpressed with the glory being heaped on Ahern's shoulders for his role as a peacemaker. A senior republican told me later the negotiations for several years were essentially between 'us and the Brits', claiming Dublin was little more than a bystander much of the time. This was a long-standing Sinn Féin contention – especially during elections.

The question on everybody's mind was: Why did Paisley do it? Could this be the same inflammatory preacher whose speeches and activities had contributed so much to inter-communal tensions over a period of four or five decades? The DUP leader was dogged by health problems in 2004 – in his own words, he walked along Death's shadows – and this may have led him to reflect on the legacy he wished to leave to the people of Northern Ireland. The Big Man himself gave a clue to his state of mind when he told the media after a meeting with Tony Blair in Downing Street: 'I would like to think that we would have a quiet province, I'd like to think that people said: "The man of war was a man of peace".'[17] Now the undisputed leader of the unionist people in Northern Ireland, Paisley clearly revelled in his new-found role. Wearing a broad and unquenchable grin on public occasions, there was no doubt that this was indeed a happy man, as I was able to observe up close when he launched the autobiography of the singer and former Member of the European Parliament, Dana, a.k.a. Dana Rosemary Scallon, in a reception at Stormont on 6 November 2007. Standing with Paisley as he spoke were Martin McGuinness, John Hume and – the first time for them to meet – Albert Reynolds. Like Bill Murray's abrasive TV presenter in *Groundhog Day*, Paisley seemed to have discovered that the secret of contentment lay in kindness and Christian charity towards one's neighbour, of whatever religion or political outlook.

Chapter 15

THE HEALING HAS BEGUN: WHAT NEXT FOR NORTHERN IRELAND?

'I have taken great care not to laugh at human actions, not to weep at them, nor to hate them, but to understand them.' Spinoza

With the Troubles apparently at an end, it is time to take stock of the situation in Northern Ireland. In the epilogue to the first edition of this book I wrote that I expected 'to live to see a united Ireland eventually'. Challenged about this by Radio Ulster's David Dunseith, I replied that I planned on living a long time! Everyone's longevity is problematic but there is also a territorial and political logic to this expectation. And it is not a question of individual wishes or desires but whether such an outcome is historically likely or inevitable. No one should underestimate for a minute the strength of unionist opposition to a 32-county state but, if the two communities are co-operating politically within Northern Ireland, surely the context could grow wider with the passage of time? In some respects it is already widening.

Unionist consent to Irish unity may still be a long way off but the basis for their objections has been seriously eroded since the time when they rebelled en masse against Home Rule in 1912. Autonomy rather than independence was the objective of Home Rule, with a native parliament taking responsibility for domestic affairs and everything else remaining with Westminster. But the overwhelming majority of the Protestant population vowed they would never accept it. The Ulster Covenant, a solemn and binding oath of resistance taken by almost half a million unionists declared that, 'Home Rule would be disastrous to the material well-being of Ulster as well as of the whole of Ireland, subversive of our civil and religious freedom, destructive of our citizenship and perilous to the unity of the Empire.'

Almost 100 years later and in defiance of the Covenant prophecy, the independent part of Ireland is thriving and prosperous, with a high measure of civil and religious freedoms enjoyed by those who live there. As for the citizenship issue, in the British–Irish Agreement which replaced the Anglo-Irish Agreement and was negotiated as part of the Good Friday pact, the two governments, 'recognise the birthright of all the people of Northern Ireland to identify themselves and be accepted as Irish or British, or both, as they may so choose, and accordingly confirm that their right to hold both British and Irish citizenship is accepted by both Governments and would not be affected by any future change in the status of Northern Ireland.'

A well-placed source involved in the talks told me the citizenship issue arose in the fortnight leading up to Good Friday. During a break in the negotiations, officials on the British side made contact with the Home Office in London. It is understood these negotiators were from the Cabinet Office and the Northern Ireland Office. The Home Office response was cautious but the Prime Minister approved the proposal to guarantee dual citizenship in perpetuity and so it went through. My source pointed out that, although the pledge is 'not justiciable' (i.e. cannot be vindicated in the courts) it is nevertheless a 'very, very big promise', which was unprecedented and was not extended to the residents of Hong Kong, for example, when the British left. The term 'people of Northern Ireland' is defined as, 'all persons born in Northern Ireland and having, at the time of their birth, at least one parent who is a British citizen, an Irish citizen or is otherwise entitled to reside in Northern Ireland without any restriction on their period of residence.'

As for the British Empire, which was felt to be under such threat from Home Rule, that once-powerful entity on which the sun never set, has to all intents and purposes been consigned to the history books. Britain is now a technocratic society with a handful of possessions such as Bermuda, the Cayman Islands, the Falklands and the Isle of Man. The imperial dream has shrunk to the role of an auxiliary to the United States in the latter's attempts to police troubled regions such as the Middle East and the Balkans.

The South has shaken off the trappings of a theocratic state to become a typical secular democracy in the European mould (this at a time when anyone who was ever a Roman Catholic, or even married to a Roman Catholic, still cannot accede to the British throne). It has also developed a thriving modern economy and Dublin-based companies are looking towards opportunities north of the Border, as seen in the Aer Lingus decision – overriding vociferous objections from a powerful lobby in the midwest of Ireland – that its critically important flights to Heathrow should originate in Belfast instead of Shannon. The airline's motivation of course was commercial rather than political. Meanwhile, Dr Alan Gillespie, chairman of the Ulster Bank Group has proposed a merger of the Republic's Industrial Development Authority (IDA) and its cross-Border equivalent, Invest Northern Ireland, with a view to attracting Foreign Direct Investment on an all-island basis. He pointed out that Tourism Ireland is already promoting the whole island as a holiday destination.[1]

Some republicans and nationalists look with misty eyes to the centenary of the 1916 Rising as the year when it could all come right. That would be a very short period in which to overcome the hatreds and suspicions of centuries. But even if one allows a longer time frame, could the 26 ever really become 32?

There have been many developments in the last half-century which came as a surprise to virtually everyone. The fall of South African apartheid and Nelson Mandela's walk to freedom would be one example: the Pretoria regime was expected to last many more years. We also had the dramatic overthrow of the Shah of Iran; the collapse of Soviet communism accompanied by the demolition of the Berlin Wall and reunification of Germany; and the rise of Islamic fundamentalism with its campaign of worldwide terror. Nearer home we have had the IRA ceasefire and Ian Paisley in government with his former arch-enemy Martin McGuinness. So perhaps we should not be completely astonished if somehow, someday, a united Ireland finally comes about by peaceful means and with the consent, freely given, of a majority in the North.

The South is no longer the economically backward and underdeveloped society of former times. In the annual United Nations Human Development Index, based on life expectancy, literacy, education and standard of living, Ireland is well ahead of the United Kingdom. The Index for 2007–8 has the Republic of

Ireland in fifth place, behind Iceland, Norway, Australia and Canada, in that order. The UK is down the field at No. 16.[2]

At the same time, the European Union is whittling away the differences between living in the North and the South. Customs posts used to be a visible sign to travellers that they were crossing the Border. As such they inevitably became a target for IRA attacks. But the EU abolished such barriers on 1 January 1993 as part of establishing the single European market.[3]

Due to the expansion of the EU, tens of thousands of Poles, Lithuanians, Latvians and Romanians are living and working relatively happily in the Irish Republic, despite linguistic and cultural differences from the indigenous population. If there was continuing peace, political co-operation and mutual goodwill, the prospect that a sufficient proportion of the Protestants of Northern Ireland would eventually decide to throw in their lot with the South in a democratic agreement, with appropriate legislative protection for their liberties and identity including a Bill of Rights, could prove to be more than a pipe-dream.

The ties that bind the constituent elements of the United Kingdom are gradually getting looser. An ICM poll conducted in England for the *Sunday Telegraph* found that only eighteen per cent of respondents believed the Union would survive indefinitely.[4] Scottish independence is a hot topic again and a 'velvet divorce' à la the Czech Republic and Slovakia cannot be ruled out. I have always maintained that Scotland would exit the United Kingdom before Northern Ireland. Welsh devolution and a certain amount of British republican sentiment (not to be confused with the Irish version) are also part of the mix.

A united Ireland, with the restoration of 'The Fourth Green Field', is a romantic vision that has captivated successive generations. It was closely intertwined with the concept of armed struggle, the heroic volunteer in a trenchcoat or, more recently, woolly anorak and balaclava, holding out against the forces of the Crown. Some say Gerry Adams and Martin McGuinness, in bringing a halt to the physical-force tradition in Irish republicanism, at least for this generation, have killed off the unity dream as well.

The implication is that unless unity is sought by physical force, it will never come about. But Germany is a recent example where peaceful means achieved what 40 years of military stand-off and belligerent posturing failed to encompass. Arguably the real achievement of Adams and McGuinness was to cut the umbilical cord between republicanism and violence, leaving Wolfe Tone's ideology to stand on its own feet in political terms.

At time of writing, the peace in Northern Ireland seems reasonably secure, although an occasional unexpected incident can still rock the boat. But there needs to be the prospect of a new society that will catch the imagination of the young people in particular. The practical day-to-day benefits of peace must be made evident to the ordinary people on the ground, especially in deprived areas such as the Falls and Shankill Roads in Belfast, the Bogside in Derry and rural communities in such counties as Tyrone and Fermanagh.

Having waged a guerrilla campaign that had few parallels anywhere in the developed world or indeed in the annals of Irish history in terms of ferocity and duration, Irish republicanism now has an opportunity to display its social dimension. Social and political deprivation and discrimination laid the groundwork for the Troubles and republicans must strive to ensure, with co-operation from their partners in government as well as from London, Dublin, Washington and Brussels, that the causes of poverty and inequality in both parts of Ireland are addressed and that a new wave of discontent does not arise in the future.

The dissidents haven't gone away, as PSNI Chief Constable Sir Hugh Orde told a seminar at Enfield, County Meath on 16 October 2007. 'They are out of date, they are behind the times,' he said. His remarks uncannily echoed similar comments made about the Provisional IRA at the time of its inception and he was wise to add a cautionary note: 'They are nonetheless dangerous.'[5]

Much of the responsibility for political progress currently rests on the shoulders of Sinn Féin as the main nationalist element in the power-sharing administration. But the party must maintain its electoral base and it is not clear at present whether Sinn Féin has begun to decline or is merely marking time before a further significant breakthrough. Can Sinn Féin go on to become the majority party throughout the island or will it gradually fade and wither, failing to make an impact in the South and yielding pride of place in Northern Ireland to a combination of Fianna Fáil and a revitalised SDLP?

The performance of Sinn Féin in the May 2007 general election in the South was an ominous sign for an organisation dedicated to achieving Irish unity through building up its strength on both sides of the Border. The party was expected to make major advances but, in the event, its tally of Dáil seats went down from five to four.

It is relatively easy for smaller parties to get into coalition in the Republic – compared with the chances of the Liberal Democrats in Britain for example – and the prospect of Sinn Féin ministers from Dublin and Belfast meeting under the auspices of the North–South Ministerial Council is anything but a fantasy, provided the party can maintain its strength in the North and build up support in the South.

Sinn Féin engaged in a highly successful voting pact with Labour in the Irish Senate elections of 2007 and afterwards Labour facilitated the reduced complement of Sinn Féin TDs in securing speaking time in the Dáil. These moves may help to explain why Fianna Fáil has now registered as a political party for the first time in Northern Ireland, with a view to challenging the 'Shinners' on their home turf. Although the Fianna Fáil initiative is still at an early stage, it could prove to be a dramatic development, particularly if the party fuses with the SDLP and contests the 2011 Assembly elections. One of the key people driving the process forward in Fianna Fáil told me it was the most significant development 'since the Good Friday Agreement' but there are mixed views in SDLP circles.

Sinn Féin leader Gerry Adams attracted much of the blame for his party's mediocre showing in the 2007 general election because of his poor performance in a television debate with other party leaders. In addition, the party's economic policies had an old-fashioned, state-centred air about them that was out of tune with the public mood.

Speculation that Adams may step down from the leadership is quietly gaining strength but, whatever the next phase of his career, the Sinn Féin leader is – for good or ill – one of the major political and historical figures of the last 40 years in Ireland. The negative critique of Adams by his detractors ranges from portraying him – above the waterline – as a superb Machiavellian manipulator who conned the Provos into becoming a pillar of partition, to the more discreet version which consists of dark mutterings that he is a puppet – or worse – of the British, who have been pulling the strings in the peace process from Day One.

The problem with this critique is that the basis of popular support for the republican movement began to be undermined when it moved from a purely defensive role in the Catholic ghettos of the North to the waging of an aggressive campaign of bombings and shootings to remove the British presence. If one could pinpoint the exact moment when this started to happen, it would be the killing of Gunner Robert Curtis during an IRA ambush on the New Lodge Road in Belfast on 6 February 1971 which, as then-IRA chief of staff Seán Mac Stíofáin points out in his autobiography, was the first time for 50 years that a British soldier was killed by an IRA unit.[6] Support for the 'armed struggle' ebbed and flowed after that, but the basic trend was downwards and Adams eventually had to come to terms with this reality.

The circumstances were quite different from what prevailed at the time of the ambush at Soloheadbeg, County Tipperary, on 21 January 1919 when Dan Breen and his IRA colleagues killed two members of the Royal Irish Constabulary, thereby starting the War of Independence. On the very same day, the majority of Irish members of parliament were holding the first meeting of the independent assembly known as Dáil Éireann. Although the connection between Soloheadbeg and Dáil Éireann could also be queried, there was no contemporary assembly or electoral mandate either implicitly or explicitly backing the Provisional IRA in 1971.

The launch, or re-launch, of an Anglo-Irish war in the early 1970s was too much for mainstream nationalist opinion to stomach. The nationalist people of the island were instinctively compassionate towards the travails of the Catholics in the ghettos of Belfast and Derry but they had not signed up for all-out war with their nearest neighbour. Despite occasional upsurges of feeling, such as after Bloody Sunday or, to a lesser extent during the Maze hunger strike of 1981, broad nationalist support for the IRA trickled away almost to nothingness over succeeding decades.

It took some time for this reality to penetrate the consciousness of the republican leadership. For example, Sean O'Callaghan, a high-level Garda agent in the IRA during the 1980s describes in his memoirs how the then-chief of staff planned to use weapons and explosives from Libya to create a 'free zone' running along the Clogher Valley from Tyrone to Fermanagh.[7]

We are told elsewhere that militants in the republican movement had plans for an Irish version of the 'Tet Offensive' which turned the tide in the Vietnamese War. The scenario for the Irish 'Tet' reportedly involved seizing areas of Armagh, Tyrone and Fermanagh. In response, the British were expected to unleash a wave of repression, including internment and massive military force.[8] The IRA had thrived in the past under such circumstances.

In a sense, it would be the 1916 Rising all over again. Instead of seizing the GPO in Dublin, the rebels would take and hold Border areas and launch audacious attacks on British personnel and equipment. Like the Easter Rising, it was meant to be a surprise.

There is an air of fantasy about these grandiose plans. The original Vietnamese Tet Offensive was carried out in January 1968 by a force of 84,000 Viet Cong guerrillas and North Vietnamese regular soldiers.[9] The strength of the IRA was probably around 700. The lack of public support would not have helped in the conduct of operations. As things stood, the IRA probably did not have enough people to use the weapons at its disposal. The Tet Offensive was a military defeat but a public relations victory because of the media coverage in the US. Unlike, perhaps, the early 1970s, there would not have been the same disposition in the Irish and British media in the mid-1980s to portray the Irish equivalent as a major success despite the cost. Atrocities like Bloody Friday, La Mon and Enniskillen left the IRA looking as bad as the British or the loyalists in many people's eyes.

British Home Secretary Reginald Maudling brought a storm down on his head when he referred in the early days of the Troubles to 'an acceptable level' of violence. But the 'Tet Offensive' would have been unacceptable. It would have engendered a wave of repression against the IRA that would in all likelihood have been tolerated by the nationalist population north and south, rather than arousing them to anger and support for the republicans. It seems unlikely the British would have repeated the ghastly blunders of the early 1970s such as the mishandled introduction of internment and the shooting of civilians in Derry on Bloody Sunday. We are told that an attenuated version of the 'Tet' plan was launched in 1988, but largely turned out to be a flop.

Provoking the British into an overreaction that will in turn create the circumstances for revolution is a recurring republican dream. I recall a conversation in the 1970s with the legendary activist, the late Séamus Costello, not long before he was murdered in an internecine feud. He outlined to me a set of circumstances whereby British forces would be drawn over the Border from the North in hot pursuit of a republican active service unit. The British would almost inevitably come into conflict with the local population and perhaps shoot some innocent civilians, thereby setting off a mass rebellion against the British presence on the island. But he was forgetting that there are times when the Irish people rebel and other times when they sit on their hands. They have been sitting on their hands since the burning of the British Embassy in Dublin in 1972.[10]

The discovery that senior republican Denis Donaldson was a British agent and widespread allegations that another very senior republican, Freddie Scappaticci, was also working for the British (which he has denied) naturally gave rise to speculation that there might be others. A senior figure from a previous administration in Dublin with a close knowledge of security matters claims the Provisionals are infiltrated up to the highest level. He said he did not know who they were and did not want to know. Likewise another senior source on the Irish side told me it was highly likely there was yet another senior republican who was a British agent because, 'The British security services are very good at what they do.'

Northern Ireland would not be the place it is and the Troubles would not have been the Troubles without this kind of suspicion and speculation. But it's not just the mainstream Provos who have been infiltrated, the dissidents also took a paid informer and agent of the FBI and MI5 to their bosom in the person of David Rupert, the giant American who received an equally massive €1.68 million for testimony that put dissident republican Michael 'Micky' McKevitt away for a twenty-year prison term. The verdict is under appeal at time of writing.

Given the duration of the Troubles and the centuries-long experience of the British in espionage and counter-insurgency, it would be surprising if there wasn't a high degree of infiltration. But it is too easy for a losing faction to blame its misfortunes on enemy 'dirty tricks'. The charge and countercharge of treachery between factions is common in revolutionary circles. Kerensky, the Russian prime minister who was ousted by the Bolsheviks, maintained that Lenin, who travelled to Russia in 1917 on a German train, was a syphilitic German agent (the writer Alexander Solzhenitsyn also portrays Lenin as a German agent – but cowardly rather than syphilitic). There are still people who believe that Michael Collins was 'turned' so that he would sign the Anglo-Irish Treaty.

In the last analysis the Provisionals made a political choice. They did it because the conflict had reached a stalemate, the recurrence of botched operations such as Enniskillen and the Shankill bomb was causing a haemorrhage of support and the movement had spent 30 years at war with no tangible result apart from sporadic electoral gains. On the plus side, there was a concurrence of political developments in Ireland, Britain and the US which offered the potential to make advances by peaceful means towards the achievement of republican aims. It was similar to the 'New Departure' of the late nineteenth century when the Fenians made common cause with constitutional nationalist Charles Stewart Parnell: I heard Sinn Féin leader Pat Doherty draw the comparison explicitly during a by-election speech in Donegal in 1996.

The dissidents lost because they had nothing new to offer, only more of the same. The Chinese leader Mao Ze Dong said that 'the people are like water and the [revolutionary] army is like fish', but by the early 1990s the water had nearly drained away for the Provisional republican movement.[11] This was the main reason the dissidents were sidelined; the fact that they may have been outmanoeuvred by Adams is a secondary consideration.

Have Adams and McGuinness sold out the republican cause or are they merely taking the scenic route, as it were, to a united Ireland? The British establishment is not a monolith but the more enlightened and intelligent elements would shed few tears at the loss of the 'Six Counties' to a united Ireland if it could be done in a peaceful way and by mutual agreement between the two main communities.

Such a move would be in line with the decolonisation process of the last 60-odd years. There is little if any material or military benefit to post-imperial, post-Cold War Britain in the current arrangement. Then-Northern Ireland Secretary Peter Brooke summed it up in his historic statement on 9 November 1990 that, 'it is not the aspiration to a sovereign, united Ireland against which we set our face, but its violent expression ... the British Government has no selfish strategic or economic interest in Northern Ireland'.

It would be damaging to Britain's prestige as a middle-ranking world power if it were seen to be forced to leave, but a more decorous form of political choreography whereby the connection could be severed following a majority vote by the populace would be a totally different thing. Did Sweden suffer greatly when Norway became independent?

The legal and parliamentary procedure for bringing about a united Ireland is clear cut. Former head of the Northern Ireland civil service Sir Kenneth Bloomfield put it succinctly in a lecture at the 2007 Merriman Summer School: 'If and when a majority of the people living in Northern Ireland vote in favour of such a step, legislation will be introduced into the parliaments of the two sovereign states to transfer the six counties from the one jurisdiction to the other.'[12]

This would come in the wake of a 'Border Poll', although relatively little attention has been paid to this issue. There is provision for it in the Good Friday Agreement. The Northern Ireland Secretary may order a poll if it appears likely to him or her that a majority wish to join a united Ireland, but there must be a seven-year gap between polls. There was what one source calls a 'slight disagreement' on the time-frame among the Irish delegation to the Good Friday talks: more senior members wanted a ten-year gap, the junior ones said five. At that point a British negotiator chipped in and suggested seven. A poll had previously been held on 8 March 1973 but nationalists and republicans boycotted the vote en masse and the result had no real standing politically.

The Northern Ireland census for 2001, published in December 2002, gave the population balance, in percentage terms, as 53–44 between Protestants and Catholics. The Northern Ireland Life and Times Survey found in 2006 that 54 per cent wished to remain in the UK and 30 per cent favoured Irish unity. Among Catholics, the balance in favour of unity was 56–22. On the Protestant side, 85 per cent backed the Union and seven per cent favoured Irish unity.[13]

Theoretically, if a relatively small percentage of unionists broke away from the consensus within their community and made common cause with the vast majority of their nationalist neighbours, a united Ireland would follow. In practice, the majority for unity would have to be considerably greater than that (ideally, there would be a strong majority in both communities) and it would have to be clear that the dissident unionist minority would accept the referendum result in a democratic spirit and refrain from violence, or at least be incapable of perpetrating more than a token level of violence. A leading constitutional nationalist has pointed out that divorce was introduced in the South by a mere 9,114 votes in a referendum but, in the words of a former loyalist activist-turned-conciliator, 'It couldn't just be a question of nailing the Six onto 26 [Counties] and carrying on regardless.' Incidentally, at time of writing, the two main unionist parties occupy only 54 or precisely half of the 108 seats in the Assembly. The remainder is made up of Sinn Féin, SDLP and Alliance as well as two independents from the nationalist or republican 'gene pool', one Green and one Progressive Unionist.

Given the lack of linguistic differences, the decline in religious sentiment south of the Border, the greater level of tolerance and civil liberty in the Republic (the dark days of censorship and overweening Church influence on government are a fading memory), the South's truly remarkable economic performance in the last fifteen years and, above all, the continuance of the power-sharing administration in the North, who knows how the unionist mindset might gradually start to shift and re-assess the constitutional position?

The functioning and performance of the North–South bodies could have a major influence in this regard. If they were seen to be beneficial to both sides of the community in the North, then hard-headed Ulster Protestants might start to look at unity as a realistic, commercial and political proposition rather than fearing it as a form of 'ethnic cleansing'.

Eamon de Valera regarded Irish membership of the Commonwealth as a form of reassurance for Britain and the unionists that could potentially ease the path to unity. Perhaps in a future final settlement there could be a quid pro quo: Ireland becomes a 32-county independent republic but forges a fresh link with the Commonwealth as a symbolic gesture of reconciliation and on the clear understanding that there are no implications for Irish sovereignty in such a move.

Unionists pride themselves on being dry-eyed realists and even the original partition arrangement had a pragmatic dimension when Carson abandoned three of the Ulster counties – Cavan, Donegal and Monaghan – in favour of the more compact 'Wee Six' where the unionists would enjoy a comfortable majority.

There are issues involved that most people, north and south, have not even started to consider. Unionists and probably even nationalists in the North would have to be reassured that Belfast would not be downgraded to the status of a provincial town. It would seem logical to offer the North some form of regional autonomy, at least on a transitional basis. Bunreacht na hÉireann, the Irish Constitution, provides in Article 15.2.2 for 'the creation or recognition of subordinate legislatures'. Interestingly, it was de Valera's granddaughter, Síle, who first drew this to my attention some years ago. The use of the word 'recognition' means that Stormont as it currently exists could be brought under the umbrella of a united Ireland although some more tactful euphemism might be needed for 'subordinate'!

Alternatively, or in addition, Belfast could be deemed the political and/or administrative capital of a united Ireland, given that Dublin is widely considered to have exceeded all reasonable levels of growth. There is an opening for this also in Bunreacht na hÉireann, which stipulates in Article 15.1.3 that the Houses of the Oireachtas [the Irish parliament] must sit in or near Dublin, 'or in such other place as they may from time to time determine'. When West Germany reunited with the East, the western capital moved from Bonn to Berlin.

But it could well be the case that a united Ireland would require a completely new constitution tailored for the entire island and its traditions, whether religious, ethnic or cultural, not forgetting the new and very diverse elements of the population that have come from abroad in recent years.

In a sense that would be the easy part. The real problem would be the question of affordability. The reunification of

Germany was an expensive process and there could also be high costs associated with Irish unity. The North receives a massive subsidy of about £7 billion or €9.6 billion each year from the British exchequer.[14] Would this continue for a period, as a type of 'dowry' from Westminster, or would the South have to assume the burden straight away? In the latter event, there could well be implications for tax levels in the South, which could, in turn, cause problems for the economy. One is mindful of the 2004 referendum on the Annan Plan for reunification of Cyprus when, amazingly, a majority of Turkish Cypriots voted in favour and the Greek Cypriots voted against.

In relation to possible Irish unity Sir Kenneth Bloomfield observed: 'Far-sighted politicians, economists and academics will have to think long and hard about the true nature, cost, ethos and dynamics of a new orientation of affairs. No crude majority vote could or should ignore or eliminate a continuing sense of "Britishness" likely to be retained by many people. How might this be done?

'And so I return to the preference for process over pre-determined conclusion. Let Catholic and Protestant, unionist and republican, learn in the first instance to work harmoniously together in the North for the public good rather than for ulterior motives. Let North and South co-operate over a widening range of issues, proceeding always on a basis of mutual consent. Let us acknowledge that, however dominant and oppressive that other island may have been in the past, today we should be the greatest and most natural of friends. Let us build on the foundations of our North–South and East–West institutions a common-wealth of common heritage and mutual understanding.'[15]

Hearing such comments from a former top civil servant and close adviser to Northern Ireland prime ministers, whose home was subjected to a terrifying bomb attack by the IRA in August 1988, underlines how far we have come in the last ten to fifteen years. Although Bloomfield was a sharp critic of the 1985 Anglo-Irish Agreement, in a sense he is picking up where he left off in early 1965, when he was involved in the mould-breaking cross-Border meetings between prime ministers Seán Lemass and Captain Terence O'Neill. When Lemass came north to see O'Neill on that cold January day, Paisley and his followers threw snowballs at the Taoiseach's car. Now it appears that his own hard-liners are throwing snowballs at Paisley.

But despite current progress there will always be a keen sense of sorrow and regret that so many people died, in such a small place and over such a long period of time. Why did it take so long to end the Troubles and are there any lessons for other areas of conflict?

One of the key messages emerging from any survey of the past 40 years is that political courage brings results while timidity perpetuates the status quo. John Hume's courage and sustained commitment to peacemaking and the political road over several decades have rightly been acknowledged with the award of the Nobel Peace Prize.

Although Albert Reynolds' tenure as Taoiseach was short-lived, he achieved a great deal. Not one of the great thinkers and analysts to tread the political stage, he was a man of action through and through; Adams described him as 'a buccaneer'. His predecessor, Charles J. Haughey, played it relatively safe by comparison although he was much more forceful than Jack Lynch.

In October 1986, following an approach from the peace process intermediary Father Alec Reid, journalist and author Tim Pat Coogan met Haughey, who was then in opposition, over lunch in a Dublin hotel. Coogan's mission was to propose a meeting between the leaders of Fianna Fáil and Sinn Féin. When Coogan suggested that peace and a united Ireland could be at stake, Haughey commented that this was 'a glittering prize' but, as Coogan writes, 'he still fought shy of meeting Adams'.[16]

Haughey returned to government in March 1987 and, the following year, he authorised two meetings between a Fianna Fáil delegation and Sinn Féin, which took place in Dundalk in March and June 1988. Fianna Fáil was represented by party official Richie Healy, Haughey adviser Martin Mansergh and local TD Dermot Ahern, who was then a backbencher but later attained ministerial office. Haughey made it clear that if the dialogue with Sinn Féin was discovered, the Fianna Fáil participants would be disowned.

Critically, Haughey decided on the basis of these discussions that a meeting between himself and Adams was out of the question, and he held to this position, as far as is known, until he left office in 1992. But not only that, he refused to sanction any further meetings of any kind with Sinn Féin. This even applied to Mansergh who was, as Father Reid said later, 'the ideal person for conducting a debate with the Republican Movement which aimed at taking the gun out of Irish politics'.[17] (Adams might not have needed much persuading but 'the boys in the back room', as they were called, certainly did.)

Mansergh's biographer Kevin Rafter describes how, apart from the two 1988 meetings, the Taoiseach's adviser on Northern Ireland had to communicate with Adams through Reid as a third party. It was only when Reynolds took over that he was allowed to meet the Sinn Féin leader face to face on a regular basis.[18] This was four years on from the Dundalk meetings of 1988 and it is very difficult not to see the gap as a wasted opportunity. Indeed, Reynolds himself did not know about the 1988 meetings until he became Taoiseach.[19] The Fianna Fáil–Sinn Féin discussions only became public knowledge in 1996.[20]

Although Haughey's name will always be inextricably linked with the North, he appeared to have lost some of his enthusiasm for the issue at this stage of his career. Former Trimble political adviser Steven King writes in his D.Phil. thesis on the Fianna Fáil leader that, when returned to the office of Taoiseach in March 1987 after an absence of four-and-a-quarter years, 'he took a less active personal interest in Northern Ireland'.[21]

In his 1989 *ardfheis* speech, Haughey hinted at the prospect of a pan-nationalist front if the IRA campaign were called off: 'If violence were to cease, the possibility would open up ... for a broad consensus among nationalists on how to achieve political stability based on justice.'

But it was little more than conference rhetoric because, unlike Hume and Reynolds, he still refrained from 'taking risks for peace'. To a considerable extent, this is understandable, given the kind of treatment meted out to Hume by the *Sunday Independent*, several of whose writers launched a sustained barrage throughout the summer of 1993 against the SDLP leader, the likes of which has not been seen in modern Ireland.[22]

Haughey had also, in fairness, embarked upon a major – and ultimately successful – effort to turn around the economic policy of the State. He appointed the tough-minded Ray MacSharry as Minister for Finance and initiated a programme of public spending cuts and fiscal rectitude that laid the foundation for the eventual emergence of the 'Celtic Tiger' economy in the South.

Haughey's reluctance to engage with the Provos may also have been influenced by the fact that he was in receipt of cash donations running into millions from a number of sources, principally the supermarket mogul Ben Dunne Jr who had been kidnapped by the IRA in 1981 and reportedly suffered very brutal treatment at the hands of his abductors. When I spoke to a key player from the early days of the peace process, he initially described Haughey's approach as 'extremely cowardly' but revised this assessment on reflection to 'prudent'. According to this source, Haughey may have been worried that British Intelligence knew about his private financial transactions and would expose them if he threw a political lifeline to the Provos. Despite bank security precautions, the 'securocrats' presumably have their own methods for monitoring movements of cash especially when, as in this case, they involved London as well as British possessions like the Caymans and the Isle of Man. It was also widely and persistently rumoured around this time that another prominent public figure was threatened with the release of videotapes of alleged amorous activities, in the event of taking an overactive role in the peace process. (Meanwhile secret contacts between the British Government and the IRA from 1990 onwards were revealed in the *Observer* newspaper in 1993.)

A source close to the Fianna Fáil delegation recalls that the meetings came to an end because parallel talks between Hume and Adams at the time had also stopped (the SDLP–Sinn Féin talks took place between March and September 1988). Haughey expressed his suspicions about Sinn Féin in unvarnished terms: 'I don't know whether we can trust these f***ers or not.' My Fianna Fáil source points out that Haughey was leading a minority government at the time which, if word of the talks had leaked out, 'wouldn't have lasted five minutes'.

If Adams' efforts were to have any credibility, it was necessary for constitutional leaders to engage with him on a fairly continuous basis. Reynolds took that risk; Haughey clearly felt that he could not. Rafter writes: 'Adams continued to argue with Reid that face-to-face dialogue would speed up the entire process. With the exception of two meetings in 1988, Haughey was unwilling to sanction direct contacts, although from the middle of 1992 his successor approved regular meetings between Adams and Mansergh.'[23] As a result, the anodyne internal talks process continued and, arguably, several years when progress could have been made were wasted.

Speaking to journalists in the years before he died, Haughey was reticent about any role he may or may not have had at the start of the peace process. 'I don't want to say too much about the peace process,' he told Kevin Rafter on 8 January 2002. 'It's a very crowded stage. What's the saying? "Success has many fathers".'[24] Haughey's reticence is understandable and it would be a kindness to his memory to refrain from claiming more for him than he claimed himself.

The moral of the story is that, for a peace process to succeed, political leaders must abide by Danton's motto in the French Revolution: *'Il nous faut de l'audace, encore de l'audace, toujours de l'audace*! (We must dare, dare again, always dare!)'

I have already dealt with the role of Adams and McGuinness who were obviously of critical and fundamental importance throughout the entire process. Bertie Ahern and Tony Blair deserve a great deal of credit for seeing the process through to the end: Blair reportedly spent up to 40 per cent of his time on Northern Ireland and the issue also took a large share of Ahern's timetable. It was fitting that the deal was done before Blair departed Downing Street: indeed, some Irish officials were heard warning from time to time that, if the Provos didn't cut a deal with Blair, they might find his successor Gordon Brown a more difficult proposition.

John Major's role in the early days should not be forgotten. Mo Mowlam was the first Northern Ireland Secretary with the possible exception of Whitelaw who won the respect of nationalists; Blair sidelined her in the latter stages of the process and the great political sage Niccolò Machiavelli would probably say her big mistake was becoming more popular than her master.

Bill Clinton took the process to his heart. But in addition to his emotional involvement, he must have known as a hard-headed politician that the effort was worth making because the deal was 'do-able'. He also put an enormous effort into the Middle East, without success, and it is said that he told Adams on one occasion, 'The difference between you and [Yasser] Arafat, Gerry, is that you delivered.' A Washington columnist, irritated that Clinton was spending so much time on a small country like Ireland, once asked me: 'What is this? Social worker foreign policy?' The encouragement Clinton received from the Kennedy family, particularly Senator Ted Kennedy and his sister, Jean Kennedy Smith, former ambassador to Ireland, as well as the lobbying conducted by Niall O'Dowd and his Irish-American friends were extremely important.

David Trimble was a rather reluctant peace process participant but nevertheless his role was crucial. Having come to the leadership of the UUP with the hardest of hard-line images, he gradually demonstrated that his approach was more complex than that of the average unionist 'no-man'. But despite many urgings and pleas from the nationalist side, he never became a salesman for the Good Friday Agreement. Indeed there were times over the years when his approach resembled passive resistance. It has been suggested that he did not share the conviction of his fellow-unionists that decommissioning should be allowed to block the formation of a power-sharing executive but had to pretend that he did, as a means of coping with and overcoming the hard-liners in the party.

Trimble's name is rapidly receding from the newspapers to the pages of the history books but his importance for the process should not be played down or forgotten. He recognised that the British – egged on by the pan-nationalist front and the Americans – were not going to back down as they had over Sunningdale. This was the lesson of the Anglo-Irish Agreement which was aptly described in Irish by a venerable Dublin civil servant as '*gunna chun cleamhnais*', roughly translated as the gun in a shotgun wedding.

Power-sharing with a North–South dimension or ultimate political marginalisation and irrelevance: this was the choice facing the unionists. Trimble opted for the former. He was a transitional figure who took a lot of abuse from his own side as he cleared away the undergrowth and rubble from a society where, apart from the brief Sunningdale interlude, politics had never really been tried before. They might not like to admit it but it was thanks to Trimble that the DUP could eventually take power with the support of a broad unionist consensus.

Trimble had his failings as a politician, particularly at the 'grip-and-grin' level. Alastair Campbell recalls a rather indelicate but colourful remark Clinton made about the UUP leader during a presidential visit to Northern Ireland: 'Someone should tell him that part of the art of politics is smiling when you feel like you're swallowing a turd.'[25] Campbell also quotes Blair as saying Trimble had the worst personal skills of any top politician he had met and that he couldn't rise to big occasions.[26] But the present writer had a chastening experience in this regard. At an American Ireland Fund dinner in Washington DC, I had just been telling an official from the State Department about the UUP leader's deficiencies in the hail-fellow-well-met department, when Trimble bounced in and confounded my pen-picture by glad-handing everyone at the table. Godson describes Trimble as a seminar leader rather than a lecturer and, during one of many frustrating moments in the process, Campbell wrote in his diary: 'The problem was DT kept going back to his own people and instead of offering leadership around a position secured by him, he took all their criticisms like a sponge.'[27]

There were others, too numerous to mention, who played critical roles in the advancement of the peace process. Father Reid was the most prominent among the clergy but he was not the only one who sought to restore Christian values to a society where killing and destruction were holding sway. Numerous civil servants and officials devoted long hours and much ingenuity to the search for a solution. Despite many differences between the various elements in the process, they shared one overriding common objective: to end the violence and the killing. Despite occasional incidents and tragic episodes, it is to the credit of all concerned that this has, by and large, been successfully achieved.

Journalists covering the peace process used to joke about getting a defining-moment watch because there were so many historical breakthroughs. Perhaps the most decisive of these was the encounter between the DUP and Sinn Féin on the weekend of 24 and 25 March 2007.

It was already understood that Monday 26 March was the date for 'devolution or dissolution'. But on Thursday 22 March Sinn Féin attended a meeting at No. 10 with Blair, who said he was being told by Paisley that the DUP would agree a date, but not 26 March. Adams responded that the DUP would have to put their proposals face to face.

The DUP executive met on Saturday 24 March and, later that day, the two parties got together at Hain's office in Stormont Castle, led by Robinson and McGuinness respectively, in what sources describe as a 'very cordial and friendly' atmosphere.

The DUP wanted to postpone devolution for twelve weeks, Sinn Féin wanted four: they finally agreed on six, with Tuesday 8 May designated as the Big Day. But this would be tied down in joint public commitments to be made on 26 March and the wording of these would be agreed in advance.

As regards seating and presentation for the Monday event, Sinn Féin wanted the party leaders sitting side by side, the DUP wanted them face to face. It came down to diagrams in the end and someone came up with the idea of having a set of tables arranged in the shape of a diamond, 'allowing the leaders to be, not side by side, but beside each other'. It would also allow the delegations to sit alongside their leaders.

Nigel Dodds had to leave the weekend deliberations early, because he was unwell. Close observers say he knocked on the door of the Sinn Féin delegation's room and said, in a very cordial tone: 'Sorry lads, I'm leaving, but there's no significance to it. I don't feel very well.' This gesture made a strong impact on Sinn Féin, because Dodds was seen as a comparative hard-liner and this was a very clear demonstration that the ice had melted.

Civility is a cornerstone of the peace process. The republican delegation would have been keenly aware that, on the night of 20 December 1996, Dodds was keeping vigil with his wife Diane at the bedside of their gravely ill six-year-old son Andrew in Belfast's Royal Victoria Hospital when the IRA launched an attack, wounding an RUC bodyguard.

NIO people were hanging around, wondering how things were going. They ordered pizzas for the two delegations and the atmosphere is described as, 'good craic'. It was almost like the tension had been broken by the very fact that the meeting was taking place.

Everything had to be worked out in advance, 'so there would be no surprises on the day'. As 26 March dawned, there was further contact between the parties to agree final details. Adams briefed the wider Sinn Féin delegation at Stormont and, as a result, Sinn Féin were a few minutes behind the DUP, who had arrived in the members' dining room at eleven o'clock sharp. Only a pool-camera and stills photographer were allowed in, the rest of the media watched on closed-circuit TV. Action, camera, history!

Ten years on from the Agreement, fresh information is still coming out. It was not known at the time that the prominent Dublin-based trade union official Daltún Ó Ceallaigh, then-general secretary of the Irish Federation of University Teachers (IFUT), travelled to Belfast that fateful week in April, at the invitation of Sinn Féin, to act as an adviser on the party's delegation.

It has also emerged that, in the run-up to Good Friday, Mitchel McLaughlin represented Sinn Féin at a meeting in the Teachers' Club in Dublin's Parnell Square on the issue of Articles Two and Three of the Irish Constitution. The well-known artist Robert Ballagh and others were prepared to mount a strong and well-resourced campaign in defence of the existing Articles. Phone calls were coming through in the course of the meeting as to the progress of the talks at Stormont and the TV news was showing footage of the delegations coming in and out of Castle Buildings. Any prospect of a strong campaign against the dilution of the Articles evaporated after Good Friday, when it became clear that Sinn Féin was assenting to the deal.

No doubt there is more to be revealed about the peace process and scholars will dispute the details long into the future. If this book settles some of the arguments, it will have achieved its objective.

Endnotes

Chapter 1: 'Who's Afraid of Peace?'

1. Richard English, in Armed Struggle: The History of the IRA (Macmillan, London 2003) p. 104, queries the use of the word 'pogrom' with some justification, but does not suggest an alternative.

2. Journalist Ed Moloney, in *A Secret History of the IRA* (Second Edition, Penguin Books, London 2007) suggests Adams was engaged in indirect discussions with the British from as early as 1986–87, using Father Alec Reid as an intermediary in contacts with successive Northern Ireland Secretaries, Tom King and Peter Brooke. This is contrary to the general view that talks only began in October 1990, involving British representative Michael Oatley of MI6 and Martin McGuinness. Father Reid has stated: 'There were no negotiations involving Mr Adams and myself with Mr King, Mr Peter Brooke or, through them, with the British government.' (*The Irish News* 3 October 2002).

3. Author's interview with John Bruton 29 December 2000.

4. See also John Major. *The Autobiography* (London 1999) pp 482–3.

5. Seat of the Irish Parliament prior to the Act of Union, the building now houses a bank

6. George J. Mitchell. *Making Peace* (New York and London 1999) p. 31 (page numbers from US edition).

7. *The Irish Times* 25 January 1996.

8. Author's interview with John Bruton 29 December 2000.

9. My colleague David Sharrock makes the point that the actual location was South Quay.

10. This was strongly rejected by John Bruton on the basis that a dynamic had already been created. Mitchell *op. cit.* p. 42 makes the point that although the decision was a huge step forward, the timing was unfortunate.

11. Pádraig Pearse (1879–1916). Educationalist, writer, Irish language activist and revolutionary. Main leader of the Easter Rising, he was executed in Kilmainham Gaol.

12. Gerry, later Lord, Fitt (1926–2005). Westminster MP for West Belfast 1966–83. Founder-member SDLP 1970, resigned 1979. Leading figure in civil rights movement, took strong stand against Provisional IRA.

13. Charles Stewart Parnell (1846–91). Nationalist leader and campaigner for Home Rule and land reform. Ruined by his involvement in a divorce case which split the Irish MPs at Westminster.

14. Strictly speaking, Mr Taylor was deputy leader of the parliamentary party but the title was usually applied to him in a more general context.

Chapter 2: Restoring the Ceasefire
1. *The Irish Times* 11 June 1996.
2. Friends of the General say he was surprised to be asked to chair Strand Two as he had expected to be dealing with decommissioning and that Mitchell would chair Strand Two. However, the appointment had the support of the two governments and Mitchell himself.
3. The Mitchell Principles provided that participants in all-party negotiations should affirm their commitment to the following: i. Democratic and exclusively peaceful means of resolving political issues; ii. Total disarmament of all paramilitary organisations; iii. Such disarmament must be verifiable to the satisfaction of an independent commission; iv. To renounce for themselves and to oppose any effort by others to use force, or threaten to use force, to influence the course or the outcome of all-party negotiations; v. To agree to abide by the terms of any agreement reached in all-party negotiations and to resort to democratic and exclusively peaceful methods in trying to alter any aspect of that outcome with which they may disagree; vi. To urge that 'punishment' killings and beatings stop and to take effective steps to prevent such actions.
4. I am grateful to my colleague Martina Purdy for assistance with the details of this episode.
5. Author's interview with John Bruton 29 December 2000.
6. See also Julia Langdon's biography, *Mo Mowlam* (London 2000) pp 271–75.
7. Author's interview with John Bruton 29 December 2000.
8. In late November 1996, German police sought Róisín McAliskey's extradition to answer questions relating to an IRA attack on a British Army barracks at Osnabrück in June 1996. She was detained in a London prison while pregnant and reportedly subjected to regular strip-searching. Her child was born while she was still in detention. The extradition was stopped on health grounds and Ms McAliskey was released. A further extradition bid was refused in November 2007.
9. *Belfast Telegraph* 11 May 1998.
10. *Belfast News Letter* 14 April 1997.
11. Bruton's reputation as a peacemaker suffered momentarily when he told a persistent radio reporter in April 1995, 'I'm sick answering questions about the f***ing peace process.' He apologised immediately for the gaffe. His efforts to reassure unionists benefited him little in the South, where critics seized on the soubriquet 'John Unionist', accidentally invented for him by Albert Reynolds in a stumbling radio interview. Some officials in the Department of Foreign Affairs reportedly were wont to refer to the

Department of the Taoiseach during Bruton's tenure as 'Glengall Street' (location of UUP headquarters at the time).

12. There was strong nationalist dissatisfaction with the previous inquiry conducted by the Lord Chief Justice of England, Lord Widgery, which was popularly known as the 'Widgery Whitewash'.

13. The election was not a foregone conclusion: in the event, Ahern's Fianna Fáil party came to power in a minority coalition with the Progressive Democrats, supported by independents.

Chapter 3: The Elephant and the Mouse
1. See Chapter 2, note 3.
2. Trimble told biographer Dean Godson that, as he was waiting outside Castle Buildings, an uncertain-sounding Blair called him on his cellphone. Blair: 'Where exactly are we now?' Trimble: 'In the outer car park.' Blair: 'They kept telling me you wouldn't do it.' Dean Godson. *Himself Alone: David Trimble and the Ordeal of Unionism* (Harper Perennial, London 2005) p. 300.
3. Burke served four-and-a-half months in jail in 2005 for submitting false tax returns. Earlier he was deemed by a planning tribunal to have received corrupt payments of approximately €250,000.
4. 'We are a Protestant parliament and a Protestant state,' Sir James Craig, first Prime Minister of Northern Ireland said in 1934.
5. The New Ireland Forum (1983–84), a body where moderate nationalist parties from both parts of the island deliberated the future of Northern Ireland, proposed three options: a 32-county state; a federal arrangement between North and South; and joint authority exercised by the two governments. The British Prime Minister at the time, Mrs Margaret Thatcher, responded on 19 November 1984: 'A unified Ireland was one solution – that's out. The second option was confederation. That's out. The third was joint authority. That's out.'
6. Charles de Gaulle (1890–1970). French general and statesman, disappointed admirers on the French right when he negotiated Algerian independence in 1962.
7. Reference to controversial comment by SDLP's Hugh Logue, prior to Sunningdale Agreement, that proposed Council of Ireland was 'the vehicle that will one day trundle through to deliver a united country'. *The Irish Times* 24 November 1973 p. 8.
8. 'Prods', derogatory abbreviation of Protestants; 'Taig' is a derogatory term for Irish Catholics, similar to 'Mick' or 'Paddy'.
9. Robert Lundy advocated the surrender of Derry in 1689 when it was under siege by the forces of the Catholic monarch, James II. Lundy's name became a synonym for 'traitor' to unionists.
10. *The Irish Times* 21 November 1997.
11. *Daily Telegraph* 17 November 1997.

12. The Northern Ireland Secretary, Peter Mandelson, told the House of Commons on 19 January 2000 that the RUC 'with 88 per cent of its members Protestant and only 8 per cent Catholic – is not representative of all sides of the community'.

13. *Bunreacht na hÉireann* (Constitution of Ireland) passed by referendum in 1937, included the following (see also note 22, p. 415–6):

Article 2: The national territory consists of the whole island of Ireland, its islands and territorial seas.

Article 3: Pending the reintegration of the national territory, and without prejudice to the right of the Parliament and Government established by this Constitution to exercise jurisdiction over the whole of that territory, the laws enacted by that Parliament shall have the like area and extent of application as the laws of Saorstát Éireann and the like extra-territorial effect.

14. *The Irish Times* 28 August 2000. The phrase was also reported as 'not unlike *a* government'.

15. Professor Mary McAleese became President of Ireland in November 1997. During the election campaign, opponents unsuccessfully sought to portray her as a Provo sympathiser. She comes from the mainly Catholic Ardoyne district in North Belfast and built a successful career as an academic lawyer, becoming Pro-Vice Chancellor of Queen's University Belfast before being chosen as the Fianna Fáil candidate for the presidency in preference to Albert Reynolds. Now serving second term.

16. *The Irish Times* 8 December 1997

17. *Ibid* 18 December 1997

18. *Ibid* 19 December 1997

19. Robert McCartney QC founded the UK Unionist Party in 1995 on a policy of full integration with Britain. He was joined by former Irish government minister Dr Conor Cruise O'Brien, who subsequently resigned in a controversy over his prediction that the growing power of Sinn Féin in the North would force unionists to consider entering a united Ireland with constitutional nationalists. Four of the five UKUP Assembly members split from McCartney in 1999 to form the Northern Ireland Unionist Party. The UKUP failed to win any Assembly seats in the 2007 elections. McCartney was MP for North Down 1995–2001.

20. Captain, later Lord, Terence O'Neill (1914-1990) became Prime Minister of Northern Ireland in 1963. His halting efforts to meet the demands of the civil rights movement caused his downfall as unionist leader and he resigned as Prime Minister on 28 April 1969.

21. Brian, later Lord, Faulkner (1921-1977) was overthrown as unionist leader when he signed the 1973 Sunningdale Agreement (see Glossary). He went on to become chief executive in the short-lived power-sharing administration of 1974.

22. *The Irish Times* 17 December 1997.

23. *Ibid.*

Chapter 4: A Road Map to Agreement
1. *Daily Telegraph* 10 January 1998.
2. Text of the Propositions on Heads of Agreement:

Balanced constitutional change, based on commitment to the principle of consent in all its aspects by both British and Irish governments, to include both changes to the Irish Constitution and to British constitutional legislation.

Democratically elected institutions in Northern Ireland, to include a Northern Ireland assembly, elected by a system of proportional representation, exercising devolved executive and legislative responsibility over at least the responsibilities of the six Northern Ireland departments and with provisions to ensure that all sections of the community can participate and work together successfully in the operation of these institutions and that all sections of the community are protected.

A new British–Irish agreement to replace the existing Anglo-Irish Agreement and help establish close co-operation and enhance relationships, embracing:

An intergovernmental council to deal with the totality of relationships, to include representatives of the British and Irish governments, the Northern Ireland administration and the devolved institutions in Scotland and Wales, with meetings twice a year at summit level.

A North–South ministerial council to bring together those with executive responsibilities in Northern Ireland and the Irish Government in particular areas. Each side will consult, co-operate and take decisions on matters of mutual interest within the mandate of, and accountable to, the Northern Ireland assembly and the Oireachtas [Irish parliament] respectively. All decisions will be by agreement between the two sides, North and South. Suitable implementation bodies and mechanisms for policies agreed by the North–South council in meaningful areas and at an all-island level.

Standing intergovernmental machinery between the Irish and British governments, covering issues of mutual interest, including non-devolved issues for Northern Ireland, when representatives of the Northern Ireland administration would be involved.

Provision to safeguard the rights of both communities in Northern Ireland, through arrangements for the comprehensive protection of fundamental human, civil, political, social, economic and cultural rights, including a Bill of Rights for Northern Ireland supplementing the provisions of the European Convention and to achieve full respect for the principles of equity of treatment and freedom from discrimination, and the cultural identity and ethos of both communities. Appropriate steps to ensure an equivalent level of protection in the Republic.

Effective and practical measures to establish and consolidate an acceptable peaceful society, dealing with issues such as prisoners, security in all its aspects, policing and decommissioning of weapons.

413

3. Mitchell *op. cit.* p. 133 .

4. *The Irish Times* 29 August 2000.

5. *Ibid* 24 January 1998.

6. *Ibid* 21 January 1998.

7. *Ibid* 5 February 1998.

8. Brendan Campbell was shot dead, apparently by Direct Action Against Drugs (a cover name for the IRA), on the Lisburn Road, Belfast, 9 February 1998; loyalist Robert Dougan was shot dead at Dunmurry, County Antrim, 10 February.

9. *The Irish Times* 14 March 1998.

10. *Ibid* 23 March 1998.

11. Mitchell *op. cit.* pp 143–6.

12. *The Irish Times* 27 March 1998.

Chapter 5: The Long Good Friday

1. Daniel O'Connell (1775–1847). Nationalist leader and founder of movement which led to Catholic Emancipation in 1829. Led unsuccessful campaign of non-violent mass action for the repeal of the Act of Union (see United Kingdom, in Glossary).

2. UUP talks delegate Thomas Hennessey reveals in his important study, *The Northern Ireland Peace Process: Ending the Troubles?* (Dublin 2000), p. 143, that Trimble had proposed a 'rather ambitious' UUP version of Article 3, in a memo to a Downing Street official, specifying that 'The Irish nation's realisation in statehood remains the hope of those of Irish nationality in both parts of Ireland' and providing that unity could only come about peacefully and with the consent of majorities in 'Éire' and Northern Ireland, voting separately.

3. Mitchell *op. cit.* p. 154–155.

4. Kate Fearon. *Women's Work: The Story of the Northern Ireland Women's Coalition* (Belfast 1999) p. 104. Martha Pope, a highly respected US public servant, had previously been the victim of a sinister smear campaign in the tabloid press, quoting British security sources who reportedly linked her romantically with republican Gerry Kelly, whom she had never even met. In Chapter 9 of his book, Mitchell recounts how Ms Pope won substantial damages and costs as well as comprehensive retractions and he chronicles his own bemusement at the failure of the NIO to deny the false allegations until several days had elapsed. He refers in this context to speculation that British security elements were trying to sabotage the talks.

5. 'The Mitchell Printables', book review in *Magill* magazine, May 1999, p. 55.

6. *Belfast Telegraph* 27 March 2000.

7. Prime Minister's spokesman Alastair Campbell, in *The Blair Years* (Hutchinson, London 2007) pp. 287–98 records that there was give and take over

North–South bodies all through the week. His account gives no indication that Ahern was warned or threatened by Blair, but notes significantly that the UUP treated Ahern 'with something close to contempt, and it was terrific the way he took it'.

8. *The Irish Times* 30 August 2000.

9. Author's interview with Peter King, Washington DC, October 1999.

10. David Andrews, in *Kingstown Republican: A Memoir* (New Island in association with First Law, Dublin 2007) pp. 279–80, writes of the 'great concern' shown for the Taoiseach by John Taylor of the UUP. 'He stopped the talks during the night a few times to ask him if he was all right and to see if he wanted a break.' Andrews also recalls a 3 am conversation with Blair, when the Prime Minister demanded to know where Mowlam was. Andrews said he didn't know and Blair replied: 'And why don't you know where she is?' He may have seen Andrews as her counterpart.

11. Channel 4 News documentary. *The Long Good Friday*. Broadcast 2 April 1999. Reporter: Eamonn Mallie. Producer: Lena Ferguson.

12. Bríd Rodgers is a native of Gweedore, County Donegal, but has lived in Northern Ireland most of her life. SDLP choice as N.I. Minister for Agriculture 1999–2002. Former Taoiseach's nominee as member of Seanad Éireann (Irish Senate).

13. Hennessey *op. cit* p.168.

14. Trimble said later that, when he told the SDLP he was accepting a full government, 'I thought Hume was going to burst into tears. Hume then hugged Taylor and Taylor responded with gusto.' Godson *op. cit.* p. 339.

15. According to a senior talks participant, when Hume and Mallon went to see Ahern around 2 am to tell him of their success in the power-sharing talks with the UUP, Mowlam arrived, 'like Lady Macbeth', in her stockinged feet. She fell asleep on Mallon's shoulder but woke up after a while and, when she heard there had been a positive development, declared: 'F***ing brill!'

16. Channel 4 News documentary.

17. BBC Northern Ireland documentary. *A Time to Choose: the Hand of History*. Broadcast 17 May 1998. Reporter: Stephen Grimason. Editor: Jeremy Adams.

18. BBC Northern Ireland documentary.

19. Channel 4 News documentary.

20. Fearon *op. cit.* p. 117.

21. BBC Northern Ireland documentary.

22. The proposed new text for Articles 2 and 3 was as follows (see Chapter 3, note 13 for existing text):

Article 2. It is the entitlement and birthright of every person born in the island of Ireland, which includes its islands and seas, to be part of the Irish nation. That is also the entitlement of all persons otherwise qualified in accordance with law to be citizens of Ireland. Furthermore, the Irish nation cherishes its special affinity with people of Irish ancestry living abroad who share its cultural identity and heritage.

Article 3. i. It is the firm will of the Irish nation, in harmony and friendship, to unite all the people who share the territory of the island of Ireland, in all the diversity of their identities and traditions, recognising that a united Ireland shall be brought about only by peaceful means with the consent of a majority of the people, democratically expressed, in both jurisdictions in the island. Until then, the laws enacted by the Parliament established by this Constitution shall have the like area and extent of application as the laws enacted by the Parliament that existed immediately before the coming into operation of this Constitution.

ii. Institutions with executive powers and functions that are shared between those jurisdictions may be established by their respective responsible authorities for stated purposes and may exercise powers and functions in respect of all or any part of the island.'

23. Fearon *op. cit.* pp 117-8.

24. Author's interview with Peter King, Washington DC, October 1999.

25. Channel 4 News documentary.

26. BBC Northern Ireland documentary.

27. Private information.

28. BBC Northern Ireland documentary.

29. BBC Northern Ireland and Channel 4 News documentaries.

30. BBC Northern Ireland documentary.

31. *Ibid.*

32. *The Irish Times* 11 April 1998 .

33. Dennis (later Lord) Rogan recorded in his diary that, 'Taylor, Maginnis and Empey spoke in favour. Trimble paused for what seemed like an eternity – he was staring impassively into the distance – and then simply declared, "Right, I'm going for the agreement".' Godson *op. cit.* p.355.

34. Trimble subsequently stated he was unaware of Donaldson's departure until some hours later. Godson *op. cit.* pp 354-5.

35. *The Irish Times* 19 May 1998.

36. *Ibid* 20 May 1998.

37. Private information.

38. Although the political parties are loosely referred to as having 'signed' the Good Friday Agreement, the only persons who actually signed anything that day were the two prime ministers.

39. *The Irish Times* 11 April 1998: the photographer was Alan Betson.

40. Mitchell *op. cit.* p. 170.

41. *The Irish Times* 30 August 2000.

Chapter 6: Lifting the Siege

1. The British–Irish Interparliamentary Body was set up in 1990 as a forum where members of the Westminster and Leinster House parliaments could meet on a regular basis to exchange ideas and discuss issues of the day. Unionists boycotted its meetings until the DUP sent a delegation in 2006.

2. See Chapter 5, note 22 for full text.

3. John McGarry and Brendan O'Leary. *Explaining Northern Ireland: Broken. Images.* (Oxford and Cambridge, Massachusetts 1995) p. 373.

4. Named after the patriot and orator Henry Grattan (1746–1820) who spearheaded the campaign that achieved legislative independence for the Irish parliament during the years 1782–1800. The parliament, which had no Catholic representation, was abolished under the Act of Union.

5. *Daily Telegraph* 13 April 1998

6. This proved to be the case although one member was regarded as a nominee of Dublin's.

7. See Chapter 3, note 10.

8. Michael Collins (1890–1922) Irish revolutionary leader who signed the Anglo-Irish Treaty of 1921 on the basis that it provided stepping-stones to an independent republic. He was shot dead in an ambush eight months later.

9. See p. 5.

10. See 'Officials' reference in Glossary.

11. See Chapter 3, note 11.

12. *The Irish Times* 16 April 1998.

13. Quintin Oliver. *Working for 'Yes': The Story of the May 1998 Referendum in Northern Ireland.* Published by The Yes Campaign, P.O. Box 833, Belfast BT1 1EZ. See also *The Irish Times* 2 May 1998.

14. The reference provoked a blistering attack on the Northern Ireland Office by Archbishop Eames who said he was 'astounded and disgusted' to find his name included in the document without his knowledge. Dr Mowlam later apologised. *Belfast Telegraph* 2 April 1998.

15. Not to be confused with Tom Clarke, one of the executed leaders of the Rising, Joe Clarke lived to a ripe old age and continued to promote the republican cause.

Chapter 7: Two Minds, One Country

1. Sir Edward, later Lord, Carson (1854–1935). Dublin-born lawyer who led the fight against Home Rule. Revered by unionists, his statue is located in front of Parliament Buildings, Stormont.

2. The d'Hondt system of allocating ministries in the Assembly is named after the nineteenth-century Belgian lawyer, Victor d'Hondt. Parties are initially ranked according to the number of seats won in the Assembly elections. The party with the highest number of seats is the first to receive a

ministry. Its seat total is divided by two, and that party rejoins the queue for further posts. If it receives a second ministry, its original seat total is then divided by three, and the party takes its place in the rank to receive a possible third executive post. The process continues until all ministerial positions have been allocated. When the d'Hondt system was applied to the allocation of the ten vacant ministerial posts after the 2007 elections, the distribution was as follows: DUP, four; Sinn Féin, three; UUP, two; SDLP, one.

3. See Orange Order reference in Glossary.

4. *The Irish Times* 19 August 1998.

5. See Chapter 1.

6. These tragedies and thousands of other deaths in the conflict are movingly chronicled in David McKittrick, Seamus Kelters, Brian Feeney and Chris Thornton, *Lost Lives: The stories of the men, women and children who died as a result of the Northern Ireland troubles* (Edinburgh and London. 1999).

7. *The Observer* 28 August 1998.

8. *The Irish Times* 24 August 1998.

9. British Deputy Prime Minister; Tony Blair visited Omagh shortly afterwards.

10. Senior member British Conservative Party.

11. Ironically Godson, *op. cit.* p. 391 writes that the wording of Trimble's remarks came mainly from Blair and Campbell. Campbell *op. cit.* p. 319 says he wrote the passage at the instigation of Blair.

12. Maskey was the Sinn Féin chief whip in the Assembly and de Brún a Dublin-born former language teacher and long-time party activist.

13. Eamon de Valera (1882–1975). Sole surviving commandant of the 1916 Rising who went on to found the Fianna Fáil party and become Taoiseach and later President of Ireland.

14. See Collins reference, Chapter 6, note 8.

15. John Taylor was Minister of State for Home Affairs, 1970–1972.

16. *The Irish Times* 22 September 1998.

17. *Ibid* 24 September 1998.

Chapter 8: The Sword of Damocles

1. David Trimble. *To Raise Up a New Northern Ireland, Speeches & Articles 1998–2000* (Belfast Press 2001). Also published on internet at http://www.davidtrimble.org/speeches_toraiseup6.htm

2. 'No battle-plan survives contact with the enemy.' Helmuth von Moltke, 'Moltke the Elder' (1800–91).

3. Popper, Sir Karl Raimund. Austrian-born British philosopher best-known for his critique of historical determinism, especially as expressed in Marxism.

4. Author's interview with Tim Attwood of the SDLP, November 2000.

5. Seán Lemass (1899–1971). Taoiseach 1959–1966 who broke with anti-partition rhetoric by visiting then-Prime Minister of Northern Ireland Terence

O'Neill in Belfast in 1965

6. *The Irish Times* 4 November 1998.

7. *Ibid* 14 November 1998.

8. See 'Officials' in Glossary.

9. The Patten Commission on police reform was set up under the Good Friday Agreement and chaired by the former Northern Ireland Minister and last Governor of Hong Kong, Christopher, later Lord, Patten. Its report in September 1999 proposing large-scale changes in the police force, including its composition, administration, title and badge, laid the basis for the transition from the Royal Ulster Constabulary to the Police Service of Northern Ireland.

10. Fianna Fáil is roughly translated as 'Soldiers of Destiny'

11. A famous photograph shows the then-Father Daly waving his handkerchief in an appeal to British soldiers to refrain from shooting while one of the victims is carried away.

12. *The Irish Times* 14 December 1998.

13. The Good Friday Agreement provided for the establishment of a consultative Civic Forum comprising representatives of the business, trade union, voluntary and other sectors.

14. Some republican propagandists tried to portray these as vigilante actions but they were generally considered to be the work of the IRA. There were also significant numbers of loyalist beatings.

15. Eamon Collins with Mick McGovern. *Killing Rage*. Granta. London. 1997

Chapter 9: The Famous Declaration

1. Hennessey *op. cit.* p. 107 writes that 'There was a feeling, among key elements of the UUP, that Ahern might be a different proposition to previous Taoisigh'.

2. This permanent secretariat, set up under the 1985 Anglo-Irish Agreement, was composed of civil servants from the British and Irish governments. It was replaced by the British–Irish Intergovernmental Secretariat, established under the British–Irish Agreement, and based at Windsor House, Belfast.

3. *The Irish Times* 17 February.

4. The UUP Manifesto for the Assembly elections, Together Within the Union, pledged that 'we will not sit in government with "unreconstructed terrorists"'.

5. Trimble made a habit of this: he had to leave a mass rally for Clinton in Belfast in December 2000 to catch a flight to Palermo.

6. Hillary Clinton subsequently went on to become a Senator for New York and contender for the Democratic nomination for President.

7. With other NATO countries, the US launched a bombing campaign to halt 'ethnic cleansing' by the former Yugoslavia in Kosovo.

8. While the President has been widely praised for his late-night phone-calls during the peace process he did have the advantage of a five-hour time difference!

Chapter 10: 'Seismic Shifts'
1. Trimble adviser Steven King wrote in his column for the *Belfast Telegraph* 11 November 1999 that he coined the phrase 'No guns, no government' in the course of a conversation with myself about the decommissioning issue although I have no recollection of this.
2. *Belfast News Letter* 26 April 1999.
3. *The Times* 25 June 1999.
4. *The Irish Times* 22 May 1999.
5. *Sunday Times* 6 June 1999.
6. The comment was made by 22-year-old accountant Timothy Johnston who went on to become DUP press officer and then special adviser to First Minister Ian Paisley.
7. *The Times* 25 June 1999.
8. *Irish Times* 24 June 1999.
9. *Independent on Sunday* 8 August 1999.
10. Campbell *op. cit*. pp 410–11 and 414–15 describes how Sinn Féin leaders raised his allegedly excessive spinning with him on 30 June and 2 July. He writes that the first encounter was 'jovial, but there was a real hint of menace' and the second, 'pretty disconcerting'.
11. Campbell *op. cit*. pp 411–16 mentions three phone calls between Blair and Clinton. Blair also spoke to Queen Elizabeth as well as arranging for Clinton to talk to Adams and Trimble.
12. *The Irish Times* 2 July 1999.
13. The scepticism was justified. Campbell *op. cit*. p. 415 describes how Trimble told Blair at 4.40 pm he would go for it. 'By five I was telling the broadcasters we were on for a deal,' writes Campbell. But at 7 pm the UUP leader returned to say he had changed his mind, due to lack of party support. However, the genie had already been let out of the media bottle. Despite Blair's upbeat announcement with the Taoiseach, Campbell reveals that his boss was totally despondent that night.
14. A noted republican activist and Maze Prison escapee, Kelly was elected to the Assembly for North Belfast in 1998. He frequently wore a traditional republican revolutionary trenchcoat to negotiations with the British.
15. *The Times* 20 July 1999.
16. *The Irish Times* 16 July 1999.
17. *Ibid* 27 May 2000.
18. *Ibid* 9 January 1999.

Chapter 11: 'We'll Burn that Bridge When We Come to it'
1. *Observer* 14 September 1997.

2. Three men and a woman, all from Ireland, were jailed in August and September 2000 on charges related to sending guns and ammunition from Fort Lauderdale to Ireland and the UK through the US mail.

3. *The Scotsman* 11 October 1999.

4. Mandelson was famed as one of the architects of 'New Labour', reshaping the party's image to attract middle-class voters and using his formidable skills as a 'spin-doctor' to combat the anti-Labour agenda in many parts of the media.

5. *The Irish Times* 12 October 1999.

6. *Belfast Telegraph* 30 March 2000: report of Trimble interview on RTE's *Prime Time* programme.

7. The UUC was composed primarily of delegates from constituency associations with 120 representatives of the Orange Order and 34 Young Unionists and 28 MLAs (Members of the Legislative Assembly).

8. *Belfast Telegraph* 20 November 1999, *Daily Telegraph* 20 November 1999, *The Irish Times* 22 November 1999.

9. In fact, John Taylor was conferred with the title Lord Kilclooney in 2001, one of many from the Northern Ireland political scene who have been elevated to the House of Lords since the beginning of the peace process. Others include David Trimble, Sir James Molyneaux, Dr Edward Haughey, John Laird, Ken Maginnis and Dennis Rogan, all from the UUP (Dr Haughey – Lord Ballyedmond – later joined the Conservatives), as well as Eileen Paisley (wife of the First Minister), Wallace Brown and Maurice Morrow of the DUP. Former Alliance Party leader and Assembly Presiding Officer Dr John Alderdice, Shankill community activist May Blood and the distinguished academic and informal Trimble adviser Paul Bew have also become peers. Knighthoods were awarded to Reg Empey, John Gorman and to ex-MP Cecil Walker and Josias Cunningham (both since deceased) of the UUP. Former UUP Environment Minister Sam Foster and ex-Trimble adviser David Campbell were both awarded the CBE (Commander of the British Empire) and UUP Assembly Member Fred Cobain received the MBE (Most Excellent Order of the British Empire).

10. Bairbre de Brún's attendance subsequently at a North-South meeting on Food Safety became a focus of controversy but because of decommissioning, not any question about its relevance to her department (*The Irish Times* 4 November 2000).

11. The block grant is the subvention by the UK Government to Northern Ireland.

Chapter 12: No Hat, No Rabbits

1.The comment was made by Sir Basil Brooke, first Viscount Brookeborough (1888–1973) Prime Minister of Northern Ireland 1943–1963.

2. Paul Berry quit the DUP in 2006 following newspaper allegations about

his private life, which he denied. These were published in the run-up to the 2005 Westminster elections. He ran unsuccessfully as an independent, anti-St Andrews Agreement candidate for the Assembly in 2007.

3. *Belfast Telegraph* 4 February 2000.

4. *The Irish Times* 19 December 1998: The LVF handed over a small quantity of weapons which were destroyed by the decommissioning body.

5. *The Irish Times* 5 February 2000

6. This group of officials, known informally as 'The Four Horsemen', provided an essential structure or framework for the interventions of the Taoiseach and the Minister for Foreign Affairs. The personnel changed, e.g. Gallagher took over as head of the Anglo-Irish Division in Foreign Affairs from Seán Ó hUiginn, who had played a crucial role in establishing and driving forward the peace process, and Michael Collins succeeded Teahon as the lead official in this area from the Department of the Taoiseach.

7. Tragically, Sir Josias Cunningham died following a car accident outside Belfast on 9 August 2000.

8. Text of de Chastelain report published in *The Irish Times* 12 February 2000.

9. The 'angel' terminology reportedly originated with the British Government.

10. *Belfast Telegraph* 14 February 2000

11. *Ireland on Sunday* 20 February 2000

12. Donald Macintyre. *Mandelson and the Making of New Labour*. HarperCollinsPublishers. London. 2000.

Chapter 13: Trimble's Risk for Peace

1. *The Irish Times* 18 March 2000.

2. The 'stalking horse' method had proven effective in the campaign to undermine Trimble's predecessor James, later Lord, Molyneaux. The candidate may have no realistic chance of winning but the precedent is set for a challenge against the current leader.

3. *Belfast Telegraph* 1 April 2000.

4. Two local incidents where Sinn Féin was accused of using 'bullyboy' tactics received wide media coverage. See 'Sinn Féin stops visit by duchess', *The Guardian* 18 January 2000 and 'Priest falls fouls of SF', *Belfast News Letter* 16 December 1999.

5. The *Sunday Tribune* 7 May 2000 and Godson *op. cit.* pp 558 and 602 attribute authorship of the memo to Britain's then-Ambassador to Ireland, Sir Ivor Roberts. Despite the use of the first person, a British diplomatic source told me a number of officials were involved in writing the document.

6. See p.347 and Note 8 below.

7. Steven King article in *The Irish Times* 19 May 2000.

8. *Building a Permanent Peace: Sinn Féin Submission to the International Body on*

Decommissioning. Republican Publications. Dublin. January 1996. (Submission made on 18 December 1995.)

9. *The Irish Times* 8 May 2000.

10. See UDR reference in Glossary.

11. *Financial Times* 29 May 2000.

12. Press Association 27 May 2000.

13. Northern Ireland security forces estimate quoted in *Belfast Telegraph* 21 July 1997. See also, Sean Boyne 'Arms and the IRA – What it Has, What it Wants, What it Can Afford to Decommission', *Jane's Intelligence Review*, 1 April 2000.

Chapter 14: Groundhog Day

1. Godson *op. cit*. p. 162.

2. Campbell *op. cit*. p. 414.

3. Campbell *op. cit*. pp 491-99.

4. The *Guardian*. 13 March 2007.

5. Too free and easy for some: Campbell describes his embarrassment at being confronted with a naked Mo, when the two of them had to share a hotel bathroom during a visit to Dublin in September 1995, *op. cit*. p. 82.

6. Martina Purdy. *Room 21: Stormont – Behind Closed Doors* (The Brehon Press, Belfast 2005) pp 215–216.

7. Purdy *op. cit*. p. 240.

8. Godson *op. cit*. p. 686.

9. The *Mirror*. 12 September 2001.

10. Although the three men were acquitted on the main charge, this was overruled on appeal and they received lengthy sentences of seventeen years each. However, they skipped bail and, in the summer of 2005, returned secretly to Ireland, which does not have an extradition treaty with Colombia.

11. Purdy *op. cit*. p. 333.

12. *The Irish Times* 8 October 2002.

13. A remarkable echo of the Book of Ecclesiastes, 3:1–8 with its reference to 'A time to love, and a time to hate; a time for war, and a time for peace.'

14. The *Guardian* 15 March 2007.

15. See http://www.standrewsagreement.org

16. Ahern had stated as early as 2003 that he intended to retire at 60, i.e. in 2011.

17. Brian Rowan. *Paisley and the Provos* (Brehon Press, Belfast 2005) p. 107.

Chapter 15: The Healing Has Begun

1. *The Irish Times* 3 October 2007.

2. The Human Development Index is included in the United Nations Development Programme's Human Development Report for 2007–8. Compiled on the basis of data from 2005, it covers a total of 177 countries.

3. Journalist John Cole describes in As it Seemed to Me: Political Memoirs (Phoenix Paperback, London 1996, pp.10–11) how even Clement Attlee, during his time as British Prime Minister, was stopped and had his car searched by customs officers while crossing the Border after a holiday in Sligo. Incidentally, the Prime Minister and his wife Violet had no police escort.

4. The *Sunday Telegraph* 9 December 2007.

5. *The Irish Times* 17 October 2007.

6. Seán Mac Stíofáin. *Memoirs of a Revolutionary* (Published by Gordon Cremonesi; printed and bound in Edinburgh, 1975) p. 166.

7. Sean O'Callaghan. *The Informer* (Bantam Press, London 1998) p. 210.

8. See numerous references in Ed Moloney. *A Secret History of the IRA* (Second edition; Penguin Books, London 2007).

9. Bernard C. Nalty, Consultant Editor. *The Vietnam War: the History of America's Conflict in South-East Asia.* (Smithmark, New York 1996) p. 190.

10. The British Embassy in Merrion Square, Dublin, was burned down on 2 February 1972 as a protest over the Bloody Sunday killings in Derry when thirteen people were shot dead and a fourteenth fatally wounded by British troops. Shortly before the embassy was burnt, Séamus Costello told the crowd: 'We have come many times to protest; this time we've come with notice to quit.'

11. Deaglán de Bréadún. 'Grim Air in a Quiet Town.' Report on Sinn Féin ardfheis in Dundalk. The Irish Times 22 February 1993.

12. Full text was published on the internet at: http://www.ireland.com/focus/2007/summerschool/index.htm with a shorter print version in The Irish Times 24 August 2007.

13. http://www.ark.ac.uk/nilt/2006/Political_Attitudes/ NIRELAND.html#religion

14. *Review of Tax Policy in Northern Ireland* by Sir David Varney, published by HM Treasury in December 2007, p. 5, note 3. The Varney Report controversially rejected calls to reduce Northern Ireland's corporation tax rate from 30 per cent to 12.5 per cent in line with the Republic, as a means of attracting investment. The former Treasury official concluded that this would disadvantage the rest of the United Kingdom.

15. Bloomfield *op. cit.*

16. Tim Pat Coogan. *The Troubles.* (Hutchinson, London 1995) p. 332.

17. Kevin Rafter. *Martin Mansergh: A Biography.* (New Island, Dublin 2002) p. 183.

18. Rafter *op. cit.* p. 183-4.

19. Rafter *op. cit.* p. 210-11.

20. Eamon Mallie and David McKittrick. *The Fight for Peace: The Secret Story Behind the Irish Peace Process.* (Heinemann, London 1996) pp 85–90.

21. Steven King. 'Charles J. Haughey and the Northern Ireland Question,

1957–92: A Study in Modern Democratic Republicanism'. (D. Phil. thesis, University of Ulster, 1995).

22. For differing viewpoints on this episode, see 'Smears, Slanders and McCarthyism: Ireland's Green-baiting Sunday Newspaper' by Patrick Farrelly in *The Irish Voice* (New York) 5 October 1993 and The *Sunday Independent* for 10 October 1993.

23. Rafter *op. cit.* p. 184.

24. Rafter *op. cit.* p. 182; see also Moloney *op. cit.* p. xv.

25. Campbell *op. cit.* p. 320.

26. Campbell *op. cit.* p. 321.

27. Campbell *op. cit.* p. 413.

SELECT BIBLIOGRAPHY

Collins, Eamon with McGovern, Mick. *Killing Rage*. Granta. London. 1997.

Coogan, Tim Pat. *The Troubles: Ireland's Ordeal 1966–1995 and the Search for Peace*. Hutchinson. London. 1995.

Devenport, Mark. *Flash Frames: Twelve Years Reporting Belfast*. The Blackstaff Press. Belfast. 2000.

Fearon, Kate. *Women's Work: The Story of the Northern Ireland Women's Coalition*. The Blackstaff Press. Belfast. 1999.

Harnden, Toby. *'Bandit Country': The IRA and South Armagh*. Hodder and Stoughton/Lir. London. 1999.

Holland, Jack. *Hope against History: The Ulster Conflict*. Hodder and Stoughton. London. 1999 (published in the US by Henry Holt and Company, New York).

Langdon, Julia. *Mo Mowlam*. Little, Brown and Company. London. 2000.

Macintyre, Donald. *Mandelson and the Making of New Labour*. HarperCollinsPublishers. London. 2000.

Major, John. *The Autobiography*. HarperCollinsPublishers. London. 1999.

Mallie, Eamonn and McKittrick, David. *The Fight for Peace: The Secret Story behind the Irish Peace Process*. Heinemann: London. 1996.

McDonald, Henry. *Trimble*. Bloomsbury. London. 2000.

McKittrick, David; Kelters, Seamus; Feeney, Brian and Thornton, Chris. *Lost Lives: The stories of the men, women and children who died as a result of the Northern Ireland troubles*. Mainstream Publishing. Edinburgh and London. 1999.

McGarry, John and O'Leary, Brendan. *Explaining Northern Ireland: Broken Images*. Blackwell Publishers. Oxford and Cambridge, Massachusetts. 1995.

Mitchell, George J. *Making Peace*. Alfred A. Knopf. New York. 1999 (Published in the UK by Heinemann).

O'Brien, Brendan. *The Long War: The IRA and Sinn Féin*. The O'Brien Press. Dublin, 1999.

O'Clery, Conor. *The Greening of the White House: The Inside Story of how America Tried to Bring Peace to Ireland*. Gill & Macmillan. Dublin. 1996. (Published in the US under the title, *Daring Diplomacy: Clinton's Secret Search for Peace in Ireland*. Roberts Rinehart. 1997.)

Oliver, Quintin. *Working for 'Yes': The Story of the May 1998 Referendum in Northern Ireland*. Published by The 'Yes' Campaign, P.O. Box 833, Belfast BT1. 1998.

Stewart, A.T.Q. *The Ulster Crisis: Resistance to Home Rule 1912–1914*. The Blackstaff Press. Belfast. 1997.

INDEX

INDEX

INDEX

INDEX